C/C++
FOR
EXPERT SYSTEMS

"Unleashes the power
of artificial intelligence."

DAVID HU

MIS:
PRESS

MANAGEMENT INFORMATION SOURCE, INC.

COPYRIGHT

DEDICATION

To Lise, Eileen, and Emily.

Special thanks to Michael Song, John Kallen, Rob Romero, Steve Janoschka, Frank Tay, Steve Chao, and Gino Wang who have contributed greatly — in software and hardware — to the preparation of this book.

ACKNOWLEDGEMENTS

The author is indebted to those whose enthusiasm inspired him to write a series of expert system books and those who contributed their ideas, cases, and reviews. These professionals include Mr. V. Daniel Hunt, Dr. Mark Fox, Dr. Rick Roth-Hayes, Dr. Frank Lynch, Mr. Richard Brimer, Dr. Craig W. Cook, Dr. Kenneth C. Hayes, Mr. Brad Netherton, Ms. Catherine Roy, Dr. Cordell Green, Dr. M. James Naughton, Mr. Mike Chamber, Mr. Eric J. Jacobs, Dr. Darryl F. Hubbard, Dr. John Kunz, Mr. Robert Fondellier, Dr. James R. Brink, Mr. Deva D. Sharma, Dr. Norman Neilson, Dr. John R. Josephson, Dr. Steven Rosenberg, Mr. Kit Sakamoto, Mr. Peter Hart, Mr. William R. Crisp, Mr. Bobby Johnson, Dr. Chee Yee Chong, Mr. Gary Martins, Mr. Thomas R. Ruschbac, and Dr. Bill Sun.

Thanks also go to Guidelines Software, Inc. (distributing Guidelines C++) and Lifeboat (distributing Advantage C++), who provided a copy of their C++ packages for preparation of the programs in this book. Sample programs included in the book are written in Guidelines C++. Ms. Chandler Vinneau and Mr. Nathaniel Stitt of Guidelines Software, Inc., Mr. Jack McAuley and Mr. Collin Purcell of Lifeboat, and Mr. Larry Edralin of Oregon Software provided constructive assistance in the preparation of the manuscript.

Every effort has been attempted to ensure the accuracy of the C/C++ source codes; however, owing to the limitation of time and the newness of C++, some sample programs may not be as bug-free as the author has hoped. Any correction by the reader is highly appreciated by both the author and future readers.

TABLE OF CONTENTS

DISK ORDER FORM
ON LAST PAGE
OF BOOK

PREFACE

This book is written for programmers who would like to introduce a new advanced software technology, AI (artificial intelligence)/ES (expert systems), into their programs by using C/C++ or who need to convert expert systems into C/C++.

Expert systems can be explained in terms comparable to those pertaining to conventional software programs. An expert system generally includes a knowledge base (comparable to a program code), an inference engine (comparable to a compiler/interpreter), and user interface facilities. The knowledge base contains rules and facts, and the inference engine consists of search control and reasoning mechanisms.

AI/expert systems have come out of laboratories and have started to gain market recognition. The expert systems market has been the fastest growing segment of the artificial intelligence "industry." This market segment grew from $9 million in 1982 and is estimated to reach $1.8 billion in the 1990s. The majority of AI experts do not believe that expert systems will replace human experts; they believe that expert systems will take over certain functions of low-level specialists, e.g., some functions of junior loan officers and computer system configurers.

However, the rapid growth path of AI/ES was truncated because many current expert systems require special software and hardware. For many expert systems, special AI workstations and sophisticated AI software packages such as KEE or ART are required. This requirement implies an advanced investment of approximately $100,000.00 before the decision-maker even has a feeling for whether AI/ES is beneficial to his or her organization.

Expert system technology written in C/C++ can bring to programming a new dimension in which the capability of capturing rule-of-thumb or heuristic expert knowledge is embedded in the program. The class structure provided in C++ enables you to represent organized knowledge/data conveniently. The efficiency and portability of C when used in expert systems gives you the speed and independence of the computing environment. Programs embedded with expert system technology may enable the user to emulate the judgmental knowledge of experts such as geologists, doctors, lawyers, bankers, or insurance underwriters.

The first-generation expert systems such as MYCIN, PROSPECTOR, and XCON were mainly applicable to scientific and engineering problems, which are not well understood theoretically in terms of decision-making processes by their experts and therefore require judgmental assessment.

The second-generation expert systems have been applied to sophisticated synthesis problems that involve a large number of choices, such as how the elements are to be composed. These problems normally entail a large search space and slower speed for the expert systems designed. Examples of these systems include factory scheduling applications such as ISIS or legal reasoning applications such as TAXMAN. The development of second-generation expert systems has focused on establishing AI/ES as a new industry different from software development. Profitable applications have been identified in almost every field from manufacturing to financial planning. Each expert tends to regard his or her field as the most useful and profitable. The three major areas that most expert systems are concentrating on are manufacturing, military operations, and financial planning. However, some companies have explored such conservative markets as operation of electric utilities, with applications for use in nuclear power plants as well as load management of industrial and commercial customers. These applications were confirmed through a grass-roots survey of 155 potential expert system end-users conducted by Macintosh International (Saratoga, CA) in 1985.

In addition to their ability to encode the expert's judgmental knowledge, expert systems generally provide the user with a more convenient man-machine interface than conventional programs, give an explanation that traces through many different aspects of the problem, and demonstrate how a decision has been derived. Many expert systems allow the user to ask why a decision is or is not made. Because of these convenient features, programmers who acquire expert system technology skills can expect to increase the user friendliness of their software products.

The third-generation expert systems are emerging in which AI/ES is no longer considered a "magic powder." AI/ES is merely a new software technique that will make programs more powerful and friendly. It will eventually be integrated into daily computer programming. Expert systems as well as expert system shells are embedded in conventional programs to make these programs smarter and friendlier to use. Such programs are empowered with reasoning capability (to obtain new facts from existing ones), query ability (to obtain data and explain to the user the reasons behind a decision), and user conveniences (e.g., error checking and natural language templates).

This book is written to enable C/C++ programmers to integrate artificial intelligence techniques, particularly expert system technology, into their programs and enable their programs to perform in the following ways:

- **Intelligent "user"**: acts as a user of databases and other software packages; interaction with the software package/database is not its primary objective but merely a convenient means to access data.

- **Intelligent "representative"**: uses mathematical logic to represent general facts about data in the software package/database to increase the ability of the package/database to respond to queries.

- **Intelligent "prober"**: supports browsing through a database or program and also supports query modification to either narrow or broaden the scope of a request to make it more understandable.

- **Natural language "interface"**: provides natural language interface software packages and allows the user to search for and process information without having to learn the specialized command language of a software package.

- **Natural language text "analyst"**: processes a user's natural language input text to produce appropriate responses to user queries. The ability of the expert system to understand natural language text in a given field permits the user to enter data in a relatively flexible form.

- **Knowledge "accumulator" and "disseminator"**: extracts expert and specialist expertise to advise or train junior personnel to perform a job at a level close to that of experts.

Because C++ doesn't allow dynamic definition of data structure at run time, an expert system shell can be used to rapidly prototype, test, and refine the structure of an expert system in response to a real-world problem. After the prototype has been approved, C++ can then be used to represent the hierarchical data and knowledge to be prepared for final delivery to multiple computing environments.

The text is written specifically for the IBM PC/XT/AT and its compatible environment; it provides the programmer with core knowledge that can be used to build the previously listed functionalities into conventional programs. This book focuses on providing you with the knowledge to embed expert system shells or expert systems in your computer programs. It consists of four sections:

- basic expert system, object-oriented programming, and C++ concepts

- C/C++ utilities and expert systems languages and tools

- programming expert system components in C/C++

- expert system applications

If you already understand expert systems and object-oriented programming, you can skip chapters in Sections I and II without limiting your comprehension of the rest of the book.

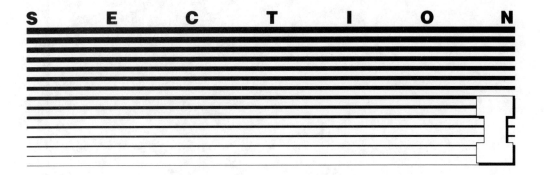

C/C++ AND EXPERT SYSTEM FUNDAMENTALS

This book introduces you to the idea of incorporating expert system technology written in C/C++ in your daily programming work by providing details on how to build each component of this innovative technology in C/C++. Section I discusses in detail the terminology and major components of expert systems and uses an object-oriented programming language, Smalltalk, to explain the desired features of C++ and examine how C/C++ is used in developing expert systems. It also examines the programming principles for expert systems. To help you comprehend the new terms easily and quickly, the description of expert system technology draws heavily upon an analogy between the new technology and conventional programming techniques.

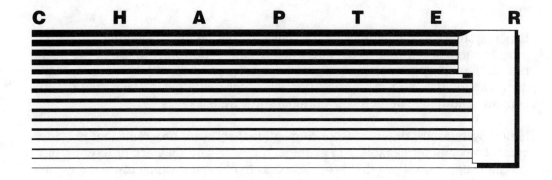

FUNDAMENTALS OF EXPERT SYSTEMS

Expert system (ES) technology is an advanced programming technique that many programmers have heard about and will have the opportunity to use in the near future. Expert system technology provides programmers with a new programming capability for incorporating symbolic representation of facts, data, and heuristic knowledge in their conventional software packages.

Expert systems are different from conventional software programs that provide access to computer capability in arithmetic power, and they are different from decision support systems that provide access to computer capability in distributing information. Expert systems capture and distribute the human expert's expertise in making judgments under various conditions. They "clone" experts by capturing knowledge that is perishable, scarce, and vague and difficult to apply, distribute, or accumulate. Expert systems afford cost-effective services in areas that require symbolic processing of knowledge and rule-of-thumb judgmental problem-solving methods. An initial application of expert systems was in the diagnosis and treatment of human physical disorders; the basic purpose of these systems was to determine what the symptoms indicated and what remedial treatment was appropriate.

Expert system technology is one of the most successful branches of artificial intelligence (AI). Other branches of AI include robotics, voice recognition and synthesis, and vision. Expert system technology started to emerge as a potent force in 1977 when Professor Feigenbaum of Stanford University presented an insight that the problem-solving power of a computer program comes from the knowledge it processes of a given domain, not just from the programming techniques and formalism it contains. However, the author's experience indicates that the programming techniques and formalism may also determine the eventual destiny of an expert system.

BASIC CONCEPTS

The structure of an expert system resembles a conventional software program, as shown in Figure 1.1. The major components of an expert system are knowledge base, inference engine, user interface mechanism (including explanation facility), and data; major components of conventional programs are data (or database), code, interpreter/compiler, and sparse user-interface mechanism, but the interpreter/compiler is not obvious to the user. Expert systems are capable of symbol processing, inferencing, and explaining.

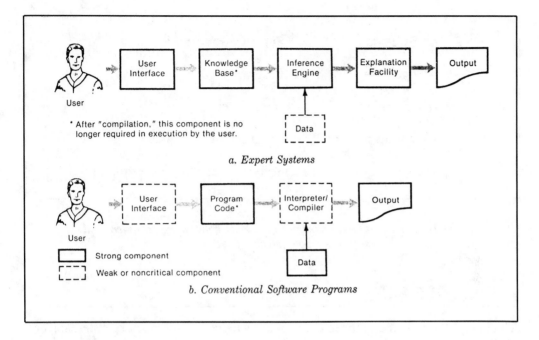

Figure 1.1   Structure of an expert system

Because of the terminology used, expert systems can be considered an advanced form of programming; however, the terminology of expert systems can be mapped on a one-to-one basis to terminology of software programs as shown in Table 1.1. For example, a knowledge base of an expert system that contains rules (likely IF-THEN rules) and facts matches the program (code) of a software program; however, a knowledge base does not correspond to a database. A knowledge base is executable, but a database is not. A database can only be queried and updated. Like an interpreter that evaluates a program in the source code and executes the statements, the inference engine takes the statements in a knowledge base and executes them because the inference engine contains search control and substitution mechanisms. AI/ES languages such as LISP, Prolog, and Smalltalk can be used to build an empty package of the knowledge base, inference engine, and user-interface. This package is called an expert system shell or tool. Expert system shells used to build expert systems are high-level programming languages with many unconventional conveniences such as explanation and tracing facilities.

Expert Systems	Software Programs
Knowledge base	Program
Inference engine	Interpreter
Expert system tool/shell	Programming language
Knowledge engineers	Software engineer/programmers

Table 1.1 One-to-one correspondence between expert system and software program technologies

KNOWLEDGE BASE

The programmer can use three types of knowledge to build expert systems: rules of thumb, facts and relations among components, and assertions and questions. To represent these types of knowledge in the knowledge base, three methods are used:

- **rules** to represent rules of thumb

- **frames** to represent structured facts and relations

- **logic** to represent assertions and queries

Rules

Rules are conditional sentences; they are expressed in the following form:

IF (premise) FACT 1, FACT 2, ...

THEN (conclusion) FACT 9, FACT 10, ...

For example, the rule of "starts per month" could be written as follows:

IF (the number of motor starts per month exceeds 20 times)

THEN (increase the operational potential of the motor)

Frames or Units

A frame is also called a unit that contains the hierarchies of objects (components) and the attributes of objects that can be assigned, inherited from another frame, or computed through procedures or other computer programs. The attributes are filled in the "slots" of a frame. Figure 1.2 shows a sample unit.

Frame name: ASD Adjustable Frequency AC Drive

Installed to: Induction motor

Inherited from: ASD

Created by: 6-30-86

Modified by: 7-5-86

Slot: Capacity
       Type: Real number, value: 0 to 1000 hp

Slot: Main-component
       Type: Alphanumeric, value: INVERTERS

Slot: USAGE
       Type: Alphabet, value: (Inherited from ASD it is kind of)

Slot: Economics
       Type: Real number, value: (Computed from PROCEDURE = ECONOMICS)

Slot: Operation
       Type: Logic, value: (Rule 5a)

Figure 1.2   Sample frame in ASD Advisor

Logic

Logic expressions consist of predicates and values to assess facts of the real world. A predicate is a statement concerning an object, such as the following:

kind-of (adjustable-Frequency-AC-Drive, aSD)

The object can be interpreted as an adjustable-frequency AC drive, which is a kind of ASD (adjustable speed drive). The object can be either a constant or a variable that may change over time. A predicate may have one or more arguments that are the objects it describes. In the example of ASD Advisor, the other kind of logic expression is appropriate for asking questions such as the following:

?- (indicator_Matrix, X) :- company (X), aSD (X), economics (X, excellent).

The question can be interpreted as "Show me all possible ASD installations in a given company that can be implemented with only induction motors that are considered to possess excellent economic potential."

INFERENCE ENGINE

Once the knowledge base is completed, it needs to be executed by a reasoning mechanism and search control to solve problems. The most common reasoning method in expert systems is the application of the following simple logic rule (also called **modus ponens**):

IF A is true, and IF A THEN B is true, then B is true.

The implication of this simple rule is that

IF B is not true, and IF A THEN B is true, then A is not true.

Another implication of the simple logic rule is as follows:

> Given: IF A, THEN B and
>   IF B, THEN C.
>
> Conclusion: IF A, THEN C.

In other words, IF A is true, THEN you can conclude C is also true.

These three simple reasoning principles are used to solve problems by examining rules, facts, and relations in expert systems; however, to minimize the reasoning time, search control methods are used to determine where to start the substitution process and to choose which rule to examine next when several rules are conflicting at the same point. The two main methods of search are forward and backward chaining. These two methods of chaining may be combined in an expert system for maximum efficiency of search control.

Forward Chaining

When the rule interpreter is **forward chaining**, if premise clauses match the situation, then the conclusion clauses are asserted. For example, in the rule of starts per month, if the real situation matches the premise (that is, the number of motor starts per month exceeds 20), the operational potential of ASDs to the motor will increase. Once the rule is used, or "fired," it will not be used again in the same search; however, the fact concluded as the result of that rule's firing will be added to the knowledge base. This cycle of finding a matched rule, firing it, and adding the conclusion to the knowledge base will be repeated until no more matched rules can be found.

Backward Chaining

A **backward chaining** mechanism attempts to prove the hypothesis from facts. If the current goal is to determine the fact in the conclusion (hypothesis), then you must determine whether the premises match the situation. For example,

Rule One:

IF you lose the key and
the gas tank is empty,

THEN the car is not running.

Rule Two:

IF the car is not running and
you have no cash,

THEN you are going to be late.

Fact One: You lost the key.

Fact Two: The gas tank is empty.

For example, if you want to prove the hypothesis "You are going to be late," given the facts and rules in the knowledge base (Facts 1 and 2, Rules 1 and 2), a backward chaining must be applied to determine whether the premises (sub-hypotheses) match the facts. Rule 2, which contains the conclusion "You are going to be late," would be fired first to determine whether the premises match the actual situation. Because the knowledge base does not contain the facts in Rule 2's premises, "the car is not running" and "you have no cash," "the car is not running" becomes the first subhypothesis. Rule 1 will then be fired to assert whether the premises "you lost the key" and "the gas tank is empty" match the facts. Because the facts (Facts 1 and 2) in the knowledge base match the premise of Rule 1, the subhypothesis "the car is not running" is proven; however, the system still has to prove "you have no cash," which is not contained in the knowledge base and cannot be asserted through rules because no rule is related to it. The system will then ask the user "IS IT TRUE THAT: you have no cash?" If the answer is "Yes," then the second subhypothesis is also proven, and the original hypothesis is therefore proven as well, concluding "You are going to be late."

MAN-MACHINE INTERFACE

The man-machine interface mechanism produces dialogue between the computer and the user. The current expert system can be equipped with templates, menus, mice, or natural language to facilitate its use and an explanation module to allow the user to challenge and examine the reasoning process underlying the system's answers.

Menus are groups of simplified instructional statements that appear on the computer screen and can be selected by the user pushing designated buttons, using a mouse or designated keys on the keyboard. The user does not need to type instructions. A semi-natural or fully natural language interface is more sophisticated than a menu interface; it allows computer systems to accept inputs and produce outputs in a language closer to a conventional language, such as English.

Several expert systems incorporate primitive forms of natural language in their user interface to facilitate knowledge base development. Explanation modules generate output statements of expert systems in language that can be understood by non-computer-user professionals.

UNCERTAINTY OF KNOWLEDGE

Rules obtained from human experts are sometimes uncertain; they describe some rules as "maybe," "sometimes," "often," or "not quite certain about the conclusion." You need some methods to handle these types of statements; furthermore, like human experts, expert systems may have to draw inferences based on incomplete information, such as unavailable, unknown, or uncertain information. Unavailable or unknown information is resolved by allowing rules to fail if the information needed is critical in evaluating the premise, i.e., the information needed is in the condition (IF) statements connected by AND. When IF statements are connected by OR, the absence of one or more of them will not affect the outcome of the rule.

Even though the reliability of knowledge that is inserted into the knowledge base is questionable, the ability to represent facts that are not guaranteed to be 100% accurate is important to expert systems.

The likelihood that a fact is true is called the fact's **certainty factor** (CF). In most expert systems, this number is between 0 and 1, where 0 represents no confidence in the fact, and 1 represents complete trust in the validity of the fact. For example, you may assign a CF of 1.0 to

"IBM is a company"

and perhaps a CF of 0.5, representing 50% certainty, to

"IBM is the best company"

The CF is an integral part of any fact and is always displayed to the user along with any display of the fact.

"IBM is a company" [CF = 1.0]

"IBM is the best company" [CF = 0.5]

Certainty factors for facts can be established in either of two ways. First, the source of the fact, generally the user, supplies a certainty factor for the fact. Second, an expert system uses rules to compute the certainty factor (see Chapter 9 for details). Any fact *not* assigned a certainty factor is assumed to have a factor of 1.0.

SUMMARY

- An expert system mimics experts or specialists in a specific field (e.g., medicine or computer configuration).

- The power of an expert system lies in the knowledge and not in the programming technique.

- The principal components of these current systems are knowledge base, inference engine, and man-machine interface.

- The knowledge base contains facts and rules that embody an expert's expertise.

- The three commonly used methods for encoding facts and relationships that constitute knowledge are rules, frames, and logical expressions.

- Inference engines are relatively simple; most commonly used methods are backward chaining and forward chaining.

- User interface is often a weak but critical element of expert systems; many current expert systems are equipped with menus and explanation modules to allow users to query expert systems and examine their output statements.

REFERENCES

Brodie Associates. "Language Workbench," a programmer's toolkit for developing natural language interfaces to applications software. *Kurzweil AI* (Waltham, MA, 1986).

Feigenbaum, E. A. "The Art of Artificial Intelligence: Themes and Case Studies." Conference Proceedings of the International Joint Conference on Artificial Intelligence, 1014-1029, 1977.

Hendrix, G. G. "The LIFER manual: A guide to build practical natural language interfaces," Tech. report, Tech. note 138, SRI, 1977.

Hendrix, G. and E. D. Sacerdoti. "Developing a natural language interface to Comp Data." Technical report. Artificial Intelligence Center, International, 1976.

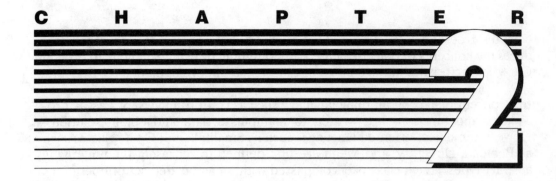

OBJECT-ORIENTED PROGRAMMING CONCEPTS AND C++ FUNDAMENTALS FOR EXPERT SYSTEM DEVELOPMENT

Chapter 1 describes the terminology of expert systems, and this chapter introduces the concepts of object-oriented programming by using Smalltalk to explain C++ characteristics in the context of expert system development.

In a conventional programming language such as C, FORTRAN, or Pascal, procedures and functions are written to manipulate data and obtain solutions. However, in object-oriented languages such as Smalltalk and C++, classes such as Boolean, Directory, and Menu are first defined to represent the underlying abstract types. Each class is encompassed with an associated set of operations (methods, analogous to procedures and functions) characterizing the behavior of the subject type. **Objects** (e.g., beta) are then declared to be of specific classes (instances) for desired operations such as sin (requesting the object name "beta" to compute the sine of itself: beta sin). Such objects inherit all the fields of data that are defined in the class to which they belong. Actions can be performed on these objects by invoking one or more of the underlying methods defined in respective classes. The process of invoking a method in the class is called sending a message to the object. A message is sent to an object to evaluate the object itself (e.g., beta sin). **Messages** perform a task similar to that of function calls in other languages. **Methods** are the internal algorithms that are performed by an object after receiving a message. They represent the internal implementation of an object. For example, a Smalltalk expression contains at least an object and a message, as in Example 2.1:

> **Example 2.1**   `3 factorial => 6`

An object-oriented programming language often has several of the following five features: information hiding, data abstraction, dynamic binding, class inheritance, message-passing, and automatic storage management (e.g., garbage collection). Smalltalk possesses all of these features.

The main vocabulary of Smalltalk consists of five words: object, message, class, instance, and method. These five words present the concepts of Smalltalk.

- **Object**: a basic element of Smalltalk, represented by private memory and operation instructions

- **Message**: a request for an object to accomplish its operations

- **Class**: a description of a set of similar objects

- **Instance**: one member object in a class

- **Method**: a description of how to perform an object's operation

Smalltalk is different from traditional procedural languages; in Smalltalk, an object carries its own operation instance, and messages represent the interaction between components by requesting them to perform operations on themselves, for example,

- **beta sin**

  Explanation: a message requesting the object named **beta** to compute the sine of itself.

- **List Addlast: newComponent**

  Explanation: a message requesting the object (a linear data structure named **List**) to add the object named **newComponent** as the last element of itself.

A Smalltalk program consists of three parts: a class name, a declaration of the variables available to the instances, and the methods used by instances to respond to messages. Smalltalk has several programming advantages, including permission to add new classes of objects without having to modify existing code due to dynamic binding capability and the ability to reuse original codes that perform a particular task to reduce the number of lines of repeated codes.

C++ provides many of the Smalltalk components, such as objects, classes, instances, methods, and messages. C++ is an excellent language for programming expert systems because of its data hiding, data abstraction, and message-passing features. It provides classes with inheritance and function overloading, which can be used to create frames and rule-set structures for knowledge representation. In addition, C++ supports many LISP-like functions, such as enumeration names, functional prototypes, default arguments, and overloading of function names, to facilitate development of expert system components.

The rest of this chapter is divided into two sections:

- becoming familiar with the Smalltalk environment

- fundamentals of C++ for expert system development

BECOMING FAMILIAR WITH SMALLTALK'S ENVIRONMENT

Smalltalk is different from conventional and other AI programming languages because thorough documentation and well-planned development programs are critical to mastering its use.

This section introduces you to the following main features of the Smalltalk environment:

- Smalltalk expressions and their evaluation

- Smalltalk classes and methods

Smalltalk Expressions and Their Evaluation

Smalltalk expressions are similar to expressions in other computer programming languages. In Smalltalk, you can enter the text for an expression in a text pane, select it, evaluate it, and display the result. In this section, simple Smalltalk expressions are illustrated and discussed.

Basic Smalltalk expressions may contain objects, messages, and variables. Simple Smalltalk programs are also composed of those three elements.

Objects

Objects are the basic building blocks of Smalltalk, analogous to pieces of data in other languages. The three elementary Smalltalk objects are integers, strings of characters, and arrays. Consider the following examples:

- Integer, 1050

- String of characters, $ABC

- Array, #('array' 'of' 4 'strings' and 6 'integer')

A $ sign is required to indicate that an object is a string of characters, and a # is required to indicate that an object is an array. As shown in the array example, not all objects contained inside of an object need to be of the same type or size.

Messages and Methods

In Smalltalk, a message is sent to an object to evaluate the object itself. Messages perform a task similar to that of function calls in other languages. Methods are the internal algorithms that are performed by an object after it receives a message. They represent the internal implementation of an object. A Smalltalk expression contains at least an object and a message, as shown in Example 2.1. In Example 2.1, **3** is an object (an integer), and **factorial** is a message that requests 3 to perform a factorial. The internal structure of **factorial** is a method. A message consists of three elements: a receiver object, a message selector, and zero or more arguments. In Example 2.1, **3** is the receiver object, **factorial** is the message selector, and no argument is used in the expression. As in functions, the message selector is the function name; the receiver object is the function parameter; and the function definition is the method. A message always returns a single object as its result.

Example 2.2   5+7 =>12

Example 2.3   10*3 =>30

Example 2.4   5+4*3 =>27

Note that in Example 2.4, the result is 27, not 17, because Smalltalk evaluates an arithmetic expression strictly from left to right.

Example 2.5   #('what' 'time' 'is' 'it?') at: 3   => 'is'

In Example 2.5, the receiver object is an array, **at:** is the message selector, and **3** is the argument. When arguments are present, a colon is added after the message. The message requests display the third element in the array:

Example 2.6   `#(7 8 9), #(10 11 12 13)`

                   `=> (7 8 9 10 11 12 13)`

In Example 2.6, the special character (non-digit and non-letter) comma (,) is the selector, which concatenates the argument with the receiver object.

Example 2.7   `3 factorial between: 2+1 and' 'Time' size *5`

                   `=> True`

Example 2.7 is a message inside messages. The expression asks whether (3 factorial) is between (2+1) and: "Time" size*5. It is true that 6 is between 3 and (4*5=20).

Expressions can be grouped as a series that can then be evaluated as a single unit. Each expression except the last one is separated from the next expression with a period. If all of the messages in the series are sent to the same receiver, they can be **cascaded**. The receiver is written only once, and each message (except the last) is terminated with a semicolon instead of a period. For example, the following two series of expressions are equivalent:

Example 2.8   `Pen up.`
                   `Pen go: length.`
                   `Pen down`

Example 2.9   `Pen`
                   `up;`
                   `go: length;`
                   `down`

Variables

Smalltalk variables are containers for objects. The two types of variables used in Smalltalk are temporary and global variables. **Temporary** variables are declared after the program is executed. You can declare them by enclosing them in pairs of vertical bars (|) at the beginning of an expression series, and their names must start with a lowercase letter, as in Example 2.10:

Example 2.10 | tempVariable   index value |

Temporary variables can be assigned values as follows:

Example 2.11   index:= 1.

tempVariable := value at: index

The first line in the example assigns the object **1** to the temporary variable **index**. Note that the symbol for value assignment is :=. The second line in the example assigns the result of a message. A caret symbol (^) is used before the value to be returned as the result of the expression series:

Example 2.12   ^value

Global variables are systemwide objects and are not automatically removed after a program has been executed; they are not confined to use in an expression. Global variable names always begin with an uppercase letter. When a global variable does not currently exist, a menu will pop up automatically to allow the user to decide whether or not to create it. The following are examples of global variables available in Smalltalk:

- Disk
- Transcript
- True

Like temporary variables, global variables can be assigned value:

Example 2.13   `Family := 'David Lise Eileen Emily '`

Programming Classes and Methods

The concept of **classes** is one of the most distinctive features of Smalltalk. Together with the other three concepts — objects, messages, and methods — classes form the basis of programming to solve problems. This section focuses on major classes available in Smalltalk and how to program classes.

Definition of Classes

Classes describe data structures (objects), algorithms (methods), and external interfaces (messages). Each object is an instance of a certain class, and all objects in a class are similiar because they share the same structure and respond to the same class messages and methods. The classes themselves are objects that are contained in global variables; consequently, all class names begin with a capital letter.

Classes form a hierarchy that consists of a root class, **Object**, and many subclasses. Subclasses, in turn, may contain more layers of subclasses. Each subclass inherits the functionality of all its superclasses in the organization and builds on its superclasses by adding its own methods and "instance variables" to characterize its behavior. **Instance variables** are internal variables accessible only to the objects they belong to; they are similar to fields of a record structure and contain either pointers, words, or bytes. Most object instance variables contain pointers.

Smalltalk makes approximately 100 classes available for selection, modification, and editing to meet user applications' needs. Figure 2.1 shows the hierarchy of these classes. The major classes that will be discussed as examples to illustrate C++ characteristics are as follows:

- Magnitude

- Collection

Each of these classes contains more subclasses, and discussion will focus on the critical subclasses of each, but first you should concentrate on how to program a class, i.e., how to modify its class methods and instance methods to meet the needs of an application.

Hierarchy Of Smalltalk Classes

I.   Object
    A. Behavior
        1. Class
        2. MetaClass
    B. BitBlt
        1. CharacterScanner
        2. Pen
            a. Animation
            b. Commander
II. Boolean
    A. False
    B. True
III. ClassBrowser
IV. ClassHierarchyBrowser
V. ClassReader
VI. Collection
    A. Bag
    B. IndexCollection
        1. FixedSizeCollection
            a. Array
            b. Bitmap
            c. ByteArray
                (1) CompiledMethod
                (2) FileControlBlock
            d. Interval
            e. String
                (1) Symbol
        2. OrderedCollection
            a. Process
            b. SortedCollection

Figure 2.1   *Hierarchy of Smalltalk classes*

```
            C. List
               1.  EmptyList
            D. Set
               1.  Dictionary
                  a. IdentityDictionary
                     1)  MethodDictionary
                  b. SystemDictionary
               2.  SymbolSet
  VII.     Complier
  VIII.       Context
  IX.      CursorManager
            A. NoMouseCursor
  X.       DemoClass
  XI.      Directory
  XII.     Directory
  XIII.    DiskBrowser
  XIV.     Dispatcher
            A. GraphDispacher
            B. PointDispatcher
            C. ScreenDispatcher
            D. ScrollDispatcher
               1.  ListSelector
               2.  TextEditor
                  a.    PromptEditor
               3.  TopDispatcher
  XV.      DispatchManager
  XVI.     DisplayObject
            A. DisplayMedium
               1.  Form
                  a.    DisplayScreen
                  b.    SelectorForm
            B. DisplayString
            C. InfiniteForm
  XVII.  File
  XVIII.Inspector
            A. Debugger
            B. DictionaryInspector
```

Figure 2.1   *Hierarchy of Smalltalk classes (cont.)*

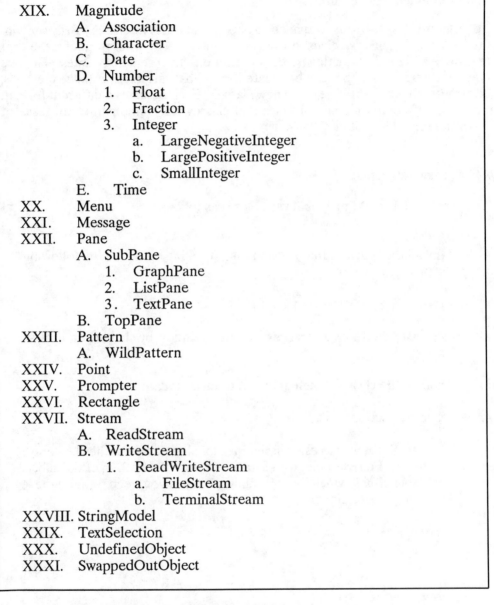

XIX. Magnitude
    A. Association
    B. Character
    C. Date
    D. Number
        1. Float
        2. Fraction
        3. Integer
            a. LargeNegativeInteger
            b. LargePositiveInteger
            c. SmallInteger
    E. Time
XX. Menu
XXI. Message
XXII. Pane
    A. SubPane
        1. GraphPane
        2. ListPane
        3. TextPane
    B. TopPane
XXIII. Pattern
    A. WildPattern
XXIV. Point
XXV. Prompter
XXVI. Rectangle
XXVII. Stream
    A. ReadStream
    B. WriteStream
        1. ReadWriteStream
            a. FileStream
            b. TerminalStream
XXVIII. StringModel
XXIX. TextSelection
XXX. UndefinedObject
XXXI. SwappedOutObject

Figure 2.1   *Hierarchy of Smalltalk classes (cont.)*

Programming Class Features

To program class features, you need to pop up the **Class Hierarchy Browser** window by selecting **browse class** in the system menu. The window allows the user to browse and modify existing method definitions and create new ones. The five types of class features that can be created are global variables, instance methods, class methods, class variables, and new classes. Each requires a different format. Examples of adding global variables and classes will demonstrate the ease of programming in Smalltalk.

Adding Global Variables

The procedure for adding global variables is as follows:

1.   Install the relevant file by evaluating (clicking on **do it**) the following expression:

```
(file pathname: 'filename') fileIn
```

2.   Activate the **Class Hierarchy Browser** Window by clicking on **browse classes**.

3.   Pop up the class list pane menu and select **update**.

4.   Select the target class.

5.   Create global variables by assigning global variables to the class and methods. For example, to create a new dog in class **Dog** of the subclass of class **animal**, which has a method of **name**, you need to write the following expressions:

```
"creating a dog, Snoopy"

Snoopy := Dog new.

Snoopy name: 'Snoopy"
```

Note the **new** is used to create a new variable, **Snoopy**.

6.   Pop up the pane menu and select **save**.

Adding a Class

The steps for adding a subclass to a class are as follows:

1—4.   Same as those for adding global variables.

5.   Pop up the pane menu, and select **add subclass**.

6.   A prompter appears to ask for the name of the subclass.

7.   Enter the name, and press the Return key.

8.   Another menu appears, select **variable Subclass**.

9.   Specify the new class's instance variables by following the template shown in the text pane.

10.   Pop up the pane menu and select **save**.

Magnitudes

The magnitude classes define objects that can be compared, measured, ordered, and counted, such as characters, numbers, dates, and times that are most frequently used. The hierarchy of the magnitude class is shown as follows:

```
Superclass (inherits from):   Object
Subclass (inherited by):      Association
                              Character
                              Date
                              Number
                                  Float
                                  Fraction
                                  Integer
                                      LargeNegativeInteger
                                      LargePositiveInteger
                                      SmallInteger
                              Time
```

Magnitude assumes its subclass implements the ordering relationship and comparison methods such as =, < =, > =, <, >, and =. Based on these methods, magnitude provides its subclasses with interval testing (between:) and max/min computation. For example:

Example 2.14   11 between: 20 and: 10 => True

             25 max: 30   => 30

             25 min: 30   => 25

The definitions of these classes can be found in *Smalltalk/V: Tutorial and Programming Handbook* by Digitalk, Inc. (Los Angeles, 1986). Now, you will examine the most frequently used subclasses: **Number**, **Character**, **Date**, and **Time**.

Number

Class **Number** supports three subclasses: **Float** (for floating point), **Fraction** (for rational), and **Integer** (for integer). Class Number implements binary arithmetic operators such as +, -, *, /, qus (integer quotient), rem (integer remainder), raisedTo (raised to the power of), and log. It also supports other unary arithmetic operators, such as sqrt, exp, COS, arcSin, tan, ln, and floor (nearest integer less than or equal to), ceiling, reciprocal, truncated, and rounded. Number also implements testing methods such as even, odd, negative, positive (true if > =0), strictlyPositive (true if >0) and sign (-1 if negative, 1 if positive, and 0 if zero). The internal testing and max/min methods are inherited from the superclass, Magnitude. All iteration methods are implemented in Number also.

The differences among Number's three subclasses are discussed below. Real numbers in class Float are represented in an 8-byte IEEE format and are given an approximate 18 digits of precision in the value range of (+/-) 4.19 e- 307 to (+/-) 1.67 e 308. A math co-processor is required to perform arithmetic operations in Float. Rational numbers are represented by instances of class fraction and are described by a pair of integers (instance variables numerator and denominator), for example,

Example 2.15   5/4

In Example 2.15, the slash message is sent to the integer receiver, 5, with an integer argument 3 to form a fraction.

Class Integer contains integers as its instance. The class is divided into three subclasses: LargeNegativeInteger, LargePositiveInteger, and SmallInteger for high efficiency in computing speed and memory requirement. For example, small integers are not represented as objects in memory. Their values are between -16,384 and 16,383. However, the large integers can be represented in up to 64K of precision.

Character

Class **Character** contains the extended ASCII character set from ASCII value 0 to ASCII 255. Characters need not be created and may be referenced by either of the two messages **asCharacter** or **value**, for example,

> **Example 2.16**   65 asCharacter => $A
>
> Character value: 65 => $A

The interval testing and comparison methods are inherited from class Magnitude, for example,

> **Example 2.17** $B <$F   =>True
>
> 75 asCharacter max: $F => $K
>
> $d between: $A and $E => False
>
> $d asUpperCase => $D

Date and Time

Instances of class **Date** represent specific dates such as January 3, 1987. Instances of class **Time** indicate specific times of day, such as 3:00 a.m. A variety of methods for classes Date and Time are listed in the Method section of Digitalk Inc.'s *Smalltalk/V: Tutorial and Programming Handbook* (Los Angeles, 1986). They can be identified by searching through the names of methods that contain terms such as day, date, month, or time. The testing and comparison methods are inherited from class Magnitude. Examples of simple date or time expressions are as follows:

Example 2.18
```
Data today

Time now

Date newday: 4 month: #January year: 1987
```

New global variables such as Birthday or Lunchtime can be created for comparison of dates. For example, if Birthday is created as follows,

Example 2.19
```
Smalltalk at: #Birthday put: '1 January 1987' asDate
```

then you can make the following comparison:

Example 2.20
```
Birthday > Date newday => false

Birthday  max: Date newday => 'January 4, 1987'
```

Collection

Class **Collection** is the superclass of all the collection classes; collections are the basic structures used to store objects in groups in a organized manner. Two kinds of collections have already been discussed: Arrays and Strings. Arrays are fixed-size sequences of objects, and strings are fixed-size sequences of characters. The hierarchy of class Collection is as follows:

```
Superclass:     Object
Superclass:     Bag
                IndexedCollection
                     FixedsizeCollection
                     Array
                     ByteArray
                     Interval
                     String
                          Symbol
                     OrderedCollection
                          SortedCollection
                List
                     EmptyList
                Set
                     Dictionary
                          IdentityDictionary
```

The definitions of these classes can be found in the previously mentioned Smalltalk/V handbook by Digitalk Inc., (Los Angeles, 1986). The most frequently used of these classes are **Dictionary**, **Bag**, and **Set**. Next, you will examine the features, attributes, and common protocol of class collection and the special characteristics of the three classes.

Features, Attributes, and Common Protocol of Class Collection

Any subclass in class Collection generally provides the following capabilities to the user:

- searching, adding, removing, accessing, and changing elements of a collection

- iterating over the elements of a collection

The four attributes that characterize a collection class are as follows:

- order of the elements in a collection

- flexibility of collection size — fixed or expandable

- duplicability of collection elements

- accessibility of a collection by a set of keys

The attributes of the three most frequently used classes are as follows:

Class	Ordered	Fixed size	Element Dup's	Key	Class
Bag	No	No	Yes	None	Any
Set	No	No	No	None	Any
Dictionary	No	No	No	Lookup	Any

A special message — **with:** — can be used to create an instance of any collection classes as follows:

```
with: firstObject

with: secondObject

with: thirdObject

with: fourthObject
```

For example, assume you want to create a parts base in which there are two global variables, Engine and Battery. Because arbitrary objects and duplicates may be used in the base class, Bag is more appropriate for it. You can initialize the variable as follows:

Example 2.21
```
Engine:= Bag with: #GM

        with: #Toyota

        with: #Ford

        with: #Nissan

Battery:= Bag with: #(Sears JCPenny)
```

Manipulating collections includes adding, removing, and testing messages and iteration messages, such as do: and select:, to process all elements of a collection. Examples are as follows:

Example 2.22
```
Engine add: #Mazda      =>Mazda

Engine remove: #GM      =>GM

Engine size             =>4

Engine addall: Battery  =>(Sears JCPenny)

Engine select: [: aPart| aPart ==#Mazda]

Engine includes: #Mazda   =>true
```

Dictionary

Class **Dictionary** stores and retrieves objects with an external lookup key. A dictionary can be easily created using Dictionary. For example, you can create a client dictionary as follows:

Example 2.23   `ClientDictionary := Dictionary new`

In Example 2.23, **ClientDictionary** is a global variable, and **new** is a message indicating it is a new variable. You can perform the following tasks with Client-Dictionary:

- Add telephone numbers to it. Use **at: put:**

```
ClientDictionary

            at: 'David' put:  '582-0000'

            at: 'Lise' put:   '583-1111'
```

- Retrieve a telephone number. Use **at:**

```
ClientDictionary at: 'David' => '582-0000'
```

- Check whether a name is in the directory. Use **at: ifAbsent**

```
ClientDictionary at: 'Emily' ifAbsent: ['not in the Directory']
```

- Review all the names in the directory. Use **inspect**

```
ClientDictionary inspect
```

Be sure to follow the above formats precisely.

Bag and Set

Class **Bag** stores an arbitrary number of objects of any kind including duplicates without implied order or sequence to the elements in the bag. Messages used to create, add, retrieve, and test elements in a bag are the common protocols available in class Collection.

Class **Set**, like Bag, stores arbitrary objects; however, Set does not store the same object more than once. The common messages available for Collection are inherited in Set. The special message that is unique to this class is **asSet**. The message asSet can be used to create a set out of the receiver collection object that eliminates duplicates from the collection. For example, to calculate the odd numbers in a string, evaluate the following expression:

Example 2.24   `'1 2 2 3 3 3 4 5 5'` asSet select: :x| x odd]

Emulation of Class and Method Structures for Expert Systems in C/C++

The discussion of classes and methods in the previous subsections gives you an understanding of how class and method structures work. C++ provides you with the core of expert systems that relies heavily on knowledge representation. Chapter 10 demonstrates a C/C++ library structure for expert system development that is similar in purpose to a structure for the classes and methods available in an object-oriented environment, such as Smalltalk.

OVERVIEW OF C/C++ FEATURES FOR EXPERT SYSTEM DEVELOPMENT

C++ was developed by Bjarne Stroustrup at the AT&T Bell Laboratories in the summer of 1983. It is an extension of C and thus retains C's efficiency and flexibility. Earlier versions of the language were collectively known as "C with Classes." The key concept in C++ is class. A **class** is a user-defined type. Classes provide object-oriented programming features such as data hiding, inheritance, user-controlled memory management, and dynamic typing.

Because C++ is an extension of C, the basic syntax and semantics of the two languages are the same. Experienced C programmers can apply their programming knowledge directly to C++ programming. As your need for stronger type checking, data abstraction, and class mechanisms such as class inheritance grows, you can gradually master the C++ facilities supporting these programming activities. C++ retains the same interface facilities that correspond directly to computer hardware and enhance the facilities for designing interfaces among program modules.

C++ modules are compatible with C modules and can be linked freely so that existing C libraries can be used with C++ programs. However, because C++ has stronger type checking, if the data type used in a C module is not rigid, errors may occur when C++ and C modules are linked. Furthermore, C++ and C functions can be used together.

This section highlights the main C++ features in ascending order; the C++ functions that are least different from C functions will be discussed first:

1. **Program Organization**

   - Header and implementation files
   - Comments

2. **LISP-like Functions**

   - Enumeration names
   - Void
   - Function prototype
   - Overloading of function names
   - Default arguments

   a) Reference parameters in function
   b) Unspecified number of parameters in function

3. **Object-Oriented Programming Features**

   - Classes and Data Encapsulation
   - Creating subclasses
   - Virtual functions and polymorphism

Program Organization

Header and implementation files and comments are discussed in this section.

Header and Implementation Files

Before using a C++ translator or compiler, you prepare your source program, using any text editor, in two distinct types of source files:

- **header files**, which have the extension **.hxx** or **.h**
- **implementation files**, which have the extension **.cpp**

As shown in Figure 2.2, a header file includes the **interface**, which is a set of related classes, functions, and data type declarations that can be manipulated by other files. In a sense, a header file collects all information and operations on an object; it may even include a mini user's guide to explain in the form of comments and examples how each function can be applied. Like classes and methods in Smalltalk, a header file is often all that is available to a programmer/user (the source code for the implementation file is usually not supplied); it is the natural place for the user to seek help in understanding how to use the functions. In the near future, when more programmers/developers have used C++, classes and methods on various specific applications similar to Bag, Dictionary, and Directory in Smalltalk will be available to C++ programmers to increase their programming productivity.

The implementation file manipulates the classes, functions, and other data types specified in the header file. Because C++ is an object-oriented language, it allows you to focus your attention on describing the objects you want to operate on. Once you have organized the objects clearly, writing the implementation file is straightforward.

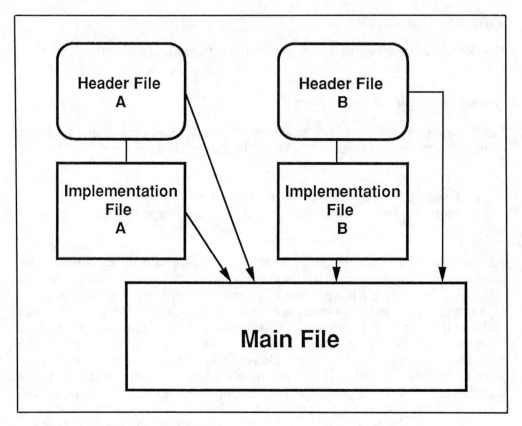

Figure 2.2   Source program files

Comments

//, /*, and */ can be used in C++ to indicate comments. The symbols // are used to signal a comment to the end of a line, and the older C-like comment delimiters, /* and */, are used to bracket a comment on a single line or over multiple lines.

LISP-like Functions

The term **LISP-like function** is used loosely to indicate that a function is frequently used in LISP-written expert systems. Main C++ functions in this area include enumeration names, void, function prototype, overloading of function names, reference parameters in functions, default arguments, and unspecified number of parameters in functions.

Enumeration Names

The declaration containing **typedef** allows users to define identifiers that can later be used as if they were type keyword:

```
typedef struct {
    int right;
    int middle;
    int left;
} mouse-button
```

The above declaration introduces the user-defined type identifier **mouse-button**. Any variables declared to be of this new type can have one of the values from the value set — right, middle, and left — for example,

```
typedef struct key-operation

{

        mouse-button  keyboard;

//...
//...
//...
};
```

This declaration provides convenience for value-choose in multiple menu selections.

Void

In C++, **void** is a type used to indicate that a function does not return a value. Pointer variables can be declared to point to void for 1) passing pointers to functions that are not allowed to make assumptions about the type of the object and 2) returning untyped objects from functions. This use of void is particularly powerful in providing menu-driven user interfaces in expert systems. For example, the declaration

```
typedef        void (*menu_driven) ( );
```

defines a point to a function, menu_driven, that returns void and has no parameters (see Listing 2.1). If there are five menu choices, (such as exit, input, output, disk, and video), the declaration

```
menu_driven    menu[5];
```

defines an array of five functions in which each specifies an operation. For this declaration to work, you need an assignment function that will actually load the array of menu functions by assigning the five function pointers to menu[0],...,menu[4].

Listing 2.1: Menu-Driven Applications

```
# include <stdio.h>
        typedef  void  (* menu driven)  ( );

        Menu driven                menu[5];

Main ( )
{
extern     void assign-fn ( );
extern     void exit ( );
extern     void input ( );
extern     void print ( );
extern     void ask-user ( );
extern     void trace ( );

int choice;
//         .
//         .
//         .
//         .
}
void       assign fn ( )
{
menu [0] = exit               ;
menu [1] = input              ;
menu [2] = print              ;
menu [3] = ask-user           ;
menu [4] = trace              ;
};
```

Function Prototype

Function prototyping, in which the parameters of a function are specified within the parameter definition section of the function, allows the compiler to perform run-time data type checking and thus minimizes serious interface problems in passing data to functions, for example,

```
void          function_name (char a, char b)
```

Overloading of Function Names

C++ allows a function name to be overloaded, i.e., to be redefined within the same scope of functions if the specifier Overload is given before the overloaded functions are declared, for example,

```
#include <stdio.h>
Overload pprint;
extern void pprint (int j);
extern void pprint (char* string);
//...
//...
//...

void pprint (int i)
{
// define pprint
}
void pprint (char* string)
{
// define pprint
}
```

Pprint is overloaded to allow printing of integers and strings. It can be further defined to print data sets, real numbers, or complex numbers.

Function name overloading is extremely important for expert system development because it provides a tool to connect classes with the inference engine in preparation for user queries (see Chapters 7 and 12 for examples).

Default Arguments, Reference Parameters in a Function, and Unspecified Numbers of Parameters in a Function

C++ features such as default arguments, reference parameters in a function, and unspecified numbers of parameters in a function provide more efficient operations for programmers.

C++ allows arguments in a function to have default values; however, the arguments with default values must appear as the last set of arguments in the function:

```
void default (int first, int second = 3, char third = 'a')
```

In C++, a **reference** acts as a name for an object. A nontrivial use of references is to ensure that the address of an object, rather than the object itself, is passed to a function (this is also called **call by reference**). References allow the use of arithmetic operators on large objects without excessive copying when pointers cannot be used. A parameter can be declared a reference parameter by using the **&** operator:

```
void      decrement      (int&  foo)

{ foo-- }

decrement (x);
```

C++ allows functions to have an unspecified number of arguments by using ellipses (...) in the argument, such as

```
int       printf (char* ...);
```

in the stdio.h. Calls to printf require at least one argument, a string. Note that argument checking is turned off when a function is declared to have an unspecified number of arguments.

Object-Oriented Programming Concepts

The concept of classes in C++ is similar to that in Smalltalk. Adding classes and associated features makes C++ closer to an object-oriented language than C is.

Object-oriented programming focuses on the data to be manipulated rather than on the procedures performing the manipulation. The main task of writing a C++ program is breaking the problem down into underlying data types (classes or subclasses) and defining the properties (method interface) of each of the classes and subclasses. The class or subclass variables correspond to the physical or logical entities constituting the actual problem. C++ provides the conveniences for creative class structures. Unlike Smalltalk, in which various classes have been created for different purposes (such as making directories and graphics), in C++ programmers must create their own classes. Perhaps in the future when more programmers have used C++, C++ class libraries will be made available by software developers. The remainder of this section will focus on classes and inheritance.

Classes and Data Encapsulation

The class construct provides the basic foundation for object-oriented programming for C++. The class encapsulates the set of values and the associated methods for an object. These values or methods can be completely or partially available to the users, and they may be completely or partially passed down to the class's subclasses. The class provides an inheritance-based hierarchy for data/knowledge representation.

The **struct** in C++ is a special case of a class with no protected section, i.e., all data (the normal struct in C) or methods (functions) are available to every call.

Special features in the C++ class include class structure (private, protected, and public sections), constructors and destructors, objects and messages, friends, and overloading of operators and function names in classes.

Structure of a Class

A class is generally constructed as follows:

```
class      class-name
{
private  :
         data and methods

//       The data and methods that cannot be accessed
//       directly by other classes

public   :
         data and methods
//       The data and methods that can be accessed directly
//       by other classes

protected :
         data and methods
//       The data and methods that can be accessed only by
//       children classes

};
```

Note that the declaration of **private** may not be required; private is the default.

Listing 2.2 shows a component class for building user-interface packages — **textscroller**. The class **KillBox** includes methods **Draw, Redraw,** and **Handle,** which are available to all classes, and also includes **HScroller, VScroller,** and **Textviewer,** which can be used by the functions declared within the class.

Listing 2.2: A Sample Program Including "Public" Data

```
// textscro.h
#ifndef TextScroller_h
#define TextScroller_h

#include <InterViews/Text/textviewer.h>
#include <InterViews/scroller.h>
#include <InterViews/box.h>
#include <InterViews/world.h>
#include <InterViews/painter.h>
#include <InterViews/frame.h>
#include <InterViews/sensor.h>
#include <InterViews/interactor.h>

class KillBox : public Interactor {
    Bitmap      *picture;
    Interactor *victim;
public:
    KillBox(Interactor *i, Painter *p);
    ~KillBox();
    void Draw();
    void Redraw(Coord, Coord, Coord, Coord);
    void Handle(Event &);
};

class TextScroller : public Frame {

    HScroller  *hs;
    VScroller  *vs;
    TextViewer *text;
public:
    TextScroller(Painter *p,int cols=COLS ,int rows=ROWS);
    ~TextScroller();
    TextViewer* Text() { return text; } ;
};


#define SCROLLERSIZE 16
#endif
```

Listing 2.3 shows another component class for user-interface — **message** (bulletins) — in which data about characteristics of the class itself (i.e., offset, length, author, subject, etc.) are declared and can be passed down to children classes. These data or methods are not accessible to outside classes.

Listing 2.3: A Sample Program to Show Inheritance

```
// message.h
#ifndef Message_h
#define Message_h

#include <InterViews/interactor.h>
#include <InterViews/painter.h>
#include "TextScroller.h"

class Message : public Interactor {
protected:
    long    offset;     // where in file the message is
    long    length;     // how long the message is
    char*   author;     // who wrote it
    char*   subject;    // what it's about
    char*   date;       // when it was written
    char*   file;       // where to read it from
    boolean selected;   // cursor is here right now
    Painter* fgpainter, *bgpainter;
    boolean seen;       // read or seen
    boolean deleted;    // has it been deleted?
public:
    Message(long, long, char*, Painter*, boolean);
    ~Message();
    void        Draw();
    void        Redraw(Coord,Coord,Coord,Coord);
    void        Handle(Event &);

    TextScroller *Read();           // return a textscroller with message
    char*        From() ;           // Who the message is from
    Message*     Add();             // add a message to the list
    char*        FindHeader(char *);  // find the specified header field
    char*        SaveHeader(char *);  // stash away an eventual header
};
#define MESSAGEWIDTH 128
#endif
```

46

After the header file is completed, methods, also called **member functions** in C++, can be defined using the double colon (::). The syntax requires the class name followed by the double colon and then the function name, for example,

```
void KillBox :: Draw ( ){
...
...

}
```

As shown in Listing 2.4, the above subroutine in the xxx.c file declares Draw ( ) as a member function of the class KillBox.

Listing 2.4: A Sample Program in Which a Member Function is Declared for a Given Class

```
/* textscro.c
*/
#include "TextScroller.h"
#include <InterViews/border.h>
#include <InterViews/bitmap.h>
#include <InterViews/shape.h>


/*
** Data for the killbox
*/


#include "killbox.icon"

KillBox::KillBox(Interactor *i,Painter *p=stdpaint) {
    shape->Rect(killbox_width,killbox_height);
    shape->Rigid();
    output = p;
    picture = new Bitmap(killbox_bits,killbox_width,killbox_height);
    victim  = i;
    Sensor *s = new Sensor(stdsensor);
    s->CatchButton(UpEvent,LEFTMOUSE);
    s->CatchButton(UpEvent,MIDDLEMOUSE);
```

continued...

...from previous page

```
    s->CatchButton(UpEvent,RIGHTMOUSE);
    s->CatchButton(DownEvent,LEFTMOUSE);
    s->CatchButton(DownEvent,MIDDLEMOUSE);
    s->CatchButton(DownEvent,RIGHTMOUSE);
    Listen(s);
}


KillBox::~KillBox() {
    delete picture;
}


void KillBox::Draw() {
    output->ClearRect(canvas,0,0,xmax,ymax);
    picture->Draw(canvas);
}


void KillBox::Redraw(Coord, Coord, Coord, Coord) {
    Draw();
}


void KillBox::Handle(Event &e) {
    Coord dummy;
    World *w;

    e.GetAbsolute(w,dummy,dummy);
    if (e.eventType == DownEvent) {
        picture->Invert();
        picture->Draw(canvas);
    }
    if (e.eventType == UpEvent) {
        w->Remove(victim);// kill the file
    }
}


/*
** TextScroller: a TextScroller will scroll a given text both horizontally
** and vertically.
*/
```

continued...

...from previous page

```
TextScroller::TextScroller(Painter *p = stdpaint,
    int cols = COLS,int rows = ROWS) : (p) {
    text    = new TextViewer(p,cols,rows);
    hs      = new HScroller(text,SCROLLERSIZE,nil,p);
    vs      = new VScroller(text,SCROLLERSIZE,nil,p);
    output = p;
    Insert(new VBox(
                new HBox(
                    text,
                    new VBorder(output),
                    vs
                ),
                new HBorder(output),
                new HBox(
                    hs,
                    new VBorder(output),
                    new KillBox(this,output)
                )
            )
    );
}
```

An object can be declared as any class in the same manner as an object is declared to be integer or real. For example, **a** in Listing 2.5 is declared to be an inside_class that has been defined earlier. The methods defined in the public section (called **public functions** hereafter) can be used by calling the class name followed by a period (.), the name of class type, two colons, and the name of the public function, as in the following example:

```
a.inside_class :: write ()
```

Listing 2.5: Initializing Classes Within a Class

```
// Program to illustrate the nesting of classes
#include <stdio.h>
class inside_class
{
        private
                int a;

        public:
                inside_class( int c ) { a = c; }
                void write ()  { printf( "\n%d", a); }
};

class outside_class
{
        private:
                int b;
                inside_class a;

        public:
                outside_class( int c);
                void write()  { printf( "\n%d", b );  }
};

outside_class::outside_class(  int c) : a(10)
{
        b = c;
}

main()
{
        outside_class object( -12 );

object.write_inside_a();
object.write();
}
```

Constructors and Destructors

Constructors are used to automatically initiate objects at their point of declaration; **destructors** are called to automatically deallocate the storage occupied by a class. As shown in Listing 2.2, the constructor **KillBox** has the same name as the class itself in which the class KillBox is initialized with **Interactor** and **Painter**. On the other hand, the tilde symbol (~), in front of "KillBox" and immediately following the constructor, is a destructor that automatically deallocates the storage occupied by the class. The destructor is used to release the storage in the heap contained by the class.

Nesting and Initializing Classes

C++ allows the nesting of classes (i.e., a class can contain one or more classes as its members either in the private or public section). As shown in Listing 2.5, the **inside_class** was first defined by giving a private member (**int a**) and two public members (the constructor **inside_class(int c) { a=c;}** and the method **write()**).

The **outside_class** is then created by declaring **int b**, **inner_class a** to be private members and the following objects to be public members:

- constructor **outside_class (int c)**
- **write()**
- **write_inside_a**, which is a *public* member function of the inside_class.

The initialization of nested classes uses constructors slightly different from those used for the simple class. For example, the variables inside the inside_class are initialized as follows (see Listing 2.5):

```
inside_class (int c)  { a = c ; }
```

The class is declared to be initialized with a constructor for int c. To assign the value of 10 to **a**, the following statement is required:

```
inside_class  (10);
```

However, to assign private data (**a**) in **inside_class** from **outside_class**, you need to write the following:

```
outside_class :: outside_class (int c) : a(10)
{ b=c;}
```

The internal data object **a** is initialized by the contractor for class outsider_class. The constructor for the internal object is executed before constructors for the class containing the internal object. In general, a list of constructors is given after a colon, each constructor separated by a comma if there is more than one data object. However, when a class that contains internal data objects is deallocated by a destructor, the order of deallocation is the reverse: the destructor of the class is executed before the destructors for a class's internal data objects.

Friends

To benefit from the efficiency of object-oriented programming, data and methods need to be defined within the same class; otherwise, a function call overhead is required because the private data and methods are available only within the class definition, and these methods might be implemented in different classes. C++ provides programmers with a convenient facility — friend — to bypass this requirement.

Friend is used to declare a method in the private section of a class or in an entire class or to declare a function to be accessible by a given class (friends of a given class), for example,

```
class     friends_example
{
          friend char* x:: list ( );
          friend class y ;
          friend vector multiply (matrix &, vector &);
          //...
}
```

In the previous example, method **char* list** () from class **x**, class **y**, and function **vector multiply** are declared to be friends of **class friends_example**. A friend declaration can be inserted into either the private or public section of a class. The location of a declaration makes no difference in the program execution.

The declaration of friends releases the software engineer from the responsibility of consistently keeping a trace of the methods required for manipulation of the underlying data for all situations that might be encountered. It also increases code efficiency and computation speed by reducing the need to apply unnecessary methods in a class when the class is called.

Static Members

If you need to have every object in the class sharing the same data, as in a corporate calendar, for example, the corporate calendar can be declared as **static** in the class calendar:

```
class calendar {
//...
calendar*          next;
static calendar*          corporate_calendar;
void          appoint (int);
//...
};
```

By declaring **corporate_calendar** as static, you are assured that only one copy of corporate_calendar exists. Corporate_calendar can be called from outside of the class:

```
calendar :: corporate_calendar
```

In a member function, a static member is referenced in the same manner as other .members. The use of static class members will help you reduce the need for global variables.

Static members are like expert systems' **own slots** in that copies aren't made for every child entity (see Chapter 7).

Creating Subclasses (Derived Classes)

You can create subclasses by using the inheritance feature of C++. **Inheritance** allows you to reuse data and functions in the classes you have created by passing all or parts of them down to children classes (i.e., subclasses). This property is extremely useful in building expert systems because it provides programmers with ready-made frame structures. In many object-oriented languages such as Smalltalk, the property of inheritance forms the backbone of the entire programming environment, in which a sophisticated baseline class organization is available to the programmer.

Each object-oriented language handles inheritance differently. C++ allows a child class to inherit or modify the methods of its parent class (sometimes, called **member slots**). C++ also allows you to add more methods not contained in the parent class (called own slots).

In the current version of C++, a class can have only one parent. (Note that in Smalltalk, a class can have several parents—called **multiple inheritance**). Unless specially authorized, a derived class cannot access the private data of its parent. This authorization can be granted by either of the following methods:

- A **friend declaration**: an entire subclass or given methods in a subclass can be declared as friends of the parent class.

- A **protected mode**: all class members can be declared as **protected** in the parent class. The protected members are hidden in the same way as private members except that they are accessible to subclasses, as shown in Figure 2.3.

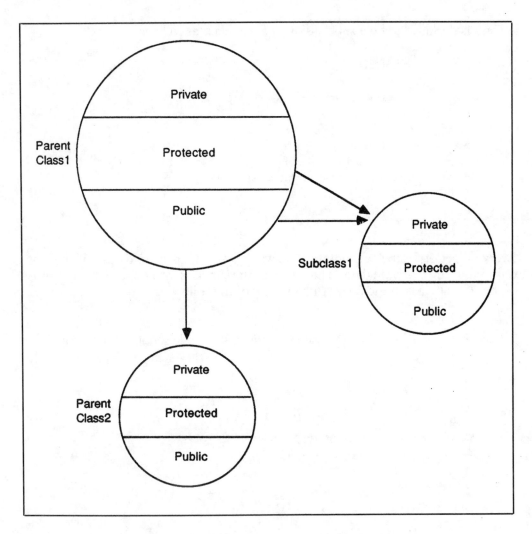

Figure 2.3   *Inheritance of the three types of class members: public,*
protected, and private

Figure 2.3 shows the inheritance of the three types of class members: public, protected, and private. The information in both the public and protected types can be accessible to subclasses. In fact, the information in the public section of the parent class can be available to anyone.

A class is declared to be a subclass of a parent class as follows:

```
class      parent_class1 ;
{
int        private1, private2 ;
public :
method1   ( )  {//...} ;
method2   ( )  {//...} ;
};
class      subclass_name:     parent_class-name
{
//...
} ;
```

Every object of a subclass contains its own copy of the private data of its parent class and its own private data. The object of the subclass may not use the methods of the parent class in the header unless one of the following two criteria is met:

- The subclass includes these methods in its public section, for example,

```
class      subclass1 : parent_class1
{
public :
void              method1 ( )
{ parent_class1 :: method1 ( );
}
//...
};
```

- The subclass is defined with the following declaration (note the word **public** before the parent_class_name), for example,

```
class subclass_name : public parent_class_name
        {
        //...
        };
```

In the first example, **method1** is available to the objects in subclass1.

However, note that in the implementation phase (main program), subclasses can assess the methods (but not the private data) of the parent class, for example,

```
main ( )
{
parent_class1 x ;
        x.method1 ( );
subclass1       y ;
        y.parent_class1 :: method2( );};
```

Initializing a Subclass with a Parent Class Constructor

When a parent class includes a constructor for initialization, you need to consider how to invoke this constructor in a subclass because objects of each subclass contain a copy of the parent class's data.

Objects of each subclass can initialize parent class data by using a constructor that contains all parameters that are required in the order: parent class first, internal class (guest) members second, and the subclass last. For example, if there are five parameters to be initialized as shown in Listing 2.6,

1.   two parameters, X1 and X2, are for the private data of the parent class: private1 and private2.

2.   two parameters, X3 and X4, are for the private data of guest member, parent_class private 4.

3.   one parameter, X5, is for the public data of the subclass, private3.

Listing 2.6: Initializing a Subclass with a Parent Class Constructor

```
#include <stdio.h>

class parent_class1
{
        private :
                int private1, private2;

        public :
        parent_class (int X1, X2)

//....
};

class  subclass1 : parent_class1
{
        private :
        int private3;
        parent_class1 private4:

        public :
        subclass1 ( int X1, int X2, int X3, int X4, int X5 ) :
                        (X1, X2), private4 (X3, X4)
        {
        private3 = X5;

        }
        //...
};
```

To initialize all five parameters, you need to declare a constructor in the public section of the subclass as follows:

```
Subclass1  (int X1, int X2, int X3, int X4, int X5)
       : (X1, X2), private4 (X3, X4)
       {
       private4 = X5;
       }
```

Virtual Functions and Polymorphism

C++ allows you to declare functions in a base (root) class that can be redefined in each subclass. These functions are called virtual functions. (The compiler guarantees the correct correspondence between objects and functions). This feature is called **polymorphism** in object-oriented programming. With polymorphism, you can send a message to an object without worrying about how the system will implement the action.

A **virtual function** must be declared in a parent class (or the class in which it is first declared) by using the keyword **virtual** in front of the function definition. The keyword virtual is used only once in the base class, and only the overloaded function name is used in the subsequently derived classes. However, not all subsequent subclasses must declare and implement the virtual function. The virtual function can thus be used even if no subclass will be derived. Like function name overload, virtual functions allow you to use the function names repeatedly in the subclasses and to slightly modify the content of the function, for example,

```
class parent_class1
{
protected
       int     version ;
public :
       parent_class1 ( ) { version = 1 ;}
       virtual void  print   ( )
       {
         printf ("\n  The parent class.  version%d," version):
       }
       };
```

continued...

...from previous page

```
class    subclass1 : public parent_class1
{
        int      layer ;

public :
//...

void print ( )
{
  printf ("\nSubclass1  layer:%d.  version%d",layer,  version);
}
};
```

In the previous example, the two **print** ( )s are slightly different even though they use the same member function name.

SUMMARY

- C++, like Smalltalk, is an object-oriented language that has the following features: information hiding, data abstraction, dynamic binding, class inheritance, and message passing.

- The main vocabulary of Smalltalk consists of five words — object, message, class, instance, and method — that present the concepts of Smalltalk.

- The concept of classes in C++ is similar to that in Smalltalk. Adding classes and associated features makes C++ closer to an object-oriented language than any conventional programming language such as C or Pascal.

- Object-oriented programming focuses on the data to be manipulated rather than on the procedures performing the manipulating. The main task of writing a C++ program is breaking the problem down into underlying data types (classes or subclasses) and defining the properties (method interface) of each of the classes and subclasses. The class or subclass variables correspond to the physical or logical entities that constitute the actual problem. C++ provides the conveniences for creative class structures.

- The class construct provides the basic foundation for object-oriented programming for C++. The class encapsulates the set of values and the associated methods for an object. These values or methods can be completely or partially available to users, and they can be completely or partially passed down to subclasses. The class construct provides an inheritance-based hierarchy for data/knowledge representation.

- Classes with inheritance and function name overloading give C++ programmers great convenience in representing structured knowledge such as frames.

REFERENCES

Digitalk, Inc. *Smalltalk/V: Tutorial and Programming Handbook*. Los Angeles, 1986.

Guidelines Software, Inc. *Guidelines C++: Installation Guide and Release Notes*. Orinda, CA, 1986.

Lifeboat Associates, Inc. *Advantage C++: User's Guide*. Tarrytown, NY, 1986.

Oregon Software, Inc. "Oregon C++: Software product description," Portland, OR, 1988.

OASYS. "Designer C++: Product description," Waltham, MA, 1987.

Strousetrup, B. *The C++ Programming Language*. Reading, MA: Addison-Wesley, 1986.

Usenix Association. "C++ Workshop. Santa Fe, NM, Proceedings, November 9-10, 1987," Berkeley, CA, 1987.

Wiener, R. and L. Pinson. *An Introduction to Object-Oriented Programming and C++*. 1988.

Zortech, Inc. "Zortech C++," Product description, Arlington, MA, 1988.

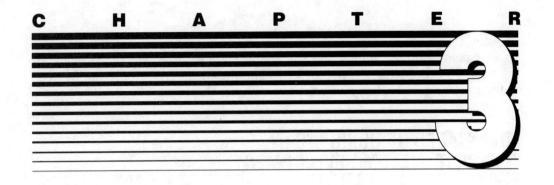

USING C/C++
IN EXPERT SYSTEM
DEVELOPMENT

Chapter 1 explains the basics of expert system technology; Chapter 2 discusses object-oriented programming and C++; this chapter examines the reasons for using C/C++ in building expert systems and the distinctive programming principles and design rules for your expert system development.

ADVANTAGES OF USING C/C++ IN EXPERT SYSTEM DEVELOPMENT

The advantages of C and C++ will be discussed separately even though C++ is a superset of C.

The Development and Strengths of C

C was developed in the early 1970s by Ken Thompson and Dennis Richies at AT&T Bell Laboratories. By the mid-1980s, C emerged as the language of choice for system development because it allowed the direct manipulation of bits, bytes, words, and pointers, which are common operations for system-level programming. As a system language, C is efficient for run-time performance.

Because C uses only 32 keywords (27 keywords from the Kernighan-and-Ritchie de facto standard and 5 keywords from the ANSI standardization committee), compilers are available for virtually all computers and operating systems. C code is portable between computers and operating systems, and thus it can be written once for one type of computer and modified with slight effort for other types of computers.

C is a structured language in which code and data can be compartmentalized (i.e., you can write subroutines in which the events occurring within these subroutines will cause no side effects in other parts of the program). All subroutines are discrete functions. All variables that are declared in a function will be known to that function. You can thus build a large program incrementally by developing, debugging, and adding functions that use only local variables and not worry about creating side effects in other parts of the program. (This incremental process is similar to the development process of expert systems, which will be discussed in later chapters.)

C usually exists with the UNIX environment in which various utilities support programming and can be called by C programs for operating system functions. Many of these functions either save programmers' time in compiling codes (such as **make,** which recompiles and relinks only those source code modules that have been changed) or allow programmers to manipulate system operations (such as **explicit memory management**) to improve run-time performance.

Many utility software packages, such as Microsoft Windows, are written in C; C programs can be integrated into these packages easily for most PC users. These programs can be treated as a master or a slave to existing packages without substantial rewriting efforts.

What Expert Systems Need from C

Undoubtedly, C can be used to write almost every function required by expert systems if you have endless financial support and time to write C code. Let us review the main elements of expert systems discussed in Chapter 1 to examine whether the strengths of C can be best used in building these components.

Expert systems contain three main elements: knowledge base, inference engine, and user-interface. The three elements play different roles from the time the expert system is being developed to the time the system is commercially implemented.

The Development Phase

In the development phase, the focus of the expert system project is on the programmers' productivity. C is most promising in implementing the inference engine and user-interface. The **inference engine** is a set of functions that will propagate appropriate rules effectively through substitution and can be performed in C fairly straightforwardly. The user-interface can be easily constructed by writing C functions to integrate readily available C packages such as windows and graphics.

The difficulty of C lies in the knowledge base in which various knowledge representation methods are needed to represent symbols, lists, and structures for complex, real-life situations, such as manufacturing process control. These methods may include frames, rules, or logic. C code can be written to represent logic and simple rules (to be discussed in later chapters). Frames and structured rules may be better handled by C++.

The Commercial Implementation Phase

Once an expert system is fully developed and tested by the focus group, it normally requires modifications or extensions to adapt to the existing user's environment. Because many existing software packages are written in C, the expert system in C can be more successfully integrated into the existing environment than systems written in other languages, such as LISP. Systems written in C can be easily ported to other computers with high run-time efficiency.

The Development and Features of C++

The key concept in C++ is **class**. A class is considered as a user-defined type. Classes provide object-oriented programming features such as data hiding, inheritance, user-controlled memory management, and dynamic typing. All these features have been discussed in Chapter 2 and are summarized next.

Summary of C++ Features

Because C++ is an extension of C, the basic syntax and semantics of the two languages are the same. C++ retains the same interface facilities that correspond directly to computer hardware and enhance the facilities for designing interfaces among program modules. C++ modules are compatible with C modules and can be linked freely so that existing C libraries may be used with C++ programs. Furthermore, C++ and C functions are interchangeable.

The main features of C++ are strong type checking and overloading, data abstraction, and object-oriented programming.

Strong Type Checking and Overloading

Type checking is an activity that a translator or a compiler carries out to ensure that the operations defined in a program are applied to the data of the correct type. Overloading is defined as giving functions the same name when they execute the same operation on objects of different types. Functions in C++ can be enhanced to perform type checking of arguments and overloading.

Type checking is performed over arguments in the function, which can also have a type. In particular, the type of the actual argument is checked against the type of the corresponding formal argument, and all standard and user-defined type conversions are performed. As discussed before, C++ requires a translator; these typed arguments help the translator better manage interfaces among modules and make the interface between a calling function and a called function safer. A special facility is provided for passing unchecked arguments or vectors or specifying default arguments. The use of type information thus makes the interface between a calling function and a called function more flexible.

Overloading includes function name and operator overloading, which allows the programmer to reuse functions defined in classes.

Data Abstraction

Data abstraction is defined as the separation of the representation of a data object from the specifications that are essential for its correct use. C++ supports data abstraction by allowing the programmer to use new types called classes. Classes provide for data hiding, guaranteeing initialization, function members, and overloaded operators. Operators may be overloaded — that is, declared to accept class objects as operands.

Data abstraction is a key feature of C++.

Object-Oriented Programming

As discussed in Chapter 2, C++ is an object-oriented programming language. In C++, the universe is a collection of different types (classes) of objects. A type is a set of values to be gathered with a set of operations on the value set. Objects of a given type have operations that they may perform. An object is a container for a value from the value set of the same type.

The type operations are called member functions; this set of operations is called the type's **public interface**. The user of an object can use it only by invoking its member functions; this user has no direct access to the data that represents the object's state.

The object-oriented model of a program in contrast to the conventional C procedural model works as follows: a program is a compilation of objects of different types that accomplish the work of the program by invoking one another's member functions. Each object determines its response, if any, to a member function. The names of the member function are resolved according to a symbol table private to the class. The member function's name is independent of the implementation of (1) the data of an object of a given type and (2) the algorithm that implements the member functions.

C++ provides a mechanism that allows calls of member functions, depending on the type of an object in cases where the actual function to be called is unknown at compile time. C++ provides dynamic binding, in which an object can determine at run time what function it will call in response to the invocation of a member function. C++ also provides new operators for controlling memory management.

This class structure, with inheritance and function name overloading, provides great convenience for programmers to represent knowledge and organized data such as frames and rule sets.

DISTINCTIVE EXPERT SYSTEM PROGRAMMING CONCEPTS

The most distinctive principle of expert system programming is rapid production of expert system prototypes, in contrast to the conventional waterfall programming approach. Rapid production of expert system prototypes is also called "rapid prototyping," which is defined as the heuristic approach to developing an expert system in that a rudimentary system is rapidly built to capture an initial set of user needs with an intent of iterative expansion and refinement of the system. The primitive system is immediately put to use by the user and is then gradually improved as the user and the developer establish a mutual understanding of the problem. The rapid prototyping approach is based on the belief that the risk of expert system projects can best be minimized by gradual learning and incremental improvement. Also, the incomplete understanding of the problem will mean that development of an expert system will be incremental, paralleling increased understanding of the problem.

The use of rapid prototyping brings together the developer and the intended user to define the requirements and design specifications for the full-scale expert system. This approach significantly reduces the risk of misidentifying the problem, experts, or problem-solving methods.

The main focus of rapid prototyping is the intended user. The internal strategy for developing a rapid prototype centers around gaining the user's cooperation and perfecting the prototype to meet the user's needs. The six elements in the strategy are as follows:

- involving the user early

- identifying functional areas for building prototypes

- establishing requirements for prototypes

- obtaining the first cut quickly, testing it, and iterating improvements between the intended user and the developer

- stressing that the purpose of the prototypes is not to replace human experts/specialists

- maintaining a small prototyping team

Getting Users Involved Early

Because application areas for expert systems are usually ill-defined, the only effective way to build the prototype is to involve the users in discussions of the functional areas of daily operations that concern them the most with respect to cost and time required, as shown in Figure 3.1. Meetings between intended users and the developers are arranged to examine the operations. Operational documents and textbooks, if available, are provided to assist the developer in understanding the requirements of the users. The underlying belief is that the intended user understands the operations and that his or her knowledge is to be extracted. In many cases, the intended user with 20 to 30 years of experience in the operations may be the only source of information for the developer; this user is generally irreplaceable for operations reliant on the use of aged but still cost-effective equipment. One example is military operations, e.g., users involved in operating long-durable battleships (as in Figure 3.1).

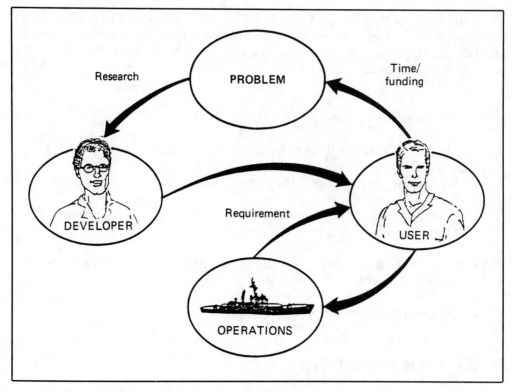

Figure 3.1   Getting users involved in developing prototypes

Identifying Functional Areas for Building Prototypes

Identifying functional areas for building prototypes is an important strategy because the selection of an "appropriate" application ensures a good likelihood of implementation success. Intended users are consulted early to identify the areas in which they need help most. Prototypes of expert systems are then built to assist the users in these functional routines and to thus free them to undertake creative work.

Figure 3.2 demonstrates this process with the military application in which large expert systems have proliferated. As shown in the illustration, when approached by the developer for an expert system, the potential user identifies the functional routines that can be replaced by expert systems. Some sophisticated methods such as Delphi techniques may be needed to reach a consensus of functional areas that are most cost-effective for expert systems. As shown in Figure 3.1, time or money saved can be used as the criterion for judging cost-effectiveness.

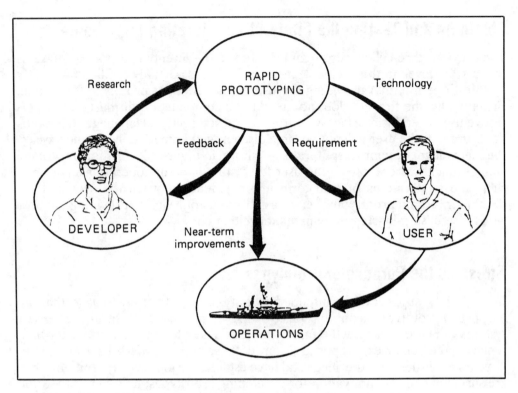

Figure 3.2   Strategic process in building rapid prototypes

Establishing Requirements for Rapid Prototypes

Establishing requirements for rapid prototypes to perform routines in the functional areas identified by the intended user is the third element in the internal strategy. In this step, the user and the developer establish the "blueprint" of the requirements for the prototype to perform the tasks of functional areas properly. Depending on application, the requirement may include physical characteristics (e.g., speed, precision, accuracy, and performance), appearance (e.g., dimension and color), and user interface (e.g., natural languages, graphics, and voice recognition). Iteration may be required to refine the requirement between the user and the developer.

Obtaining and Testing the First Cut and Iterating Improvements

The previous three elements might have raised the intended user's expectations to a certain level; in this element, the expectation is partially fulfilled by quickly (within three months) providing the user with a first-cut prototype for testing. Functionally, the first cut does not need to be complete, but it must have an effective user-friendly interface with graphic and semi-natural language commands to ensure that the user will not become discouraged immediately. In most cases, the user will not be computer literate. As shown in Figure 3.2, the rapid prototype is built quickly, presented to the user for testing in actual operations, and then subjected to iterations of near-term improvements between the user and the developer. Rapid prototyping serves as a formal approach to providing the user with a useful step-by-step incremental development.

Stressing the Purpose of Prototypes

In gaining the support of the intended user, it is crucial to stress to users that the purpose of prototypes is not to replace users. In most cases, it is true that expert systems will take over only the functional routines of human experts rather than replacing the human expert per se. Many of these human experts have more than 20 years of on-the-job experience and have established job security. Initially, they are suspicious of the motivation for developing prototypes; however, if their job security is assured, their cooperation can be gained quickly and their enthusiasm will also develop shortly. This crucial step in the internal strategy can easily be ignored and can result in failure of the prototyping project due to a lack of cooperation by human experts.

Maintaining a Small Prototyping Team

Development of rapid prototypes by large groups is difficult; a prototyping team should be composed of no more than three or four individuals to avoid the need for elaborate project management such as formal documentation, checkpoints, and reviews. A large team impedes speed, unity of objective, unity of approach, and communication and increases overhead in a rapid prototyping environment where speed, communication, and cost-effectiveness are essential to success.

DESIGN RULES

The five principles in designing rapid prototypes are modularity, object-oriented programming, simple inference engine, redundancy of knowledge, and good man-machine interface.

Modularity

Modularity refers to building the components in the prototypes as modules that can be reused over and over. These modules consist of "black boxes" that have input-output characteristics and can be recombined for use in other prototypes. Modules are portable, and if the approach of a prototype is unsatisfactory, the modules of knowledge in the prototype can then be transferred to a new prototype. Modularity may also imply simple, consistent knowledge representation.

Object-Oriented Programming

In object-oriented programming, the entities in a program are viewed as objects that communicate with each other via messages. Each object has distinct properties and rules/procedures associated with it. When a message arrives at an object, attachments (properties and rules/procedures) to the object process the message and carry out its effects. Object-oriented programming can thus be highly modular, can perform local actions such as display or self-modification, and can both receive information from and return information to the other objects. The purpose of object-oriented programming is also reusability in that objects representing knowledge can be reused over and over — either in the same prototype or in other prototypes. Object-oriented programming also provides a simple means for unifying the major knowledge representation methodologies such as rules, frames, or graphic images and prevents the developer from writing "spaghetti" code in which all subroutines are intertwined.

Simple Inference Engine

In the knowledge lies the power: inference is not critical in prototypes. A simple inference engine is helpful in two ways. First, explanations are easier to produce because they are currently generated by replaying the actions taken in the system. Keeping those actions simple ensures that less work is needed to generate comprehensive explanations the users can understand. Second, knowledge acquisition is simpler because less effort is needed to determine the exact knowledge to be added to improve system performance. The work of building prototypes becomes less complicated and errors can be more easily traced when the inference engine is simple.

Redundancy of Knowledge

Redundancy of knowledge, the fourth principle, is a convenient remedy for incomplete and inexact knowledge because the human experts themselves do not always know exactly what it is they comprehend most thoroughly in their areas of expertise. To build redundancy of knowledge into prototypes, you must obtain multiple overlapping sources of knowledge with different areas of strength and weakness. Proper use of multiple sources of knowledge can enrich the knowledge representation in the knowledge base.

Good Man-Machine Interface

The last design principle is good man-machine interface, which is the most important principle for developing rapid prototypes. Without it, prototypes will not be properly used and tested, and they eventually will be forgotten because of difficulties in use. Good man-machine interface, which includes effective display and data input/output and easy-to-use functions, is often ignored by many developers because they are so involved in computers they forget that users may not be computer literate. Good man-machine interface offers the only assurance that prototypes developed will be accepted by users.

SUMMARY

- In the development phase, the focus of the expert system project is the programmers' productivity; C is most promising in implementing inference engine and user interface. The inference engine is a set of functions that will propagate appropriate rules effectively through substitution and can be performed in C fairly straightforwardly. The user interface can be easily constructed by writing C functions to integrate readily available C packages such as windows and graphics.

- Once an expert system is fully developed and tested by the focus group, it normally requires modifications/extensions to adapt to the existing user's environment. Because many existing software packages are written in C, the expert system in C can be more successfully integrated to the existing environment than systems written in other languages such as LISP. C can be easily transported to other computers with high run-time efficiency.

- The key concept in C++ is class. A **class** is considered as a user-defined type. Classes provide object-oriented programming features such as data hiding, inheritance, user-controlled memory management, and dynamic typing.

- C++ modules are compatible with C modules, and the two can be linked freely so that existing C libraries may be used with C++ programs. Furthermore, C++ and C functions are interchangeable.

- The class structure with inheritance and function name overloading provides great convenience for programmers to represent knowledge and organized data such as frames and rule sets.

- Rapid prototyping is a heuristic approach to developing an expert system in that a rudimentary system is rapidly built to capture an initial set of user needs with an intent of iterative expansion. This approach reduces the risk of expert system projects. The four aspects of rapid prototyping are as follows: internal strategy, design principles, a step-by-step method and selection of experts, and acquisition of knowledge.

- The main focus of rapid prototyping is the user; the internal strategy for developing a rapid prototype centers around gaining the user's cooperation and perfecting the prototype to meet the user's needs by involving the users early, identifying functional areas for building prototypes, establishing requirements for prototypes, obtaining the first cut quickly, testing it, and iterating improvements.

- The five rules in designing rapid prototypes are modularity, object-oriented programming, simple inference engine, redundancy of knowledge, and good man-machine interface.

REFERENCES

Martino, Joseph P. *Technological Forecasting for Decision Making.* (New York: American Elsevier, 1983).

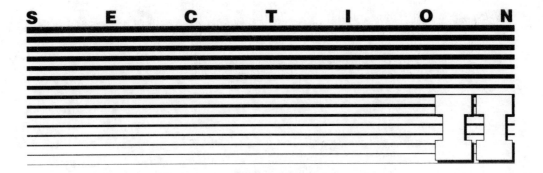

EXPRESSING LANGUAGES AND TOOLS FOR EXPERT SYSTEMS/ARTIFICIAL INTELLIGENCE IN C/C++

Section I presents the basic vocabulary for AI/expert systems and the C++ language. Section II focuses on the main task you are likely to encounter, i.e. to translate existing AI/expert system programs into C/C++ or to compare and select an expert system tool (shell). Section II contains three chapters. Chapters 4 and 5 provide you with C/C++ utility programs to express the two most popular AI/expert system languages. Chapter 6 discusses expert system tools.

The reason for this presentation is simple: most AI/expert systems and tools have been written in LISP; some are in Prolog because these languages provide sophisticated utilities for programmers to rapidly prototype an expert system in a relatively short period of time. However, when the system is ready for commercial distribution, C is the most efficient and convenient vehicle for mass installation, so utility programs in C/C++ may become handy when a conversion is required.

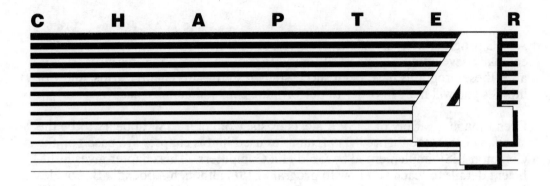

UTILITIES FOR LISP

As a C programmer, one of the tasks you are likely to perform if you are with a company developing AI/expert systems is to convert LISP programs into C/C++ after these programs have been successfully tested. This chapter arms you with utilities you will need in order to perform the conversion more easily.

Even though a variety of LISP dialects exists, Common LISP appears to be the standard LISP (see Figure 4.1). Examples used in this chapter are based on the Common LISP implemented by Gold Hill Computers. This chapter gives insufficient details to teach you how to program LISP, although Appendix B provides further discussion on LISP functions. If you are interested in skills of a good LISP programmer, read the definitive book, *Common LISP: Reference Manual*, by Guy L. Steele, Jr. (Digital Press, 1984).

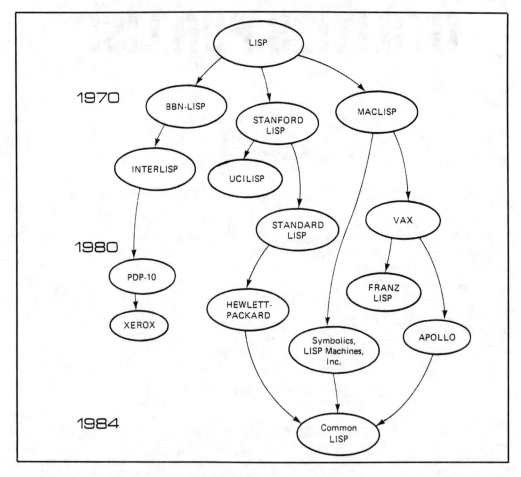

Figure 4.1   Development of LISP dialects

This chapter shows the similarities of and differences between LISP and C/C++ through examples in LISP and then discusses utility programs that can be used to convert LISP programs into C/C++. This chapter covers the following sections:

- Becoming Acquainted with LISP

- Program Structure

- List Operations

- C/C++ Utility Functions for List Operations

- Sample Conversions from LISP to C: Substitution

This chapter concentrates on supplementing C with utility functions that emulate LISP list operations. See Appendix B for a more detailed discussion of LISP programming.

BECOMING ACQUAINTED WITH LISP

Programming languages in general have their own idiosyncrasies. The LISP idiosyncracy is embracing parentheses for every statement in a program, and non-matching parentheses are often the sources of errors in a long program. In the following examples, the statements beginning with * signs are LISP expressions; the statements without them are the computer's responses:

```
* (sqrt 25);this is a comment for the square root of 25

  5

* 9

  9

* ()

  nil

  (expt 5 2
```

Note that at least one blank space is used to separate elements in a statement, and comments begin with a semicolon. Program accuracy is not affected by the use of upper- or lowercase letters or the number of spaces between parentheses or between elements. The last expression will not return anything until the right parenthesis is supplied. An error will occur if anything but a matching parenthesis is inputted.

In LISP, everything is accomplished by executing functions; all programs receive zero or more arguments and return 0, 1, or more values, for example,

```
* (- 4.98  7.38)

 2.40

* (abs -9.50)

 9.50
```

In these examples, function - (**minus**) requires two arguments, but function **abs** requires only one argument. Functions can be defined either internally in the package by the developer, such as **plus** (+), or externally by the programmer.

Programs and data use the same symbolic expressions (also called s-expressions or simply expressions), which consist of atoms and lists. Indivisible characters such as 9, 5, and 3.1416 are called **numeric atoms**; symbols such as +, sum, total, verb, and dog are called **symbolic atoms**. Numeric atoms include both integers and floating point numbers. A **list** is composed of a left parenthesis, followed by zero or more atoms or a list and then a right parenthesis.

Everything in a LISP expression is evaluated immediately after the right parenthesis is typed unless the evaluation is blocked with a **quote**:

```
*(expt 5 2)

 25

*(quote (I love you.))

 (I love you.)
```

The three rules for evaluating expressions are as follows:

1. Numbers evaluate to themselves, and nil ,(), evaluates to nil:

```
* 120

120

* ()

nil
```

2. Symbols evaluate to the last value assigned to them:

```
* L

Error
```

The above statement produces an **Error** because no value has been previously assigned to L. You can assign a value to L by using **setq**:

```
*(setq L 'a)
```

The ' is similar to a quote that indicates that atoms or lists after the symbol require no evaluation when L is re-evaluated:

```
* L

A
```

3.   Lists are evaluated by considering the first element as a function and the remaining elements as arguments for that function:

```
*(min 7 4 9 5 7)

4
```

In this example, **min** means the minimum of the arguments: 7, 4, 9, 5, 7.

PROGRAM STRUCTURE

LISP programs consist of forms and functions. A form is an object that can legally be evaluated, i.e., an expression that can be evaluated and that returns a value. Functions are invoked by applying them to arguments; they return a value.

Forms are divided into the following five categories:

- **Self-evaluating form**: includes all numbers, characters, strings, and bit-vectors; when evaluated, they are simply returned.

- **Variable**: represented by a symbol, including local (lexical or static) and global (special or dynamic) variables.

- **Special form**: represented by a list in which the first element is a special symbol reserved by Common LISP as shown in Table 4.1.

- **Macro call**: represented by a list in which the first element is a symbol that is not the name of a special form and is defined by a **macro**.

- **Function call**: represented by a non-empty list in which the first element is neither the name of a special form nor the name of a macro.

block	if	progv
catch	labels	quote
compiler-let	let	return-from
declare	let*	setq
eval-when	macrolet	tagbody
flet	multiple-value-call	the
function	multiple-value-prog1	throw
go	progn	unwind-protect

Table 4.1   Names of all common LISP special forms

Functions include named functions and lambda expressions. **A named function** begins with a special form of **defun** (see Table 4.1), while a **lambda expression** is an unnamed function in which the first element is the symbol lambda.

Like most other computer languages, declared global variables need to appear at top-level (i.e., the beginning of a program) in a function, lambda, or macro.

LISP is strong in list operations, which provide excellent functionalities for symbolic manipulation; it is relatively weak in number crunching. Like C, LISP enables you to perform conditional actions, recursion, iteration and binding, user-defined functions, macros, declaration of global variables and named constants, as well as to create record structures.

LIST OPERATIONS
(LISP FUNCTIONS THAT CAN BE EMULATED WITH C/C++)

Lists are the most frequently used data type in LISP. Basic functions include **list**, **append**, **cons**, **display**, **member**, **car**, **cdr**, **set**, **setq**, **length**, **reverse**, **subst**, and **last**. Because these functions are new to programmers, they will be discussed in greater detail.

Assign Values: setq, psetq, set

The three functions setq, psetq, and set perform assignment in a slightly different way although they all are used to alter the value of a variable.

setq

The **setq** function causes the value of the second argument to become the value of the first argument, which can only be a symbol, for example,

```
* (setq x (+2 3))

 5

* (setq Hometown '(San Francisco))

(San Francisco)

* (setq)

nil
```

The setq function can assign an unlimited even number of arguments sequentially:

```
* (setq x (-9 4) y x)

 5
```

In this example x is set to 5, y is set to x (which is 5), and setq returns 5.

psetq

The **psetq** function is similar to **setq**, except that assignment happens in parallel; the variables are set to the resulting values at the same time:

```
*(setq x 5)

5

*(setq y 7)

7

*(psetq x y y x)

*x

7

*y

5
```

In this example, the values of x and y are exchanged by executing **psetq**.

set

The **set** function is similar to **setq** except that because the former evaluates the first argument and works only with dynamic (global) variables but not locally bound variables, quotes are needed on the first arguments. Note that **setq** does not require the quote:

```
* (set 'x 7)    ;; if x has not been assigned by setq

7
```

Take Lists Apart: car, cdr, and Their Derivatives

Car and cdr are the most distinctive concepts to the conventional programmer. They can be combined to create new functions.

Car causes the returning value of the first element of the list:

```
*(car '( x y z))

x

*(car '(( USA Washington-DC) China))

(USA Wash-DC)
```

Cdr is complementary to car; it causes the return of the rest of the list, which is always a list with all but the first element of the original list:

```
*(cdr '(x y z))

(y z)
```

Occasionally, several cars and cdrs are needed to "dig" out from deep within a nested expression:

```
*(car(car(cdr'((plus 7 8) (x y) 1))))

x
```

A convenient name for the new function that performs the combination of these cars and cdrs is **cxxxr**; each x represents **cars (a)** or **cdrs (d)**. In the previous example, the abbreviated name is **cdaar**.

Second returns the second element of a list; it is equivalent to **cadr**, for example,

```
*(second '(a b c d ))

b
```

Construct and Display: list, append, cons

List, append, and cons are used to assemble lists, while car and cdr take lists apart. **List** is a function that puts together elements of all lists called upon:

```
*(setq x '(p q))

(p q)

*(list x x x)

((p q) (p q) (p q))

*(list 'U 'S 'A)

(U S A)
```

Note that parentheses around p and q are not removed. To remove them, **append** is used to run the elements of its arguments together:

```
*(append x x x)

(p q p q p q)
```

If for some reason the elements in the first x need to be kept intact, then **cons** is used to insert a new first element into a list:

```
*(cons x x x)

((p q) p q p q)
```

An inverse relationship can be drawn between cons and the pair car and cdr:

```
*(cons (car x) (cdr x))

x
```

Note that the effect of (cons 'p ()) is the same as (list 'p).

To display a list that has been assigned, enter the name of the list:

```
* x

(p q)
```

Reorganize Lists: member, reverse, length, subst, etc.

Functions to reorganize lists and their elements include member, union, intersection, setdifference, length, last, nth, remove, reverse, and subst.

Member determines whether an item is a member of a list. If the item is found in the list, then the sublist beginning with that item is returned; otherwise, nil is returned:

```
* (member Dave '(Peter Lin Dave Linda))

(Dave Linda)
```

Union takes the union of two sets in the list and returns a list of items that appear in either set:

```
*(union '(Peter Lin Dave Linda) '(Dave Lisa Eileen Emily))

(Peter Lin Dave Linda Lisa Eileen Emily)
```

Intersection takes the intersection of two sets and returns a list of only those items that appear in both sets:

```
*(intersection '(Peter Lin Dave Linda) '(Dave Lisa Eileen Emily))

(Dave)
```

Setdifference subtracts from the elements of the first set the elements of the second set that are common to both sets:

```
*(setdifference '(Peter Lin Dave Linda) '(Dave Lisa Eileen  Emily))

(Peter Lin Linda)
```

Length counts the number of top-level elements in a list:

```
*(length '(p q))

2

*( length '((p q) (p q) (p q))

3
```

Last returns a list that contains only the last element of the original list:

```
*( last '(Peter Lin Dave Linda))

(Linda)
```

Nth takes the car of the nth cdr of a list; the first element of the list is nth 0, the second element is nth 1, and so on:

```
*(nth 1 '(p q r))

q
```

Remove returns a copy of list with all top-level elements except those to be excluded:

```
*(remove 'p '(p q r p s))

(q r s)
```

Reverse returns the reversal of a list; it works only on lists and does not change the value of any variables:

```
*(setq love '(I love you))

(I love you)

*(reverse love)

(you love I)

*love

(I love you)
```

Subst substitutes one symbol for another wherever that symbol appears in a list; it takes three arguments as in "substitute a for b in c":

```
*(subst 'like 'love '(I love you))

(I like you)
```

Predicates: atom, listp, null, numberp, eq, eql, equal, and, or, not

These predicates are functions for use in decision making; they respond to queries as true or false. True is represented in LISP by t; false is represented in LISP by nil.

The two predicates atom and listp are used to test the content of a list; **atom** tests its argument to determine whether that argument is an atom, while **listp** tests to determine whether that argument is a list:

```
*( atom 'expert)

t

*(listp '(expert system))

t

*(listp 'expert)

nil
```

Null tests to determine whether its argument is empty:

```
*(null 'AI)

nil
```

Eq and equal test the sameness of two lists. **Eq** tests to determine whether two LISP objects are in the same storage location:

```
*(setq p 'x)

x


*(setq q 'x)


x

*(eq p q)

nil


*(eq p (car (list p q)))

t


*(eq (float 3) (float 3))

 nil
```

Eql is similar to eq, except that it is true only if the two arguments are eq or are numbers with the same type and value:

```
*(eq (float 3) (float 3))

nil
```

Equal tests whether two expressions look alike, that is, whether they are printed the same way:

```
*(equal 5 (- 7 2))

t
```

And, or, and not are logical operators. **Not** returns true only if its argument is nil; **and** returns true only if all arguments are non-nil; **or** returns true only if any one argument is non-nil:

```
*(not nil)

t

*(and t t nil nil)

nil

*(or nil nil t t t)

t
```

In evaluation, **and** and **or** are treated slightly differently from the standard logical operators. Both evaluate their arguments from left to right. If a nil is encountered by **and**, or something other than nil is encountered by **or**, the argument is returned. Any remaining arguments are not evaluated; otherwise, the value of the last argument is returned, for example,

```
*(setq family '(David Lisa Eileen Emily))

(David Lisa Eileen Emily)

*(and ( member 'Lisa family) (member 'Eileen family))

(Eileen Emily)

*(or (member 'Lisa family) (member 'Tam family))

(Lisa Eileen Emily)
```

For more discussion on LISP functions, see Appendix B.

C/C++ UTILITY FUNCTIONS FOR LIST OPERATIONS

This section discusses fundamental list operation utility functions that may expedite the conversion of LISP programs to C/C++. List operations are the strengths of LISP and can greatly enhance the expression power of C/C++. Major functions discussed are car, cdr, append, cons, nth, member, length, reverse, subst, equal, atoms, variablep, copy-list, push, killcons, lread, and lprint.

car and cdr

Car and cdr are the most distinctive LISP concepts. **Car** causes the returning value of the first element of the list. **Cdr** is complementary to car; it causes the return of the rest of the list, which is always a list with all but the first element of the original list. In C, **union** and **define** can be used to write an emulation program for car and cdr as shown in Listing 4.1 and briefly illustrated in the following example:

```
typedef struct _cons {          /* a cons-cell */
    union {
      struct _cons  *p;
      char          *s;
    } car;
    struct _cons  *cdr;         /* usually points to a sublist */
    unsigned char type;         /* the types of the pointers in the cells */
} cons;


#define CAR(x) (x)->car.p
#define CDR(x) (x)->cdr
```

Listing 4.1: C/C++ Program CAR, CDR, and ATOM

```
/* cons.h
typedef struct _cons {          /* a cons-cell */
    union {
      struct _cons  *p;
      char          *s;
    } car;
    struct _cons  *cdr;         /* usually points to a sublist */
    unsigned char type;         /* the types of the pointers in the cells */
} cons;

#define CAR_STRING      1
#define CAR_INTEGER     2
#define CAR_LIST        4
#define CDR_STRING      8
#define CDR_INTEGER     16
#define CDR_LIST        32

#define C_FILE          0
#define C_STRING        1

#define ATOM(x) ((x)->type != CAR_LIST)
#define CAR(x) (x)->car.p
#define CDR(x) (x)->cdr
#define HEAD CAR
#define TAIL CDR
```

continued...

...from previous page

```
cons *mkcons(),*lread();
cons *nsubst(),*copy_list(),*mklist2();
cons *member(),*nconc(),*nreverse();
cons *unify_equal(),*unify_term_c(),*unify_pred_c(),*unify_list_c_1();
cons *unify_pred_nv(),*unify_list_nv_1();

cons *twotees(),*ltwotees();
cons *join_subst(),*subst_list();
```

Append and Cons

The function **append** is used to run the elements of its arguments together. If for some reason the elements in the first set, x, need to be kept intact, then **cons** is used to insert a new first element into a list:

```
*(cons x x x)

((p q) p q p q)
```

In Listing 4.2, nconc_lisp and mkcons emulate append and cons, respectively.

Listing 4.2: Utility Functions for LISP Conversion

```
/*
** UTIL.C
**
** Emulation of LISP utilities
*/

#include <stdio.h>
#include "cons.h"
#include "goal.h"
```

continued...

...from previous page

```
/*
** nsubst(): replace surgically every occurrence of _old_ with _new_ in the
** list _list_.
*/


/*--------------------------------------------------nth_list()-----------*/


/*
**   Usage:
**   E.x.   n = 2, list = (((?x 3)(?y 5))(?z 1)((?m 4)))
**          nth_list(n,list) ===> (?z 1)
**
*/

cons   *nth_list(n,list)
int    n;
cons   *list;
{
       int   i;
       cons *substp = list;

       for(i = 1;  i < n;  i++)
       {
               substp = CDR(substp);
       }
       return(mkcons(CAR_LIST,CAR(substp),NULL));
}



/*---------------------------------------------------mkcons()-----------*/


/*
**   Usage:
**   E.x.    mkcons(CAR_LIST,(?x 1),(?y 2)) ===> ((?x 1)(?y 2))
**
*/
```

continued...

...from previous page

```c
cons *mkcons(type,head,tail)
cons *head,*tail;
{
  cons *p;

  if (p = (cons *) malloc(sizeof(cons))) {
    p->type  = type;
    p->car.p = head;
    p->cdr   = tail;
  } else {
    puts("\n*** Yow! Out of core ***\n");
  }
  return p;
}



/*--------------------------------------------------killcons----------*/


killcons(p)
cons *p;
{
  if (p != NULL) {
    if ((p->type & CAR_LIST) == CAR_LIST) {
      killcons(p->car.p);
      killcons(p->cdr);
    } else if ((p->type & CAR_STRING) == CAR_STRING) {
      free(p->car.s);                          /* get rid of the string */
    }
    free(p);
  }
}
```

continued...

...from previous page

```
/*-----------------------------------------------nsubst()-----------*/

cons *nsubst(new,old,list)
char *new,*old;
cons *list;
{
  cons *t;
  char *strsave();

  if (list == NULL) {
    t = NULL;
  } else if (list->type == CAR_STRING) {
    if (!strcmp(list->car.s,old)) {
      killcons(list);
      t = mkcons(CAR_STRING,strsave(new),NULL);
    } else {
      t = list;
    }
  } else {
    list->car.p = nsubst(new,old,list->car.p);
    list->cdr   = nsubst(new,old,list->cdr);
    t = list;
  }
  return t;
}



/*-------------------------------------------------copy_list()-------*/

/*
** copy_list(): copy a list structure, down to the last atom, string &c.
*/
```

continued...

...from previous page

```
cons *copy_list(list)
cons *list;
{
  cons *t;
  if (list == NULL) {
    t = NULL;
  } else if (list->type == CAR_STRING) {
    t = mkcons(CAR_STRING,strsave(list->car.s),NULL);
  } else {
    t = mkcons(CAR_LIST,copy_list(list->car.p),copy_list(list->cdr));
  }
  return t;
}




/*-----------------------------------------------------length()---------*/

/*
** length(): returns the length of a list (counting only the 'top' or
** backbone elements, i.e.:
** length( '(a b (c d) e)) == 4, not 5
*/

int length(lp)
cons *lp;
{
  int l = 0;

  if (ATOM(lp))
    return 0;
  while (lp != NULL) {
    ++l;
    lp = lp->cdr;
  }
  return l;
}
```

continued...

...from previous page

```
/*--------------------------------------------------mklist2()----------*/

/*
** mklist2(): make a two-element list out of the given string arguments.
**
** Usage: E.x. mklist2("x","y") ===> (x y)
**
*/

cons *mklist2(foo,bar)
char *foo,*bar;
{
  return mkcons(CAR_LIST,mkcons(CAR_STRING,strsave(foo),NULL),
                      mkcons(CAR_LIST,mkcons(CAR_STRING,strsave(bar),NULL),
                                  NULL));
}



/*-----------------------------------------------member_list()----------*/

/*
** member_list(): searches for the first occurrence of list1 in the list2.
** Searches are done on the top-level only, and only deal with length(list1)
** equal 1.
** Return SUCCEED or FAIL
** Usage: E.g. member_list((?x 1),((?y 2)(?x 1))) ===> SUCCEED
**             member_list((?x 1),(((?x 1)))) ===> FAIL
**
**
*/

cons *member_list(list1,list2)
cons *list1,*list2;
{
  int  i;
  cons *temp1;
```

continued...

...from previous page

```
if(list1 == NULL)
{
     return SUCCEED;
}
for(i = 1; i <= length(list2); i++)
{
      temp1 = nth_list(i,list2);
      if(equal(list1,CAR(temp1)))
      {
             return SUCCEED;
      }
}
return FAIL;
}

/*----------------------------------------------------variablep()----------*/

/*
** variablep(): Quick function, returns 'true' if the first character of
** var is '?' and 'false' if not.
*/

int variablep(var)
cons *var;
{
   return (ATOM(var) && *(var->car.s) == '?');
}



/*---------------------------------------------------equal()------------*/

/*
** equal(): determine whether two lisp constructs are equal
*/
```

continued...

...from previous page

```
int equal(l1,l2)
cons *l1,*l2;
{
  if (l1 == NULL && l2 == NULL) {
    return 1;
  } else if (l1 == NULL || l2 == NULL) {
    return 0;
  } else if (l1->type == CAR_STRING && l1->type == CAR_STRING) {
    return !strcmp(l1->car.s,l2->car.s);
  } else if (l1->type == CAR_LIST && l2->type == CAR_LIST) {
    return (equal(l1->car.p,l2->car.p) && equal(l1->cdr,l2->cdr));
  }
}
```

```
/*----------------------------------------------nconc()---------------*/

/*
** nconc(): surgically concatenate two lists. Appends list2 to the end of
** list 1 and returns the modified list1/list2 complex.Only used in backward
** chaining.
** Modified from nconc_lisp. Add some test cases.
** Usage: E.g. nconc(((?x 1)(?y 2)),(?z 3)) ===> ((?x 1)(?y 2)(?z 3))
**        E.g. nconc((t t),(t t)) ===> (t t)
**        E.g. nconc((?x 1),(?x 1)) ===> (?x 1)
**
*/
```

continued...

...from previous page

```
cons *nconc(list1,list2)
cons *list1,*list2;
{
  cons *olist1;

  olist1 = list1;
  if (list1 == NULL)
  {
        return list2;
  }
  if(equal(list1,ltwotees()) && equal(list2,ltwotees()))
  {
        olist1 = ltwotees();
        return olist1;
  }
  if(!equal(list1,ltwotees())&&equal(list2,ltwotees()))
  {
        return list1;
  }
  if(!equal(list2,ltwotees())&&equal(list1,ltwotees()))
  {
        return list2;
  }
  if(equal(list1,list2))
  {
        return list1;
  }
  if(!ATOM(CAR(list1))&&member_list(list1,list2))
  {
        return list2;
  }
  while (list1->cdr != NULL) {
    list1 = list1->cdr;
  }
  list1->cdr = list2;
  return olist1;
}
```

continued...

...from previous page

```
/*----------------------------------------------nconc_lisp()----------------*/

/*
** nconc_lisp():surgically concatenate two lists. Appends list2 to the end of
** list 1 and returns the modified list1/list2 complex.
*/

cons *nconc_lisp(list1,list2)
cons *list1,*list2;
{
  cons *olist1;

  olist1 = list1;
  if (list1 == NULL)
  {
          return list2;
  }
  while (list1->cdr != NULL) {
    list1 = list1->cdr;
  }
  list1->cdr = list2;
  return olist1;
}



/*----------------------------------------------------nreverse()------------*/

/*
** nreverse(): destructively reverses a list
*/

cons *nreverse(list)
cons *list;
{
  cons *tmpcdr;
```

continued...

...from previous page

```
  if (list == NULL || list->cdr == NULL) {
    return list;
  }
  tmpcdr = list->cdr;
  list->cdr = NULL;
  return nconc(nreverse(tmpcdr),list);
}



/*--------------------------------------------------fgetword()------------*/

/*
** read a space-delimited word from the input file _fp_ and put it in _buf_
*/

void fgetword(fp,buf)
FILE *fp;
char *buf;
{
  int c;

  while ((c = getc(fp)) != EOF && strchr(" \t\n",c)) /* skip whitespace */
    ;
  *buf++ = c;
  while ((c = getc(fp)) != EOF && !strchr(" \t\n()",c)) { /* get all reals */
    *buf++ = (char) c;
  }
  *buf = '\0';                                    /* delimit */
}

/*------------------------------------------------push()---------------*/

/*
**   push(item,list): the item is consed onto the front of the list.
**   Usage: E.g. push(((?x 1)),((?y 2))) ===> (((?x 1))(?y 2))
**
*/
cons    *push(item,list)
cons    *item,*list;
{
        return mkcons(CAR_LIST,item,list);
}
```

Member, Length, Nth, Reverse, and Subst

Member, length, nth, reverse, and subst are functions to reorganize lists and their elements. **Member** determines whether an item is a member of a list. If the item is found in the list, then the sublist beginning with that item is returned; otherwise, nil is returned. **Length** counts the number of top-level elements in a list. **Nth** takes the car of the nth cdr of a list. **Reverse** returns the reversal of a list; it works only on lists and does not change the value of any variables. **Subst** substitutes one symbol for another wherever it appears in a list. The C subroutines — member_list, length, nth_list, nreverse, and nsubst — in Listing 4.2 can be used to emulate the above functions for reorganizing lists.

Predicates: Atom, Variablep, Equal

The predicates atom, variablep, and equal are functions for use in decision making; they respond to queries as true or false.

The two predicates atom and variablep are used to test the content of a list; **atom** tests its argument to determine whether it is an atom, while **variablep** tests to determine whether it is a variable. **Equal** tests sameness of two LISP constructs. Atom is shown in Listing 4.1 and repeated as follows:

```
#define ATOM(x) ((x)->type != CAR_LIST)
```

Variablep and equal are shown in Listing 4.2.

Copy_list, push, and killcons

Copy_list, push, and killcons are three useful utilities for converting LISP to C/C++. **Copy_list** allows you to copy a list structure down to the last atom, string, and character; **push** allows an item to be concatenated onto the front of a list; and **killcons** frees up the memory space allocated by a mkcons.

These subroutines are shown in Listing 4.2.

Lread and Lprint (Reading and Printing in S_expressions)

The **Lread** and **Lprint** subroutines read and print lists in LISP fashion (i.e., in the form of an s_expression within parentheses). These two subroutines are further discussed in Chapter 9. (Listings 9.1 and 9.2 give examples of Lread and Lprint, respectively.)

SAMPLE CONVERSIONS FROM LISP TO C/C++: SUBSTITUTION

Listing 4.3 shows four sample C/C++ subroutines that compose most requirements for substitution in backward and forward chaining.

Listing 4.4 shows the original LISP code that has been translated to C/C++. Comparison of the two listings indicates a distinctive difference in the purpose of the two computer languages: In prototyping, LISP is good for formulating concepts. Once the concept has been formulated, C/C++ can be used to gain maximum efficiency and portability.

Examine the subroutine that performs a variable substitution on list, nonrecursively, in both listings. Neither subroutine (C nor LISP) deals with nonrecursiveness, and only one substitution can be applied to each atomic term. Example usage follows:

```
subst_list((p ?x ?y),((?x 1)(?y 2))) ===> (p 1 2)
```

The core of the subroutine in LISP is

```
(mapcar #'(lambda (term) (aif (assoc term subst) (cdr it) term) list))
```

This LISP expression is converted into the following C code:

```
while (list != NULL) {
  term = list->car.p;
  substp = substi;              /* get 1st substitution */
  while (substp != NULL) {
    if (term->type == CAR_STRING && !strcmp(term->car.s,
                                    substp->car.p->car.p->car.s)) {
      term = substp->car.p->cdr->car.p;
      break;
    }
    substp = substp->cdr;       /* make more subst's */
  }
  new_list = nconc(new_list,mkcons(CAR_LIST,copy_list(term),NULL));
  list = list->cdr;
}
return new_list;
}
```

The previous C code includes the code for a LISP user-defined macro, **aif**, in the following LISP expression, which is also contained in Listing 4.4:

```
(defmacro aif (test-form &rest body)
  '(let ((it ,test-form))
     (if it ,@body)))
```

Listing 4.3: Substitution—A Sample LISP-C Conversion Program

```
/*
**  substitu.c:  Functions for manipulating substitutions.
**
*/

/*---------------------------------------------------include-------------*/

#include <stdio.h>
#include "cons.h"


/*-----------------------------------------------twotees()-----------*/

cons *twotees()
{
  static cons *tt = NULL;

  if (tt == NULL) {
    tt = mklist2("t","t");
  }
  return tt;
}




/*-----------------------------------------------ltwotees()-----------*/

cons *ltwotees()
{
  static cons *ltt = NULL;

  if (ltt == NULL) {
    ltt = mkcons(CAR_LIST,twotees(),NULL);
  }
  return ltt;
}
```

continued...

...from previous page

```
/*-------------------------------------------------lltwotees()------------*/

cons *lltwotees()
{
  static cons *lltt = NULL;

  if (lltt == NULL) {
    lltt = mkcons(CAR_LIST,ltwotees(),NULL);
  }
  return lltt;
}




/*-------------------------------------------------join_subst()------------*/

/*
** z1 is subst for ONE term.
*/

cons *join_subst(z1,z2)
cons *z1,*z2;
{
  cons *retval;

  if (equal(z1,ltwotees())) {
    return z2;
  } else if (equal(z2,ltwotees())) {
    return z1;
  } else {
    return(mkcons(CAR_LIST,z1,z2));
  }
}
```

continued...

...from previous page

```
/*--------------------------------------------------subst_list()------------*/
/*
/* THIS EXAMPLE DISCUSSED IN THE TEXT
/*
** Variable substitution
** %% Use of system fn like subst would be real efficient, except that it
** does not deal with nonrecursiveness.
** Performs a variable substitution on list, nonrecursively
** (only one substitution applied to each atomic term).
** Usage: E.g. subst_list((p ?x ?y),((?x 1)(?y 2))) ===> (p 1 2)
*/


cons *subst_list(list,substi)
cons *substi,*list;
{
  cons *new_list = NULL;
  cons *substp;
  cons *term;
  cons *tmp;

  while (list != NULL) {
    term = list->car.p;
    substp = substi;                         /* get 1st substitution */
    while (substp != NULL) {
      if (term->type == CAR_STRING && !strcmp(term->car.s,
                                       substp->car.p->car.p->car.s)) {
        term = substp->car.p->cdr->car.p;
         break;
      }
      substp = substp->cdr;                  /* make more subst's */
    }
    new_list = nconc(new_list,mkcons(CAR_LIST,copy_list(term),NULL));
    list = list->cdr;
  }
  return new_list;
}
/*
/* THE ABOVE IS THE EXAMPLE DISCUSSED IN THE TEXT.
/*
```

continued...

...from previous page

```
/*-----------------------------------------------subst_prop()------------*/

/*
** subst_prop(): performs a variable substitution on proposition
** Returns a copy of the proposition with replacements according to the
** substitution list.
** Usage:  E.g. subst_prop(((p ?x)(q ?y)),((?x 1)(?y 2))) ===> ((p 1)(q 2))
**
*/

cons *subst_prop(list,substi)
cons *substi,*list;
{
        int        i;
        cons       *temp1,*temp2;

        temp1 = NULL;
        if(list == NULL)
        {
                killcons(temp1);
                killcons(temp2);
                return NULL;
        }
        for(i = 1; i <= length(list); i++)
        {
                temp2 = nth_list(i,list);
                temp1 = nconc(temp1,
                        mkcons(CAR_LIST,subst_list(CAR(temp2),substi),NULL));
        }
        killcons(temp1);
        killcons(temp2);
        return temp1;

}
```

continued...

...from previous page

```
/*--------------------------------------------------subst_pred()------------*/

/*
** subst_pred(): Performs nonrecursive variable substitution on a predicate
** Would be more mem-efficient if result SHARED with pred.
** Usage: E.g. subst_pred((p ?x ?y),((?x 1)(?y 2))) ===> (p 1 2)
*/

cons *subst_pred(pred,subst)
cons *pred,*subst;
{
  return subst_list(pred,subst);
}


cons *substitute_pred(pred,subst)
cons *pred,*subst;
{
        int   i,j;
        cons *new_list = NULL;
        cons *substp;
        cons *term;
        cons *tmp;

        for(i = 1; i <= length(pred); i++)
        {
                substp = subst;
                for(j = 1; j <= length(subst); j++)
                {
                            ;
                }
        }
}
```

continued...

...from previous page

```
/*-------------------------------------------------subst_substlist()-----*/

/*
** subst_substlist(): perform a substitution on a substitution list
** s-s( (((?x 1)) ((?x 2))) , ((?x ?y)) ) ==> (((?y 1)) ((?y 2)))
*/

cons *subst_substlist(substlist,subst)
cons *substlist,*subst;
{
  cons *new_substlist = NULL;
  cons *new_subst     = NULL;
  cons *new_pair      = NULL;
  cons *term,*substp,*substip,*tmp;

  while (substlist != NULL) {            /* for each substitution */
    new_subst = NULL;
    substp = substlist->car.p;
    while (substp != NULL) {             /* for each pair */
      term = substp->car.p->car.p;
      substip = subst;
      while (substip != NULL) {          /* for each substitution-pair */
        if (!strcmp(term->car.s,substip->car.p->car.p->car.s)) {
          term = substip->car.p->cdr->car.p;
          break;
        }
        substip = substip->cdr;
      }
      new_subst = nconc(new_subst,
          mkcons(CAR_LIST,
                 mkcons(CAR_LIST,
                        copy_list(term),
                        mkcons(CAR_LIST,
                               copy_list(substp->car.p->cdr->car.p),
                               NULL)),
                 NULL));
```

continued...

...from previous page

```
        substp = substp->cdr;
    }
    new_substlist = nconc(new_substlist,mkcons(CAR_LIST,new_subst,NULL));
    substlist = substlist->cdr;
  }
  return new_substlist;
}




/*-----------------------------------------------test_subst_used()-----*/

/*
** test_subst_used():Tells if substitution has been used.
** Usage: E.g.
**      test_subst_used(((?x  5)),((((?x  1)))) ===>  0
**      test_subst_used(((?x  5)),((((?x  5)))) ===>  1
**
*/

int test_subst_used(list1,prev_subst)
cons  *list1,*prev_subst;
{
        int   i,j;
        int   flag = 0;
        cons  *temp1,*temp2;

        for(i=1;i<=length(list1);i++)
        {
           flag = 0;
           temp1 = nth_list(i,list1);
           for(j=1;j<=length(prev_subst);j++)
           {
               temp2 = nth_list(j,prev_subst);
               if(equal(temp1,CAR(temp2)))
               {
                   flag = 1;
                   break;
```

continued...

...from previous page

```
            }
        }
        if(flag == 1)
        {
            return 1;                  /*at least one not used*/
        }
    }
    return 0;                          /*all used*/
}
```

Listing 4.4: The LISP Code for Substitution

```
;;; **********************************************************************
;;; Variable substitution
;;; %% Use of system fn like subst would be real efficient, except that it
;;; does not deal with nonrecursiveness.

;;; Performs a variable substitution on list, nonrecursively
;;; (only one substitution applied to each atomic term).

(defmacro aif (test-form &rest body)
  '(let ((it ,test-form))
     (if it ,@body)))

(defun Subst-List (list subst)
  (declare (special subst))
  (mapcar #'(lambda (term) (aif (assoc term subst) (cdr it) term)) list))
;;;
;;; THE ABOVE IS THE EXAMPLE DISCUSSED IN THE TEXT
;;;
;;; Performs a variable substitution on expression, nonrecursively
;;; Used backtrack
```

continued...

...from previous page

```lisp
(defun Subst-Exp (exp subst)
  (declare (special exp subst))
  (cond ((not exp) nil)
        ((atom exp)
         (or (some #'(lambda (s) (when (eq (car s) exp) (cdr s))) subst)
             exp))
        (t (mapcar #'(lambda (piece) (subst-exp piece subst)) exp))))


;;; Performs nonrecursive variable substitution on a predicate
;;; Would be more mem-efficient if result SHARED with pred.
;;; NB: Subst not applied to first term!!
(defun Subst-Pred (pred subst)
  (declare (special subst))
  (cons (car pred)
        (mapcar #'(lambda (term) (aif (assoc term subst) (cdr it) term))
                (cdr pred))))


;;; Performs a variable substitution on proposition, nonrecursively
;;; (only one substitution applied to each atomic term).
;;; NB: Subst not applied to first term!!
(defun Subst-Prop (prop subst)
  (declare (special prop subst))
  (cond ((not prop) nil)
        ((atom prop)
         (or (some #'(lambda (s) (when (eq (car s) prop) (cdr s))) subst)
             prop))
        (t (cons (car prop)
                 (mapcar #'(lambda (piece) (subst-Prop piece subst))
                         (cdr prop))))))
;;; This is slower, but more memory-efficient...
;      (t (let ((car (substitute-nonrecursive (car proposition) substitution))
;               (cdr (substitute-nonrecursive (cdr proposition) substitution)))
;           (if (and (eq car (car proposition)) (eq cdr (cdr proposition)))
;               proposition (cons car cdr))))))
```

continued...

...from previous page

```lisp
(defun Subst-Substlist (substlist subst)
  (declare (special subst))
  (mapcar #'(lambda (sl)
              (mapcar #'(lambda (s) (aif (assoc (car s) subst)
                                         (list* (cdr it) (cdr s)) s))
                      sl))
          substlist))
```

```lisp
;;;  ***********************************************************************
;;;; Tells if substitution has been used.   **** Used everywhere ***
;;;; I.e., there is a prev-subst in prev-substs that is contained in poss-subst.
;;;; (subst-used? '((?x . 5)) '(((?x . 1))))  --> NIL
;;;; (subst-used? '((?x . 5)) '(((?x . 5))))  --> T
;;;; (subst-used? '((?x . 5)) '(((?x . 5) (?y . 3))))  --> NIL
;;;; {because there might be some other way to get ?y}
;;;; (subst-used? '((?x . 1) (?y . 1)) '(((?x . 1))))  --> T
;;;; {Because this is clearly not a new solution when we just want a new ?x}
;;;;   Heuristic is, "I don't want a solution that is the Same (for my
;;;;   purposes) as any of these"
(defun Subst-Used? (poss-subst prev-substs)
  (declare (special poss-subst))
;   (find subst prev-substs :test #'equal))
  (some #'(lambda (prev-subst)
            (subset-equal prev-subst poss-subst))
        prev-substs))
```

```lisp
;;;; Tells if containee is a condensed version of container.
;;;; Used in find-goal-stack.
(defun Condensed-Substs? (containee container)
  (and (equal (list-length containee) (list-length container))
       (every #'subset-equal containee container)))
```

SUMMARY

- Even though a variety of LISP dialects exists, Common LISP appears to be the standard LISP.

- This chapter shows the similarities of and differences between LISP and C/C++ through examples in LISP and then discusses utility programs that can be used to convert LISP programs into C/C++. This chapter covers the following topics: becoming acquainted with LISP, program structure, list operations, C/C++ utility functions for list operations, and sample conversions from LISP to C.

- This chapter has examined fundamental list operation utility functions that may expedite the conversion of LISP programs to C/C++. List operations are the strengths of LISP and can greatly enhance the expression power of C/C++. Major functions discussed are car, cdr, append, cons, nth, member, length, reverse, subst, atoms, equal, variablep, copylist, killcons, push, lread, and lprint.

REFERENCES

Gold Hill Computers. "Golden Common LISP," various versions. (Cambridge, MA, 1986).

Steele, G. et al. *Common LISP References Manual.* Digital Press, 1984.

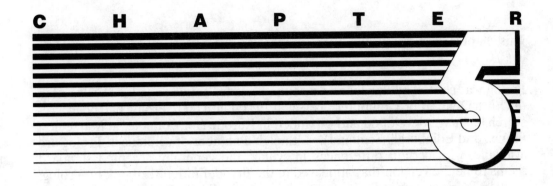

UTILITIES FOR PROLOG

This chapter discusses Prolog functions that can be used to build expert systems in C/C++.

Prolog was chosen by the Japanese as the basis for software to be developed in the Fifth Generation Computer Project in 1981. Until then, Prolog had been a research language developed and expanded in Europe (for example, in Marseilles, France and Edinburgh, Scotland). Although a number of versions of Prolog are available, with certain differences in syntax, the generally accepted standard seems to be the version that appeared in the first definition textbook on Prolog, entitled *Programming in Prolog* (second edition) by W. F. Clocksin and C. S. Mellish at the Edinburg University, Edinburgh, Scotland (Springer-Verlag, 1981). The examples executed in Prolog-86 are used in this chapter. The discussion focuses primarily on the strengths that can be expressed in C/C++ for use in building expert systems: unification and backtracking.

The main topics in this chapter are "Becoming Acquainted with Prolog" and "Utility Prolog Functions Using C."

BECOMING ACQUAINTED WITH PROLOG

Prolog is a programming language that allows the user to declare relationships between objects, to accumulate and organize these relationships, and to draw logical deductions from facts in relationships that the user has supplied. Unlike other conventional programming languages such as C or Pascal, the user need not input data to specify step-by-step procedures that the computer must carry out to obtain the desired output.

Prolog programming consists of the following three steps:

1. Declare facts about objects and their relationships.

2. Define rules that govern objects and their relationships.

3. Ask questions about objects and their relationships.

Step 3 can be placed before step 2 in many cases. After the facts about the objects and their relationships have been declared, questions can be asked about them without rules.

Declaring and Querying Facts

To declare a fact such as **David likes Lise** in Prolog, you need to identify the objects and relationships. The objects are **David** and **Lise**, and the relationship is **likes**. This fact is expressed as follows:

> **Example 5.1**   likes(david, lise).

Note that in Example 5.1 the names of the objects and relationships are in lowercase letters. Prolog distinguishes between uppercase and lowercase letters, and the names that begin with a capital letter or and underscore (_) are reserved for variables. You can use any sequence surrounded by single quotation marks, for example, 'X', 'Apollo', '_add'. The relationship between the objects (i.e., **likes**) appears first and is called a **predicate**. The objects (i.e., **david** and **lise**) following the predicate are enclosed in parentheses and are separated by a comma. The order of the objects makes a difference. The statement **likes (david, lise)** is different from **likes (lise, david)** in Prolog.

Each expression must be terminated by a period.

A statement such as Example 5.1 in Prolog is referred to as a **clause**. Each clause can be translated into pseudo-English by putting the predicate between the arguments. For example,

> **Example 5.2**   professor(david, tim).

Example 5.2 can be translated into **David is the professor of Tim.** The predicate **professor** stands for the phase **is the professor of**. The names in the example refer to particular objects. Each given name has only one meaning in Prolog. The programmer must carefully differentiate between the name that represents the class of an object and the name that represents an instance of a class. For example, in developing an expert system to identify a particular catfish that is active in a pond, two facts are used:

A catfish resembles an eel.

The catfish in the pond is extremely active.

You need to give the catfish different names to distinguish the two facts, as in Example 5.3:

Example 5.3   ```resembles(catfish, eel).```

```active(catfish1).```

```is_a (catfish1, catfish).```

As with other programming, names a programmer uses to represent the predicate or arguments do not affect the accuracy of a Prolog program as long as they begin with a lowercase letter. However, the names of objects should be meaningful for later program review or review by someone else.

Examples 5.2 and 5.3 can be used to translate relationships about a particular set of objects that constitute a real-world problem into Prolog clauses. The collection of all facts (relationships) that have been inputted is called a **database** in Prolog. This database can be queried. Once the facts have been stored in the database, you can query the database about the objects and their interrelationships. For example, the fact of Example 5.1 can be inquired into as follows:

Example 5.4   ```?-likes(david, lise).```

or

```likes(david, lise)?```

Prolog answers questions by searching through the database for a clause that matches the question. The question will match a fact in the database if the predicate (e.g., likes) of the question (i.e., Example 5.4) matches the predicate of a fact in the database (i.e., Example 5.1) and each argument of the question matches the corresponding argument in the fact. Consequently, the question in Example 5.4 matches the fact in Example 5.1 because the predicate as well as the two arguments are the same. The answer to the question in Example 5.4 is yes; however, note what happens if the order of the argument changes, such as in the following example:
```

Example 5.5   `likes(lise, david)?`

Prolog will answer

no

The above answer indicates that as far as the computer "knows," the database does not contain a fact that matches the question in Example 5.5. The fact **likes(david, lise)** is different from the fact **likes(lise, david)**.

Constants and Variables

In the previous section, constants have been used. A constant is a name that stands for a specific object (such as **david**, **lise**) or a relationship between objects (such as **likes**). The two types of constants are integers and atoms.

An **integer** is a positive or negative whole number ranging from -32,765 to 32,764, depending on the implementation.

Examples of integers are as follows:

-15, 0, 32, 5001

An **atom** is a sequence of letters, numbers, and special characters denoting the name of a given object or relationship and not starting with an underscore or a capital letter. If an atom must contain an uppercase letter or other characters (e.g., a space), it must be enclosed in single quotation marks. The following are examples of atoms:

`abc, chapter_10, david,`

`'This is an atom.'`

As previously mentioned, the name of an atom cannot start with integers, a capital letter, or the underscore character, and it cannot be hyphenated. The following are *not* atoms:

```
479 145street large-number, Vector, _tax
```

A variable is any sequence that begins with the underscore or an uppercase letter. It is a special type of name that can match any object. Consequently, X, _ten, Y, Z, David, and Lise are all variables. When variables are used in facts, they usually stand for words such as "everybody," "everyone," and "everything." For example, to add the fact **Everyone likes Lise**, enter the following clause:

Example 5.5   likes(X, lise).

You can ask the question **Does Eileen like Lise?** by entering the following:

Example 5.6   likes(eileen, lise)?

Prolog answers:

yes

Any atom replacing X in Example 5.5 will make Prolog answer "yes." For the convenience of future memory or the understanding of other programmers, X in Example 5.5 can be given a more meaningful name such as **Her_friend**.

The misuse of variables such as those used in Example 5.5 can destroy the special interrelationships between objects in the database; a variable can be removed using the command **retract**, as in the following:

Example 5.7   retract(likes(X, lise))!

Note that Example 5.7 contains another Prolog expression as its argument. The command retract ends with a ! symbol rather than with a period.

Structures (Compound Predicates)

Example 5.7 is a **compound predicate**, which is also called a structure or a compound term. A typical structure takes the form

predicate (argument1, argument2, ...)

where **argument** can be a constant, a variable, or a structure, for example,

Example 5.8   `likes(david, lise)`

`union(R, Y, Z)`

`asserta(is_a(Animal, mammal, how))`

`owns(david, book(X, author(western)))`

Structures can contain an **and** or an **or** to further narrow or expand the answer spaces. Prolog provides the comma (,) operator to stand for "and," and either a semicolon (;) or a vertical bar (|) to denote "or," for example,

Example 5.9   `likes(david, lise), likes (david, eileen)?`

Example 5.10   `likes(david, lise); likes (david, eileen)?`

Example 5.11   `likes(david, lise)| likes (david, eileen)?`

Example 5.9 uses an **and** operator. Examples 5.10 and 5.11 are the same, both using an **or** operator.

In answering a question containing the **and** operator, such as in Example 5.9, Prolog first tries to match the left-most clause. If this match fails, the answer to the question is "no." If the first match succeeds, then Prolog attempts to match the next clause after the comma. If the match fails again, then the answer will still be "no." Otherwise, Prolog answers "yes" to the conjunctive question.

When attempting to answer questions containing the **or** operator, such as in Example 5.10, Prolog first attempts to match the left-most clause in the disjunctive question against the facts in the database. If the match succeeds, Prolog answers "yes," or if the question contains a variable, the variable is binding. If the first match does not succeed, Prolog will try to satisfy the next clause. If this match succeeds, it will answer "yes" or will return the variable bindings. Otherwise, the answer will be "no."

Instantiation and Backtracking

You can build a small database to examine instantiation and backtracking.

> **Example 5.12**   likes(david, lise).
>
> likes(david, eileen).
>
> likes(david, emily).
>
> likes(david, frank).
>
> likes(david, rob).
>
> likes(eileen, lise).

Then, ask the following question:

> **Example 5.13**   likes(david People_David_likes)?

The variable **People David likes** is said to be "uninstantiated" before Prolog determines that David likes Lise. Once a variable stands for a given object, such as People_David_likes = lise, People_David_likes is said to be "instantiated" to lise.

Examine how the variable is instantiated. Prolog searches through the Example 5.12 database from the beginning to locate a clause that matches the question in Example 5.13. Note that the variable People_David_likes will match any object. The question in Example 5.13, likes (david, People_David_likes)? matches likes (david, lise) in Example 5.12 because the predicates and the first argument are the same, and the variable matches anything. When Prolog finds a match, it instantiates the variable to the name of the first object it matches. In this case, People_David_ likes becomes instantiated to lise.

Once a match is found, Prolog marks the database location in which the match was found. In some implementations, such as Prolog-86, Prolog will automatically return to this mark and attempt to find another match until all matches in the database have been found. If there are numerous matches in the database, a method such as **cut** will be needed to eliminate unlimited returns (cut will be discussed later in this chapter). The process of returning to the mark to attempt to unify the variable with the object is called **backtracking**. For example, the question contains the following compound clause:

Example 5.14   `like(david, People_liked), likes(eileen, people_liked)?`

Example 5.14 queries the database "who is the person both David and Eileen like?" In this example, the first clause was matched against the database in Example 5.12, and People-liked is instantiated to lise. Prolog will then attempt to satisfy the second clause, likes (eileen, People_liked). It fails when Prolog tries to match the clause with likes (david, eileen). However, by backtracking, Prolog will return to the database as many times as required until the clause is matched with the facts in the database and Prolog instantiates the variable to the given object or no fact remains in the database. In Example 5.14, the People_liked in the second clause is instantiated with lise after five trials.

Adding Comments to the Program

To add comments to the program, you need to check the symbol for comments in each implementation of Prolog. For example, in Prolog-86, the % operator is used to write comments as follows:

```
likes(david, lise). % David likes Lise.
```

In Clocksin and Mellish's definitive book, a pair of /* */ symbols is used as follows:

```
likes(david, lise). /* David likes Lise.*/
```

Adding Rules to the Database

The format for adding a rule to the database is as follows:

```
P:-

Q,

R,

"
"
"

Z.
```

where P is true if Q, R, ... , Z are true. To satisfy goal P, all subgoals of Q, R, ... Z must be satisfied first. For example, rules to express whether a person is the brother of another person are as follows:

Example 5.15   `brother_of(Person1, Person2):-`

`parent(X, Person1),`

`parent(Y, Person2),`

`sex(Person1, male),`

`diff(Person1, Person2).`

`diff(X, Y):- X/=Y.`

Example 5.15 reveals that Person1 is the brother_of Person2 if X is the parent of both Person1 and Person2, if Person1 is male, and if Person1 is different from Person2.

The rules in Example 5.15 can be used to query the relationship of objects in the database as follows:

Example 5.16   `brother_of(X, david)?`

Arithmetic Operations

Arithmetic operations take a back seat in Prolog to the pattern matching discussed above. Prolog includes mostly integers. The **is** operator is used to accomplish the task of the equal sign (=) in many computer languages, as shown in Example 5.17.

Example 5.17   `X is 10 + 20?`

which is equivalent to X = 10 + 20.

The sophistication of arithmetic operations depends on each implementation of Prolog. Most implementations include the following operators:

Operators	Meanings	Example	Result
+	add	2+3	5
-	subtract	3-1	2
*	multiply	3*5	15
/	divide	7/4	4
mod	integer remainder	7mod4	3
^	power	2^3	8
=	equal	2=2	True
/=	not equal	3/=2	True
>	greater than	3>5	False
<	less than	3<5	True
<=	less than or equal to	X<=Y	Undetermined
>=	greater than or equal to	X>=Y	Undetermined

Writing Programs

A Prolog program consists of rules, facts, and queries. Rules usually appear first in a program. The format for each of the three compounds is summarized as follows:

Rules:
P:- Q,R,...,Z means

(a) P is true if Q,R,...,Z are true.

(b) To satisfy goal P, subgoals Q,R,..., and Z must be satisfied.

Facts:
P. means

(a) P is true.

(b) Goal P is satisfied.

Queries:
P,Q? or ?_P,Q. means

(a) Are P and Q true?

(b) Satisfy goals P and Q.

P;Q? or ?_P,Q. means

(a) Is P or Q true?

(b) Satisfy goal P or Q.

A sample Prolog program to solve the "Tower of Hanoi" game that is played with three poles and a set of disks of various diameters is as follows:

```
hanoi(I) :- move (I,left,center,right).

move(0,_,_,_) :- !.
move((I,A,B,C) :-
        M is I - 1,
        move(M,A,C,B),
        show(A,B),
        move(M,C,B,A).

show(X,Y) :-
    print('Move the disk on ',X, to ,Y),
    n1. % n1 indicates a new line on the current output stream
```

The predicate **print** and ! (the cut operator to stop automatic backtracking after the goal is satisfied once) will be discussed later.

Display All Clauses

To display all clauses in the current interpreted program, the predicate **Listing** is used:

```
Listing!
```

This predicate does not list any clauses in prolog.lib.

Input/Output

This section discusses saving and loading files, executing large programs, and input and output of data and single characters.

Saving and Loading Source Files on Disk

To save a source file, use **save.**

Example 5.18   Save 'a:testfile.pro'!

Example 5.18 causes the program (the database) to be saved under the filename **testfile.pro** on disk A.

There are three ways to load a source file: load it when the Prolog interpreter is loaded, use the load command, or use the consult command:

Load the source file when the Prolog package is loaded by using the following command:

Example 5.19   `Prolog testfile.pro`

If you are already in Prolog, a source file can be brought in by entering either of the following two commands:

Example 5.20   `load 'testfile.pro'!`

Example 5.21   `consult('testfile.pro')!`

The difference between load and consult is as follows:

- **load** removes all existing clauses in the current database before the new file (testfile.pro) is brought into the database.

- **consult** adds the clauses in the new file into the current database without removing the existing clauses.

Running Large Prolog Programs

To avoid an "environment stack full" error in running a large program, you can increase the size of the variable stack when the Prolog interpreter is loaded:

Example 5.22   `prolog -s1500`

Note that **-s** is used before the number of desired units of stack size (e.g., 1500).

Input and Output of Data

To read data from the terminal or a disk file, predicate **read** is used. For example, to read the next term from the terminal, enter

Example 5.23   `read(X)?`

When the > prompt appears, enter a term:

`friends(X,Y).`

Prolog will respond with

`X = friends(X,Y).`

To input an atom or a sentence, use the single quotation marks and the predicate **ratom**:

Example 5.24   `ratom(X)?`

When the prompter appears, enter

`'This is a test'.`

Prolog will answer

`X = 'This is a test'.`

To output data into the terminal, use **print**:

```
print('This is a test.')!
```

The single quotation marks are not printed. Each call to **print** causes the output to be printed on a new line. The predicate **print** can be combined with '\n' and '\t' to produce a new line and tab, respectively. The character '\t' inserts four spaces into the print line.

The predicate **prin** will eliminate the newline character, as in the following:

Example 5.25   `prin('This is  line one.'), prin('This is line two.')!`

will result in

This is line one. This is line two.

Input and Output of Single Characters

To read a single character (e.g., **a**) from the terminal or a disk file, enter

Example 5.26   `getc(X)?a`

Prolog will respond with

`X = a`

Note that **a** is typed on the same line as the predicate before the Return key is pressed.

To output a single character (e.g., **c**), use the predicate **putc**:

Example 5.27   `putc(c)!`

Modifying the Database

This section discusses predicates that can be used to modify an existing database. The predicates **assert**, **asserta**, and **assertz** add new clauses to the database while **retract** and **retractall** remove clauses from the database.

Adding Clauses: asserta, assert, and assertz

The predicate asserta adds new clauses at the beginning of the database while assert and assertz add new clauses at the end of the database:

Example 5.28   `asserta(likes(lise,emily))!`

`assert(likes(lise,eileen))!`

`assertz(likes(eileen,david))!`

Prolog will add these facts into the database accordingly.

Removing Clauses: retract

The predicate **retract** removes the first clause in the database but **retractall** removes all clauses that match the clause in question, for example,

Example 5.29   `retract(likes(X,Y))!`

will only remove the first clause in the database in Example 5.12, which is **likes(david,lise)**. However, note the following example:

Example 5.30   `retractall(likes(X,Y))!`

All the clauses in the database that are in the form
likes(X,Y) will be removed. When you enter

`likes(david,emily)?`

the response from Prolog is

no

Writing LISP Functions in Prolog

Prolog can be used to write LISP functions for processing lists. A list is either an
atom representing an entry list or a structure with two arguments, a head and a
tail, enclosed in a pair of brackets ([ ]). The head of a list is its first element and
the tail is the remaining elements in the list. Note the following example:

Example 5.31   `friends([a,b,c,d,e])`

To find the head and tail of the list, enter

`friends([H|T])?`

or

`friends([H, ..T])?`

Prolog answers

H = a

T = [b,c,d,e]

LISP functions, such as car, append, and member, can be built using a recursive procedure. Member is used here as an example to describe the procedure. The rules to define member are as follows:

- A is a member of list P if A is the first element of P.

- If A is not the first element of list P, then A is a member of P only if A is a member of the tail of list P.

These two rules can be implemented as follows:

Example 5.32
```
member(A,[A|_]).

member(A,[_|Y]):- member(A,Y)
```

The definition can then be tested by entering

```
member(x,[x,y,z])?
```

Prolog answers

yes

because x is the member of list [a,b,c].

List- and set-processing predicates frequently defined for use in Prolog include car, cdr, last, nextto, cons, append, list, reverse, efface, delete, subst, sublist, map-car, member, subset, disjoint, intersection, and union.

Cut Operator in Backtracking

The cut operator is one of the most important operators in Prolog for controlling the effect of automatic backtracking. It is represented by the **!** character. The cut operator allows the programmer to tell Prolog which previous choice it need not consider again when Prolog automatically backtracks. This operator enables programs to run faster and use less memory and prevents programs from generating large or infinite numbers of solutions. Note the following example:

Example 5.33   `member(X,[a,b,c,d,e])?`

Some implementations of Prolog may return all the answers as follows:

X = a

X = b

X = c

X = d

X = e

The cut operator can be written into the procedure of member, which has been defined in Example 5.27 to reduce the number of solutions as follows:

Example 5.34
```
member(X,[X|_]) :- !.

member (X,[_|Y]) :- member (X,Y).
```

If you enter

```
member(X,[a,b,c,d,e])?
```

Prolog will answer

```
X = a
```

When the first clause in Example 5.34 was satisfied, the cut was marked; consequently, when Prolog attempted to backtrack, it stopped at the cut mark, and the second clause in Example 5.34 was never executed more than once.

PROLOG UTILITY FUNCTIONS IN C/C++

This section focuses on two main Prolog functions: unification and backtracking. These two functions are essential if you want to write a Prolog-based expert system in C/C++.

Unification in C/C++

Unification provides you with an elementary mechanism to bind or combine data/facts in the knowledge (data) base of a Prolog program. For example, a knowledge base has the following relations (the expression of relation has slightly deviated from the Prolog convention discussed in the previous section):

(p 2 3)

(p 2 4)

(p 2 2)

P in these relations indicates less than or equal (< =). If you query the knowledge base with the statement

```
(p 2 ?X)
```

unification will bind the variable ?X as follows:

```
((?X 2)) ((?X 3)) ((?X 4))
```

If the following two relations are in the knowledge base (predicate calculus statements),

```
(p ?X ?Y)

(p 2 ?Y))
```

they can be combined by unification as

```
((?X . 2))
```

by using the following command:

```
(unify-Pred-C '(p ?X ?Y) '(p 2 ?Y))
```

The unification subroutines to accomplish the above tasks are shown in Listing 5.1, and their usages are shown in the following corresponding examples:

unify_equal():   Compares whether the two terms are equal; however, it does not handle variable terms such as (?X, ?X). Two terms are considered equal for the purposes of unification if one of two conditions is met:

1. They are #' equal, i.e., numbers with the same type and value (a la LISP).

2. They denote an equivalent number.

Example: `unify-equal ('3, '3) --> ((t.t))`

`unify-equal ('p, ?X) --> NIL`

unify_term_c: Unifies terms and makes sure the first argument is a variable, with second argument unsubstitutable.

Example: `unify_term_c(?a, 3) --> ((?a . 3))`

`unify_term_c(3, ?a) --> nil`

unify_pred_c: Unifies predicates with second predicate constant. Typically, the first argument is a goal, and the second is a fact with no variables.

Example: `unify-pred-C '(P ?X 5) '(P 3 ?Y) ==> nil`

`unify-Pred-C '(P ?X ?Y) '(P 2 ?Y) ==> '((?X . 2))`

unify_pred_nv: Like unify_pred_c, but only returns substitution for terms that are nonvariables in constant predicates (second term) to be used in backward chaining. The second value returned is for the elements that are variables in both predicates (for use in translating previous substitution, prev-substs).

Example: `(unify_pred_nv ((p 1 ?X ?Z),(p ?Y 1 ?X)) --> (((?X .`

`1)) ((?X . ?Z)))`

Listing 5.1: Unification in C for Prolog

```
/***********************************************************************


          Unification Implementation

Convention:  Substitutions returned by unify-xxx are for the FIRST argument.

It makes no sense to mix substitutions of two expressions!! the variable names
are relative to each expression, so that it makes no sense to mix them.
Ex:  (unify-pred '(p ?x 1) '(p 2 ?x))  should work fine, but what to return?

PRED is LIST w/first term nonvar symbol assumed
PROP is EXP w/first term nonvar symbol assumed, rest terms are PROPS.

Could make all unify-xxx fns faster by making loop, instead of recursion.

**********************************************************************/

/*--------------------------------------------------include-----------*/

#include <studio.h>
#include "cons.h"
#include "goal.h"



/*--------------------------------------------------unify_equal()------*/

/*
** unify_equal: Does not handle varterms
** This is the KEY, inner loop operation performed for unification
** in the reasoning system.  As such, we would like to make it as efficient
** as possible.  Two terms are considered equal for the purposes of
** unification if one of two conditions are met:
** * They are #'equal (a la lisp)
**
** * They denote an equivalent number
**
**   Example:unify-equal ('3, '3) --> ((t t))
**           unify-equal ('p, ?X) --> NIL
**
*/
```

continued...

...from previous page

```
cons *unify_equal(term1,term2)
cons *term1,*term2;
{
  return (!strcmp(term1->car.s,term2->car.s)) ? mklist2("t","t") : NULL;
}


/*-------------------------------------------------unify_term_c()------*/

/*
** unify_term_c:
** Term unification, with second arg unsubstitutable.
**
** Example: unify_term_c(?a, 3) --> ((?a . 3))
**          unify_term_c(3, ?a) --> nil
**
** Used for slot and variable values.
*/

cons *unify_term_c(accom_term,const_term)
cons *accom_term,*const_term;
{
  if (variablep(accom_term)) {
    return mklist2(accom_term->car.s,const_term->car.s);
  } else {
    return unify_equal(accom_term,const_term);
  }
}


/*-------------------------------------------------unify_term()------*/

/*
** unify_term: Handles var-terms
** Used for predicate EQUAL.
**
** Example: unify_term(?a, 3) --> ((?a . 3))
**          unify_term(3, ?a) --> ((?a . 3))
**
*/
```

continued...

...from previous page

```c
cons *unify_term(term1,term2)
cons *term1,*term2;
{
  if (variablep(term1)) {
    return mklist2(term1->car.s,term2->car.s);
  } else if (variablep(term2)) {
    return mklist2(term2->car.s,term1->car.s);
  } else {
    return unify_equal(term1,term2);
  }
}
```

```c
/*--------------------------------------------------unify_pred_c()------*/

/*
** unify_pred_c: Predicate Unification with second predicate constant.
** finds substitution s that makes accom-exp . s = const-exp
**
**   Example: unify-pred-C '(P ?X 5) '(P 3 ?y) ==> nil
**            unify-Pred-C '(P ?X ?Y) '(P 2 ?Y) ==> '((?X . 2))
**
** Typically first arg is goal and second is fact w/no vars.
*/

cons *unify_pred_c(accom_pred,const_pred)
cons *accom_pred,*const_pred;
{
if(equal(accom_pred,const_pred))
  return ltwotees();
  if (length(const_pred) == length(accom_pred) &&
      !strcmp(const_pred->car.p->car.s,accom_pred->car.p->car.s)) {
    return unify_list_c_1(accom_pred->cdr,const_pred->cdr);
  } else {
    return NULL;
  }
}
```

continued...

...from previous page

```
/*-------------------------------------------------unify_list_c_1()------*/

/*
** unify_list_c_1() Aux fn that does not check length.
** This is an auxiliary for unify_pred_c.
*/

cons *unify_list_c_1 (ap,cp)
cons *ap,*cp;
{
  cons *subst = NULL;
  cons *apterm = ap->car.p;
  cons *cpterm = cp->car.p;
  cons *tmp;

  while (apterm != NULL) {
    if (tmp = unify_equal(apterm,cpterm)) {
      killcons(tmp);
    } else if (variablep(apterm)) {
      tmp = mkcons(CAR_LIST,mklist2(apterm->car.s,cpterm->car.s),NULL);
      subst = nconc(subst,tmp);
    } else {
      return NULL;
    }
    ap = ap->cdr; cp = cp->cdr;
    apterm = ap->car.p;
    cpterm = cp->car.p;
  }
  if (subst == NULL) {
    return mkcons(CAR_LIST,mklist2("t","t"),NULL);
  } else {
    return subst;
  }
}
```

continued...

...from previous page

```
/*---------------------------------------------------unify_pred_nv()------*/

/*
** unify_pred_nv(): Like U-P, but only returns substitution for terms
** that are nonvar in const_pred.  Used in backward-chain.
**
** Example:  (unify_pred_nv ((p 1 ?x ?z),(p ?y 1 ?x)) --> (((?x . **
**                1)) ((?x . ?z)))
**
** the second value returned is for the terms that are var in both (for use
** in translating prev-substs.)
*/

cons *unify_pred_nv(accom_pred,const_pred)
cons *accom_pred,*const_pred;
{
  if(equal(accom_pred,const_pred))
    return mkcons(CAR_LIST,ltwotees(),mkcons(CAR_LIST,ltwotees(),NULL));
  if (length(const_pred) == length(accom_pred) &&
      !strcmp(const_pred->car.p->car.s,accom_pred->car.p->car.s)) {
    return unify_list_nv_1(accom_pred->cdr,const_pred->cdr);
  } else {
    return NULL;
  }
}




/*--------------------------------------------unify_list_nv_1()------*/

/*
** unify_list_nv_1(): Aux fn that does not check length.
*/
```

continued...

...from previous page

```
cons *unify_list_nv_1(ap, cp)
cons *ap,*cp;
{
  cons *subst = NULL,*subst2 = NULL;
  cons *apterm = ap->car.p;
  cons *cpterm = cp->car.p;
  cons *tmp,*retval;
  while (apterm != NULL) {
    if (tmp = unify_equal(apterm,cpterm)) {
       killcons(tmp);
    } else if (variablep(cpterm)) {
      if (variablep(apterm)) {
        subst2 = nconc(subst2,mkcons(CAR_LIST,
                                 mklist2(cpterm->car.s,apterm->car.s),
                                 NULL));
      }
    } else if (variablep(apterm)) {
      subst = nconc(subst,mkcons(CAR_LIST,
                              mklist2(apterm->car.s,cpterm->car.s),
                              NULL));
    } else {
      return NULL;
    }
    ap = ap->cdr; cp = cp->cdr;
    apterm = ap->car.p;
    cpterm = cp->car.p;
  }
  return mkcons(CAR_LIST,
              (subst == NULL) ? mkcons(CAR_LIST,mklist2("t","t"),NULL)
                      : subst,
              mkcons(CAR_LIST,(subst2 == NULL) ? mkcons(CAR_LIST,
                                                   mklist2("t","t"),
                                                   NULL)
                                     : subst2));

}
```

Backtracking

Backtracking is used when conjunctive conditions are applied in a query of the database. For example, if the query is

```
(a ?X)(b  ?X)  /* Explanation: look for a and b that are equal in
                  the database */
```

and the database has the following facts:

(a 1) 1.0   /* Explanation: a is 1 with certainty factor of 1.0 */

(a 2) 0.8

(b 3) 1.0

(b 2) 0.7

In a Prolog-like system, **a** will be substantiated with 1 and **b** with 3 first. It is apparent the answer is wrong. A backtrack through the database is required to receive a correct answer:

(a 2)

(b 2)

Backtracking is a complex procedure. Listing 5.2 shows the C/C++ program for backtracking, which is further analyzed in Chapter 8.

Listing 5.2: Backtracking Program

```
/**********************************************************************
          Implementation of Backtracking

The first call to a conjunction will leave this data structure around.
#s(GOAL-STACK :GOAL (AND (Q ?Y) (P ?X)) :PREV-SUBSTS (((?Y . 1) (?X . 1)))
              :GOAL-STACK (#s(GOAL-FRAME :GOAL (P ?X) :SIT ((?Y . 1)) :PS NIL
                                 :ROC NIL :SOLN ((?X . 1)) :CERT 1.0)
                           #s(GOAL-FRAME :GOAL (Q ?Y) :SIT NIL :PS NIL
                                 :ROC ((P ?X)) :SOLN ((?Y . 1))
                                 :CERT 0.8)))

We save a goal stack for every conjunction that is called initially.  When
that conjunction is called again, we use the same goal stack.  Possible
problem: a conjunction called in two places might need two different goal
stacks!!

********************************************************************** */


/*-------------------------------------------------------include-----------*/

#include    <stdio.h>
#include    <math.h>
#include    "cons.h"
#include    "goal.h"


/*-----------------------------------------------------global variable---*/

Goal_Stack  *GOAL_STACK;                /*declare the global GOAL_STACK*/

/*-----------------------------------------------------backtrack()--------*/

/*
**    backtrak.c
**    Description:   This program is to implement backtrack step in reasoning.
*/
```

continued...

...from previous page

```
/* Gets another solution to the current goal.  As above, only returns
** solution for strictly current goal.  Caller should add s_i_t.
** If Once? is t, then backtracking will only happen by one frame.
*/


Ret_Pair  *Backtrack(gs_obj,once)

Goal_Stack   *gs_obj;                    /*goal stack object*/
int          once;                       /*tried or not flag*/


/*-------------------------------------------------------------------------*/


{
        Ret_Pair        *ret_pair;          /*return pair: subst,cert*/
        Ret_Pair        *temp_pair1,*temp_pair2;
        Goal_Frame      *gf;
        cons            *new_prev_substs,*tmp1;
        double          *cert;

        ret_pair  = init_ret_pair();    /*initialize the return pair*/
        temp_pair1 = init_ret_pair();

        gf = pop_a_frame(gs_obj);       /*pop a goal frame from goal_stack*/
        if(gf != NULL)                  /*pop up success*/
        {
            new_prev_substs = mkcons(CAR_LIST,gf->soln,gf->ps);
            temp_pair1 = achieve(gf->goal,new_prev_substs);
            if(temp_pair1->subst != NULL)
            {
                gf->ps = new_prev_substs;
                gf->soln = temp_pair1->subst;
                gf->cert = temp_pair1->certainty;
                push_a_frame(gf,gs_obj);
                tmp1 = gf->sit;
                temp_pair2 = Frwdtrack(gs_obj,
                            subst_prop(gf->roc,temp_pair1->subst),
                                nconc(tmp1,temp_pair1->subst),FALSE);
                if(temp_pair2->subst != NULL)
                {
```

continued...

...from previous page

```
            tmp1 = temp_pair1->subst;
            ret_pair->subst = nconc(tmp1,temp_pair2->subst);
            Min(temp_pair1->certainty,temp_pair2->certainty,cert);
            ret_pair->certainty = (*cert);
            return ret_pair;
        }
        else
        {
            return Backtrack(gs_obj,once);
        }
    }
    else if(once == FALSE)
        {
            return Backtrack(gs_obj,FALSE);
        }
    }
}
```

SUMMARY

- Prolog is a programming language that allows the user to declare relationships between objects, to accumulate and organize these relationships, and to draw logical deductions from facts in relationships that the user has supplied. Unlike other conventional programming languages such as C or Pascal, with Prolog the user need not input data to specify step-by-step procedures that the computer must carry out to obtain the desired output.

- Prolog programming consists of the following three steps:

    1.   Declare facts about objects and their relationships.

    2.   Define rules that govern objects and their relationships.

    3.   Ask questions about objects and their relationships.

- This chapter has focused on two main Prolog functions: unification and backtracking. These two functions are essential if you want to write a Prolog-based expert system in C/C++.

- Unification provides you with an elementary mechanism to bind or combine data/facts in the knowledge (data) base of a Prolog program.

- Backtracking is used when conjunctive conditions are applied in a query of the database.

REFERENCES

Clocksin W. and C. Mellish. *Programming in Prolog.* New York: Springer-Verlag, 1981.

Micro-AI. *Prolog-86 User's Guide and Reference Manual.* Rheem Valley, CA, 1985.

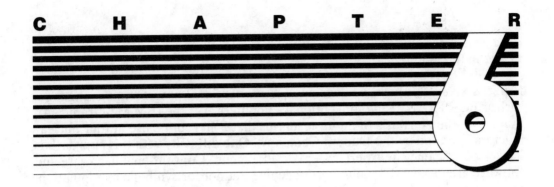

EXPERT SYSTEM TOOLS AND C/C++

Expert system tools commercially available for developing expert systems are discussed in this chapter.

Expert systems (ES) can be developed in conventional programming languages such as FORTRAN, using conventional computers, e.g., the IBM Mainframe. An example is the diagnosis of multiple alarms that is in routine use at four nuclear reactors operated by the Dupont Company. One difficulty with this approach is its lack of efficiency in expert system development. Conventional hardware and software are designed for number crunching but not for symbolic manipulation. Special-purpose LISP machines tend to have huge memories with automatic "garbage collection" and "free" data types (data types are assigned at run time). They provide flexibility and ease of programming. Supporting facilities in ES tools such as debugging aids provide programmers with a means for increasing their productivity in building and testing expert systems.

However, note that efficiency in developing expert systems is no guarantee of cost-effectiveness of delivering the systems, which is the ultimate goal of system development. Many ES knowledge engineers and managers may in the past have overlooked the commitment to delivery vehicles and the ultimate users. The trade-off between the compatibility of the facility used for development and that used for delivery should be considered before an expert system project is undertaken and a facility or tool is selected.

Tools for expert system development offer many facilities to software engineers and managers. The three major expert system programming languages are LISP, Prolog, and Smalltalk, which are used to create tools. A majority of tools are written in LISP; however, a few of them are in Prolog and Smalltalk. These tools provide many conveniences that are not available in conventional programming packages. With greater effort, LISP, Prolog, or Smalltalk can also be used directly to build expert systems; these languages have been discussed in the previous chapters. This chapter focuses on tools that may be convenient and efficient to use in developing large systems.

Among the tools, a significant difference exists between those developed for personal computers and those developed for special-purpose workstations; most of the differences concern memory size and speed.

This chapter discusses facilities available in tools, range of tools, tools available in personal computers, and tools available for special-purpose workstations.

FACILITIES AVAILABLE IN TOOLS

As shown in Figure 6.1, in addition to the supporting facilities such as debugging aids and input/output menus that may also be available to conventional programs, facilities that may also be available to expert systems developers include explanation processors and system building aids (i.e., expert system tools/shells).

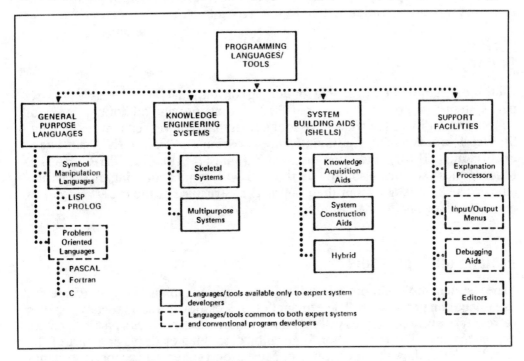

Figure 6.1   Tools/facilities for expert systems and conventional programs

Debugging Aids

Debugging aids include tracing and break points. Tracing provides the user with the display of operation by either listing the names and numbers of rules fired (in expert systems) or by showing the subroutines called (in conventional programs). A breakpoint enables the user to predefine program stops so he or she can test the program execution just before suspending the error line. Most tools have this facility.

Input/Output Menus

Input/output menus assist the user in writing input/output routines. Many advanced conventional programs have these facilities. Some expert systems, such as EMYCIN or EXPERT, request needed information from the user through menu-driven routines when the system cannot locate it in the knowledge base. ROSIE even has special commands that allow a ROSIE expert system to communicate with an operating system as if it were a user.

Editors

Editing mechanisms are available for editing conventional programs as well as expert systems. However, some expert system tools provide additional powerful editors for modifying knowledge bases and rules that require frequent refinement. Special features include **automatic bookkeeping** (in EMYCIN), **consistency checking** (TIMM), and **knowledge extraction** (TIMM and EXPERT-EASE). Most of these systems also provide the user with **syntax checking**, in which the editors use knowledge about the grammatical structure of the expert system to correct spelling and format.

Explanation Processors

Expert system tools that provide software support for explanation are referred to as **explanation processors**. The explanation processor will automatically perform **retrospective reasoning** (i.e., will explain how the system reaches a particular state or conclusion). The explanation is given by describing or displaying part of the rules that led to the state or conclusion. Most expert systems incorporate explanation processors.

RANGE OF TOOLS

Tools/shells can be used to shorten expert system development time. Because tools are built by a third party, they are usually less flexible and cannot be broken into in order to modify the structure to meet the user's particular need.

Because AI languages, such as LISP and Prolog, can sometimes be considered tools, ES tools can be placed on a one-dimensional plane from language to shells, as shown in Figure 6.2 (Chart A) or can be placed on a two-dimensional plane that indicates the trade-off between two characteristics of tools: freedom of expression and the amount of AI programming required (Chart B).

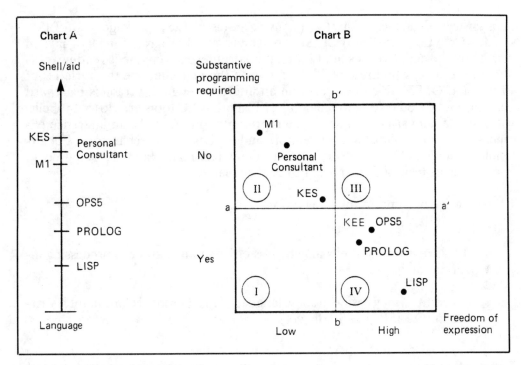

Figure 6.2   Range of ES tools

When an ES tool for expert system development is closer to a language, e.g., LISP, users must be more proficient in programming the tool before they can actually use it for acquiring knowledge. Because of the need to program the expert system from scratch, the user has more freedom and flexibility in using the tool to the most efficient structure that can be configured to represent knowledge. On the other hand, when an ES tool is closer to a shell (e.g., KEE), more facilities — such as input processor, explanation mechanism, and natural language inter-face — may be available to the user; however, the user then is constrained by the limitation in tool structure (e.g., editor), representation method (e.g., rule-based), and inference engine (e.g., backward chaining) embedded in the tool.

As shown in Figure 6.2, Chart A, many varieties of LISP packages — MuLISP, Golden Common LISP, and CLISP — resemble an AI programming language in which no knowledge representation method or inference engine is readily available to the user, who must build it. Between the extremes are the varieties of Prolog and OPS5, which both contain an inference engine; Prolog is backward chaining and OPS5 is forward chaining. Most other PC tools are closer to shells, which contain a variety of knowledge representation methods, an inference engine, and other facilities such as editors and explanation mechanisms. For example, among PC tools, Personal Consultant has many facilities required in knowledge acquisition, which will be discussed later.

Following are two important observations:

- Tools resembling shells may be less efficient and slower in processing information.

- These tools may reside in some language (e.g., Personal Consultant is written in IQ LISP, a LISP dialect).

Because these tools must support many facilities, more memory and slower speed result. These tools may be used for experimenting in knowledge acquisition from experts when the structure and source of knowledge are not completely understood by the developer. The objective of so doing is to save development time. However, after knowledge has been well documented, it can be converted and restructured by other languages, e.g., C/C++.

The trade-off between the programming requirement and freedom is demonstrated in Figure 6.2, Chart B. The four boxes in the chart represent different combinations of programming requirements and freedom of expression. For example, most PC tools belong to Box II in which no programming is required but little freedom exists for the user to change the way the tool functions, e.g., M.1. At the other extreme is Box IV in which most of the tools resembling a language are located. Tools in Box IV require significant programming and user skills, but they allow the user freedom to design a more efficient expert system with a long lead time because many facilities need to be tailored by the user. The tools in Boxes II and IV require a large trade-off in freedom or skill level needed.

Tools in Box II are more suitable for both beginners and experts/specialists who neither can afford to learn a new language quickly nor have the desire to learn it. Tools that are located closer to line aa' may require more programming experience; those closer to line bb' provide for greater freedom. For example, a user may require more training and programming in applying Personal Consultant than in applying M.1. The situation is reversed for tools in Box IV. Those in the box that are located closer to line aa' require less effort from the user to use; tools closer to line bb' provide less freedom for the user to change the features provided. Clearly the tools in Box IV are aimed at conventional software programmers who desire to learn and program in AI.

Selection of ES tools depends on individual preference and usage. However, a general rule is that tools resembling a shell are easier for beginners because they do not require knowledge of programming AI languages.

TOOLS AVAILABLE FOR PERSONAL COMPUTERS

Most of the tools available for personal computers lack sophistication and capability for developing a sophisticated expert system. A list of the majority of PC tools is presented in Appendix C and a simple comparison of sample PC tools is presented in Table 6.1. These tools can be classified according to four criteria: transferability, sophistication, knowledge acquisition requirements, and the language tools based on C/C++.

(Table 6.1 on next page)

	Personal Cons	XSYS	KES	KDS	M.↑	MacKIT	Exper OPS5	NEXPERT	OPS5+ IBM	OPS5+ Mac
Requirements										
Hardware										
Machine — IBM PC	✓	✓	✓	✓	✓			✓	✓	
Machine — Mac 512						✓	✓			✓
Memory — ≥128k										
Memory — ≥192k					✓					
Memory — ≥256k				✓					✓	
Memory — ≥640k	✓	✓	✓							
Disk drive — >1	✓	✓	✓				✓		✓	
Hard disk — 10 MB										
Other — IBM mouse	✓									
Other — 8087 coproc		✓	✓							
Other — Graphics card		✓	✓							
Software — IQLISP	incl.									
ExperLISP						✓				
Text editor					✓		✓			
micro-PROLOG3.1										
Capabilities										
Scope — Tool	✓	✓	✓	✓	✓	✓	✓	✓	✓	✓
Engine — Language							✓	✓	✓	✓
Fwd Chain	✓	✓	?	✓	✓	✓	✓	✓	✓	✓
Bkwd Chain	✓	✓	✓	✓	✓	✓		✓		
Knowledge Rep — Rules			✓					✓		
Frames				✓				✓		
Induction										
Certainty Factors	✓	✓	✓	✓	✓					
Hooks — Language	✓		✓	✓	✓	✓		✓	✓	✓
Applications			✓	✓					✓	
Emphasis — Prototype/demo	✓	✓				✓	✓			
Educational										
Price	$950	$995	$4,000	$795	$10,000	$149	$325	$5,000	$3,000	$3,000

Table 6.1   Comparison of sample PC tools

Requirements		INSIGHT 1	INSIGHT 2	micro-Prolog	PROLOG 1	PROLOG 2	Expert-Ease	EXSYS 3.0	APES 1.1	Exper-Teach	ES/P Advisor
Hardware											
Machine	IBM PC	✓	✓	✓	✓	✓	✓	✓	✓	✓	✓
	Mac 512										
Memory	≥ 128k	✓									
	≥ 192k			✓	✓	✓	✓		✓		✓
	≥ 256k		✓					✓		✓	
	≥ 640k										
Disk drive	> 1										
Hard disk	10 MB		✓								
Other	IBM mouse										
	8087 coproc										
	Graphics card										
Software	IQLISP										
	ExpertLISP										
	Text editor										
	micro-PROLOG3.1								incl.		
Capabilities											
Scope	Tool	✓	✓				✓	✓	✓	✓	✓
Engine	Language			✓	✓	✓			✓		
	Fwd Chain	✓	✓				?		✓	✓	?
	Bkwd Chain	✓	✓				?	✓		✓	?
Knowledge Rep	Rules										✓
	Frames										
	Induction						✓				
	Certainty Factors	✓	✓					✓			
Hooks	Language	✓	✓			✓		✓			✓
	Applications		✓					✓	✓		
Emphasis	Prototype/demo	✓	✓	✓	✓		✓	✓		✓	✓
	Educational										
Price		$95	$485	$250	$276.50*	$1,326*	$695	$395	$425	$475	$895

* price to academic institutions

Table 6.1   Comparison of sample PC tools (cont.)

Transferability of PC Tools

PC tools for expert system development can be classified according to whether they can be transferred to other environments: PC, minicomputers, and mainframe computers (particularly IBMs). For example, KES, KEE, and S.1 are three tools that have been transferred from minicomputers to PCs, and they present three completely different methods in tool transformation.

KES (Knowledge Engineering System) was originally developed by Software Architecture and Engineering, Inc., for operating on minicomputers such as Univac, VAX, Apollo, Sun, and Tektronix systems. It was converted into C for portability on the IBM PC and is called KES II. Knowledge bases created with KES II are compatible with existing KES knowledge bases.

KEE (Knowledge Engineering Environment) was originally developed by Intelli-Corp for operating minicomputers such as Symbolic 3600 and Xerox 1100 computer systems. It was posted to 386-based systems. A PC can be linked to a host minicomputer system that supports a full implementation of common LISP. The PC terminal downloads part of the application knowledge base, and the terminal can be a member of the IBM PC family or compatibles (e.g., COMPAQ and Sperry PCs) as well as the Apple Macintosh. Because of special features of object programming in KEE, the delivery system can interface with several popular PC application packages, e.g., Lotus 1-2-3 or dBASE.

M.1 is similar to S.1, and both tools were launched in 1984. M.1 was developed for the PC system, and the S.1 (System 1) system was developed for minicomputers such as VAX or Xerox. Both use the rule-based knowledge representation method and a backward chaining control scheme from EMYCIN. However, S.1 also supports frame-based and procedure-oriented representation methods. S.1 is implemented in INTERLISP (a variation of LISP), and M.1 is implemented in Prolog. In a sense, M.1 is a simplified version of S.1 for use in PC systems.

Sophistication of Tools

Tools for PCs normally cannot be as sophisticated as tools for LISP workstations; however, sophistication varies among PC tools. Based on tool complexity, PC tools can be classified as simple rule-based, structured rule-based, logic-based hybrid, frame-based hybrid, or object-oriented hybrid.

Simple rule-based tools use IF...THEN production rules for uncomplex knowledge that can be expressed by 50 to 500 rules in an expert system. These tools are adequate for instructional problems. Examples include INSIGHT-1 and INSIGHT-2, KES, and M.1.

Structured rule-based tools use IF...THEN rules subdivided into groups that can be stuctured in a hierarchy. Different groups of rules can be examined without going through every rule each time the system is called upon. These systems are more suitable for complex problems. A good example is PERSONAL CON-SULTANT.

Logic-based hybrid tools use logical analysis (predicate calculus) to represent knowledge and can be combined with simple rule-based or induction features to help input knowledge in expert systems. The logic-based method uses predicate logic to control the analysis of declarative clauses in the form of consequents, e.g., antecedent-1, antecedent-2, . . . antecedent-n, or where both consequent and antecedents are predicates. The antecedents are predicates that can be tested for their true value, and the consequent can only be true if all antecedents can be proved true. Logic-based hybrid tools are more widely used in Europe, where Prolog is used, than in the United States, where LISP is popular, and they are powerful with complex problems. ES/P ADVISOR is an example of a logic-based hybrid tool in which simple rule-based and logic-based features are combined.

Frame-based hybrid tools use frames as well as rules to represent knowledge. These tools are useful for complex problem areas in which the form and content of the data are important in problem solving, e.g., interpreting visual scenes, understanding speech, or representing a variety of information in a single set of data structures. These tools tend to use both backward and forward chaining control schemes. IQ-200 is a good example.

Object-oriented hybrid tools represent the problem elements as objects that can contain facts, IF...THEN rules, or pointers to other objects. The tools facilitate the development of expert systems that incorporate complex, graphical user interfaces. If these tools also combine induction features, they can be very powerful for experts/specialists to use in developing intelligent job aids. This type of tool is not fully developed as yet.

Knowledge Acquisition Requirement

Knowledge acquisition requirement can also be used to classify PC tools for expert system development into three categories: induction, induction hybrid, and noninduction tools.

Induction tools take examples from the user, convert them into rules, and then apply specific algorithms to the rule to determine the order the system follows in inferencing. These systems are user-friendly but weak and inflexible in performance; they are useful only for very simple tasks. Examples include Expert-Ease and TIMM. Induction tools can be used to test rules extracted by knowledge engineers even though rules induced from examples often are not useful in a structured knowledge base because these tools can extract only simple rules. These tools can be used as "test stones" in identifying shortcuts and appropriate knowledge areas for software engineers to undertake in knowledge acquisition.

Induction hybrid tools use the induction method to obtain rules and are combined with frame-based or object-oriented methods to assist in putting knowledge into expert systems. These tools can be very powerful in solving real-time complex problems. No induction hybrid tools are available in the market yet.

Noninduction tools include most PC tools available in the market that do not use induction methods to extract rules. These tools include all those discussed previously that are not inductive.

The Language Tools Based on C/C++

Most tools are based in LISP; however, several tools are written in C, such as NEXPERT and VP Expert, and some can produce C code, e.g., RuleMaster 2.

NEXPERT represents knowledge by using a combination of simple production rules, as well as contexts and categories. Knowledge base structure can be represented either as a tree or a network. NEXPERT supports backward chaining, forward chaining, or a combination of both. VP-Expert features simple backward and forward chaining, inductive front-end, windows, text editor, and confidence factors. RuleMaster is also based in C and can generate C and FORTRAN source codes; it also automatically induces rules from sets of examples supplied by the expert.

TOOLS FOR SPECIAL-PURPOSE WORKSTATIONS

Tools for special-purpose workstations have been the focus of AI development in the past decade; more than 90 research-grade tools have been developed. Approximately one dozen of them are in commercial use and are supported, maintained, and upgraded regularly. These tools are categorized according to their main features in this section.

Tools used for developing large expert systems are designed for use by knowledge engineers in AI workstations. These tools are classified into three groups: specific tools, hybrid tools, and aids.

Specific Tools

The specific tools have evolved through the improvement in laboratory-type expert systems developed in the past two decades. These tools constrain the user to limited (one or two) knowledge representation methods such as frame-based or rule-based methods; however, they allow the user to create large specific expert systems quickly and effectively by providing efficient user interface. Many of these tools are empty skeletal languages, as discussed previously. The developers of these tools are generally also the developers of the "parent" expert system, e.g., KAS out of PROSPECTOR by SRI International.

Frame-based tools use mainly frames to represent knowledge. Frame-based tools are useful for problem areas where the form and content of the data are important in problem solving. Examples include CSRL, SRL, and UNIT PACKAGE. Most of these tools are research-grade.

Rule-based tools use structured "IF...THEN" rules to represent knowledge for building large expert systems. Examples include AL/X, ARBY, EXPERT, GLIB, HEARSAY-III, and KAS (a "shell" of PROSPECTOR).

Logic-based tools use logical analysis (predicate calculus) to structure the knowledge for building large expert systems. Examples include ALICE, FIT, and Prolog.

Object-oriented tools represent the problem elements as objects that communicate with one another by sending and receiving messages. Examples include FLAVORS and Smalltalk.

Hybrid Tools

Hybrid tools combine at least two representative and programming methods discussed. Common combinations are rule-based plus frame-based (KES), rule-based plus logic-based (MRS), rule-based plus procedure-oriented (ROSIE), frame-based plus procedure-oriented (AIMDS), and logic-based plus frame-based representation methods (DUCK).

Some large sophisticated hybrid tools contain three or four representation and programming methods: rule-based, frame-based, logic-based, object-oriented, or procedure-oriented methods. The number of these tools available is limited:

- ART is rule-based, frame-based, and procedure-oriented.

- KC is rule-based, frame-based, object-oriented, and procedure-oriented.

- KEE is frame-based, rule-based, procedure-oriented, and object-oriented.

- LOOPS is object-oriented, procedure-oriented, and rule-based.

- PICON is object-oriented, frame-based, and rule-based.

- S1 is rule-based, frame-based, and procedure-oriented.

- SRL+ is frame-based, rule-based, logic-based, and object-oriented.

Many of the tools being developed require steep learning curves; however, they are powerful for developing complex expert systems.

Aids to System Building

Aids help acquire and represent the domain knowledge and also help design and construct expert systems. Examples of these tools are ACLS, ADVISE, TEIRESIAS, and TIMM. Among these tools, ACLS and TIMM are commercially available.

SUMMARY

- Although expert systems can be developed in conventional programming languages in the conventional hardware environment, the efficiency of development in time and cost is compromised.

- Tools for expert system development offer many facilities. A majority of tools are written in LISP; however, only a few of them are in Prolog and Smalltalk. These tools provide many conveniences that are not available in the conventional programming packages.

- Among the tools, a significant difference exists between those developed for personal computers and those developed for special-purpose workstations; most of the differences concern memory size and speed. Facilities that may be available to expert system developers include debugging aids, input/output menus, editors, and explanation processors.

- ES tools can be placed on a one-dimensional plane from language to shells/aids or can be placed on a two-dimensional plane that indicates the trade-off between two characteristics of tools: freedom or flexibility and the amount of programming effort required. When an ES tool for expert system development resembles a language more than it does a shell, users must be more proficient in programming the tool before they can actually use it for acquiring knowledge. Because of the need to program the tool, the user has more "freedom of expression" in using the tool with the most efficient structure.

- Tools for PCs normally cannot be as sophisticated as tools for LISP workstations. However, sophistication varies among PC tools. PC tools can be classified as simple rule-based, structured rule-based, induction, logic-based hybrid, frame-based hybrid, and object-oriented hybrid. Tools used for developing large expert systems are designed for use by knowledge engineers in AI workstations. These tools are classified into three groups: specific tools, hybrid tools, and aids.

- ES tools can be used to experiment in acquiring knowledge from experts when the structure and source of knowledge are not completely understood by the developer. The objective of doing so is to save development time; however, after knowledge has been well documented, it can be converted and restructured by other languages, such as C/C++.

REFERENCES

Aiello, N., C. Bock., H. P. Nii., et al. "Joy of AGEing: an introduction to the AGE-1 system." Report HPP-81-23. Computer Science Department, Stanford University, 1981.

"Artificial intelligence publications, the personal consultant." *The AI Report.* vol.1, no. 12, 1984.

Balzer, R., L. D. Erman, P. London, et al. "HEARSAY-III: a domain-independent framework for expert systems." *Proceedings of the First Annual National Conference on Artificial Intelligence*, 1980.

Bobrow, D. G. and M. Stefik. *The LOOPS Manual.* Xerox Corporation, December 1983.

Boley, H. "FIT-PROLOG: a functional/relational language comparison." Report SEKI-83-14. Fachbereich Informatik, Universitat Kaiserslautern, Postfach 3049, D-6750 Kaiserslautern 1, West Germany, December 1983.

Buchanan, B. and E. Shortliffe. "The problem of evaluation." In Buchanan and Shortliffe (eds.) *Rule-Based Expert Systems* Reading, Mass: Addison-Wesley, 1984, 571-596.

Bylander, T., S. Mittal, and B. Chandrasekaran. "CSRL: A language for expert systems for diagnosis." *Proceedings IJCAI-83*, 1983, 218-221.

Carnegie Group, Inc. "Knowledge craft, an environment for developing knowledge based systems." Pittsburgh, PA, 1985.

Clayton, B. D. "ART programming primer." Report. Inference Corporation, Los Angeles, CA, 1984.

Clocksin, W. and C. Mellish. *Programming in Prolog* New York: Springer-Verlag, 1981.

Duda, R.O. and R. Reboh. "AI and decision making: the PROSPECTOR experience." In W. Reitman (ed.) *Artificial Intelligence Applications for Business.* Norwood, NJ: Ablex, 1984.

Davis, R. "Representation as a basis for system construction and maintenance." In D. A. Waterman and F. Hayes-Roth (eds.) *Pattern-Directed Inference Systems* (Academic Press, 1978).

"DUCK builds intelligent systems." *Applied Artificial Intelligence Reporter.* vol. 2, no. 2, November 1984.

Ennals, J. *Beginning Micro-Prolog.* 2nd rev. ed. New York: Harper & Row, 1984.

Expert Systems International. "ES/P advisor product description." King of Prussia, PA, 1985.

Fain, J., F. Hayes-Roth, H. Sowizral, et al. "Programming in ROSIE: an introduction by means of examples." Report N-1646-ARPA (Rand Corporation, February 1982).

Freiling, M. and J. Alexander. "Diagrams and grammar: tools for mass-producing expert systems." *Proceedings of the First Conference on Artificial Intelligence Applications.* IEEE Computer Society, December 1984.

Gimmy, K. "Plant experience with an expert for alarm diagnosis." *Proceedings of the Society for Computer Simulation Multiconference.* (San Diego, CA, January, 1986), 23-25.

Goldberg, A. *Smalltalk-80: The Interactive Programming Environment.* Reading, MA: Addison-Wesley, 1984.

Goldberg, A. and D. Robson. *Smalltalk-80: The Language and Its Implementation.* Reading, MA: Addison-Wesley, 1983.

Human Edge Software, Inc. "EXPERT-EASE product description." Palo Alto, CA, 1985.

IBM Corporation. *Expert System Consultation Environment/vm and Expert System Development Environment/vm.* General information manual. GH 20-9597 (Menlo Park, CA, 1985).

IBM Corporation. *Expert System Development Environment/vm.* Reference manual. SH20-6909 (Menlo Park, CA, 1985).

IBM Corporation. *Expert System Development Environment/vm*. User guide. SH20-9608 (Menlo Park, CA, 1985).

Kaehler T. and D. Patterson. *Taste of Smalltalk*. New York: W. W. Norton & Co., 1986.

Kunz, J. C., T. P. Kehler, and M. D. Williams. "Applications development using a hybrid AI development system." *The AI Magazine*. vol. 5, no. 3, Fall 1984.

Lauriere, Jean-Louis. "A language and a program for stating and solving combinatorial problems." *Artificial Intelligence*, vol. 10, 1978, 29-127.

Level Five Research, Inc. "Insight 1 and 2 product description." Melbourne Beach, FL, 1985.

Malix, K. "Led the dataflow in a machine like alice." *Computing*. 24 Nov. 1983. 26.

McDermott, D. and R. Brooks. "ARBY: diagnosis with shallow casual models." *Proceedings AAAI-82*, 1982, 370-372.

Michalski, R. S. and A. B. Baskin. "Integrating multiple knowledge representations and learning capabilities in an expert system: the ADVISE system." *Proceedings IJCAI-38*, 1983, 256-258 .

Michie, D., S. Muggleton, C. Reise, et al. "RULEMASTER: a second-generation knowledge-engineering facility." *Proceedings of the First Conference on Artificial Intelligence Applications*. IEEE Computer Society, December 1984.

Moore, R. L., L. B. Hawkinson, C. G. Knickerbocker, et al. "A real-time expert system for process control." *Proceedings of the First Conference on Artificial Intelligence Applications*. IEEE Computer Society, December 1984.

Parker, R. E. and S. J. Kiselewich. "The modeling of human cognitive decision processes in the intelligent machine model (TIMM)." Report (Santa Barbara, CA: Artificial intelligence laboratory, General Research Corporation, 1984).

Paterson, A. and T. Niblett. "ACLS user manual." Report. Intelligent Terminals, Ltd., 15 Canal Street Oxford, UK 0S2 6BH, 1982.

Reboh, Rene. "Knowledge engineering techniques and tools in the PROSPECTOR environment." SRI technical note 243, Stanford Research Institute, 333 Ravenswood Avenue, Menlo Park, CA, June 1981.

Reiter, J. E. "AL/X: an inference system for probabilistic reasoning." MS thesis. Computer Science Department, University of Illinois. Champaign-Urbana, 1981.

Software Architecture and Engineering, Inc. "Knowledge engineering systems." Artificial Intelligence Center, Suite 1220, 1401 Wilson Blvd., Arlington, VA 22209, November 1983.

Sridharan, N. S. "AIMDS user manual version 2." *Technical Report CBM-TR-89.* Computer Science Department, Rutgers University, New Brunswick, NJ, June 1978.

Stefik, M. "An examination of a frame-structured representation system." *Proceedings IJCAI-79*, 1979, 845-852.

Teknowledge. M.1 product description. Palo Alto, CA, 1984.

Teknowledge. S.1 product description. Palo Alto, CA, 1984.

Touretzky, D. *LISP, a Gentle Introduction to Symbolic Computation.* New York: Harper & Row, 1984.

Van Meele, Shortliffe, and Buchanan. "EMYCIN: a knowledge engineer's tool for constructing rule-based expert systems" in B. Buchanan and E. Shortliffe (eds.) *Rule-Based Expert Systems* New York: Addison-Wesley, 1984, 302-328.

Waterman, Donald A. *A Guide to Expert Systems.* Reading, MA: Addison-Wesley, 1986.

Weinreb, D. and D. Moon. "Objects, message passing, and flavors." *LISP Machine Manual.* Symbolics, Inc., July 1981, 279-313.

Weiss, S. M. and C. A. Kulikowski. "Expert consultation systems: the EXPERT and CASNET projects" in A. H. Bond (ed.) *Machine Intelligence.* Infotech State of the Art Report, series 9, no. 3 (Pergamon Infotech Limited, 1981), 339-353.

"Which computer?" *Expert-Ease* (April 1984), 68-71.

Winston, P. H. and B. K. P. Horn. *LISP* (2nd edition). Reading, MA: Addison-Wesley Publishing Company, 1984.

Wright, J. M. and M. S. Fox. "SRL/1.5 user manual." Pittsburgh, PA: Robotics Institute. Carnegie-Mellon University, December 1983.

Wyle, F. "Artificial intelligence in the commercial marketplace." *LISP Machine, Inc.*, 23 Feb. 1984.

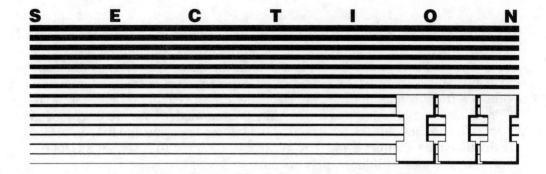

PROGRAMMING EXPERT SYSTEMS IN C/C++

Chapters 4, 5, and 6 have examined LISP, Prolog, and expert system tools. Various C/C++ utility programs to emulate functions of LISP and Prolog have been presented. This section deals with knowledge representation using C/C++.

The power of an expert system resides in its knowledge, not in the computing formalism, as discussed in Chapter 1. Because knowledge is often abstract and ambiguous, a well-specified language for encoding this knowledge becomes essential. This language is called **knowledge representation language**. The knowledge representation language may use any one or a combination of frames, rules, and logic to represent facts explicitly; however, an expert system must also provide access to the facts implicit in the knowledge represented that can be derived through its inference mechanism. Finally, an expert system would remain empty if no particular domain of knowledge were extracted and encoded in it. In essence, the four major components of expert system technology to be addressed in the remaining part of this book are the knowledge representation language, inference engine, user interface, and specific domain knowledge.

Section III includes four chapters to present methods for building the three major components of an expert system that provides a user-friendly environment for experts/specialists to encode explicit descriptions of how they solve real-world problems (see Figure III.1).

The knowledge representation language is used to build the knowledge base of an expert system, and an inference engine in the expert system then probes the knowledge base and infers the implicit data in the base. However, as discussed in Chapter 1, a very critical element of an expert system is the user interface. Without a friendly man-machine interface, the expert system becomes essentially "deaf" and "dumb." Methods for building the knowledge base are discussed in Chapter 7, and methods for constructing the inference engine and user-interface are discussed in Chapters 8 and 9, respectively. Chapter 10 describes a C/C++ library structure for building expert systems.

Section IV concerns methods to build real-world expert systems by extracting and organizing expert knowledge, using the components developed in Section III. Chapter 11 discusses historical applications and approaches of expert system technology, and Chapter 12 discusses building and delivering expert systems in selected domains.

Methods and examples used in the discussion and design rules for building expert systems are followed closely. Note that the two important rules in writing code, which have been discussed previously, are modularity and object-oriented programming.

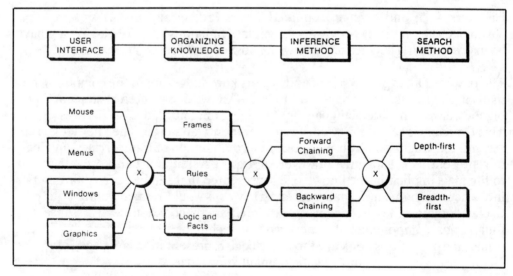

Figure III.1   Structure of an expert system/tool

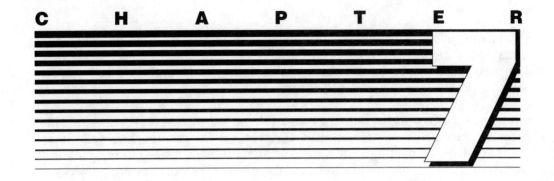

BUILDING KNOWLEDGE REPRESENTATION LANGUAGE STRUCTURES

This chapter discusses methods for building knowledge representation language structures. Chapter 8 examines approaches to building an inference engine that interprets these structures and infers implicit information, and Chapter 9 discusses the user interface that connects the user with the expert system in a computer.

Most current PC expert system tools use a single knowledge representation language, i.e., rules, frames, or logic. Rules are best for representing knowledge that facilitates decision-making. For a sophisticated problem, a single representation language may be inconvenient and, after all, inefficient in representing knowledge. A structure will be discussed that will combine all three languages to provide the user with all conveniences available in representing various types of knowledge.

This chapter includes the following main sections:

- Building Frame Structures
- Building Rule Structures
- Building Logic Structures

BUILDING FRAME STRUCTURES

Frame structures are also called "units" or "schemas" in some AI workstation tools, such as KEE (distributed by IntelliCorp.). **A frame structure** can provide the expert/specialist with a uniform set of representation services for complex data collections or databases. A frame is more than a structure that is used in other computer languages such as C or Pascal. It is a generalized structure that contains spaces (called **slots**) that can be filled with information describing various aspects of that structure, in addition to just the value of that slot. For example, the slots can in turn contain a default value, a restriction of value to be added, a procedure activated to compute a needed value, or a rule activated when certain conditions are met. Furthermore, a frame is a generalization hierarchy in which information is inherited from its parent class. This section discusses the fundamental assumptions about, advantages/disadvantages of, and methods for designing frame structures.

Fundamental Assumptions

A fundamental assumption about the frame representation language is that frames can be used to unify and denote a loose collection of objects, e.g., related ideas, concepts, facts, experiences, etc. Frames can be linked into a classification system. Each frame represents a class of objects that is connected to a parent class (called **superclass**) or a child class (called **subclass**). A **frame** contains slots that can be filled with other expressions such as frames, names, identifiers, specifications, relationships between slots, or procedural attachment. Clearly it is assumed that both **declarative knowledge** ("knowing that," such as facts, relationships) and **procedural knowledge** ("knowing how," such as when to do something and how to do it) can be represented in a frame. An AI programmer frame is shown in Tables 7.1 and 7.2. Table 7.1 shows the declarative knowledge of the AI programmer frame, and Table 7.2 demonstrates the procedural knowledge of the programmer frame.

Slot	Procedure
Languages/ Tools used	LISP, Prolog, shells
Educational background	Generalist plus AI courses
Programming approach	Heuristic programming*
Major tasks	Acquiring domain knowledge
	Defining and structuring the problem
	Interviewing experts
	Encoding knowledge
	Prototyping the system
	Testing the system
	Refining the system

*Programming by experience; no general guidelines.

Table 7.1   Declarative knowledge of AI programmer frame

Slot	Procedure/Condition
Languages/ Tools used	When apply
Educational background	Test qualification
Programming approach	Test applicability
Major tasks	How to perform

Table 7.2   Procedural knowledge of AI programmer frame

Tables 7.1 and 7.2 clearly indicate the combined and powerful features of a frame.

It is further assumed that the operation of classifications is one basic reasoning method, i.e., the property of an object in the superclass will be passed down to the object in the subclass if no restriction is specified in the object of the subclass. Through this operation, you can apply a whole set of specific knowledge in a particular class to objects in the downstream classes, guide your search for specific facts about the object in the frame, or make assumptions about properties that must be true for the entire class of frames, without checking specific slots.

Advantages/Disadvantages

The advantage lies in the powerful features of a frame, such as default values, declarative knowledge, and procedural attachments that are available to experts/specialists to extract their knowledge. In particular, the concept of a classification system is analogous to the real-world structure of facts and organization. It is natural for the user to relate the concept of frame to daily activities. Properties, relationships, and events can be easily fitted into slots of an object from conditions and situations; restrictions can also be attached to the slots to trigger a sequence of actions to be taken by the program.

Two difficulties arise in the design of a frame structure. First, the theoretical foundation of the frame to support the assumption that the frame can contain both declarative and procedural knowledge cost-effectively requires further research. Some even suggest that the frame is only an organized extension of logic representation. Second, the implementation of frames in the context of class deserves attention for two reasons. The class structure that a frame belongs to should allow the user to change the order of the hierarchy and create subclasses or superclasses to any given class; however, because of the inheritance feature of frames, special care is needed when a superclass is inserted into an existing classification system to ensure that the properties of the slots are properly passed down to subclasses. Furthermore, because a frame can be attached to a slot, the depth (number of layers) of the frame can become infinite and thus prohibit an efficient search in consultation.

Methods to Design Frame Structures

To design a frame structure that will provide classification and inheritance, four essential elements are required: class, unit (entity), slot, and inheritance. Note that "unit" is a term that can refer to both class units and entity units. Some systems do not make such a marked distinction between a class and its instances (entities). This treatment is less efficient but allows for incremental refinement of knowledge. The functions of these four essential elements are described briefly as follows:

- **Class**: provides a hierarchical structure through an inheritance tree with links (nodes) so that you can locate a frame by traversing either subclass (child) or superclass (parent) links.

- **Unit**: provides an organization to host slots that will be used to store both declarative and procedural information on a given subject.

- **Slot**: provides a data structure to hold information regarding a particular attribute of a unit, i.e., certainty factors, inheritance, etc.

- **Inheritance**: modes that will either enable or disable a class to inherit value and default value from the parent class (superclass) and pass the value and default value to the child class (subclass).

The relationships among the four elements are shown in Figure 7.1, in which a class contains another class, a unit, or a slot.

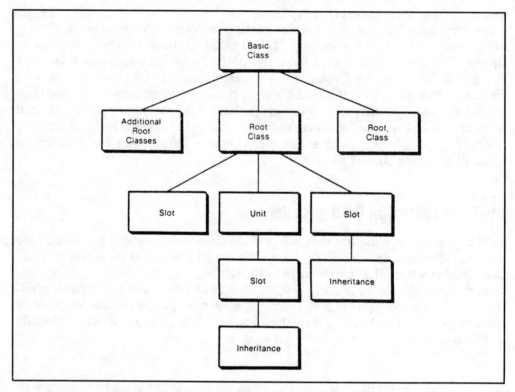

Figure 7.1   Relationships among classes, units, slots, and inheritance

Note that a class does not "contain" other classes in the same way as it contains slots: it only has inheritance with child classes or entities. A unit, in turn, may contain many slots. Slots contain inheritance modes and other attributes inputted by the users. As shown in Figure 7.2, a class can have a superclass, a class can also contain many units, and a unit can contain as many slots as desired. Depending on whether the value of the slots can be passed down to those of the subclass, slots can be classified as member slots or own slots:

- **Member slots:** the value of the slot will be inherited by those of the sub-class.

- **Own slots**: the value of the slot as well as the whole slot itself will not be inherited.

C++ provides facilities to build most of these features. Next you will examine how to program each of the four elements.

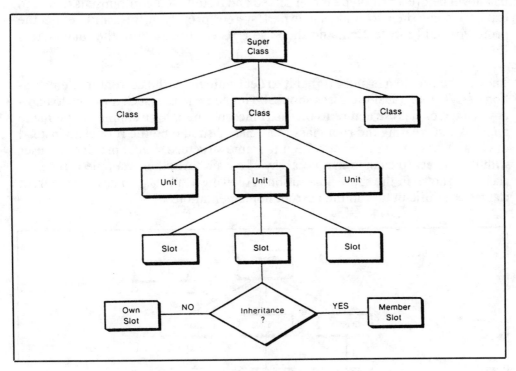

Figure 7.2   The organization of a frame structure

Class

A **class** is a set of closely related objects that share the same attributes. The initial class is always the basic class that is the root class of any classes; every other class created thereafter is a subclass of the root class, as shown in Figure 7.2. A class can have slots that will be inherited by subclasses, other classes, or units. The values in the slots of the basic class will also be inherited by all classes.

C++ has a readily available capability for implementing these features into a frame structure. The two difficulties in using C++ to build a frame structure are nondynamic defining of data during run time and inflexibility of class hierarchy. Because C++ provides no dynamic defining to allow the user to define problem structures at run time, when using C++ to create a frame structure, you need to know in advance the complete structure of the problem, which normally cannot be known before a prototype is completed and tested. A compromise is to use an expert system shell to build an expert system prototype, test and refine the prototype until satisfaction, and then use C/C++ to structure the final system for delivery.

The second problem is more difficult to deal with under the current implementation of C/C++. Ideally, classes should be implemented in such a way as to allow any change of class structure to be easily incorporated, for example, if you make a mistake in creating the root class (e.g., class 0 should be the root class instead of class 1). As shown in Figure 7.3, the frame structure should provide the user with the facility to change the hierarchy of a class. Another example is the sub-class 112 shown in the same illustration. Allowing a subclass to have two parent classes is a difficult task in the current implementation.

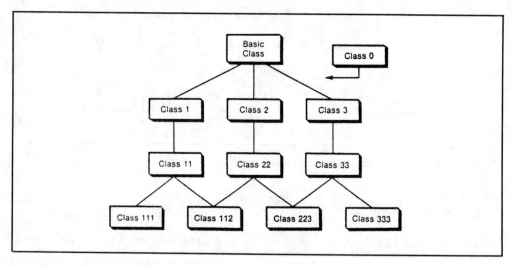

Figure 7.3   Difficulties in editing the class structure

Because of the current implementation of C/C++, a simplified version of class hierarchy will be discussed with the following assumptions:

- Classes are not separated from units; i.e., their structures are similiar.

- A class can have only one parent class (superclass) but can include as many child classes (subclasses) as you want; the root class has the basic class as its parent class.

- The hierarchy of a class cannot be changed easily. When it is changed, care must be given to the detail of the attributes that can be inherited.

Unit (Entity)

The **unit** (for clarity, sometimes "entity" is used rather than "unit"; the terms are interchangeable in this discussion) structure is similar to the class structure, except that a unit is like a table, which stores all data regarding characteristics of specific objects but cannot have any subclasses.

Slot and Inheritance

A **slot** is an object that holds information regarding a particular attribute of a unit. A unit can have as many slots as you want. The primary items of information include the following:

- **Slot Name**: is the name of the slot.

- **Slot Value**: is the value given by the user.

- **Slot Type-Restriction**: is a restriction on the type of value that can be inputted for this slot.

- **Slot Source**: is the source from which the attribute is inherited.

- **Slot Destination**: is the location to which the attribute is passed.

- **Slot Default-Value**: is the value used if no value is given.

- **Slot Certainty**: indicates how sure the user feels about the information.

- **Slot Prompt**: is used by the user to enter value.

- **Slot Documentation**: documents the purpose, function, etc. of the slot.

- **Slot Assertable?**: tells whether the value of the slot can be asserted.

Slot name and value are self-explanatory. Slot type-restriction is used to restrict the value of the slot that can be accepted when inputted by the user. To restrict a slot value, set its type-restriction as follows:

- **Expression**: the value can be any expression.

- **Number**: the value can be any number.

- **String**: the value can be any string.

- **Boolean**: the value must be yes or no.

- **(member (<atom>*))**: the value must be one of the atoms in the list.

- **(predicate <predicate>)**: the value must satisfy the LISP predicate.

- **(class <classname>)**: the value must be an entity of class *classname*.

- **Name:** the value must be a name.

Slot source and slot destination are used for inheritance to indicate from which unit the slot originates and where it destines to (the slot destination is either :own or :member). Slot default value is used if the user does not input a value. Slot certainty indicates the confidence level of the user about the value he or she is inputting. For the purpose of probability calculation, slot certainty is selected to range between zero and one. Slot prompt is used to allow the user to input value. In a more sophisticated tool, a procedure name can be inputted to compute the appropriate value. The procedure is called a method, or a demon; however, this procedure can also be implemented in the rule structure. Slot documentation is provided for the user to input information regarding the slot for the future user. Slot assertable? is either yes or no; it is activated when it is necessary for the value to be asserted for future reasoning. If the slot is nonassertable, when reasoning is evoked, the information it contains will not be checked; it is considered merely a document.

Not all of the slot features are needed in a specific domain, depending on the requirement of an application. You may need to tailor the slot features for each application.

Implementation of the Frame Structure with C++

As discussed before, because C+ + is not dynamic-defining, you may not be able to use it to create run-time classes. The following steps are required to build an applications knowledge representation in C/C+ +:

1.   Draw a class hierarchical chart similar to Figure 7.1 that is pertinent to a specific application domain.

2.   For each class in the organizational chart, define the slot data structure; for each class at the lowest layer, such as HAYWARD-INV, STANFORD-CUSTS, link all entities into a tree for efficient searches in querying the expert system.

3.   For the private slots, define the member functions that manipulate these slots' values, i.e., get_slot_value(), set_slot_value(), print_slot_value(), etc.

4.   For the relationship between parent and children classes, use the C++ inheritance mechanism to define the inheritance. For example, the relation between class 1 and class 11 in Figure 7.1 can be defined as

```
class_11: class_1 /* .... */
```

An inventory control system is used as an example to demonstrate how C++ is used to represent frame knowledge.

Inventory Control System—An Example

The application is entitled Inventory Control System (ICS); its purpose is to gather information about the availability and pricing of certain automobile parts from a warehouse that uses databases, such as dBASE III, to keep track of its inventory.

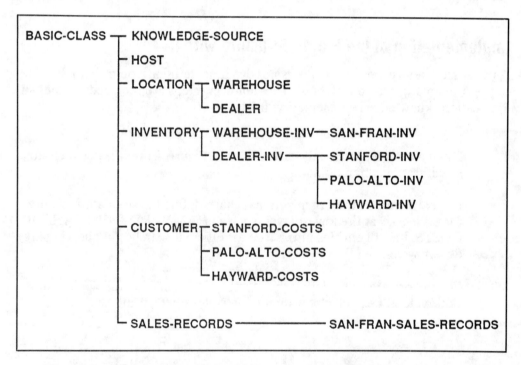

Figure 7.4   The class structure for the Inventory Control System

Assume that you have an automobile dealership and you want to gather information from other dealers and its warehouse database (as shown in Figure 7.4). Currently, to get information about the availability or price of a part, you must do the following:

- Find the Part ID number the warehouse uses for ordering the part.

- Call the warehouse and request information about availability or pricing.

- Wait two to three days for the request to be processed and a reply initiated.

In addition to this procedure, there are two problems associated with the responsibilities of the warehouse:

- Warehouse personnel must be familiar with dBASE III.

- Information requested may be inaccurate due to processing lag times or inaccuracies associated with a high volume of requests.

For this simple exercise, an expert system (ICS) written in C/C++ will be used to perform the following:

- Ask for inventory and pricing information, using clear, simple English queries.

- Gather the information quickly.

- Remove all dependency on learning/using dBASE III.

- Remove the need for warehouse processing personnel.

- Represent the information in a clear, consistent manner.

To simplify the process of representing and obtaining information to perform the above functions, ICS does the following:

- Uses structures called **objects** to represent groups of information, such as an inventory on a specific part at the warehouse.

- Uses structures called **knowledge-sources** to represent various sources of information, such as a warehouse's dBASE III program files.

- Uses structures called **hosts** to represent the location of information from external sources (the phone number and logon procedures of the warehouse computers).

- Uses structures called **rules** to serve as guidelines for making decisions based upon the information in other objects or on a host.

- Uses a **reasoning system** (inference engine) to gather information from the knowledge source objects.

The warehouse in the sample application stores the inventories of parts in dBASE III files. The warehouse file used here is fairly simple. Below is an exact listing of the dBASE file WARE.DBF:

Record#	NAME	CIL	OIL	COST	DISCOUNT	MIN_ORD	ORDER_TIME
1	oil_pump	20	30	50.00	0.00	2	21
2	oil_pan	10	50	15.00	0.00	2	21
3	cooling_fan	2	23	45.00	0.00	1	28
4	fan_belt	10	45	8.00	1.00	5	14
5	battery	30	50	22.00	5.00	5	14
6	headlight	50	50	20.00	3.00	41	4
7	parking_brake	28	30	17.50	0.00	1	21
8	distributor	30	23	80.00	0.00	1	28
9	spark_plug	100	120	0.50	0.10	20	14
10	tire	100	125	80.00	10.00	4	28
11	fuel_pump	20	25	45.00	0.00	1	28
12	ignition_coil	30	31	25.00	0.00	1	28

As you can see from the listing, the warehouse contains inventories on 12 different parts. Selecting the first part as a example gives you the following:

Record#	NAME	CIL	OIL	COST	DISCOUNT	MIN_ORD	ORDER_TIME
1	oil_pump	20	30	50.00	0.00	2	21

This dBASE III record describes the inventory on a part called OIL_PUMP:

Current Inventory Level (CIL)	20
Optimal Inventory Level (OIL)	30
Cost	$50.00
Discount$	0.00
Minimum Order Quantity (MIN_ORD)	2
Days Until Delivery (ORDER_TIME)	21

For each part, you will be using the information from four of the fields: CIL, OIL, COST, and DISCOUNT.

For the inventory control system, you will want to keep track of the inventories of a number of automobile parts. An inventory of a part consists of the part's name, its current inventory level (CIL), its optimal inventory level (OIL), its cost, and an optional discount. (You will not use the MIN_ORD and ORDER_TIME fields in these examples.) The following is a sample inventory of Battery:

NAME:	Battery
CIL:	30
OIL:	50
COST:	22.00
DISCOUNT:	5.00

To store this information, you will create an object called an entity with slots called NAME, CIL, OIL, COST, and DISCOUNT (thus an ICS Entity corresponds to a dBASE record, and ICS slots correspond to dBASE fields). Each of these slots has a value that is limited by a constraint that defines the type of value the value can assume. For this entity, you have the following slot values (constraints are in braces):

```
Battery    {:NAME}
30         {:INTEGER}
50         {:INTEGER}
22.00      {:NUMBER}
5.00       {:NUMBER}
```

However, because there are many parts, you know you will be creating more than one of the above inventories and can simplify the creation of many entities by creating a class object that will group all the inventories together. Assuming you call this class object PARTS, you would want to create a tree structure similar to the following:

```
BASIC-CLASS---PARTS
{Battery-Parts, Distributor-Parts, ...}
```

Note: Basic-Class is the root of the tree structure. In the Objects section, a class tree was created:

```
BASIC-CLASS----PARTS
{Battery-Parts, Distributor-Parts}.
```

The class PARTS contained the slots NAME, CIL, OIL, COST, and DISCOUNT. The same principle can be applied to encode all information regarding part inventory control, as shown in Figure 7.4.

ICS Frame Representation in C++

The class structure for the inventory control system is shown in Figure 7.4. This structure is a result of rapid-prototyping by using an expert system tool, IQ-200 (presented in Appendix A). Listing 7.1 shows a C++ implementation of the class structure. The subprograms for individual classes are shown in Figure 7.4, and their associated slots are self-explanatory.

The objective of Listing 7.1 is to translate the hierarchy of the dealership inventory relationship shown in Figure 7.4 into a C++ class structure. The root (base) class is the basic class and has four subclasses: location, inventory, customer, and sales records. These four classes are declared to be friend classes so their data and methods can be shared. Their own data and methods are subsequently declared.

The subclasses of these four classes and the children classes of the subclasses (e.g., Stanford_inventory) are further declared.

Listing 7.2 exhibits the programs that initialize classes by using constructors and define member functions in the classes shown in Listing 7.1, such as the following:

```
Inv* location::get_slot_value2()
{
        Inv* temp = NULL;

        temp = invntory->get_slot_value();
        return temp;
}
```

Listing 7.3 shows subroutines that define units/slots and test the C++ representation of the frame knowledge structure.

Listing 7.1: The Inventory Control System Class Structure in C++

```
/*****************************************************************************
        This header file defines the knowledge representation data structure
    in inventory control system in C++.

    Inventory Control System Class structure :
```

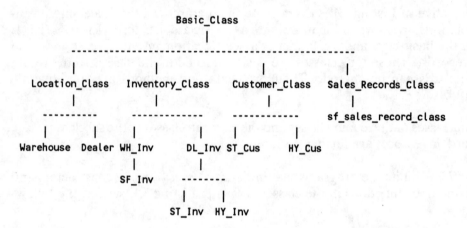

```
*****************************************************************************/
/*
**   icsclass.h
**
**   Define each class.
**
**   Date:        9/6/88
*/
```

continued...

...from previous page

```
/*------------------------------------------------define class-----------*/


class basic_class {
        friend class   location;
        friend class   inv;
        friend class   cust;
        friend class   sales_records;
};




/*--------------------------------------------------cust class-------*/
class cust : public basic_class {
        char_slot        *dealer;
        char_slot        *name;
        char_slot        *part;
        int_slot         *number;
        char_slot        *order_date;
        char_slot        *time;
        friend class st_cust;
        friend class hayward_cust;
public:
        cust();
        ~cust() { delete dealer; delete name; delete part;
                    delete order_date; delete number; delete time;
                }   /*destructor*/
        void  set_slotval();                    /*set the slot value*/
        Cust* get_slotval();                    /*get the slot value*/
        void  prn_value();
};

/*-------------------------------------------------st_cust class---*/
/*Inheritence from class cust
*/

class st_cust : public cust {};
```

continued...

...from previous page

```
/*-------------------------------------------------inv class-------*/

class inv : public basic_class {
        char_slot    *name;                    /*part name*/
        int_slot     *cil;                     /*current inv level*/
        int_slot     *oil;                     /*optimal inv level*/
        friend class dealer_inv;
        friend class warehs_inv;
public:
        inv();
        ~inv() { delete name; delete cil; delete oil;}
        void set_slotval();
        Inv* get_slotval();
        void prn_value();
};



/*-----------------------------------------dealer_inv class-----*/
/*Inherited from class inv
*/
class dealer_inv : public inv {};


/*---------------------------------------------st_inv class--------*/
/*Inherited from class dealer_inv
*/
class st_inv : public dealer_inv {};



/*-----------------------------------------warehs_inv class-----*/
/*Inherited from class inv
*/

class warehs_inv : public inv {
        double_slot   *cost;
        double_slot   *discount;
        int_slot      *min_order;
        char_slot     *order_time;
```

continued...

...from previous page

```
public:
        warehs_inv();
        ~warehs_inv() { delete order_time; delete cost;
                                delete min_order; delete discount;}
        void set_slotval1();
        Ware_Inv* get_slotval1();
        void prn_value1();
};



/*----------------------------------------sf_inv class-----*/
/*Inheritence from class warehs_inv
*/


class sf_inv : public warehs_inv {};



/*----------------------------------------------location class----------*/

class location : public basic_class {
        char_slot           *address;              /*address of the location*/
        char_slot           *phone;                /*phone number of the loc*/
        class  invent : public inv {} *invntory;   /*inventory subclass*/
        friend class dealer;
        friend class warehs;
public:
        location();
        ~location() {   delete address; delete phone;}
        void set_slotval();                    /*set the slot value*/
        Loc* get_slotval1();                   /*get the address, phone*/
        Inv* get_slotval2();               /*get the subclass inventory value*/
        void prn_value();
};



/*--------------------------------------------dealer class----------*/
/*Inherited from class location
*/
```

continued...

...from previous page

```
class dealer : public location {
        class  custmers : public cust {} *custm;
public:
        dealer() { custm = new custmers;}
        ~dealer() { delete custm;}
        void set_cust_slotval();
        Cust* get_cust_slotval();
        void prn_cust_slotval();
};




/*----------------------------------------------sales_records class-------*/

class sales_records : public  basic_class {
        int_slot            *sale_number;
        char_slot           *date;
        char_slot           *part;
        int_slot            *number_sold;
        double_slot         *cost;
        double_slot         *total_sale;
        char_slot           *sold_to;
        friend class sf_sales_records;
public:
        sales_records();
        ~sales_records() { delete date; delete part;
                           delete sold_to; delete sale_number;
                           delete number_sold; delete cost;
                           delete total_sale;}
        void set_slotval();
        Sales_Rec* get_slotval();
        void prn_value();
};




/*-------------------------------------------------sf_sales_records class--*/
/*Inherited from class sales_records
*/

class sf_sales_records : public sales_records {};
```

continued...

...from previous page

```
/*-------------------------------------------------warehs class---------*/
/*Inherited from class location
*/

class warehs : public location {
      class  sales_recs : public sales_records {} *sales_rec;
public:
      warehs() {sales_rec = new sales_recs;}
      ~warehs() { delete sales_rec;}
      void set_sales_recs_slotval();
      Sales_Rec* get_sales_recs_slotval();
};




/*
*****************************************************************
**
**   ics.h
**
**   Define the overloaded functions which are used in building up KB.
**   Date:    9/6/88
**
*/




#define    FAIL         0
#define    SUCCEED      1




struct slot_node {                      /*slot node used in slot list*/
      char*  name;
      slot_node*  next;
};

struct cls_slot {
      char*           name;
      slot_node*      sllist;
};
```

continued...

...from previous page

```
/*-------------------------------------------------------For ICS -------------*/
/*
**  Define each class node and entity node structure for the leaves of class
**  tree. Because C++ is compiler language instead of intepreter language.
**  So it is impossible to dynamic define the data structure in the run time.
*/


/*
** st_cust class
*/
struct stcust_etynd {              /*st_cust class entity node*/
      char*                        name;
      st_cust*                     entity;
      stcust_etynd*                next;
};

struct stcust_class {              /*st_cust class node*/
      char*                        name;
      slot_node*                   slist;
      stcust_etynd*                elist;
};


/*
** st inv  class
*/
struct stinv_etynd {               /*st_inv class entity node*/
      char*                        name;
      st_inv*                      entity;
      stinv_etynd*                 next;
};

struct stinv_class {               /*st_inv class node*/
      char*                        name;
      slot_node*                   slist;
      stinv_etynd*                 elist;
};
```

continued...

...from previous page

```
/*
** san francisco inv  class
*/
struct sfinv_etynd {          /*sf_inv class entity node*/
       char*                  name;
       sf_inv*                entity;
       sfinv_etynd*           next;
};

struct sfinv_class {           /*sf_inv class node*/
       char*                  name;
       slot_node*             slist;
       sfinv_etynd*           elist;
};

/*
**   warehouse class
*/
struct warehs_etynd {
       char*                  name;
       warehs*                entity;
       warehs_etynd*          next;
};

struct warehs_class {
       char*                  name;
       slot_node*             slist;
       warehs_etynd*          elist;
};

/*
**   dealer class
*/
struct dealer_etynd {
    char*                     name;
    dealer*                   entity;
    dealer_etynd*             next;
};
```

continued...

...from previous page

```
struct dealer_class {
    char*                   name;
    slot_node*              slist;
    dealer_etynd*           elist;
};


/*
**  sf_sales_records class
*/
struct sfsalrec_etynd {
    char*                   name;
    sf_sales_records*       entity;
    sfsalrec_etynd*         next;
};


struct sfsalrec_class {
    char*                   name;
    slot_node*              slist;
    sfsalrec_etynd*         elist;
};



/*------------------------------------------------Overload define----------*/
/*
** The best way to generalize the routines.
*/
overload addslot_clsnd;
void addslot_clsnd(cls_slot*,stcust_class*);    /*for st_cust class*/
void addslot_clsnd(cls_slot*,stinv_class*);     /*for st_inv class*/
void addslot_clsnd(cls_slot*,sfinv_class*);     /*for sf_inv class*/
void addslot_clsnd(cls_slot*,warehs_class*);    /*for warehs class*/
void addslot_clsnd(cls_slot*,dealer_class*);    /*for dealer class*/
void addslot_clsnd(cls_slot*,sfsalrec_class*);  /*for sf_sales_rec class*/

overload addety_clsnd;
void addety_clsnd(char*,st_cust*,stcust_class*); /*for st_cust class*/
void addety_clsnd(char*,st_inv*,stinv_class*);   /*for st_inv class*/
void addety_clsnd(char*,sf_inv*,sfinv_class*);   /*for sf_inv class*/
void addety_clsnd(char*,warehs*,warehs_class*);  /*for warehs class*/
void addety_clsnd(char*,dealer*,dealer_class*);  /*for dealer class*/
void addety_clsnd(char*,sf_sales_records*,sfsalrec_class*);  /*for sf_sales_rec class*/
```

continued...

...from previous page

```
overload print_entity_name;
void print_entity_name(stcust_etynd*);        /*for st_cust class*/
void print_entity_name(stinv_etynd*);         /*for st_inv class*/
void print_entity_name(sfinv_etynd*);         /*for sf_inv class*/
void print_entity_name(warehs_etynd*);        /*for warehs class*/
void print_entity_name(dealer_etynd*);         /*for dealer class*/
void print_entity_name(sfsalrec_etynd*);        /*for sf_sales_rec class*/


overload print_clsnode;
void print_clsnode(stcust_class*);        /*for st_cust class*/
void print_clsnode(stinv_class*);         /*for st_inv class*/
void print_clsnode(sfinv_class*);         /*for sf_inv class*/
void print_clsnode(warehs_class*);        /*for warehs class*/
void print_clsnode(dealer_class*);        /*for dealer class*/
void print_clsnode(sfsalrec_class*);      /*for sf sale rec class*/


overload find_entity_node;
st_cust* find_entity_node(char*,stcust_class*); /*for st_cust class*/
st_inv*  find_entity_node(char*,stinv_class*);  /*for st_inv class*/
sf_inv*  find_entity_node(char*,sfinv_class*);  /*for sf_inv class*/
warehs*  find_entity_node(char*,warehs_class*); /*for warehs class*/
dealer*  find_entity_node(char*,dealer_class*); /*for dealer class*/
sf_sales_records*  find_entity_node(char*,sfsalrec_class*); /*for sf sale class*/


overload find_all_entities;
stcust_etynd* find_all_entities(stcust_class*);  /*for st_cust class*/
stinv_etynd* find_all_entities(stinv_class*);    /*for st_inv class*/
sfinv_etynd* find_all_entities(sfinv_class*);    /*for sf_inv class*/
warehs_etynd* find_all_entities(warehs_class*);  /*for warehs class*/
dealer_etynd* find_all_entities(dealer_class*);  /*for dealer class*/
sfsalrec_etynd* find_all_entities(sfsalrec_class*);  /*for sf sal rec class*/


overload find_e_with_slot;
stcust_etynd* find_e_with_slot(char*,char*, stcust_class*);     /*for st_cust class*/
stinv_etynd* find_e_with_slot(char*,char*, stinv_class*);      /*for st_inv class*/
sfinv_etynd* find_e_with_slot(char*,char*,sfinv_class*);       /*for sf_inv class*/
warehs_etynd* find_e_with_slot(char*,char*, warehs_class*);    /*for warehs_inv class*/
dealer_etynd* find_e_with_slot(char*,char*,dealer_class*);     /*for dealer_inv class*/
sfsalrec_etynd* find_e_with_slot(char*,char*,sfsalrec_class*); /*for sf sales records class*/
```

continued...

...from previous page

```
/*
**************************************************************
**
**    slotdef.h
**
**    Define the slot structure
**    Date:    9/6/88
*/

struct char_slot {                      /*the slot value is char*/
        char*           slot_name;
        char*           slot_value;
};

struct double_slot {                    /*the slot value is double*/
        char*           slot_name;
        double          slot_value;
};

struct int_slot {                       /*the slot value is int*/
     char*              slot_name;
     int                slot_value;
};

#define     SLOTNAME        30
#define     SLOTVALUE       30
#define     SLOT_END        "END"


/*
*****************************************************
**
**    parse.h
**
**    Define the structure used in parsing the query.
**    Date:    9/6/88
**
*/


#define   CASE1   1    /*C and E are instantiated without slot*/
#define   CASE2   2    /*C is instantiated but E isn't without slot*/
```

continued...

...from previous page

```
#define   CASE3   3    /*C and E are instantiated with slot var*/
#define   CASE4   4    /*C is instantiated but E isn't with slot var*/
#define   CASE5   5    /*C and E are instantiated with slot constant*/
#define   CASE6   6    /*C is instantiated but E isn't with slot constant*/
#define   CASE7   7    /*entity is instantiated and class isn't*/
#define   ZERO    0
#define   ONE     1
#define   TWO     2
#define   THREE   3
#define   FOUR    4
#define   FIVE    5
#define   SIX     6
#define   SEVEN   7
#define   EIGHT   8



/*
**
**********************************************************************
**      tempstru.h
**
**      This header file defines some structures for inputing and outputing
**      the class slot data.
**
**      Include:    Location,Inventory,Customer
**      Date:       7/22/88
*/

struct Loc {                         /*location*/
        char_slot       *address;    /*address of the location*/
        char_slot       *phone;      /*phone number of the loc*/
};


struct Inv {                         /*inventory*/
        char_slot       *name;       /*part name*/
        int_slot        *cil;        /*current inventory level*/
        int_slot        *oil;        /*optimal inventory level*/
};
```

continued...

...from previous page

```
struct Cust {                                  /*customer*/
        char_slot          *dealer;
        char_slot          *name;
        char_slot          *part;
        int_slot           *number;
        char_slot          *order_date;
        char_slot          *time;
};

struct Sales_Rec {                             /*sales records*/
        int_slot           *sale_number;
        char_slot          *date;
        char_slot          *part;
        int_slot           *number_sold;
        double_slot        *cost;
        double_slot        *total_sale;
        char_slot          *sold_to;
};

struct Ware_Inv {                              /*warehouse inventory*/
        double_slot        *cost;
        double_slot        *discount;
        int_slot           *min_order;
        char_slot          *order_time;
};
```

Listing 7.2: The ICS Class Constructors and Member Functions

```
/*
**  icskb0.cpp
**  Define the member functions of each class.
**
**  Date:    9/6/88
*/

#include <stream.h>
#include <string.h>
#include <slotdef.h>
#include <tempstru.h>
#include <icsclass.h>

/*--------------------------------------------------------cust_class----*/

cust::cust()
{

     dealer->slot_name = new char[SLOTNAME];
     dealer->slot_name = "dealer";
     dealer->slot_value = new char[SLOTVALUE];
     *dealer->slot_value = NULL;
     name->slot_name = new char[SLOTNAME];
     name->slot_name = "name";
     name->slot_value = new char[SLOTVALUE];
     *name->slot_value = NULL;
     part->slot_name = new char[SLOTNAME];
     part->slot_name = "part";
     part->slot_value = new char[SLOTVALUE];
     *part->slot_value = NULL;
     number->slot_name = new char[SLOTNAME];
     number->slot_name = "number";
     number->slot_value = 0;
     order_date->slot_name = new char[SLOTNAME];
     order_date->slot_name = "order_date";
     order_date->slot_value = new char[SLOTVALUE];
     *order_date->slot_value = NULL;
     time->slot_name = new char[SLOTNAME];
```

continued...

...from previous page

```
        time->slot_name = "time";
        time->slot_value = new char[SLOTVALUE];
        *time->slot_value = NULL;
}


Cust* cust::get_slotval()                    /*get the slot value*/
{
        Cust* temp = new Cust;

        temp->dealer->slot_value = dealer->slot_value;
        temp->dealer->slot_name = dealer->slot_name;
        temp->name->slot_value = name->slot_value;
        temp->name->slot_name = name->slot_name;
        temp->part->slot_value = part->slot_value;
        temp->part->slot_name = part->slot_name;
        temp->number->slot_value = number->slot_value;
        temp->number->slot_name = number->slot_name;
        temp->order_date->slot_value = order_date->slot_value;
        temp->order_date->slot_name = order_date->slot_name;
        temp->time->slot_value = time->slot_value;
        temp->time->slot_name = time->slot_name;
        return temp;
}



void cust::set_slotval()                     /*set the slot value*/
{


        cout << "\n" << dealer->slot_name << ":  ";
        cin >> dealer->slot_value;
        cout << name->slot_name << ":  ";
        cin >> name->slot_value;
        cout << part->slot_name << ":  ";
        cin >> part->slot_value;
        cout << number->slot_name << ":  ";
        cin >> number->slot_value;
        cout << order_date->slot_name << ":  ";
```

continued...

...from previous page

```
    cin >> order_date->slot_value;
    cout << time->slot_name << ":  ";
    cin >> time->slot_value;
}


void cust::prn_value()
{
    cout << "\n" << dealer->slot_name << ": " << dealer->slot_value;
    cout << "  " << name->slot_name << ": "  << name->slot_value;
    cout << "  " << part->slot_name <<  ": " << part->slot_value;
    cout << "  " << number->slot_name <<  ": " << number->slot_value;
    cout << "  " << order_date->slot_name << ": " << order_date->slot_value;
    cout << "  " << time->slot_name << ": " << time->slot_value;
}


/*-------------------------------------------------------inv_class----*/


inv::inv()
{
    cil->slot_name = new char[SLOTNAME];
    cil->slot_name = "cil";
    cil->slot_value = oil->slot_value = 0;
    oil->slot_name = new char[SLOTNAME];
    oil->slot_name = "oil";
    name->slot_name = new char[SLOTNAME];
    name->slot_name = "name";
    name->slot_value = new char[SLOTVALUE];
    *name->slot_value = NULL;

}
```

continued...

...from previous page

```
void inv::set_slotval()
{
    cout << "\n" << name->slot_name << ":   ";
    cin >> name->slot_value;
    cout << cil->slot_name << ":   ";
    cin >> cil->slot_value;
    cout << oil->slot_name << ":   ";
    cin >> oil->slot_value;
}



Inv* inv::get_slotval()
{
    Inv* temp = new Inv;

    temp->name->slot_name = name->slot_name;
    temp->name->slot_value = name->slot_value;
    temp->cil->slot_name = cil->slot_name;
    temp->cil->slot_value = cil->slot_value;
    temp->oil->slot_name = oil->slot_name;
    temp->oil->slot_value = oil->slot_value;
    return temp;
}

void inv::prn_value()
{
    cout << "\n" << name->slot_name << ":   " << name->slot_value;
    cout << "   " << cil->slot_name << ":   " << cil->slot_value;
    cout << "   " << oil->slot_name << ":   " << oil->slot_value;
}



/*------------------------------------------warehs_inv class-----*/
```

continued...

...from previous page

```
warehs_inv::warehs_inv()
{
    cost->slot_name = new char[SLOTNAME];
    cost->slot_name = "cost";
    cost->slot_value = 0.0;
    discount->slot_name = new char[SLOTNAME];
    discount->slot_name = "discount";
    discount->slot_value = 0.0;
    min_order->slot_name = new char[SLOTNAME];
    min_order->slot_name = "min_order";
    min_order->slot_value = 0;
    order_time-<>slot_name = new char[SLOTNAME];
    order_time->slot_name = "order_time";
    order_time->slot_value = new char[SLOTVALUE];
    *order_time->slot_value = NULL;

}



void warehs_inv::set_slotval1()
{
    cout << "\n" << cost->slot_name << ":  ";
    cin >> cost->slot_value;
    cout << discount->slot_name << ":  ";
    cin >> discount->slot_value;
    cout << min_order->slot_name << ":  ";
    cin >> min_order->slot_value;
    cout << order_time->slot_name << ":  ";
    cin >> order_time->slot_value;
}


Ware_Inv* warehs_inv::get_slotval1()
{
    Ware_Inv* temp = new Ware_Inv;
```

continued...

...from previous page

```
        temp->cost->slot_name = cost->slot_name;
        temp->cost->slot_value = cost->slot_value;
        temp->discount->slot_name = discount->slot_name;
        temp->discount->slot_value = discount->slot_value;
        temp->min_order->slot_name = min_order->slot_name;
        temp->min_order->slot_value = min_order->slot_value;
        temp->order_time->slot_name = order_time->slot_name;
        temp->order_time->slot_value = order_time->slot_value;
        return temp;
}


void warehs_inv::prn_value1()
{
        cout << "\n" << cost->slot_name << ":  "<< cost->slot_value;
        cout << "  " << discount->slot_name << ":  " << discount->slot_value;
        cout << "  " << min_order->slot_name << ":  " << min_order->slot_value;
        cout << "  " << order_time->slot_name << ":  " << order_time->slot_value;
}


/*------------------------------------------------location_class------------*/
location::location()
{
        address->slot_name = new char[SLOTNAME];
        address->slot_name = "address";
        address->slot_value = new char[SLOTVALUE];
        *address->slot_value = NULL;
        phone->slot_name = new char[SLOTNAME];
        phone->slot_name = "phone";
        phone->slot_value = new char[SLOTVALUE];
        *phone->slot_value = NULL;
        invntory = new invent;
}
```

continued...

...from previous page

```
void location::set_slotval()
{
    cout << "\n" << address->slot_name << ":  ";
    cin >> address->slot_value;
    cout << phone->slot_name << ":  ";
    cin >> phone->slot_value;
    invntory->set_slotval();
}

Loc* location::get_slotval1()
{
    Loc* temp = new Loc;

    temp->address->slot_name = address->slot_name;
    temp->address->slot_value = address->slot_value;
    temp->phone->slot_name = phone->slot_name;
    temp->phone->slot_value = phone->slot_value;
    return temp;
}

Inv* location::get_slotval2()
{
    Inv* temp = new Inv;

    temp = invntory->get_slotval();
    return temp;
}


void location::prn_value()
{
    cout << "\n" << address->slot_name << ":  " << address->slot_value;
    cout << "  " << phone->slot_name << ":  " << phone->slot_value;
    invntory->prn_value();  /*print out the subclass inventory value*/
}
```

continued...

...from previous page

```
/*-------------------------------------------------------dealer_class-------*/


void dealer::set_cust_slotval()
{
    custm->set_slotval();
}
Cust* dealer::get_cust_slotval()
{
    Cust* temp = new Cust;

    temp = custm->get_slotval();
    return temp;
}


void dealer::prn_cust_slotval()
{
    custm->prn_value();
}


/*-------------------------------------------------------warehs_class------*/

void warehs::set_sales_recs_slotval()
{
    sales_rec->set_slotval();
}

Sales_Rec* warehs::get_sales_recs_slotval()
{
    Sales_Rec* temp = new Sales_Rec;

    temp = sales_rec->get_slotval();
    return temp;
}
```

continued...

...from previous page

```
/*------------------------------------------------sales_records class--*/

sales_records::sales_records()
{
     sale_number->slot_name = new char[SLOTNAME];
     sale_number->slot_name = "sale_number";
     sale_number->slot_value = 0;
     number_sold->slot_name = new char[SLOTNAME];
     number_sold->slot_name = "number_sold";
     number_sold->slot_value = 0;
     date->slot_name = new char[SLOTNAME];
     date->slot_name = "date";
     date->slot_value = new char[SLOTVALUE];
     *date->slot_value = NULL;
     part->slot_name = new char[SLOTNAME];
     part->slot_name = "part";
     part->slot_value = new char[SLOTVALUE];
     part->slot_value = NULL;
     sold_to->slot_name = new char[SLOTNAME];
     sold_to->slot_name = "sold_to";
     sold_to->slot_value = new char[SLOTVALUE];
     sold_to->slot_value = NULL;
     cost->slot_name = new char[SLOTNAME];
     cost->slot_name = "cost";
     total_sale->slot_name = new char[SLOTVALUE];
     total_sale->slot_name = "total_sale";
     cost->slot_value = total_sale->slot_value = 0.0;
}


void sales_records::set_slotval()
{
     cout << "\n" << sale_number->slot_name << ":  ";
     cin >> sale_number->slot_value;
     cout << date->slot_name << ":  ";
     cin >> date->slot_value;
     cout << part->slot_name << ":  ";
     cin >> part->slot_value;
     cout << number_sold->slot_name << ":  ";
```

continued...

...from previous page

```
        cin >> number_sold->slot_value;
        cout << cost->slot_name << ":  ";
        cin >> cost->slot_value;
        cout << total_sale->slot_name << ":  ";
        cin >> total_sale->slot_value;
        cout << sold_to->slot_name << ":  ";
        cin >> sold_to->slot_value;
    }

Sales_Rec* sales_records::get_slotval()
{
        Sales_Rec* temp = new Sales_Rec;

        temp->sale_number->slot_name = sale_number->slot_name;
        temp->sale_number->slot_value = sale_number->slot_value;
        temp->date->slot_name = date->slot_name;
        temp->date->slot_value = date->slot_value;
        temp->part->slot_name = part->slot_name;
        temp->part->slot_value = part->slot_value;
        temp->number_sold->slot_name = number_sold->slot_name;
        temp->number_sold->slot_value = number_sold->slot_value;
        temp->cost->slot_name = cost->slot_name;
        temp->cost->slot_value = cost->slot_value;
        temp->total_sale->slot_name = total_sale->slot_name;
        temp->total_sale->slot_value = total_sale->slot_value;
        temp->sold_to->slot_name = sold_to->slot_name;
        temp->sold_to->slot_value = sold_to->slot_value;
        return temp;
}

void sales_records::prn_value()
{
    cout << "\n" << sale_number->slot_name << ":  " << sale_number->slot_value;
    cout << "  " << date->slot_name << ":  " << date->slot_value;
    cout << "  " << part->slot_name << ":  " << part->slot_value;
    cout << "  " << number_sold->slot_name << ":  " << number_sold->slot_value;
    cout << "  " << cost->slot_name << ":  " << cost->slot_value;
    cout << "  " << total_sale->slot_name << ":  " << total_sale->slot_value;
    cout << "  " << sold_to->slot_name << ":  " << sold_to->slot_value;
}
```

continued...

...from previous page

```
/*
******************************************************************
**
** Building up slot name lists and their initialization
**
**   icskb1.cpp
**   Define some funtions which  will be used to do initialization.
**   Date:    9/6/88
*/

#include <stream.h>
#include <string.h>
#include <slotdef.h>
#include <tempstru.h>
#include <icsclass.h>
#include <ics.h>

extern stcust_class* STCUST_CLASS;      /*st_cust class node*/
extern stinv_class*  STINV_CLASS;       /*st_inv class node*/
extern sfinv_class*  SFINV_CLASS;       /*sf_inv class node*/
extern warehs_class* WAREHS_CLASS;      /*warehs class node*/
extern dealer_class* DEALER_CLASS;      /*dealer class node*/
extern sfsalrec_class* SFSALREC_CLASS;  /*sf sale rec class node*/


/*
**   Because C++ does not support the dynamic defining the data structure.
**   In order to do the reasoning in an object oriented knowledge base, the
**   developer should initialize each class name, the slot names which defined
**   in the class definition before doing the reasoning.
*/


/*
** Make up the slot name list of the class
** Generic function.
*/
```

continued...

...from previous page

```
cls_slot* make_up_cls_slot(char* clsname,char* slot[])
{
    cls_slot* temp = new cls_slot;
    int i = 0;

    temp->name = clsname;
    temp->sllist = NULL;
    while(strcmp(slot[i],SLOT_END))
    {
        slot_node*  temp1 = new slot_node;
        temp1->name = slot[i];
        temp1->next = temp->sllist;
        temp->sllist = temp1;
        i++;
    }
    return temp;
}



/*
**  Insert slot name list into the class node.
**  Overloaded function.
*/


/*for sf_inv class*/
void addslot_clsnd(cls_slot* c,stcust_class* s)
{
    /* The following are same for different class. Overloaded!!*/
    s->name = c->name;
    s->slist = c->sllist;
}


/*for sf_inv class*/
void addslot_clsnd(cls_slot* c,sfinv_class* s)
{
    /*...... same as above ....*/
}
```

continued...

...from previous page

```
/*for st_inv class*/
void addslot_clsnd(cls_slot* c,stinv_class* s)
{
     /*...... same as above ....*/
}


/*for warehs class*/
void addslot_clsnd(cls_slot* c,warehs_class* s)
{
     /*...... same as above ....*/
}


/*for dealer class*/
void addslot_clsnd(cls_slot* c,dealer_class* s)
{
     /*...... same as above ....*/
}


/*for sf sale rec class*/
void addslot_clsnd(cls_slot* c,sfsalrec_class* s)
{
     /*...... same as above ....*/
}



/*-------------------Below is not generic function----------------------*/
/*
** Initialize class node.
*/

void initstcustcls()          /*for st_cust class*/
{
    STCUST_CLASS = new stcust_class;

    *STCUST_CLASS->name = NULL;
    STCUST_CLASS->slist = NULL;
    STCUST_CLASS->elist = NULL;
}
```

continued...

...from previous page

```
void initstinvcls()          /*for st_inv class*/
{
     STINV_CLASS = new stinv_class;

/*   *STINV_CLASS->name = NULL;*/
     STINV_CLASS->slist = NULL;
     STINV_CLASS->elist = NULL;
}

void initstinvcls()          /*for st_inv class*/
{
     STINV_CLASS = new stinv_class;

     *STINV_CLASS->name = NULL;
     STINV_CLASS->slist = NULL;
     STINV_CLASS->elist = NULL;
}


void initwarehscls()         /*for warehs class*/
{
     WAREHS_CLASS = new warehs_class;

     *WAREHS_CLASS->name = NULL;
     WAREHS_CLASS->slist = NULL;
     WAREHS_CLASS->elist = NULL;
}

void initdealercls()         /*for dealer class*/
{
     DEALER_CLASS = new dealer_class;

     *DEALER_CLASS->name = NULL;
      DEALER_CLASS->slist = NULL;
      DEALER_CLASS->elist = NULL;
}
```

continued...

...from previous page

```
void initsfsalreccls()        /*for sf sale rec class*/
{
    SFSALREC_CLASS = new sfsalrec_class;

    *SFSALREC_CLASS->name = NULL;
    SFSALREC_CLASS->slist = NULL;
    SFSALREC_CLASS->elist = NULL;
}




/***************************************************************
**
**
** Linking entity nodes into a tree structure for query
**
**   icskb2.cpp
**   Define some utility functions which are used to build up the KB.
**   Date:   9/6/88
*/



#include <stream.h>
#include <string.h>
#include <slotdef.h>
#include <tempstru.h>
#include <icsclass.h>
#include <ics.h>



/*-----------------------------------------Class Node------------------*/
extern stcust_class* STCUST_CLASS;  /*st_cust class node*/
extern stinv_class* STINV_CLASS;    /*st_inv class node*/
extern sfinv_class* SFINV_CLASS;    /*sf_inv class node*/
extern warehs_class* WAREHS_CLASS;  /*warehs class node*/
extern dealer_class* DEALER_CLASS;  /*dealer class node*/
extern sfsalrec_class* SFSALREC_CLASS;  /*sf sale rec class node*/
```

continued...

...from previous page

```
/*
**  Insert entity into the class node
**  Overloaded function.
*/

/*For st cust class*/
void addety_clsnd(char* ename,st_cust* s,stcust_class* s1)
{
      stcust_etynd* temp = new stcust_etynd;

      /* The following are same for different class. Overloaded!!*/
      temp->name = ename;
      temp->entity = s;
      temp->next = s1->elist;
      s1->elist = temp;
}


/*For st inv class*/
void addety_clsnd(char* ename,st_inv* s,stinv_class* s1)
{
      stinv_etynd* temp = new stinv_etynd;

      /*...... same as above ....*/

}


/*For sf inv class*/
void addety_clsnd(char* ename,sf_inv* s,sfinv_class* s1)
{
      sfinv_etynd* temp = new sfinv_etynd;

      /*...... same as above ....*/

}
```

continued...

...from previous page

```
/*For warehs class*/
void addety_clsnd(char* ename,warehs* s,warehs_class* s1)
{
    warehs_etynd* temp = new warehs_etynd;

    /*...... same as above ....*/
}


/*For dealer class*/
void addety_clsnd(char* ename,dealer* s,dealer_class* s1)
{
    dealer_etynd* temp = new dealer_etynd;

    /*...... same as above ....*/
}


/*For dealer class*/
void addety_clsnd(char* ename,sf_sales_records* s,sfsalrec_class* s1)
{
    sfsalrec_etynd* temp = new sfsalrec_etynd;

    /*...... same as above ....*/
}


/*
**  Print slot name
**  Generic function.
*/
void print_slot_name(slot_node* c)
{
    slot_node* temp;

    temp = c;
    cout << "\n" << "SLOT NAME :  ";
    while(temp != NULL)
    {
        cout <<  temp->name << "    ";
        temp = temp->next;
    }
}
```

continued...

...from previous page

```
/*
**  Print out entity.
**  Overloaded function
*/

/*For st cust class*/
void print_entity_name(stcust_etynd* ety)
{
    stcust_etynd* temp;

    /* The following are same for different class. Overloaded!!*/
    temp = ety;
    cout << "\n" << "ENTITIES:  ";
    while(temp != NULL)
    {
        cout << "\n" << temp->name << ":";
        temp->entity->prn_value();
        temp = temp->next;
    }
}


/*For st inv class*/
void print_entity_name(stinv_etynd* ety)
{
    stinv_etynd* temp;

    /*...... same as above ....*/
}


/*For sf inv class*/
void print_entity_name(sfinv_etynd* ety)
{
    sfinv_etynd* temp;

    /*...... same as above ....*/
}
```

continued...

...from previous page

```
/*For dealer class*/
void print_entity_name(dealer* ety)
{
     dealer* temp;

     /*...... same as above ....*/
}



/*
** Print out class node.
** Overloaded function
*/

/*For st cust class*/
void print_clsnode(stcust_class* st)
{
     /* The following are same for different class. Overloaded!!*/
     cout << "\n" << "ClASS NAME:  " << st->name;
     print_slot_name(st->slist);
     print_entity_name(st->elist);
}

/*For st inv class*/
void print_clsnode(stinv_class* st)
{
     /*...... same as above ....*/
}

/*For sf inv class*/
void print_clsnode(sfinv_class* st)
{
     /*...... same as above ....*/
}

/*For warehs class*/
void print_clsnode(warehs* st)
{
     /*...... same as above ....*/
}
```

continued...

...from previous page

```
/*For dealer class*/
void print_clsnode(dealer_class* st)
{
     /*...... same as above ....*/
}


/*For sf sale rec class*/
void print_clsnode(sfsalrec_class* st)
{
     /*...... same as above ....*/
}
```

Listing 7.3: Main Programs to Define Slots and Test Knowledge Representation

```
/*
**
*/
/*
**    icsmain.cpp
**
**    This program is to implement the connction between Knowledge Base which
**    is made up of objects and the query about the KB. There are some steps
**    required before doing such kind of reasoning.
**
**    The steps are:
**    1) define the class. e.g. structs.h.
**    2) define the kb. e.g. kbstruct.h
**    3) do the query.
**
**    The query's format is:
**         (entity ?x is-a ?y with slot_name = ?z)
**
**    Date:    8/5/88
**
*/
```

continued...

...from previous page

```
#include <stream.h>
#include <string.h>
#include <slotdef.h>
#include <tempstru.h>
#include <icsclass.h>
#include <ics.h>
#include <parse.h>

#define MAXQUERY     60


/*
** Because C++ does not support the dynamic defining the data structure.
** In order to do the reasoning in an object oriented knowledge base, the
** developer should initialize each class name, the slot names which defined
** in the class definition before doing the reasoning.
*/


/*----------------------------------------Class Node-------------------*/
stcust_class* STCUST_CLASS;      /*st_cust class node*/
stinv_class*  STINV_CLASS;       /*st_inv class node*/
sfinv_class*  SFINV_CLASS;       /*sf_inv class node*/
warehs_class* WAREHS_CLASS;      /*warehs class node*/
dealer_class* DEALER_CLASS;      /*dealer class node*/
sfsalrec_class* SFSALREC_CLASS;  /*sf sale rec class node*/

/* The initialization for each class's slot as follow.
** the SLOT_END must be added in the end of each initialization.
*/


/*for cust class*/
char* cust_slot[7] = { "dealer", "name", "part", "number", "order_date",
                         "time", SLOT_END};

/*for inv class*/
char* inv_slot[4] = { "name", "cil", "oil", SLOT_END};

/*for warehs class*/
char* warehs_inv_slot[8] = { "name", "cil", "oil", "cost", "discount",
                                 "min_order", "order_time", SLOT_END};
```

continued...

...from previous page

```
/*for location class*/
char* loc_slot[3] = { "address", "phone", SLOT_END};

/*for sales record class*/
char* salrec_slot[8] = { "sale_number", "date", "part", "number_sold", "cost",
                         "total_sale", "sold_to", SLOT_END};
/*---------------------------------------------------------------------*/


main()
{
    cls_slot* temp1;
    extern void initstcustcls();
    extern void initstinvcls();
    extern void initsfinvcls();
    extern cls_slot* make_up_cls_slot(char*,char*[]);

/*For st_cust*/
    initstcustcls();
    char* temp = new char[40];
    temp = "st_cust";
    temp1 = make_up_cls_slot(temp, cust_slot);
    addslot_clsnd(temp1,STCUST_CLASS);

/*For entity creating and setting for st_cust*/
    st_cust* janoschka_stephen = new st_cust;
    char* te;
    te = "janoschka_stephen";
    addety_clsnd(te,janoschka_stephen,STCUST_CLASS);

    st_cust* lisa_hu = new st_cust;
    addety_clsnd("lisa_hu",lisa_hu,STCUST_CLASS);


    cout << "\n" << "Enter Janoschka Stephen's Data, Please";
    janoschka_stephen->set_slotval();
    cout << "\n" << "Enter Lise Hu's Data, Please";
    lisa_hu->set_slotval();

    print_clsnode(STCUST_CLASS);
```

continued...

...from previous page

```
/*----------------------------------------------------do some queries------*/
    char x[MAXQUERY];
    cout << "\nEnter query: ";
    gets(x);
    int i;
    extern int check_entity_pred_syntax(char*);
    i = check_entity_pred_syntax(x);

    extern char query_word[8][30];
    char* class_name;
    class_name = query_word[THREE];

    switch (i)
    {
            case CASE1:

            if(!strcmp(class_name,"st_cust"))
            {
                    stcust_class* x;
                    st_cust* y;
                    x = STCUST_CLASS;
                    y = find_entity_node(query_word[ONE],x);
                    if ( y != NULL)
                        cout << "\nQuery is true!";
                    else
                        cout << "\nQuery is not true!";
            }
            if(!strcmp(class_name,"st_inv"))
            {
                    stinv_class* x;
                    st_inv* y;
                    x = STINV_CLASS;
                    y = find_entity_node(query_word[ONE],x);
                    y->prn_value();
```

continued...

233

...from previous page

```
        }
        if(!strcmp(class_name,"sf_inv"))
        {
                sfinv_class* x;
                sf_inv* y;
                x = SFINV_CLASS;
                y = find_entity_node(query_word[ONE],x);
                y->prn_value();
        }
        if(!strcmp(class_name,"warehs"))
        {
                warehs_class* x;
                warehs* y;
                x = WAREHS_CLASS;
                y = find_entity_node(query_word[ONE],x);
                y->prn_value();
        }
        if(!strcmp(class_name,"dealer"))
        {
                dealer_class* x;
                dealer* y;
                x = DEALER_CLASS;
                y = find_entity_node(query_word[ONE],x);
                y->prn_value();
        }
        if(!strcmp(class_name,"sfsalrec"))
        {
                sfsalrec_class* x;
                sf_sales_records* y;
                x = SFSALREC_CLASS;
                y = find_entity_node(query_word[ONE],x);
                y->prn_value();
        }
                break;
```

continued...

...from previous page

```
case CASE2:

if(!strcmp(class_name,"st_cust"))
{
        stcust_class* x;
        stcust_etynd* y;
        x = STCUST_CLASS;
        y = find_all_entities(x);
        print_entity_name(y);
}
if(!strcmp(class_name,"st_inv"))
{
        stinv_class* x;
        stinv_etynd* y;
        x = STINV_CLASS;
        y = find_all_entities(x);
        print_entity_name(y);
}
if(!strcmp(class_name,"sf_inv"))
{
        sfinv_class* x;
        sfinv_etynd* y;
        x = SFINV_CLASS;
        y = find_all_entities(x);
        print_entity_name(y);
}
if(!strcmp(class_name,"warehs"))
{
        warehs_class* x;
        warehs_etynd* y;
        x = WAREHS_CLASS;
        y = find_all_entities(x);
        print_entity_name(y);
```

continued...

...from previous page

```
        }
        if(!strcmp(class_name,"dealer"))
        {
                dealer_class* x;
                dealer_etynd* y;
                x = DEALER_CLASS;
                y = find_all_entities(x);
                print_entity_name(y);
        }
        if(!strcmp(class_name,"sfsalrec"))
        {
                sfsalrec_class* x;
                sfsalrec_etynd* y;
                x = SFSALREC_CLASS;
                y = find_all_entities(x);
                print_entity_name(y);
        }
                break;
        case CASE6:

        if(!strcmp(class_name,"st_cust"))
        {
                stcust_class* x;
                stcust_etynd* y;
                x = STCUST_CLASS;
                char* s1;
                char* s2;
                s1 = query_word[FIVE];
                s2 = query_word[SEVEN];
                y = find_e_with_slot(s1,s2,x);
                print_entity_name(y);
```

continued...

...from previous page

```
}
if(!strcmp(class_name,"st_inv"))
{
        stinv_class* x;
        stinv_etynd* y;
        x = STINV_CLASS;
        char* s1;
        char* s2;
        s1 = query_word[FIVE];
        s2 = query_word[SEVEN];
        y = find_e_with_slot(s1,s2,x);
        print_entity_name(y);
}
if(!strcmp(class_name,"sf_inv"))
{
        sfinv_class* x;
        sfinv_etynd* y;
        x = SFINV_CLASS;
        char* s1;
        char* s2;
        s1 = query_word[FIVE];
        s2 = query_word[SEVEN];
        y = find_e_with_slot(s1,s2,x);
        print_entity_name(y);
}
if(!strcmp(class_name,"warehs"))
{
        warehs_class* x;
        warehs_etynd* y;
        x = WAREHS_CLASS;
        char* s1;
        char* s2;
        s1 = query_word[FIVE];
        s2 = query_word[SEVEN];
        y = find_e_with_slot(s1,s2,x);
        print_entity_name(y);
```

continued...

...from previous page

```
        }
        if(!strcmp(class_name,"dealer"))
        {
                dealer_class* x;
                dealer_etynd* y;
                x = DEALER_CLASS;
                char* s1;
                char* s2;
                s1 = query_word[FIVE];
                s2 = query_word[SEVEN];
                y = find_e_with_slot(s1,s2,x);
                print_entity_name(y);
        }
        if(!strcmp(class_name,"sfsalrec"))
        {
                sfsalrec_class* x;
                sfsalrec_etynd* y;
                x = SFSALREC_CLASS;
                char* s1;
                char* s2;
                s1 = query_word[FIVE];
                s2 = query_word[SEVEN];
                y = find_e_with_slot(s1,s2,x);
                print_entity_name(y);
        }

                break;

        }

}
```

BUILDING RULE STRUCTURES

Rule structures are also called "production rules," "production systems," or "rule-based systems," which are the most used and the simplest form of knowledge representation. Most PC tools are in this category. Examples include M.1, Personal Consultant, and EXSYS. In this form of knowledge representation, heuristic knowledge or experience is expressed. Fundamental assumptions, advantages/disadvantages, and methods to design rule structures are discussed in this section.

Fundamental Assumptions

A rule structure in its simplest form consists of templates that enable programmers or experts/specialists to input IF-THEN rules to build expert systems. The five fundamental assumptions about the rule structure are acceptance of rule formalism, modus ponems, limited interaction between factors in rules, limited attributes of a given object, and common understanding between various users.

Acceptance of **rule formalism** by the user or the expert/specialist is the most important assumption. Experts/specialists must be able to transform their knowledge into rules (i.e., they must recognize and then formalize chunks of their knowledge and experience and express them in rules). Unfortunately, not every field of knowledge will support this assumption. The ability to transform knowledge into rules appears to require a field that has attained a certain level of formalization but has not yet achieved a thorough, scientific formalization of the problem-solving process. The fields that are inclined to accept rules in representing knowledge generally have a broadly recognized set of conceptual primitive factors and a minimum understanding of basic processes, such as diagnosis or configuration. It is further assumed that the IF-THEN format of rules is sufficiently simple, expressive, and intuitive to provide a useful knowledge representation language for experts to express their knowledge.

Modus ponens, as discussed in Chapter 2, provides a simple, basic logic rule that allows new facts to be deducted from other facts, as follows:

IF A is true, and IF A THEN B is true, then B is true.

The implication of this simple rule is

> IF B is not true, and IF A THEN B is true, then A is not true.

The rule can then be further extended to cover the following:

IF A THEN B, and	(Rule 1)
IF B THEN C, then	(Rule 2)
IF A THEN C	(Rule 3)

From rules 1, 2, and 3, if A is known, then C can be deduced; however, for the rule structure to be useful in representing knowledge, the rules' simple modus ponems chaining must appear natural enough that a user can readily identify with it.

Limited interaction between factors in rules entails three assumptions:

- Only a small number of factors (about six clauses) in the premise can be considered simultaneously to trigger an action in the consequence.

- The presence or absence of each of these clauses can be determined without adverse effects on the others.

- The clauses of rule premise connected by AND/OR can be set up toward nonconflicting subgoals so that action clauses in the consequence will not depend on the order in which the evidence is collected.

Having a limited number of attributes for a given object and a limited number of objects will prevent the exponential growth in search time for the expert system when the number of rules in the knowledge base grows considerably. Therefore, newly acquired rules will reference only established attributes of a given object, and the use of these rules will not cause further branching because the attributes appearing in the premises of these rules will have already been traced.

Common understanding between various users assures that the same representation language is communicative between different classes of users, i.e., the domain experts who "train" the expert system and the inexperienced users who possess little knowledge of the expert system but who want to use it to gain its knowledge. Assume that common understanding is feasible.

Advantages and Disadvantages

The advantages of the rule structure are in three areas: modular coding, ease of explanation, and ease of knowledge acquisition.

Each rule in the rule structure is a simple conditional statement in which the premise consists of a limited number of conditional clauses, the action contains one or more conclusions, and each statement is modular and independent of the others. Such modular coding provides an easy way to identify contradiction and subsumption in the knowledge base by examination of premises and conclusions. Individual rules can be manipulated to facilitate automatic detection and correction of undesirable interactions among rules. Because rules are retrieved only when they are relevant to a specific goal (i.e., the goal appears in their action part), the addition of new rules becomes easy: the premise and action parts of rules can be systematically scanned to search the desired goals, and the rules can then be added to the appropriate internal lists according to the parameters found in their actions. These rules can simply be added to the rule set in the knowledge base without changing other rules because rules in the knowledge base are relatively independent; i.e., one rule never directly calls another. This advantage is particularly significant when you compare an addition of rules to the addition of a new procedure to a typical FORTRAN program.

Ease in explanation is another benefit; inquiries of an expert system can be answered by retrieving rules in which premise and action (consequence) contain the relevant items, and the reason for these actions can then be easily explained by tracing the passage of rules fired. Explanation evokes the tracing of the consultation process in searching through an AND/OR goal tree. In general, inquiries are of two types: *how* a conclusion is reached and *why* a question is asked. In how-type inquiries, rules are traced from the top down, as shown in Figure 7.5. For example, if you ask the expert system, "How is C11 obtained?" the system will answer that C11 is obtained because of the following:

Rule A and B1

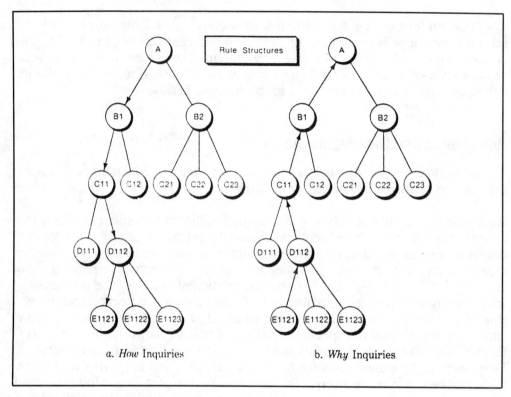

Figure 7.5   Rule tracing: how and why

However, in why-type inquiries, rules are traced from the bottom up, as shown in Figure 7.5. If you ask "Why is C11 obtained?" the answer will be

Rule E1121 and D112

Ease of knowledge acquisition lies in the fact that rules are a reasonably intuitive way of expressing chunks of inferential knowledge and experience that are significant without requiring the user to know any programming language. Because it may be impossible to write a complete set of rules, the rule structure provides a capability for incremental improvement of competence in response to new research that produces new results and modifications of old principles and rules. The rule structure further facilitates the explanation of errors in the conclusion process. This tracing facility supplies the expert with subsequent clues for fixing errors and a set of expectations about the form and content of the anticipated correction.

The disadvantages of the rule representation language include inflexibility of rule expression, sequence of rules, and insufficient power.

Inflexibility of rule expression, i.e., a predetermined format, reduces the freedom of expressing the experts' knowledge and experience and at times appears difficult to the inexperienced user. Furthermore, to meet the requirement of modularity, all contextual information must be stated explicitly in the premise and the consequence. This requirement often results in rules with long and complicated premises that entail many subgoals. Rules are inflexible and cannot learn from mistakes. It may be difficult to determine which rules to add/change to correct the behavior of the expert system.

Sequence (ordering) of rules affects the efficiency of production systems in consultation. The requirement of correct sequence for either backward or forward chaining means substantial effort is needed in arranging rules to meet the appropiate sequence.

The rule structure provides insufficient power for expressing complex, large, or dynamic concepts because rules are simple conditional statements. In particular, mapping a sequence of events to a set of rules has at times proven extremely difficult. Goal-directed chaining may require excess human effort to structure the appropriate sequence for large chunks of knowledge that cannot easily be subdivided into separate pieces.

Methods to Implement Rule Structures

The two primary components of a rule are the premise and the conclusion. The premise is the condition under which the rule is said to "fire"; it is a proposition that is not assumed to be true given an unknown environment, whose truth value will be occasionally evaluated. The conclusion of the rule is the result of firing the rule; it is a proposition that will be become true when the rule fires, for example:

Premise (IF): `(todays-date "5/29/87")`
Conclusion (THEN): `(todays-day Friday)`

When a rule is **attempted**, the ICS needs to find a fact in the knowledge base that complies with the conditions of the premise. In the previous example, if the knowledge base contained the fact,

```
(todays-date "5/28/87")
```

then the rule would fire upon being attempted and

```
(todays-day Friday)
```

would be put in the knowledge base. If the fact in the premise did not appear in the knowledge base, then nothing would happen; the rule would not fire.

The firing of a rule frequently affects the knowledge base through the addition or modification of facts. A rule is affected by its certainty. The certainty of these new facts is determined by a combination of the following:

- the certainty of the facts used to fire the rule

- the certainty of the rule itself

In general, the attributes of a rule needed to enable the user to extract knowledge may include the following:

- Rule premise

- Rule conclusion

- Rule action

- Rule explanation

- Rule certainty

- Rule askable?

Rule premise provides the facility to record the premise of a rule. The premise can contain conjunctive (**and**) and disjunctive (**or**) phrases; **Rule premise** can be a logical expression. **Rule conclusion** is the rule's "then" part; it can contain conjunctive and disjunctive phrases and also can be a logical expression. **Rule action** indicates the set of actions to be taken if the rule is invoked. **Rule explanation** contains the explanation for the rule that is an English-language description of why the rule is true. **Rule certainty** indicates the likelihood of the conclusion given that the premise is true. It represents the degree of confidence in a rule or a fact. In determining the confidence factor of a conjunction of rules or facts, the minimum confidence factor among the factors for the rules or facts is given. For a disjunction, the maximum confidence factor is used. Once the confidence factor of the premise of a rule is determined, the confidence factor of the conclusion is then calculated as the product of the confidence level of the premise and the confidence level of the rule. **Rule askable?** indicates whether the premise of the rule can be obtained from the user if it cannot be determined internally by the system in achieving a goal.

Implementing a rule structure is a relatively straightforward process, as shown in Listing 7.4. The sample program in the listing contains the following features:

- Reads rules as they appear the the following order:

    a) the IF part

    b) the THEN part

    c) the certainty factor

- Adds rules to the rule database.

- Locates and prints rules when they are requested and deletes those that have been fired.

The implementation of certainty factors is discussed in detail in Chapter 9. More functions can be added to the program to increase the attributes of the rule structure.

Listing 7.4: Sample Program for the Rule Structure

```
/*
** Rule.h
*/

typedef struct _rule {
  char *name;                         /* the name of the rule */
  cons *premise;                      /* the premise predicates */
  cons *conclusion;                   /* the conclusion predicate */
  double certainty;                   /* the certainty of this rule */
  struct _rule *next;                 /* the next rule in the database */
} rule;

extern rule *make_rule();
extern rule *delete_rule();
extern rule *find_rule();
extern void add_rule();
extern void kill_rule();
extern void print_rule();
extern void printall_rules();

extern rule *RuleDatabase;            /* pointer to all rules */

/*
**********************************************************************

**
** Rule.c
*/
/*
**
** (new format of rules)
*/


#include <math.h>
#include <stdio.h>
#include "cons.h"
#include "rule.h"

rule *RuleDatabase = NULL;            /* pointer to all rules */
```

continued...

...from previous page

```
/*
** read_rule(): reads the rule from the standard input. Rules look like
** this:
** Rule-name IF (pred*) THEN pred
** E.g:
** Fuel-rule-1 IF ((fuel-level low)) THEN (out-of-fuel)
*/

rule *read_rule()
{
  rule *rp;
  cons *pp;

  if (rp = (rule *) malloc(sizeof (rule))) {
    pp = lread(C_FILE,stdin);             /* first the name */
    rp->name = pp->car.s;                 /* save the name */
    free(pp);                             /* junk the cons */
    pp = lread(C_FILE,stdin);             /* get the 'IF' */
    if (strcmpi(pp->car.s,"IF")) {        /* not if? */
      free(rp);                           /* not a rule! */
      killcons(pp);
      return NULL;
    }
    killcons(pp);                         /* get rid of it */
    rp->premise = lread(C_FILE,stdin);
    pp = lread(C_FILE,stdin);             /* get the 'THEN' */
    if (strcmpi(pp->car.s,"THEN")) {      /* not then? */
      killcons(rp->premise);              /* not a rule! */
      killcons(pp);
      free(rp);
      return NULL;
    }
    killcons(pp);                         /* get rid of 'then' */
    rp->conclusion = lread(C_FILE,stdin);
    pp = lread(C_FILE,stdin);             /* lastly, the certainty */
    rp->certainty  = atof(pp->car.s);
    killcons(pp);                         /* junk the certainty */
    rp->next = NULL;
  }
  return rp;
}
```

continued...

...from previous page

```
/*
** _add_rule(): adds the rule _rp_ to the database _dbp_
*/

static rule *_add_rule(rp,dbp)
rule *rp,*dbp;
{
  rule *rp2 = dbp;

  if (dbp == NULL) {
    return rp;
  }
  while (rp2->next) {
    rp2 = rp2->next;
  }
  rp2->next = rp;
  return dbp;
}


/*
** add_rule(): adds the rule _rp_ to the RuleDatabase
*/

void add_rule(rp)
rule *rp;
{
  RuleDatabase = _add_rule(rp,RuleDatabase);
}

rule *delete_rule(rp,dbp)
rule *rp,*dbp;
{
  rule *rrp;
```

continued...

...from previous page

```
  if (dbp == NULL) {
    return NULL;
  } else if (rp == dbp) {
    rrp = dbp->next;
    kill_rule(rp);
    return dbp->next;
  } else {
    dbp->next = delete_rule(rp,dbp->next);
    return dbp;
  }
}


/*
** find_rule: find rule by name
*/

rule *find_rule(s,dbp)
char *s;
rule *dbp;
{
  if (dbp == NULL) {
    return NULL;
  } else if (!strcmp(s,dbp->name)) {
    return(dbp);
  } else {
    return find_rule(s,dbp->next);
  }
}

void kill_rule(rp)
rule *rp;
{
   killcons(rp->premise);
   killcons(rp->conclusion);
   free(rp);
}
```

continued...

...from previous page

```
void print_rule(rp)
rule *rp;
{
  printf("Name: %s\nPremise: ",rp->name);
  lprint(rp->premise,C_FILE,stdout);
  printf("\nConclusion: ");
  lprint(rp->conclusion,C_FILE,stdout);
  printf("\nCertainty: %g\n",rp->certainty);
}

void printall_rules(rule_base)
rule *rule_base;
{
  rule *db = rule_base;

  while (db != NULL) {
    print_rule(db);
    db = db->next;
  }
}
```

The Inventory Control System Example

Rules are used to create new data that are not available in the knowledge base. For example, you will now create rule objects that will use the information in the classes and entities created earlier in the chapter to calculate new information. One useful piece of information is the cost of a part to a potential customer. This value is the true cost of the part, calculated by subtracting any applicable discounts from the cost of the part by creating a rule that calculates the true cost of any part:

```
Rule: TRUE-COST

PREMISE:
The cost of ?entity is ?cost
AND
The discount of ?entity is ?discount
AND
?cost - ?discount = ?true-cost

CONCLUSION:
The true-cost of ?entity is ?true-cost
```

In obtaining this rule, first note the need for two pieces of information to find a part's true cost: Cost and Discount. Because you do not know which entity you will be using (you will actually use many entities), the unknown terms of the statement are given variables:

```
"The Cost of ?ENTITY is ?COST"

"The Discount of ?ENTITY is ?DISCOUNT"
```

Note that the variable ?ENTITY is used twice in the premise of the rule. This is because you are trying to find the Cost and Discount of the same entity, and once the variable ?ENTITY is bound to a particular entity, you will be assured of using the same one. Using the same variable names in this way is the most common technique used to relate two or more separate statements. To simply combine statements, use the logical AND and OR operators.

Once you have found the Cost and Discount of the entity, you need to subtract the two to find the true cost. If you can find these values (i.e., if the PREMISE portion of the rule is TRUE), then you can store this information (the CONCLUSION portion of the rule). The processes of searching, calculating, and storing are performed by the inference engine (reasoning system), which will be explained in Chapter 8. For this particular example, the reasoning system performs the following steps:

1. Because the premise is an AND statement, an attempt is made to match every English expression to make the premise true.

2.   An attempt is made to match the first expression,

   "The Cost of ?ENTITY is ?COST"

   by finding a match with the first entity that has a Cost slot, binding the ?ENTITY variable to the name of that entity and binding ?COST to the value of the Cost slot of that entity.

3.   If a true sentence is found, the reasoning system continues to match with the second statement,

   "The Discount of ?ENTITY is ?DISCOUNT"

   by binding ?DISCOUNT to the value of the Discount slot in the same entity named by the previously bound variable ?ENTITY.

4.   Then, if the second statement has matched, the reasoning system attempts to match the third statement,

   "?COST - ?DISCOUNT = ?TRUE-COST"

   by evaluating the bound values of the ?COST and ?DISCOUNT variables, using subtraction and then binding ?TRUE-COST to the value returned.

5.   Finally, if successful, the rule can "fire" because the premise of the rule is TRUE. When the rule fires, the conclusion of the rule (True-Cost ?entity ?true-cost) is asserted by substituting the values of the previously bound variables and asserting the statement in the knowledge base for future use.

You have defined a rule in which, given that a part entity has a cost value and a discount value, you can immediately calculate the true cost of the part entity and place that value in the knowledge base for later use.

To create the rule, enter the name, premise, and conclusion of the rule as specified above. Upon completion, the menu should appear as follows:

Specify Rule to Create

Rule name: TRUE-COST

Explanation:

Premise (in English):

> The COST of ?ENTITY is ?COST
>
> AND
>
> The DISCOUNT of ?ENTITY is ?DISCOUNT
>
> AND
>
> ?COST - DISCOUNT = ?TRUE-COST

Conclusion (in English):

> The TRUE-COST of ?ENTITY is ?TRUE-COST

Certainty: 1.0

Has rule fired?:   NO

As another example, you can create a rule that does not store new information into the knowledge base but will nevertheless tell you information about the existing entity objects.

Suppose you need to know if a part is available in a certain quantity. You will need to compare the current inventory level of the part to a requested number of parts. Again, make the rule as powerful as possible by using variables to stand for the specific part about which the information is desired:

```
Rule: AVAILABLE

PREMISE:
"Entity ?ENTITY is-a PARTS with CIL = ?CIL
AND
?NUMBER <  ?CIL"

CONCLUSION:
"There are ?NUMBER ?ENTITY Available"
```

This rule will be used only for querying. Given a number and an entity name in the form of "There are *number entity-name* Available", the rule will attempt to compare the current inventory level with the number specified. A query for this information will notify the user of the results of this attempt.

Now create the rule as usual:

```
Rule name:          AVAILABLE
Explanation:
Premise (in English):
        ENTITY ?ENTITY IS-A PARTS WITH CIL = ?CIL
        and
        ?NUMBER  < ?CIL
Conclusion (in English):
There are ?NUMBER ?ENTITY AVAILABLE
Certainty:          1.0
Has rule fired?:    NO
```

Meta Rules

In implementing a rule, the rule can be designated as a **forward chaining rule** that can be used in forward chaining only, a **backward chaining rule** that can be used in backward chaining only, or a **bidirectional rule** that can be called upon in both chaining directions. This feature is called **meta level** or **rule set**. An even more advanced concept is the meta-level rule, which is a rule describing the feature of all rules in a given rule set. The meta-level rule that can refer to object rules by description rather than by name is also called **meta rule**. Meta rules express strategies of how to use other knowledge in rules, frames, or other sources in the knowledge base to invoke subsequent rules in a situation in which more than one chunk or source of knowledge may be applicable. For example, given a problem that is solvable by either a forward chaining search through rules first or a tree search through the frame structure first, a meta rule might indicate which approach to take, based on the characteristics of the problem domain and other specifications of the desired solution, such as speed of search and accuracy of solution.

A meta rule makes a conclusion about other rules. It either makes deductions about the likely use of certain groups of rules or determines a partial ordering among subsets of rules or among rule sets. However, a meta rule makes conclusions about rule classes in rule groups but does not indicate circumstances under which some rule classes are invalid.

Implementing meta rules requires only a minor change to the control structure, i.e., before the system attempts to retrieve the entire classes of rules relevant to the current goal, it determines if there are any meta rules relevant to that goal. If so, these meta rules are invoked first to determine the likely utility and relative ordering of rule classes and rules. As a result, the search space can be pruned or the branches of the search tree can be reordered to increase system efficiency.

BUILDING LOGIC STRUCTURES

Logic can be used to represent facts about objects and their relations, properties, and functions, as shown in Figure 7.6.

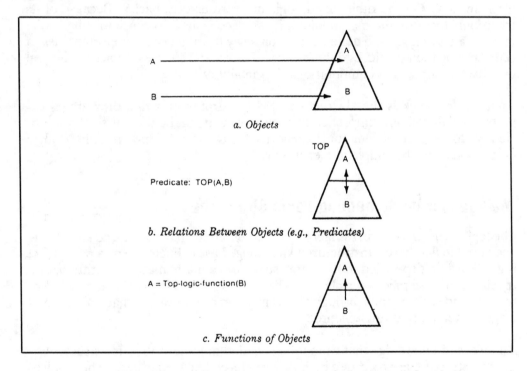

a. Objects

b. Relations Between Objects (e.g., Predicates)

c. Functions of Objects

Figure 7.6   Logic in representing facts about objects, relations, and functions

These facts can be expressed in a formula such as the following:

```
(there-is (x) (bird (x))     //"there is a bird"

(For-all(x) (Feathers (x)) (Animal (x)) => (Bird (x))
```

This equation is used to indicate the fact that all animals that have feathers are birds. It is a formula in which Feathers, Animal, and For-all are predicates to express relations or properties between objects such as x. X represents objects but not relations (predicates); consequently, this type of logic is called first-order logic or first-order predicate calculus. Times, events, kinds, organizations, worlds, and physical objects can be treated as logic predicates (facts). Logic provides methods that allow the user to assert these facts.

Logic is a powerful addition for knowledge representation, but it also has advantages and disadvantages. Logic expressions are usually concise and universally understood. Logicians have over the centuries proven rigorously and structurally what can be achieved with knowledge in certain domains, such as mathematics. On the other hand, logic has serious drawbacks. Because of its traditional focus on the methodology, it can deceive us into concentrating on the mathematics of logic and deflect attention away from the really important task of representing the key pieces of knowledge that are the source of power. The real drawback of logic is its computational intractability.

Another drawback is the abstractness of logic expressions that discourages experts/specialists from comprehending the true meanings behind the symbols. Obviously, for expert system tools to be useful to experts and specialists, logic expressions must be simple and expressive.

Methods for Implementing Logic Structures

The logic structure to express facts is implemented in an unstructured knowledge and variable database (unstructured knowledge base). Facts can be a partial fact regarding a unit specified in the frame structure, a mathematical operation, or a special relationship between classes. They are expressed in predicate calculus internally and can be input through the translation of natural language if a natural language template is implemented.

All pieces of knowledge that cannot be encoded in either the frame structure or the rule structure are recorded in the unstructured knowledge base. The features available to the user to operate on the logic structure include the following:

- **Display**: Allows the user to display the unstructured knowledge base. Each fact is followed by its certainty factors.

- **Assert**: Allows the user to insert a fact into the knowledge base. Forward chaining is performed; any rules whose antecedent matches the facts are triggered. The user is prompted for certainty factor.

- **Stash**: Allows the user to stash a fact into the knowledge base. No forward chaining is performed. The user is prompted for certainty factor.

- **Lookup**: Allows the user to search for a fact and its certainty factor.

- **Delete**: Allows the user to delete a fact from the knowledge base.

- **Edit**: Allows the user to edit a fact in the knowledge base.

- **Clear**: Allows the user to delete all facts from the knowledge base; it requires confirmation.

Listing 7.5 shows a sample program for a simple logic structure to store unstructured facts. Listing 7.5 provides only stash and lookup.

Listing 7.5: Program for Logic Structure (Unstructured Fact Base)

```
/*
** fact.h
*/
typedef struct _fact {
  struct _fact *next;
  cons          *predicate;
  double         cert;
} fact;
```

continued...

...from previous page

```
extern fact *PkbList;

/*
***********************************************************************
**
** Facts.c
**
**
** facts are stored as predicate-certainty pairs.
** stash(): add a fact to the data base
**
*/


/*--------------------------------------------------------include-----------*/

#include <stdio.h>
#include "cons.h"
#include <yyyymath.h>
#include "fact.h"
#include "goal.h"


/*-------------------------------------------------------global variables---*/

fact *PkbList = NULL;


/*------------------------------------------------------read_fact----------*/

fact *read_fact()
{
    fact *fp;
    cons *pp;
```

continued...

...from previous page

```
    if(fp = (fact *)malloc(sizeof(fact)))
    {
         fp->predicate = lread(C_FILE,stdin);
         pp = lread(C_FILE,stdin);
         fp->cert = atof(pp->car.s);
         killcons(pp);
         fp->next = NULL;
    }
    return fp;
}


/*-------------------------------------------------------_pkb_stash()-------*/
static fact *_pkb_stash(fp,fbp)
fact *fp,*fbp;
{
  fact *fp2 = fbp;

  if (fbp == NULL) {
    return fp;
  }
  while (fp2->next) {
    fp2 = fp2->next;
  }
  fp2->next = fp;
  return fbp;
}
```

continued...

...from previous page

```
/*-------------------------------------------------------pkb_stash()-------*/

void pkb_stash(predicate,cert)
cons *predicate;
double cert;
{
  fact *fp = (fact *) malloc(sizeof(fact));
  if (fp) {
    fp->predicate = predicate;
    fp->cert      = cert;
    fp->next      = NULL;
    PkbList = _pkb_stash(fp,PkbList);
  }
}




/*-------------------------------------------------------print_fact()-------*/

void print_fact(fp)
fact *fp;
{
  printf("Predicate: "); lprint(fp->predicate,C_FILE,stdout);
  printf("\nCertainty: %lg\n\n",fp->cert);
}




/*-------------------------------------------------------print_facts()-------*/

void printall_facts() {
  fact *fp = PkbList;

  while (fp != NULL) {
    print_fact(fp);
    fp = fp->next;
  }
}
```

continued...

...from previous page

```
/*-----------------------------------------------lookup_pkb_fact()------*/

/*
**    lookup_pkb_fact(): Look up the pkb.
**    Return struct Ret_Pair (substitution,certainty).
**    Author:   Sony Y. Song
**    Date:     7/8/88
*/


Ret_Pair *lookup_pkb_fact(pattern,prev_subst)
cons       *pattern;
cons       *prev_subst;
{
  Ret_Pair   *ret_pair;
  fact *fp = PkbList;
  cons *subst;

  subst = NULL;
  if (ret_pair = (Ret_Pair *) malloc(sizeof(Ret_Pair)))
  {
          ret_pair->subst = NULL;
          ret_pair->certainty = 0.0;
  }
  else
  {
          puts("\n*** Yow! Out of core ***\n");
  }
  while (fp != NULL) {
    subst = unify_pred_c(pattern,fp->predicate);
    if (subst != NULL && !test_subst_used(subst,prev_subst))
    {
      ret_pair->subst = subst;
      ret_pair->certainty = fp->cert;
      break;
    } else {
```

continued...

...from previous page

```
      fp = fp->next;
    }
  }
  killcons(subst);
  return ret_pair;
}



/*-------------------------------------------------delete_PKB()-------*/

void delete_PKB()
{
          fact *PkbList = NULL;
}
```

Assert, Stash, and Lookup

Assert will trigger forward chaining to be performed, and any rules in which the antecedent matches the facts are invoked. The procedure for assert is as follows:

1.   Choose the value of the attributes of the fact given by the user.

2.   Compare the fact; if the fact is null, then inform the user, "Nothing asserted." If the fact is already in the knowledge base, inform the user, "Fact is already in the knowledge base." Otherwise, assert the fact and certainty factor through forward chaining.

3.   Push the fact into the knowledge base.

Stash is slightly different from assert. Instead of asserting the fact, stash adds it to the knowledge base without performing forward chaining by using the function add-fact, which pushes the fact and its certainty factor into the last of the stack in the knowledge base.

Lookup enables a user to search for a fact and its associated certainty factor in the unstructured knowledge base. Because the unstructured knowledge base can be stashed with a large quantity of unrelated facts, lookup may prove to be quite useful in a search.

SUMMARY

- The power of an expert system resides in its knowledge. Because knowledge is often abstract and ambiguous, a well-specified language for encoding this knowledge becomes essential. This language is called **knowledge representation language**. The knowledge representation language may use any one or a combination of frames, rules, and logic to represent facts explicitly.

- Frame structures are also called "units" or "schemas" in some AI workstation tools, such as KEE (distributed by IntelliCorp.). A frame structure can provide the expert/specialist with a uniform set of representation services for complex data collections or databases. A frame is more than a structure that is used in other computer languages such as C or Pascal. It is a generalized property list that contains spaces (called slots) to specify more than one property value. For example, the slots can in turn contain a default value, a restriction of value to be added, a procedure activated to compute a needed value, or a rule activated when certain conditions are met. Furthermore, a frame is a generalization hierarchy in which information is inherited from the superclass.

- C++ has a readily available capability for implementing these features into a frame structure. The two difficulties in using C++ to build a frame structure are nondynamic defining and inflexibility of class hierarchy. Because C++ provides no dynamic defining when C++ is used to create a frame structure, you need to know in advance the complete structure of the problem, which normally cannot be known before a prototype is completed and tested. A compromise is to use an expert system shell to build an expert system prototype, test and refine the prototype until satisfaction, and then use C/C++ to structure the final system for delivery.

- Rule structures are also called "production rules," "production systems," or "rule-based systems," which are the most used and the simplest form of knowledge representation. Most PC tools are in this category. In this form of knowledge representation, every piece of knowledge or experience is expressed.

- Logic can be used to represent facts about objects—their relations, properties, and functions. This type of logic is called first-order logic or first-order predicate calculus. Times, events, kinds, organizations, worlds, and physical objects can be treated as logic individuals (facts). Logic provides methods that allow the user to assert these facts. All pieces of knowledge that cannot be encoded in either the frame structure or the rule structure are recorded in the unstructured knowledge base.

REFERENCES

Hayes, P. "The Logic of Frames." In R. Brachman and H. Levesque. (eds.) *Readings in Knowledge Representation*. Los Altos, CA: Morgan Kaufmann Publishers, 1985.

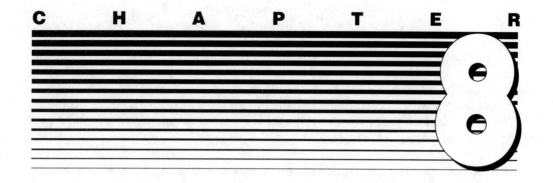

BUILDING AN INFERENCE ENGINE

The approaches to designing the first component of an expert system—a knowledge base that uses frames, rules, and logic—have been discussed. This chapter covers design of one of the remaining two components—the inference engine. The inference engine, as introduced briefly in Chapter 1, empowers an expert system with a reasoning mechanism and search control to solve problems. The user interface that provides the user with the convenience to use the expert system is discussed in Chapter 9.

This chapter examines the following main topics: designing an inference engine, forward chaining, backward chaining, justification, and search strategy.

DESIGNING AN INFERENCE ENGINE

An inference engine can be either simple or complicated, depending on the structure of the knowledge base. For example, if the knowledge base consists of simple rules (i.e., no structured rule set) and facts, a forward chaining will suffice. However, for a knowledge base that consists of structured frames and rules and unstructured logic (facts, data, and variables), sophisticated forward and backward chaining with a well-planned search strategy may be required. First, examine the main elements of an inference engine: forward chaining, backward chaining, justification, and search strategy.

FORWARD CHAINING

Forward chaining in its simplest form is an interactive program that performs a loop of substitution. It steps through the rule list until it finds a rule in which premises match the fact or situation. The rule will then be used or "fired" to assert a new fact. As discussed in Chapter 1, once the rule has been used, it will not be used again in the same search; however, the fact concluded as the result of that rule's firing will be added to the knowledge base. This cycle of finding a matched rule, firing it, and adding the conclusion to the knowledge base will be repeated until no more matched rules can be found. Variations of the simple forward chaining form can be suggested to enrich the inference mechanism. You will first examine the implementation of a simple forward chaining form and then a variation of the form.

Implementation of a Simple Chaining Form

Forward chaining is used to assert a fact that matches the premise of a rule and can be applied to determine further facts.

The detailed procedure for forward chaining is as follows:

1.   A fact is asserted.

2.   The fact matches the premise of a rule.

3.   The system computes the substitution that unifies the fact and the premise.

4.   The substitution is applied to the conclusion of the rule.

5.   This result is asserted and is available for further forward chaining.

6.   Steps 1 through 5 are repeated.

Listing 8.1 shows a sample forward chaining program.

Listing 8.1:   A Sample C Program for Forward Chaining

```
/*
**    forward.c
**
**    Description: This program is to implement the forward chain in reasoning
*/


/*--------------------------------------------------include------------*/

#include <stdio.h>
#include <math.h>
#include "cons.h"
#include "rule.h"
#include "fact.h"
```

continued...

...from previous page

```
/*------------------------------------------------forward_chain()--------*/

/*
** E.g.
**
** Rule Base:
**      1 IF ((d ?x)) THEN (c ?x) 1.0
**      2 IF ((a ?x)(c ?x)) THEN (b ?x) 1.0
** Predicate Base:
**      ((d 2), 0.7);
**
** predicate = (a 2), certainty = 0.9, rule_base = RuleDataBase
**
** forward_chain(predicate,certainty,rule_base) ===>
** New Predicate Base:
**      ((d 2), 0.7), ((a 2), 0.9), ((c 2), 0.7), ((b 2), 0.7)
**
*/

void forward_chain(predicate,certainty,rule_base)

cons    *predicate;                 /*predicate of beginning fact*/
double  certainty;                  /*certainty of beginning fact*/
rule    *rule_base;                 /*rule base*/


/*------------------------------------------------------------------------*/
{
        int     i;                  /*loop variable*/
        int     flag = 0;           /*flag to show rule base status*/
        double  *cert,cert1;        /*certainty of new fact*/
        double  *fact_cert;
        rule    *rulep;             /*rule base pointer*/
        fact    *factp,*new_fact;
        cons    *subst = NULL;
        cons    *new_concl,*temp;
        extern  cons *lookup_pkb_fact1();

        cert1 = 1.0;
        factp = PkbList;            /*initial to fact base*/
        rulep = rule_base;          /*initial to rule base*/
```

continued...

...from previous page

```
pkb_stash(predicate,certainty);  /*stash the fact into fact_base*/
while(rulep != NULL)             /*search all the rule base*/
{
                                 /*only concern conjunction*/
    for(i = 1; i <= length(rulep->premise); i++)
    {
        temp = nth_list(i,rulep->premise);
        subst=lookup_pkb_fact1(CAR(temp),fact_cert);
        if(subst != NULL)        /*find a matched rule's part*/
        {
            flag = 1;                /*set up success flag*/
            rulep->premise = subst_prop(rulep->premise,subst);
            rulep->conclusion = subst_pred(rulep->conclusion,subst);
            Min(cert1,(*fact_cert),cert); /*MYCIN certainty calcul*/
            cert1 = (*cert);
        }
        else
        {
            flag = 0;
            break;
        }
    }
    if (flag == 1)          /*find fact unified with premise*/
    {
        flag = 0;                    /*reset the flag*/
                        /*get the substituted rule conclusion*/
        new_concl = rulep->conclusion;
        cert1 = cert1*rulep->certainty;/* MYCIN certainty cal*/
        pkb_stash(new_concl,cert1);
        cert1 = 1.0;                 /*reset the certainty*/
        rule_base = delete_rule(rulep,rule_base);/*the fired rule is kicked out*/
        rulep = rule_base;    /*restart search rule base*/
    }
    else
    {
        rulep = rulep->next;    /*search for next rule*/
    }
    factp = PkbList;            /*restart search fact base*/
}
}
```

continued...

...from previous page

```
/*
**      stash_fact_pkb(predicate,cert)
**      Before stash the fact into pkb, check whether it is already there or not
**
*/
stash_fact_pkb(pred,cert)
cons        *pred;                  /*predicate calculus format of fact*/
double      cert;                   /*fact's certainty*/
{
        cons        *fp;
        double      *cert_out;

        fp = lookup_pkb_fact(pred,cert_out);
        if(fp == NULL)
        {
            pkb_stash(pred,cert);
        }
        else /*the fact is already there*/
        return;
}




/*---------------------------------------------lookup_pkb_fact1()--------*/

/*
** Different from the lookup_pkb_fact() in facts.c file. The difference is
** the argument.
*/

cons *lookup_pkb_fact1(pattern,cert)
cons *pattern;
double *cert;
{
  fact *fp = PkbList;
  cons *subst = NULL;
```

continued...

...from previous page

```
 *cert = 0.0;
 while (fp) {
   subst = unify_pred_c(pattern,fp->predicate);
   if (subst != NULL) {
     *cert = fp->cert;
     break;
   } else {
     fp = fp->next;
   }
 }
 return subst;
}
```

As shown in Listing 8.1, the implementation of this forward chaining procedure involves three elements:

- Unify

- Substitute

- Stash

The three elements are first examined, and then forward chaining is discussed to illustrate how to integrate these elements in forward chaining.

The purpose of **unify** is to return a substitution that will make the fact unify with the premise in the rule, i.e., will test the compatibility of the fact and the premise. You can either design unify in a narrow sense that exactly matches the fact and the premise or you can design it in broad terms that allow substitution of parts of the fact and the premise to make the fact and the premise compatible. For example, if the fact is that the size of an engine order is $x, and the premise is that the size of any order is 10, you can unify the two statements as follows:

```
Unify (( Order-size Engine $x) (Order-size $y 10)

==> (($x . 10) ($y . Engine))
```

The two statements are combined to obtain the size of an engine order, 10. The new statement can then be used to derive a conclusion from the rule containing an antecedent that matches it.

A sample program for a broadly defined unify is shown in Listing 5.1 (Chapter 5). The program initially determines whether the two expressions, p1 and p2, are equal. If not, it tries to substitute the components of the two expressions and compose a new statement that combines both expressions. Note that the program uses substitution to replace components.

Substitute is used to compute the substitution that unifies the fact and the premise; it performs a variable substitution on the proposition, as shown in the previous equation. A sample program for substitution is shown in Listing 4.3 (Chapter 4).

Stash is needed to incorporate the proposition (conclusion) into the knowledge base. Because the conclusion may include a conjunctive or disjunctive statement, each statement as well as its certainty factor needs to be asserted. The certainty factor for a conjunctive statement is simply copied from that of the premise. Listing 8.1 includes a subroutine to implement a stash that handles conjunctive propositions.

Enhancement of the Simple Chaining Form

The simple forward chaining form can be enhanced in two ways: (1) by using a conflict resolution method (a tie-breaking procedure) to select one of the eligible rules when the premises of more than one rule match the fact and (2) by considering the combination of conjunctive and disjunctive propositions in the premise or conclusion.

The first enhancement includes two features: (1) discarding those rules that would add only duplicates to the knowledge base and (2) executing a conflict resolution method to select one of the eligible rules. The enhanced procedure is as follows:

1.   Make eligible all rules in which the premise unifies with the fact.

2.   Substitute the premises.

3.   Discard rules in which the conclusion would have a nullifying effect.

4.   If no eligible rules remain, stop.

5.   Use a conflict resolution method to select one of the eligible rules if more than one rule is eligible.

6.   Stash the conclusion proposition to the knowledge base.

7.   Repeat the previous six steps.

The procedure is not much different from the one in the previous section, "Implementation of a Sample Chaining Form"; the only difference is that all eligible rules are first stored in the group of eligible rules, and a conflict resolution method will indicate the way these rules are to be selected. If no other methods are preferred, a first-in-last-out method is used to break ties among all eligible rules.

Combining conjunctive premises is discussed next in "Backward Chaining"; the same principles can be applied in forward chaining.

BACKWARD CHAINING

Backward chaining reasoning is used when the user makes a query as to whether a certain fact is true and when there is a rule that can determine the query from known information in the knowledge base or from answers given by the user.

In other words, backward chaining attempts to prove the hypothesis from facts. If the current goal is to determine the fact in the conclusion (hypothesis), then it is necessary to determine whether the premises match the situation. The example discussed in Chapter 1 will be repeated to show the logic of backward chaining:

Rule One:

IF you lose the key and

the gas tank is empty,

THEN the car is not running.

Rule Two:

IF the car is not running and

you have no cash,

THEN you are going to be late.

Fact One: You lost the key.

Fact Two: The gas tank is empty.

For example, if you want to prove the hypothesis "you are going to be late," given the facts and rules in the knowledge base (Facts 1 and 2, Rules 1 and 2), backward chaining can be applied to determine whether the premises match the situation. Rule 2, which contains the conclusion, would be fired first to determine whether the premises match the fact. Because the knowledge base does not contain the facts in the premises of Rule 2, "the car is not running" and "you have no cash," "the car is not running" becomes the first subgoal, or subhypothesis. Rule 1 will then be fired to assert whether the premises "you lost the key" and "the gas tank is empty" match the facts. Because the facts (Facts 1 and 2) in the knowledge base match the premise of Rule 1, the subhypothesis "the car is not running" is proven. However, the system still must prove the subgoal "you have no cash," which is not contained in the knowledge base and cannot be asserted through rules because no rule is related to it. The system will then ask the user "IS IT TRUE THAT: you have no cash?" If the answer is "yes," then the second subgoal is also satisfied, and the original hypothesis is therefore proven, concluding that "you are going to be late."

In summary, the procedure for backward chaining is as follows:

1.   A request is made to achieve a fact (the goal).

2.   The goal does not match any known fact.

3.   The goal matches the conclusion of a rule.

4.   The system computes the substitution that unifies the goal with the conclusion.

5.   The substitution is applied to the premise of the rule.

6.   This result becomes a new goal of the system.

7.   This new goal can do the following:

- match a fact in the knowledge base
- match a conclusion of a rule, leading to further backward chaining
- ask the user for the needed information
- fail, in which case the original goal fails

8.   Steps 1 through 7 are repeated.

A sample program for backward chaining is shown in Listing 8.2.

Listing 8.2: A Sample Program for Backward Chaining

```
/*
**      backward.c
**      Description:    This program is to implement backward chain in the
**                     reasoning.
**      Usage:  E.g.
**              Rule Base:
**                      1. IF ((a ?x)(b ?x)) THEN (c ?x) 1.0
**              Predicate Base:
**                      ((c 2), 1.0)
**              previous substitutions: NULL
**              backward_chain((c ?y),NULL) ===> ((?y 2), 1.0)
*/

/*-----------------------------------------------------------include-----*/

#include <stdio.h>
#include <math.h>
#include "cons.h"
#include "rule.h"
#include "fact.h"
#include "goal.h"
```

continued...

...from previous page

```
/*-----------------------------------------------------------define-------*/

#define ONE        1
#define TWO        2

/*
** backward_chain
*/

/*-------------------------------------------------------backward_chain()---*/

Ret_Pair    *backward_chain(goal,prev_subs)

cons        *goal;                         /*the goal trying to achieve*/
cons        *prev_subs;                    /*previous substitution list*/

/*-------------------------------------------------------------------------*/
{
   int      flag = 0;
   rule     *rp;
   cons     *subs,*concl_pred_subst,*subst_for_vars,*subbed_prem;
   cons     *prem_prev_substs,*prem_subs,*true_concl_pred_subst;
   cons     *true_concl_pred,*tmp1,*tmp2;
   cons     *possible_subst;
   Ret_Pair *ret_pair,*temp1;

#ifdef DEBUG
   printf("\nIn backward_chain:");
   printf("\ngoal:  ");
   lprint(goal,C_FILE,stdout);
   printf("  prev_substs:  ");
   lprint(prev_subs,C_FILE,stdout);
#endif
```

continued...

...from previous page

```
possible_subst=NULL;
subs = NULL;
true_concl_pred = NULL;
rp = RuleDatabase;                          /*point to Rule base*/
ret_pair = init_ret_pair();                 /*initialize the ret_pair*/
temp1    = init_ret_pair();
while( rp != NULL)                          /*trying to find a match rule*/
{
        subs = unify_pred_nv(rp->conclusion,goal);
        if(subs != NULL)                    /*find a rule match goal*/
        {
                flag = 1;                   /*find a rule*/
                break;
        }
        rp = rp->next;
}

if(!flag)                                   /*not find match rule, back*/
{
      return ret_pair;
}
tmp1 = nth_list(ONE,subs);
tmp2 = nth_list(TWO,subs);
concl_pred_subst = CAR(tmp1);
subst_for_vars = CAR(tmp2);
subbed_prem = subst_prop(rp->premise,concl_pred_subst);
if(length(subbed_prem) == 1)                      /*not conjunction premise*/
{
      subbed_prem = CAR(subbed_prem);
}
prem_prev_substs = subst_substlist(prev_subs,subst_for_vars);
temp1 = achieve(subbed_prem,prem_prev_substs);
prem_subs = temp1->subst;
if(prem_subs != NULL)
{
```

continued...

...from previous page

```
        true_concl_pred_subst = nconc(concl_pred_subst,prem_subs);
        true_concl_pred = subst_pred(rp->conclusion,true_concl_pred_subst);
        possible_subst = unify_pred_c(goal,true_concl_pred);
        if(!test_subst_used(possible_subst,prev_subs)) /*not used in prev*/
        {
                ret_pair->subst = possible_subst;
                ret_pair->certainty = rp->certainty * temp1->certainty;
        }
    }
#ifdef DEBUG
    printf("\nreturn from backward_chain:");
    printf("\nret_pair->subst::");
    lprint(ret_pair->subst,C_FILE,stdout);
    printf("  ret_pair->certainty::%g",ret_pair->certainty);
#endif
    return ret_pair;
}
```

As shown in Listing 8.2, the implementation of a backward chaining procedure involves the following major elements:

- unify

- substitute

- achieve

- backtrack

- forwardtrack

The coding of backward chaining in C is fairly complicated, involving multiple recursions of backtracking (detailed in Chapter 5), achieve, forwardtracking, and backward chaining. This complication arises when matching the facts/data in the knowledge base fails during a conjunctive proposition. For example, if the query is

```
(a ?x)(b ?x)(c ?x)  */ Explanation: look for a, b, and c that
                       are equal in the database
```

the database contains the following facts:

```
(a 1) 1.0  */ Explanation: a is 1 with certainty factor of 1.0
```

```
(a 2) 0.8
```

```
(b 3) 1.0
```

```
(b 2) 0.7
```

```
(c 2) 0.9
```

```
(c 4) 0.5
```

In backward chaining, **a** will be instantiated with 1, but (b 1) will not be found in the database. Therefore, the system will **backtrack** and try to find a new way to obtain (a ?x). It will find (a 2), and this will also lead to (b 2) being found:

```
(a 2)
```

```
(b 2)
```

At the same time, a forwardtrack through the database is requested to check whether (c 2) is a right answer to avoid getting wrong answers.

Figure 8.1 shows the flowchart for a complete backward chaining.

Note that the flowchart does not show two subroutines, unify and substitute, which are the backbone of forward and backward chaining.

Achieve ( )

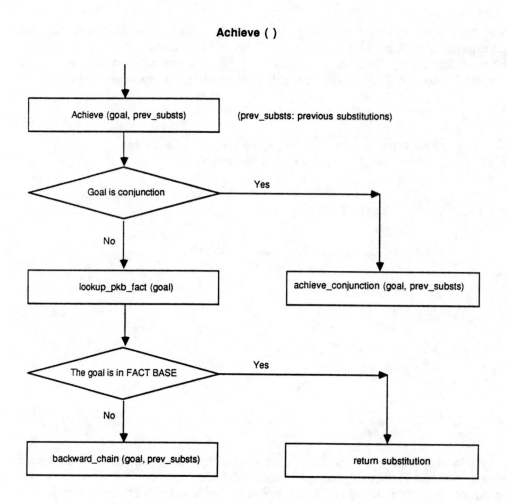

Figure 8.1   Flowchart for backward chaining

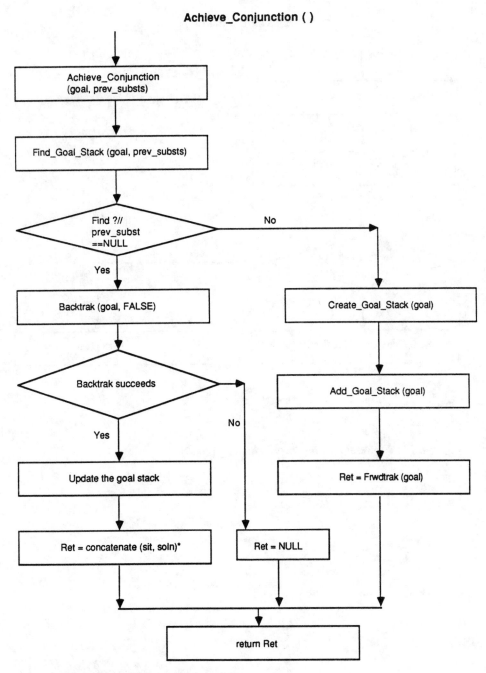

Achieve_Conjunction ( )

*sit = substitute is there (already good); soln = solution

Figure 8.1   Flowchart for backward chaining (cont.)

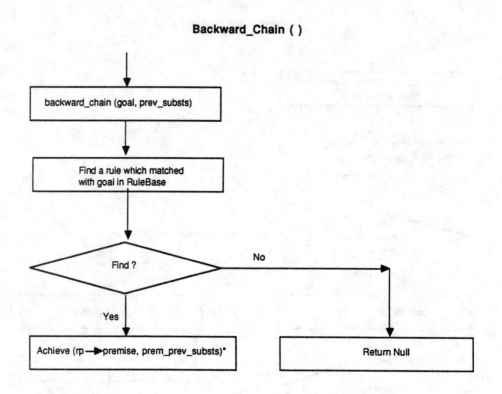

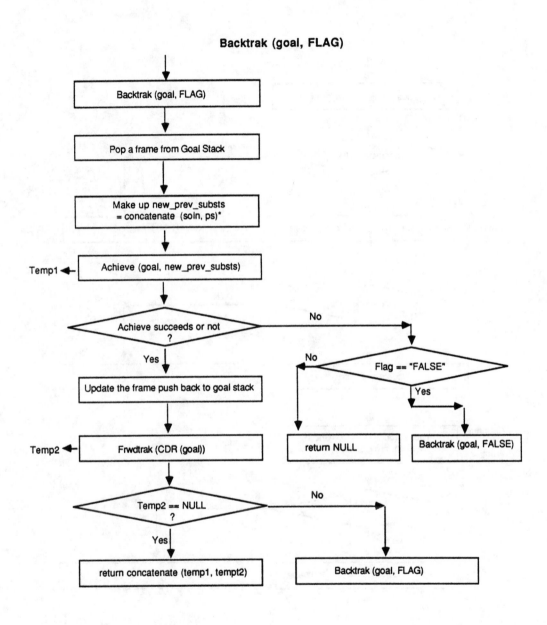

Backtrak (goal, FLAG)

*ps = previous substitute

Figure 8.1   Flowchart for backward chaining (cont.)

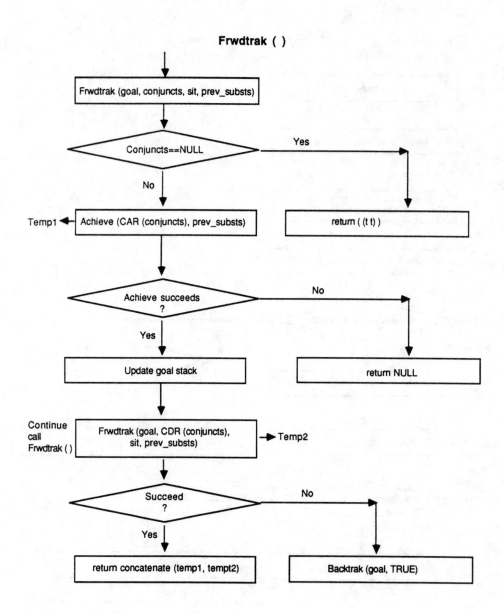

Figure 8.1   Flowchart for backward chaining (cont.)

The objective of **achieve** is to achieve the goal required by the user and return a substitution by checking if the substitution is a conjunction, a disjunction, or a fact in units, or if it is a proposition in the unstructured knowledge base. A sample program is shown in Listing 8.3. As demonstrated in the example of whether you are going to be late, the difference between a conjunctive and a disjunctive statement is the requirement of achieving the subgoals. When a conjunction appears in the subgoals, every subgoal must be proven true for the final goal to be true. In the case of disjunction, only one subgoal is required to be true. A sample program in Listing 8.3 deals with conjunction.

Listing 8.3: A Sample Program for Achieve

```
/*
**      achieve.c
**
**      Description:    This program is to implement backward reasoning.
**
**      Include:       achieve(),achieve_conjunction();
**
*/


/*----------------------------------------------------------include--------*/

#include <stdio.h>
#include <math.h>
#include "cons.h"
#include "rule.h"
#include "fact.h"
#include "goal.h"



/*-------------------------------------------------achieve_conjunction----*/

/*
** achieve_conjunction():
**
** If we're backtracking with prev_substs and there is no saved
** goal on the stack, that could mean
```

continued...

...from previous page

```
** that we haven't tried the goal yet at all and the prev_substs
** are from somewhere else.
**
** Return struct Ret_Pair (pair of substitution,certainty).
**
** E.g.
**
** Predicate Base:
**       ((a 1), 1.0), ((a 2), 1.0), ((b 2), 0.9)
**
** achieve_conjunction(((a ?x)(b ?x)),NULL) ===> (((?x 2)), 0.9)
**
**
*/


Ret_Pair   *achieve_conjunction(conjunction,prev_substs)

cons       *conjunction;
cons       *prev_substs;

/*-------------------------------------------------------------------------*/
{
        Ret_Pair       *ret_pair,*temp1;
        Goal_Stack     *gs_obj;
        Goal_Frame     *gf;
        cons           *tmp1;

        #ifdef  DEBUG
               printf("\nIn Achieve_Conjunction");
               printf("\nconjunction == ");
               lprint(conjunction,C_FILE,stdout);
               printf("  prev_substs == ");
               lprint(prev_substs,C_FILE,stdout);
        #endif

        gs_obj = NULL;
        ret_pair = init_ret_pair();
        gs_obj = Find_Goal_Stack(conjunction,prev_substs);
        if(prev_substs == NULL || gs_obj == NULL)
```

continued...

...from previous page

```
        {
            gs_obj = Create_Goal_Stack(conjunction);
            Add_Goal_Stack(gs_obj);          /*push into goal stack*/
            ret_pair = Frwdtrack(gs_obj,conjunction,NULL,prev_substs);
        }
        else
        {
            temp1 = Backtrack(gs_obj,FALSE);
            if(temp1->subst != NULL)
            {
                    gf = gs_obj->goal_frame_list;
                    tmp1 = gf->sit;
                    ret_pair->subst = nconc(tmp1,gf->soln);
                    ret_pair->certainty = temp1->certainty;
            }
        }
        if(ret_pair->subst != NULL)
        {
                gs_obj->prev_subst = push(ret_pair->subst,gs_obj->prev_subst);
        }
        #ifdef  DEBUG
            printf("\nreturn from Achieve_conjunction");
            printf("\nret_pair.subst == ");
            lprint(ret_pair->subst,C_FILE,stdout);
            printf("ret_pair.cert ==  %g",ret_pair->certainty);
        #endif
        return ret_pair;
}




/*--------------------------------------------------------achieve()-------*/

/*
** Attempts to achieve goal, returning a substitution and certainty
** Only dealing with the conjunction premises.
**
```

continued...

...from previous page

```
** E.g.
**
** Rule Base:
**      1 IF ((a ?z)) THEN (b ?z) 1.0
**      2 IF ((b ?w)) THEN (c ?w) 0.9
**      3 IF ((c ?x)(d ?x)) THEN (e ?x) 1.0
**      4 IF ((e ?x)) THEN (f ?x) 0.8
** Predicate Base:
**      ((a 6), 0.8), ((a 3), 0.6), ((d 3), 1.0)
**
** achieve((f ?y),NULL)  ===>  (((?y 3)), 0.432)
**
*/


Ret_Pair  *achieve(goal,prev_substs)

cons      *goal;
cons      *prev_substs;


/*------------------------------------------------------------------------*/
{
        Ret_Pair  *ret_pair;

        #ifdef  DEBUG
                printf("\nIn achieve.c");
                printf("\ngoal == ");
                lprint(goal,C_FILE,stdout);
                printf("  prev_substs == ");
                lprint(prev_substs,C_FILE,stdout);
        #endif

        ret_pair = init_ret_pair();
        if(!equal(prev_substs,ltwotees()))
        {
                if(!ATOM(CAR(goal)))            /*only deal with conjunction*/
                {
```

continued...

...from previous page

```
            {
                    ret_pair = achieve_conjunction(goal,prev_substs);
            }
            else
                {
                ret_pair = lookup_pkb_fact(goal,prev_substs);
                if(ret_pair->subst == NULL)      /*not find in pkb*/
                {
                    ret_pair = backward_chain(goal,prev_substs);
                }
                }
        }

}
```

Listing 8.3 uses recursion to reach the deep "nest" of conjunctive propositions that need to be substituted one by one. Backward and forward tracking is then used to return a substitution that makes conjuncts true. A sample program for backtracking is shown in Listing 5.2 (Chapter 5). Listing 8.4 exhibits a sample program for forwardtracking.

Listing 8.4: A Sample Program for Forwardtracking

```
/*
**      frwdtrack.c
**      Description:  This program is to implement forward tracking step
**                    in reasoning.
*/

/* Returns the substitution that makes conjuncts true.  (Does NOT return
** solution with s_i_t; that should be prepended by caller)
** If prev_substs is specified then we're calling the conjunct for the first
** time, but where some solutions have been tried already elsewhere
*/
/*-----------------------------------------------------include---------*/
```

continued...

...from previous page

```c
#include    <tdio.h>
#include    <math.h>
#include    "cons.h"
#include    "goal.h"


/*--------------------------------------------------------frwdtrack()------*/


Rt_Pair    *Frwdtrack(gs_obj,conjuncts,subs_in_there,prev_substs)

Goal_Stack        *gs_obj;                    /*goal stack object*/
cons              *conjuncts;                 /*conjuncts list*/
cons              *subs_in_there;             /*substitutions in there*/
cons              *prev_substs;               /*previous substitution list*/

/*------------------------------------------------------------------------*/
{
        Ret_Pair          *ret_pair;          /*return pair: subst,cert*/
        Ret_Pair          *temp_pair1,*temp_pair2;
        Goal_Frame        *goal_frame;
        cons              *temp1,*tmp1;
        double            *cert;

        #ifdef DEBUG
                printf("\nIn Frwdtrack");
                printf("\ngs_obj ::");
                print_goal_obj(gs_obj);
                printf("\nconjuncts :: ");
                lprint(conjuncts,C_FILE,stdout);
                printf(" sit :: ");
                lprint(subs_in_there,C_FILE,stdout);
                printf(" prev_substs :: ");
                lprint(prev_substs,C_FILE,stdout);
        #endif
        ret_pair = init_ret_pair();
        temp_pair1 = init_ret_pair();
        if(conjuncts == NULL)
```

continued...

...from previous page

```
{
        ret_pair->subst = mkcons(CAR_LIST,mklist2("t","t"),NULL);
        ret_pair->certainty = 1.0;
        return ret_pair;
}
else
{
        temp_pair1 = achieve(CAR(conjuncts),prev_substs);
        if(temp_pair1->subst != NULL)
        {
            if (goal_frame = (Goal_Frame *) malloc(sizeof(Goal_Frame)))
            {
                goal_frame->goal = CAR(conjuncts);
                goal_frame->sit = subs_in_there;
                goal_frame->ps = prev_substs;
                goal_frame->roc = CDR(conjuncts);
                goal_frame->soln = temp_pair1->subst;
                goal_frame->cert = temp_pair1->certainty;
                push_a_frame(goal_frame,gs_obj);
                tmp1 = subs_in_there;
                temp_pair2 = Frwdtrack(gs_obj,
                            subst_prop(CDR(conjuncts),temp_pair1->subst),
                                nconc(tmp1,temp_pair1->subst),prev_substs);
                if(temp_pair2->subst != NULL)
                {
                    ret_pair->subst =
                            nconc(temp_pair1->subst,temp_pair2->subst);
                    Min(temp_pair1->certainty,temp_pair2->certainty,cert);
                    ret_pair->certainty = (*cert);
                    return ret_pair;
                }
                else
                {
                    return Backtrack(gs_obj,TRUE);
                }
```

continued...

...from previous page

```
                    }
                    else
                    {
                            puts("\n*** Yow! Out of core ***\n");
                    }
            }
            else
            {
                    ret_pair->subst = NULL;
                    ret_pair->certainty = 0.0;
                    return ret_pair;
            }
        }
}
```

The second issue is to determine whether the new goal can match the fact in the knowledge base. This fact can be either a proposition in the unstructured database or structure information in the frame structure, e.g., slot of a unit or class. Listing 8.5 shows sample programs to initialize and search the knowledge base of the sample Inventory Control System.

Listing 8.5: Sample Programs to Search the Knowledge Base of the Inventory Control System

```
/*
** icskb3.cpp
**
** Contains:
** 1). find_entity_node(entity_name,class_node).
**      where:
**              entity_name: is the entity name which you try to find data.
**              class_node: is the class which the entity belongs to.
**      return:
**              entity data(slot data).
**      e.g.    find_entity_node("lisa_hu",STCUST_CLASS) -> lisa_hu slot data
```

continued...

...from previous page

```
**
** 2). find_all_entities(class_node).
**      where:
**              class_node: is the class.
**      return: all entities which belong to that class.
**      e.g.    find_all_entities(STCUST_CLASS) -> "lisa_hu", "david_hu", etc.
**
** 3). find_e_with_slot(class_node,slot_name,slot_value).
**      where:
**              class_node: is the class name.
**              slot_name:  is the slot name you try to find.
**              slot_value: is the value of this slot.
**      return: all entities of that class with specified slot.
**      e.g.    find_all_entities_with_slot(STCUST_CLASS,"dealer","vallejo").
**
*/


#include <stream.h>
#include <string.h>
#include <slotdef.h>
#include <tempstru.h>
#include <icsclass.h>
#include <ics.h>


/*-----------------------------------------Class Node-------------------*/
extern stcust_class* STCUST_CLASS;   /*st_cust class node*/
extern stinv_class*  STINV_CLASS;    /*st_inv class node*/
extern sfinv_class*  SFINV_CLASS;    /*sf_inv class node*/
extern warehs_class* WAREHS_CLASS;   /*warehs class node*/
extern dealer_class* DEALER_CLASS;   /*dealer class node*/
extern sfsalrec_class* SFSALREC_CLASS;  /*sf sale rec class node*/


/*
** Find the entity from the OKB
** Overloaded function.
*/
```

continued...

...from previous page

```
/*for st_cust class*/
st_cust* find_entity_node(char* s,stcust_class* sl)
{
        stcust_etynd* temp1;

        /* The following are same for different class. Overloaded!!*/
        temp1 = sl->elist;
        while(strcmp(s,temp1->name) && temp1 != NULL)
        {
                temp1 = temp1->next;
        }
        if(temp1 == NULL)
        {
                cout << "\n" << "Not such entity !";
                return NULL;
        }
        else
        {
                return temp1->entity;
        }
}


/*for st_inv class*/
st_inv* find_entity_node(char* s,stinv_class* sl)
{
        stinv_etynd* temp1;

        /*...... same as above ....*/
}


/*
** for sf_inv class
*/
sf_inv* find_entity_node(char* s,sfinv_class* sl)
{
        sfinv_etynd* temp1;
```

continued...

...from previous page

```
        temp1 = sl->elist;
        while(strcmp(s,temp1->name) && temp1 != NULL)
        {
                temp1 = temp1->next;
        }
        if(temp1 == NULL)
        {
                cout << "\n" << "Not such entity !";
                return NULL;
        }
        else
        {
                return temp1->entity;
        }
}


/*
** for warehs class
*/
warehs* find_entity_node(char* s,warehs_class* sl)
{
        warehs_etynd* temp1;

        temp1 = sl->elist;
        while(strcmp(s,temp1->name) && temp1 != NULL)
        {
                temp1 = temp1->next;
        }
        if(temp1 == NULL)
        {
                cout << "\n" << "Not such entity !";
                return NULL;
        }
        else
        {
                return temp1->entity;
        }
```

continued...

...from previous page

```
}

/*
** for dealer class
*/
dealer* find_entity_node(char* s,dealer_class* sl)
{
        dealer_etynd* temp1;

        temp1 = sl->elist;
        while(strcmp(s,temp1->name) && temp1 != NULL)
        {
                temp1 = temp1->next;
        }
        if(temp1 == NULL)
        {
                cout << "\n" << "Not such entity !";
                return NULL;
        }
        else
        {
                return temp1->entity;
        }
}

/*
** for sf sale rec class
*/
sf_sales_records* find_entity_node(char* s,sfsalrec_class* sl)
{
        sfsalrec_etynd* temp1;

        temp1 = sl->elist;
        while(strcmp(s,temp1->name) && temp1 != NULL)
        {
                temp1 = temp1->next;
        }
        if(temp1 == NULL)
```

continued...

...from previous page

```
            {
                    cout << "\n" << "Not such entity !";
                    return NULL;
            }
            else
            {
                    return temp1->entity;
            }
}



/*
**   Find the all entities
**   Overloaded function.
*/

/*for st_cust class*/
stcust_etynd* find_all_entities(stcust_class* sl)
{
        /* The following are same for different class. Overloaded!!*/
cout << "\nsosssss";
        return sl->elist;
}

/*for st_inv class*/
stinv_etynd* find_all_entities(stinv_class* sl)
{
        /*...... same as above ....*/
}



/*
**   Find the all entities with specified slot
**   Overloaded function.
*/
```

continued...

...from previous page

```
/*for st_cust class*/
stcust_etynd* find_e_with_slot(char* slot_nm, char* slot_val,stcust_class* sl)
{
        /* The following are same for different class. Overloaded!!*/
        stcust_etynd* tmp2;
        tmp2 = NULL;
        slot_node*  temp1;
        temp1 = sl->slist;
        while(strcmp(slot_nm,temp1->name) && temp1 != NULL)
        {
            temp1 = temp1->next;
        }
        if(temp1 == NULL)
        {
            cout << "\n" << "This class has not this slot name !";
            return NULL;
        }
        else
        {
            stcust_etynd* temp;
            temp = sl->elist;

            extern stcust_etynd* make_up_etylist(stcust_etynd*,stcust_etynd*);
            while(temp != NULL)
            {
                Cust*  tpm;
                tpm = temp->entity->get_slotval();
                if(!strcmp(slot_nm,"dealer"))
                {
                    if(!strcmp(tpm->dealer->slot_value,slot_val))
                    {
                      stcust_etynd* tpp = new stcust_etynd;
                      tpp->name = temp->name;
                      tpp->entity = temp->entity;
                      tpp->next = NULL;
                      tmp2 = make_up_etylist(tmp2,tpp);
                    }
```

continued...

...from previous page

```
                }
                if(!strcmp(slot_nm,"name"))
                {
                      if(!strcmp(tpm->name->slot_value,slot_val))
                        make_up_etylist(tmp2,temp);
                }
                if(!strcmp(slot_nm,"part"))
                {
                      if(!strcmp(tpm->part->slot_value,slot_val))
                        make_up_etylist(tmp2,temp);
                }
                if(!strcmp(slot_nm,"order_date"))
                {
                      if(!strcmp(tpm->order_date->slot_value,slot_val))
                        make_up_etylist(tmp2,temp);
                }
                if(!strcmp(slot_nm,"time"))
                {
                      if(!strcmp(tpm->time->slot_value,slot_val))
                        make_up_etylist(tmp2,temp);
                }
                temp = temp->next;
          }
        }
        return tmp2;
}


/*
** The same as other class for find_e_with_slot().
*/


stcust_etynd* make_up_etylist(stcust_etynd* el1,stcust_etynd* el2)
{
        /* The following are same for different class. Overloaded!!*/
        el2->next = el1;
        el1 = el2;
        return el1;
}
```

Ask-user is sometimes required when no fact in the knowledge base can be matched and no rule can be applied to derive new facts. The user is asked whether the fact is true; you can add this feature on to the sample backward chaining program.

JUSTIFICATION

Justification provides the user with a tracing facility to indicate the history of goal substitution regarding the last conclusion; the achievement method via rules, units, and facts in the unstructured database; or the answer that is user provided. Justification gives the source name of the rule, unit, or fact used, as well as the fact in the rule or unit that has been used. Justification uses the combination of car and cdr to retrieve the history of goal achievement and uses conditionals to print out the tracing results. Utility programs for car and cdr are shown in listings in Chapter 4 and can be used for writing a C subroutine to print out the path of rule firing.

SEARCH STRATEGY

The three common search strategies are depth-first, breadth-first, and best-first. Each of the three strategies uses a slightly different approach to search for the target solution.

Depth-First Search

In the discussion of forward and backward chaining, you used an implied search strategy, depth-first. Certain terms must be defined to explain the concept of a depth-first search. In both forward and backward chaining, there is always a starting point (either a fact or a goal). The starting point is called the **root node**. There are choices (**branch nodes**) after the starting point and more subbranches at each branch as the matching and substitution process goes along. This decision process is called a **tree** because every branch has a unique parent, with only one exception (the root node).

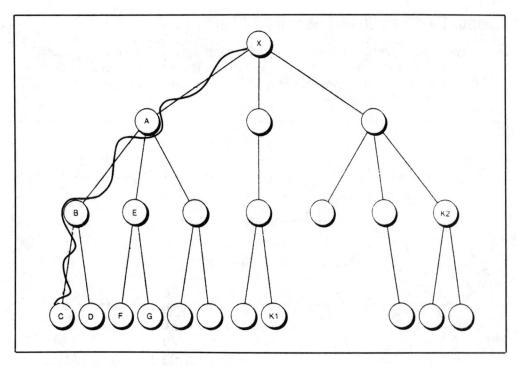

Figure 8.2   Depth-first search

In a **depth-first** search, as illustrated in Figure 8.2, the search starts from X down to A, B, and C. Only the left-most child of each node is examined. If the node is not the desired node, the process goes down to the next level and chooses the left-most child of that node, always moving downward. If it reaches the bottom level without finding the desired choice, the process returns to the last node that contained a choice. Then the downward motion is repeated. For example, if the target node for the search is K2 in Figure 8.2, it will take a great effort for the depth-first strategy to reach the K2 node because the process has to go through almost all nodes, down from X to C, returning from C to B and moving down again to D, returning to A, descending to E and F, and so on to get to K2.

The depth-first search entails a recursive procedure in which the recursion occurs for moving down one tree branch and then moving across all the branches. This recursion is implemented in both forward and backward chaining programs as discussed previously.

Breadth-First Search and Best-First Search

In a **breadth-first** search, movement is performed level by level; the process examines all the nodes on the same level one by one. If the target node is not found, then the process looks at those on the next level, as shown in Figure 8.3.

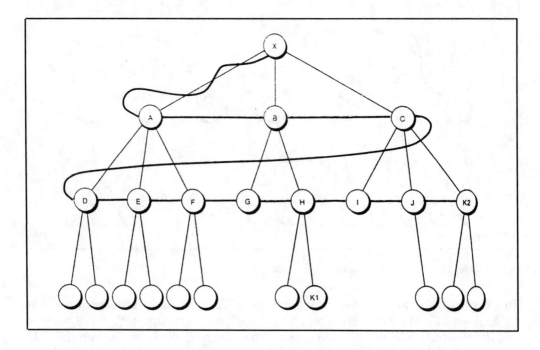

Figure 8.3   Breadth-first Search

The same example of searching for K2 is used to compare the difference in efficiency. Because K2 is on the third level, the search process will need to examine only 10 nodes to reach K2, in comparison with 19 nodes in the depth-first search. Whether the breadth-first search is more efficient than the depth-first search depends on where the target node is. Consequently, it sometimes pays to make a good guess about how far the target node is from the current node and select the shortest path leading to the target node. This strategy is called the **best-first** search.

The two elements required in a best-first search are (1) complete ordering of the paths and (2) a method to determine the distance remaining between the current node and the target node. In theory, the ordering of the paths can be undertaken by using **Sort,** and the straight-line distance between the target node and the current node can be used as the starting point if the nodes' locations can be identified. The straight line distance is estimated as follows,

```
Distance = SQRT ((N1-X) (N1-X) + (N2-Y) (N2-Y))
```

where (N1, N2) is the position of the target node, and the X-Y coordinate is the location of the current node on a travel map.

The implementation of a breadth-first and best-first search into the forward and backward chaining programs requires a careful estimation of the trade-off between complexity and efficiency for the actual application of the expert system and tool; you can explore the possibility of implementing these two strategies in actual applications.

SUMMARY

- The inference engine empowers an expert system with a reasoning mechanism and search control to solve problems.

- An inference engine may include forward chaining, backward chaining, justification, and search strategy.

- An inference engine can be either simple or complicated, depending on the structure of the knowledge base. For example, if the knowledge base consists of simple rules (i.e., no structured rule set) and facts, a forward chaining may suffice. However, for a knowledge base that consists of structured frames and rules and unstructured logic (facts, data, and variables), sophisticated forward and backward chaining with a well-planned search strategy may be required.

- Forward chaining in its simple form is an interactive program that performs a loop of substitution. It steps through the rule list until it finds a rule whose promises match the fact or situation. The rule will then be used or "fired" to assert a new fact.

- A backward chaining reasoning is used when the user makes a query as to whether a certain fact is true and there is a rule that can determine the query from known information in the knowledge base or from answers given by the user.

- Backward chaining attempts to prove the hypothesis from facts. If the current goal is to determine the fact in the conclusion (hypothesis), then it is necessary to determine whether the premises match the situation.

- Justification provides the user with a tracing facility to indicate the history of goal substitution regarding the last conclusion; the achievement method via rules, units, and facts in the unstructured database; or the answer that is user provided. It gives the source name of the rule, unit, or fact used, as well as the fact in the rule or unit that has been used.

- The three common search strategies are depth-first, breadth-first, and best-first. Each of the three strategies uses a slightly different approach to search for the target solution.

- In both forward and backward chaining, there is always a starting point (either a fact or a goal). The starting point is called the root node. There are choices (branch nodes) after the starting point and more subbranches at each branch as the matching and substitution process continues. This decision process is called a **tree** because every branch has a unique parent, with only one exception (the root node).

- In a depth-first search, the search moves from top to bottom. Only the left-most child of each node is examined. If the first node is not the desired node, the process goes down to the next level and chooses the left-most child of that node, always moving downward. If it reaches the bottom level without finding the desired choice, the process returns to the last node that contained a choice. Then the downward motion is repeated. The depth-first search entails a recursive procedure in which the recursion occurs for moving down one tree branch and then moving across all the branches. This recursion is implemented in both forward and backward chaining programs as discussed before.

- In a breadth-first search, movement is performed level by level, and the process examines all the nodes on the same level one by one. If the target node is not found, then the process looks at those on the next level. Consequently, it sometimes pays to make a good guess about how far the target node is from the current node and select the shortest path leading to the target node. This strategy is called a best-first search.

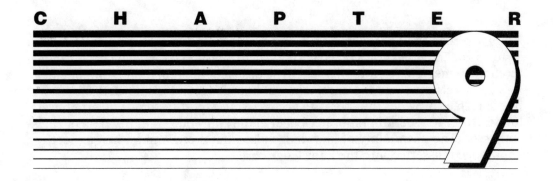

INCORPORATING USER INTERFACE AND UNCERTAINTY OF KNOWLEDGE

You have seen the approaches to designing the first two components of expert systems and tools: a knowledge base that uses frames, rules, and logic; and an inference engine. This chapter discusses the design of the remaining component — the user interface — and the uncertainty of knowledge in the knowledge base. A user interface provides the user with access to the expert system. Uncertainty allows the user to ascertain his or her belief in the knowledge — either data or rules gathered. The uncertainty of knowledge also affects reasoning when a piece of knowledge is asserted into the knowledge base.

Because programs for user interface generally involve input/output facilities that are system-specific, this chapter presents largely generic concepts that may be applicable to most systems. Topics in this chapter include an overview of user interface, user-interface options, and dealing with uncertain knowledge.

OVERVIEW OF USER INTERFACE

The man-machine interface mechanism produces dialogue between the computer and the user. The current expert system may be equipped with "menus" or a natural language to facilitate its use and an explanation module to allow the user to challenge and examine the reasoning process underlying the system's answers.

Menus refer to groups of simplified instructional statements that appear on the computer screen and can be selected by pushing designated buttons on a mouse or designated keys on the keyboard. The user does not need to type instructions. A semi-natural or fully natural language interface is more sophisticated than a menu interface; it allows computer systems to accept input and produce output in a language closer to a conventional language such as English. Several expert systems incorporate primitive forms of natural language in their user interface to facilitate knowledge base development. Explanation modules generate output statements of expert systems in language that can be understood by noncomputer-professional users. Most expert systems are equipped with this type of module.

The three aspects of the user interface mechanism that affect its efficiency are as follows:

- **User modes**: client, tutor, and pupil

- **Interface purpose**: testing, applications, and modifications

- **User groups**: domain expert, knowledge engineer, and general public

User mode is defined as how users will use the expert system when they interface with it. Three different user modes are associated with an expert system, in comparison with the single mode of obtaining answers to problems characteristic of general computer software applications. The user can act as a client to obtain answers to problems from the expert system, as a tutor to increase or improve the knowledge of the expert system, and as a pupil to harvest the knowledge of the expert system for increasing his or her skill in a specified subject.

Interface purpose is defined as the objective of the user's interaction with the expert system. Interface with the expert system can occur for testing the expert system before it is completely refined, for applying it to the real-world situation for consultation of problems, and for modifying it when the experts find the answers are invalid or insufficient. Users are classified into three groups: domain experts, knowledge engineers, and the general public.

Domain experts are experts or specialists in a given application field who assist in building the expert system initially, test it, and then apply it to solve problems later when it is completed. **Knowledge engineers** are computer programmers who obtain knowledge from experts to develop expert systems and then refine the system; they frequently apply the system to real world problems. The **general public** does not develop or refine the system, but benefits by using expert systems. The effectiveness of a man-machine interface for an expert system can be determined once its user modes, interface purpose, and user groups are identified.

A commercial display screen package, such as Cview, can be used to provide a mechanism for creating forms, displaying forms, and acquiring input with menus from the user through the forms. A commercial graphics package, such as BPS Business Graphics, can be used to create graphics of the results to give the user a better understanding of the expert system results.

User interface is the weakest but most critical element of expert systems because it determines how well the systems will be accepted by the end users. Major research efforts have been undertaken in natural language interface, voice recognition, and voice synthesis to make expert systems more user friendly. Now you are ready to examine these items in greater detail.

Semi-Natural or Fully Natural Language Interfaces

A semi-natural or fully natural language interface provides the user with near-natural comprehension and text generation in the context of a focused dialog. By the use of parsing, ellipses, imperfect input handling, fail-recovery technique, and with the constraint on vocabulary and concepts because of domain specificity, a natural language interface can free the user from the need to learn cognitive commands and allow the user to focus on the problem. Whether a language interface is considered semi-natural or fully natural depends on how closely it "comprehends" natural language dialogs and generates natural language text.

Because of the complexity of database systems, most natural language interfaces were designed for database query, such as Clout (by Microrim of Bellevue, WA) and G&A (by Symantec of Cupertino, CA). Few interfaces are designed specifically for expert systems.

XCALIBUR, which is one such interface, presents a good example in that it was designed to interact with XCON and XCEL, two early and successful expert systems (XCON is discussed in detail in Chapter 11). Two samples of XCALIBUR's dialogs are as follows:

User: What is the largest 11780 fixed disk under $40,000?

XCALIBUR: The rp07.aa is a 516 MB fixed pack disk that costs $38,000.

User: Tell me about the lxy 11.

XCALIBUR: The lxy11 is a 240 LPM line printer with plotting capability.

The three major modules in XCALIBUR, as shown in Figure 9.1, are a natural language parser (DYPAR), an information manager, and a natural language generator. The core of the interface is the natural language parser that integrates several diverse parsing techniques such as multi-strategy parsing, semantic grammar, pattern matching, and the recursive case-frame method to recognize action (verbs), complex nouns, and other sentence elements. The information manager handles the communications between the parser, the underlying expert system (such as XSEL and XCON), and the natural language generator. The generator reverses the process of the parser by converting a request from the information manager or the parser into English. A sample of the output of the generator is as follows:

User: Requests the price of all 120-volt graphics terminals that are less than $3,200.

Generator: The vt105-ma is a 120-volt terminal with graphics capability that costs $3,100.

The generator prints only the vt105 terminal because there is only one such terminal available.

Natural language interfaces that are integrated into expert systems are domain-specific and need to be modified for each domain. Programmer's toolkits for developing natural language interfaces such as Language Workbench (Brodie Associates, Boston, MA) are available.

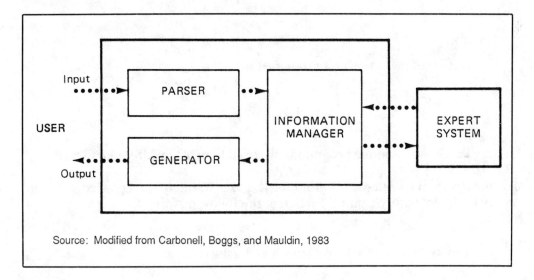

Source: Modified from Carbonell, Boggs, and Mauldin, 1983

Figure 9.1   Major components of XCALIBUR

USER-INTERFACE OPTIONS

A user interface encompasses a large variety of selections, ranging from a simple input/output utility to sophisticated voice recognition. The mouse, window, and menu operations are familiar to most programmers and are system dependent and language dependent.

Simple Input/Output Utilities

Input/output utilities allow the user to read, to print statements in a certain format or via certain media, or to query the expert system conveniently. Listing 9.1 contains a sample program to allow the user to input LISP-like statements such as

```
((p q) p q p q)

(Peter Lin Dave Linda Lisa Eileen Emily)

((p q) (p q) (p q))
```

Listing 9.2 shows a sample program to write statements in LISP-like format.

Listing 9.3 shows a sample program for the user to query the knowledge for an entity in the Inventory Control System in the following format:

```
(entity ?x is-a ?y with slot_name = slot_value)

(entity ?x is-a ?y)
```

Similar input/output programs can be written in C/C++ to better enable users to input data, ask queries, or understand the results of their queries.

Listing 9.1: Sample Program to Read LISP Expressions

```
/*
** INPUT.C
**
**
** History:
**
** Routines to read lists in lisp fashion, i.e. of the form
** s_expression ::= atom | ( list )
** list         ::= list atom |
**
*/

#include <ctype.h>
#include <stdio.h>
#include "cons.h"

#define LEFT_PAREN  64
#define RIGHT_PAREN 128

cons *lread(type,where)
int type;
char *where;
{
   int dummy;
   cons *read_s_expr();

   return read_s_expr(type,where,&dummy);
}

static cons *read_s_expr(type,where,etype)
int   type,*etype;
char *where;
{
   int         ty;
   cons        *f,*read_list();
   char        *strsave();
   static char buf[512];
```

continued...

...from previous page

```
switch (get_token(type,where,buf)) {
  case 0:                           /* empty list */
    f = NULL;                       /* return a NIL pointer */
  break;

  case CAR_STRING:                  /* a string */
    if (f = mkcons(CAR_STRING,strsave(buf),NULL)) {
      *etype = CAR_STRING;
    }
  break;

  case LEFT_PAREN:
      f = read_list(type,where);
      *etype = CAR_LIST;
      break;

      case RIGHT_PAREN:
      f = (cons *) 1;                /* for right parens */
      *etype = ')';
      break;
  }
  return f;
}


cons *read_list(type,where)
int type;
char *where;
{
  cons *t, *z;
  int     first = 0,etype;

  z = read_s_expr(type,where,&etype);
  if (etype == ')') {
    t = NULL;
  } else {
    if (t = mkcons(CAR_LIST,z,read_list(type,where))) {
      return t;
```

continued...

...from previous page

```
    } else {
      t = NULL;
    }
  }
  return t;
}

int get_token(type,ip,store)
int type;                           /* file or string input */
char *ip;                           /* input source */
char *store;                        /* place to store strings */
{
  int  c;
  char *s;

  c = skip_whitespace(type,ip);
  if (c=='"') {
    for (s=store;;s++) {
      switch (*s = Getc(type,ip)) {
          case '"':
          if ((c = Getc(type,ip)) != '"') {
            Ungetc(type,c,ip);
            *s = '\0';
            return CAR_STRING;
          }
          break;
          case '\\':
          switch (c=Getc(type,ip)) {
            case 'n':
            *s = '\n';
            break;

            case 'r':
            *s = '\r';
            break;

            case 'd':
            *s = '\004';
            break;
```

continued...

...from previous page

```
/*          case '0':
            Ungetc(type,c,ip);
            *s = (char) c;
            break;
*/
            case 'p':
            *s++ = '\\';
            *s   = 'p';
            break;

            case '(':
            *s++ = '\\';
            *s   = '(';
            break;

            case ')':
            *s++ = '\\';
            *s   = ')';
            break;

            case '\0':
            *s = '\0';
            return CAR_STRING;
            break;

            default:
            *s = c;
            break;
          }
          break;
      }
    }
  }
  if (isalpha(c) || c == '?') {
    Ungetc(type,c,ip);
    for (s=store; isalpha(*s=Getc(type,ip)) || isdigit(*s) || *s == '-'
                                  || *s == '?'; s++)

      ;
```

continued...

...from previous page

```
   Ungetc(type,*s,ip);
   *s='\0';
   return CAR_STRING;
 }

 if (isdigit(c)) {
   int n = c - '0';
/*
   while (c = Getc(type,ip),isdigit(c)) {
     n *= 10;
     n += c - '0';
   }
   Ungetc(type,c,ip);
   *((int *) store) = n;
*/
   *store++ = c;
   while (c = Getc(type,ip),isdigit(c) || c == '.') {
     *store++ = c;
   }
   *store = '\0';
   Ungetc(type,c,ip);
   return CAR_STRING;
 }

 if (c == '(') {
   if ((c = skip_whitespace(type,ip)) == ')') {
     return 0;                          /* empty list */
   } else {
     Ungetc(type,c,ip);
     return LEFT_PAREN;
   }
 }
 if (c == ')') {
   return RIGHT_PAREN;
 }
 return c;
}
```

continued...

...from previous page

```
char *strsave(s)
char *s;
{
  char *t;

  if (t = (char *) malloc(strlen(s)+1)) {
    strcpy(t,s);
  }
  return t;
}
int Getc(type,source)
int type;
char *source;
{
  if (type == C_STRING) {
    return (*(*((char **) source))++);          /* whew! */
  } else {
    return getc((FILE *) source);
  }
}


int Ungetc(type,c,source)
int type;
char c;
char *source;
{
  if (type == C_STRING) {
    *--(*((char **) source)) = c;
  } else {
    ungetc(c,(FILE *) source);
  }
}


int skip_whitespace(type,ip)
int type;
char *ip;
{
  int c;
```

continued...

...from previous page

```
  while ((c = Getc(type,ip)) == ' ' || c == '\t' || c == '\n' || c == ';')
   if (c == ';')                       /* a comment */
     while (Getc(type,ip) != '\n')     /* read up to & including the EOL */
       ;
  return c;
}
```

Listing 9.2: Sample Program to Print Output in LISP Fashion

```
/*
** OUTPUT.C
**
**
** Routines to print lists in lisp fashion.
**
*/

#include <stdio.h>
#include "cons.h"

static int sputs(s,where)                        /* similar to fputs */
char *s, *where;
{
    strcat(where,s);
    return 0;
}


/***************/

lprint(l,type,target)
cons *l;
int  type;
char *target;
```

continued...

...from previous page

```
{
  switch (type) {
    case C_STRING:
    _print_s_expr(l,sputs,target);
    break;

    case C_FILE:
    _print_s_expr(l,fputs,target);
    break;

    default:
    ; /**/ /* Error-message */
    break;
  }
}


/************/

static _print_s_expr(node,output,target)
cons *node;
int (*output)();
char *target;
{
    static char slask[80];

  if (node->type == 0 & node->car.p == NULL) {
    printf("()");
  } else if (node->type == CAR_STRING) {
    (*output) ((char *) node->car.s,target);
  } else if (node->type == CAR_LIST) {
    _print_list(node,output,target);
  } else {
    ;    /**/ /* Error message */
  }
}
```

continued...

318

...from previous page

```
/*
** _print_list():
*/

static _print_list(node,output,target)
cons *node;
int (*output)();
char *target;
{
  (*output) ("(",target);
  do {
    _print_s_expr((cons *) node->car.p,output,target);
    node = node->cdr;
    (*output) ((node == NULL) ? ")" : " ",target);
  } while (node != NULL);
}
```

Listing 9.3: Sample Program for Querying the Inventory Control System

```
/*
**   knlparse.cpp
**
**   check_entity_pred_syntax()
**
**   Checks if class name and slot names are valid, but NOT ENTITY name
**   (It could be a remote entity from a ks)
**   If class-must-be-inst is nil, lets class-name be var-term.  In this case,
**   However, there may be no slot-specs.
**
**   Ex1.  (entity ?x is-a ?y with slot_name = slot_value)
**   Ex2.  (entity ?x is-a ?y)
**
**
*/
```

continued...

...from previous page

```
#include "stream.h"
#include "string.h"
#include "cons.h"
#include "malloc.h"


#define    CASE1    1     /*C and E are instantiated without slot*/
#define    CASE2    2     /*C is instantiated but E isn't without slot*/
#define    CASE3    3     /*C and E are instantiated with slot var*/
#define    CASE4    4     /*C is instantiated but E isn't with slot var*/
#define    CASE5    5     /*C and E are instantiated with slot constant*/
#define    CASE6    6     /*C is instantiated but E isn't with slot constant*/
#define    CASE7    7     /*entity is instantiated and class isn't*/
#define    ONE      1
#define    TWO      2
#define    THREE    3
#define    FOUR     4
#define    FIVE     5
#define    SIX      6
#define    SEVEN    7
#define    EIGHT    8


int   check_entity_pred_syntax(cons* pred)
{
        extern cons* nth_list(int,cons*);       /*defined in util.c*/
        extern int length(cons*);               /*defined in util.c*/
        extern int variablep(cons*);            /*defined in util.c*/

        if(length(pred) < 4 || length(pred) > 6)
        {
                cout << "\n" << "Bad number of terms";
                return FAIL;
        }
        if(strcmp((CAR(nth_list(ONE,pred)))->car.s,"entity"))   /*1st term not entity*/
        {
                cout << "\n" << "entity is expected in beginning";
                return FAIL;
```

continued...

...from previous page

```
}
if(strcmp((CAR(nth_list(THREE,pred)))->car.s,"is-a"))    /*3rd term not is-a*/
{
        cout << "\n" << "is-a connector is expected";
        return FAIL;
}
cons*    class_name = CAR(nth_list(FOUR,pred));
cons*    entity_name = CAR(nth_list(TWO,pred));
if(variablep(class_name) && length(pred) > 4)
{
   cout << "\n" << "No slots can be specified when class_name is a variable";
   return FAIL;
}
if(variablep(class_name) && !variablep(entity_name))
{
        return CASE7;
}
if(!variablep(class_name) && !variablep(entity_name)
                                    && length(pred) == FOUR)
{
        return CASE1;
}
if(!variablep(class_name) && variablep(entity_name)
                                    && length(pred) == FOUR)
{
        return CASE2;
}
if(!variablep(class_name) && !variablep(entity_name)
    && length(pred) == EIGHT && !variablep(CAR(nth_list(EIGHT,pred))))
{
        return CASE5;
}
if(!variablep(class_name) && variablep(entity_name)
    && length(pred) == EIGHT && variablep(CAR(nth_list(EIGHT,pred))))
{
        return CASE4;
}
```

continued...

...from previous page

```
if(!variablep(class_name) && variablep(entity_name)
    && length(pred) == EIGHT && !variablep(CAR(nth_list(EIGHT,pred))))
{
        return CASE6;
}
if(!variablep(class_name) && !variablep(entity_name)
    && length(pred) == EIGHT && variablep(CAR(nth_list(EIGHT,pred))))
{
        return CASE3;
}
}
```

The Mouse Operation

The mouse operation involves design of the following elements: the structure, environment, utility function, and documentation of the mouse operation. For some computers, such as the Macintosh, the mouse operation occurs automatically.

The mouse structure is designed to pop up menus in a designated area on the screen so users can select the menu they want, highlight the area when the mouse passes over it, and hide the mouse when the keyboard is used for input. The following elements are needed in menu design:

- sensitive text (menu) shown on screen

- documentation

- value to return from the screen

- starting column position for the menu area

- starting row position for the menu area

- starting (x,y) mouse position

- other features such as text highlighting

To design the environment for the mouse structure, you need to define the color for any line drawing during mouse tracking, the color of menu items, and the color of the backward screen. Utility functions required for the mouse to operate smoothly include initializing the mouse, showing or hiding the mouse, and highlighting the menu text with a given color. Many of these functions use a low-level system function, such as **%sysint**, that generates a software (internal) interrupt.

- **Mouse_init**: initializes the mouse by putting the screen in graphics mode.

- **Mouse_show**: shows the mouse to the user.

- **Mouse_hide**: hides the mouse from the user.

- **Highlight**: highlights the menu text item with a given color when the mouse passes over that item.

Documentation of the mouse operation is required to inform the user of the mouse button's function, i.e., the meanings of the right, middle, and left buttons. Because mouse operation is system specific, no sample programs are presented here, but you can use commercial mouse programs.

The Window Operation

The window operation organizes the screen skillfully to provide the user with maximum visual comfort and convenience. Designing a window operation involves two major tasks: making windows and operating windows. In Listing 9.4, the window operation is built to meet a given system and application need. This program sample creates a small window to print diagnosis output on the screen.

Listing 9.4: Sample Program for Creating Windows

```c
/*
** WINDOW.C
**
** Supports a little window in the region (1,19) - (78,22) on the screen.
** Diagnostic output from REMOTE will be routed to this window. It is
** deliberately very stupid, and will only accept <CR>, <LF> and <BS> as
** valid control characters. Everything else is output directly to the
** screen in the region specified above.
*/

#include <dos.h>

#define LOX 1
#define HIX 78
#define LOY 19
#define HIY 22
#define WIN_COLOR 0x0E
#define VIDEO 0x10

static int winx, winy,display_page;

wclear()
{
  union REGS in,out;

  in.h.ah = 0x0F;                               /* get current video mode */
  int86(VIDEO,&in,&out);
  display_page = out.h.bh;                       /* current screen */
  out.h.ah = 0x02;                               /* set cursor position */
  out.h.bh = display_page;
  out.h.dl = winx = LOX;                         /* move to home position */
  out.h.dh = winy = HIY;
  int86(VIDEO,&out,&in);
}


/*
** wputs(): window puts: put string to window using BIOS services
*/
```

continued...

...from previous page

```
wputs(s)                                         /* put string using BIOS IO */
char *s;
{
  while (*s) {
    wputc(*s++);
  }
}
wputc(c)
char c;
{
  union REGS regs;

  if (winy < LOY) {
    winy = LOY;
    winx = LOX;
  }
  regs.h.ah = 0x02;                              /* set cursor position */
  regs.h.bh = display_page;
  regs.h.dl = winx;                              /* move to home position */
  regs.h.dh = winy;
  int86(VIDEO,&regs,&regs);
  switch (c) {
    case '\b':
    if (winx > LOX)
      --winx;
    break;

    case '\r':
    winx = LOX;
    break;

    case '\n':
    wnl();
    break;

    default:
    regs.h.ah = 0x09;                            /* draw character */
    regs.h.al = c;
    regs.h.bl = WIN_COLOR;
```

continued...

...from previous page

```
      regs.h.bh = display_page;
      regs.x.cx = 1;                              /* only 1 char */
      int86(VIDEO,&regs,&regs);                   /* dumpit */
      if (++winx > HIX) {
        winx = LOX;
        wnl();
      }
    }
    regs.h.ah = 0x02;                             /* set cursor position */
    regs.h.bh = display_page;
    regs.h.dl = winx;                             /* move to home position */
    regs.h.dh = winy;
    int86(VIDEO,&regs,&regs);
  }

wnl() {
  union REGS in;
  if (winy < HIY) {                               /* not at bottom line */
    ++winy;
  } else {
    winy = HIY;                                   /* force to bottom line */
    in.h.ah  = 0x06;                              /* scroll window up */
    in.h.bh  = display_page;                      /* current screen */
    in.h.al  = 1;                                 /* scroll one line */
    in.h.cl  = LOX;                               /* region. */
    in.h.ch  = LOY;
    in.h.dl  = HIX;
    in.h.dh  = HIY;
    in.h.bh  = WIN_COLOR;
    int86(VIDEO,&in,&in);
  }
}
```

The Menu Operation

The menu operation integrates the mouse and window operations, receiving input from the mouse as well as from the keyboard and returning output streams to windows. Because the number of menu items and restrictions and the type of each item differ in each individual menu group (e.g., classes, units, rules, unstructured database, and variables), common menu operations must be defined to enable the user to select menus in those menu classes. The main menu operations include the following:

- create menus

- initialize menu windows

- erase menus

- choose menus

- display menus

- input menus

Because the menu operation is system specific, no sample program is included here.

Natural Language Front Ends

Natural language (in comparison to computer language) front ends translate the query or prompt from natural language to predicate calculus used efficiently by AI professionals. Predicate calculus (PC) enables you to conveniently calculate the truth of propositions because it consists of a language for expressing propositions and rules for inferring new facts from the facts existing in the knowledge base. However, a PC form is not as understandable to the user as natural language; consequently, natural language front ends can provide a useful service to the user in communicating with the expert system and tool. An unconstrained natural language front end can be extremely complicated. Fortunately, the PC form is fairly concise because it is used to express the following relationships:

1. **Class**

   - A fact about the own-slot value of a class can be expressed as follows:

     (<slot-name> <class name> <value>)

   - A fact about the memberships of a class in another class can be expressed as follows:

     (subclass <class-name1> <class-name2>)

2. **Unit**

   - A fact about the slot value of a unit can be expressed as follows:

     (<slot-name> <unit-name> <value>)

   - A fact about the class of a unit can be expressed as follows:

     (in-class <unit-name> <class-name>)

3. **Variable**

   - A fact about the value of a variable can be expressed as follows:

     (value <variable-name> <variable-value>)

A preliminary natural language front end can be used to add appropriate terms such as "the," "of," "is," "a," and "all" to those relationships so that they can be more understandable to the user. The preliminary front end would allow the following simple translation of the previously shown PC formats:

1. **Class**

   - Own-slot value of a class can be expressed as follows:

     the <slot-name> of <unit-name> is <value>

- Membership of a class in another can be expressed as follows:

  all <class-name1> are <class-name2>

2. **Unit**

   - Slot value of a unit can be expessed as follows:

     the <slot-name> of <unit-name> is <value>

   - The class of a unit can be expressed as follows:

     <unit-name> is a type of <class-name>

3. **Variable**

   - The value of a variable can be expessed as follows:

     <variable name> is <variable-value>

To translate this natural front end to the PC form, you need a simple parsing of the input string to delete the add-on English words such as "the," "of," etc. Commercial packages, such as Language Workbench, can be used to implement transparent, near-natural language templates.

Voice Recognition and Synthesis, Video Display, and Other User Conveniences

Commercial expert systems used in the industrial environment may require a compact, portable man-machine interface unit that provides a video display, keyboard, printer, voice recognition and synthesis, and communications. One such unit has been designed by Honeywell (See Figure 9.2). Some less expensive systems that can be integrated with expert systems in the IBM PC/AT environment are also available. Samples that have been tested include the VocaLink voice recognition system and DecTalk speech synthesis box. VocaLink (Interstate Voice Products, Orange, CA) is relatively inexpensive ($395, complete with PC half card, microphone, and software) and performs well under ideal conditions. DecTalk (Digital Equipment Corporation) has eight preprogrammed voices and a virtually infinite number of user definable voices, and can convert ASCII strings sent to it via a standard COM port to speech. IBM, Texas Instruments, and Kurzweil AI also offer similar products that can be installed to provide better man-machine interface.

Figure 9.2   Honeywell's design concept for compact, portable man-machine
             user interface

DEALING WITH UNCERTAIN KNOWLEDGE

In developing facts and rules for expert systems, it becomes clear that data and rules obtained from experienced specialists are somewhat uncertain; they may describe some rules as "maybe," "sometimes," "often," or "not quite certain about the conclusion." You need some methods to handle these types of probabilistic statements. Further, expert systems, like human experts, may need to draw inferences based on unavailable, unknown, or uncertain information. Unavailable or unknown information is resolved by allowing rules to fail if the information needed is critical in evaluating the premise, i.e., the information needed is in the condition (if) statements connected by **and**. When **if** statements are connected by **or**, the absence of one or more of them will not affect the outcome of the rule.

Theoretical Approaches

As discussed in Chapter 1, uncertainty of facts or rules can be represented by the use of either the Bayesian theory or the theory of belief function. The latter is also called the Dempster-Shafer Theory of Evidence in the AI community. Because of circumstances and assumptions regarding facts and rules, the two probabilistic judgment approaches are often modified to meet the need of the circumstances. Following are two examples:

- The case of PROSPECTOR in which a set of quasi-Bayesian rules for combining probabilities were used.

- The case of MYCIN, in which an ad hoc set of rules for combining belief functions (that were called "certainty factors, or CFs," in MYCIN) were established.

The Bayesian and belief function approaches will find their respective niches in the development of expert systems, and they will fit only certain narrow kinds of problems. In general, the Bayesian approach will function more efficiently in representing probability judgment in expert systems that are applied under constant conditions so that solutions are determined randomly with known chances such as in the diagnostics of physical, man-made machineries. Belief function designs, on the other hand, will be more effective in representing uncertainty of knowledge involving personal experience in a specialty field, such as medicine.

However, modification of either approach is often required to fully represent the flexibility of human probability judgment. In any modification of the two probability approaches, you must carefully establish rules for the following issues:

- how uncertainty will be represented

- how uncertainty probabilities will be combined

- how premise clauses are connected and how they will affect the joint probability

As long as these issues are resolved, the modification will represent uncertainty in knowledge.

In some cases, the uncertainty is approximated through a "pseudo-Bayesian" function that maintains separate measures of belief (positive) and disbelief (negative) for each hypothesis. A single-valued certainty factor is computed from the belief values on the basis of a linear weighting function that combines two sets of weights; one set of weights is collected from the user (representing the user's priorities on the various factors), and the other set of weights is built into the system, allowing for a predetermined bias of judgment. All values of certainty factors are "translated" into English before they are displayed to the user with terms such as "slightly," "significantly," or "definitely."

Implementation of Uncertainty in C

Uncertainty arises from two sources: premises (facts or data) and rules themselves. A MYCIN approach is used for computing certainties of conjunctions (**and** propositions) and disjunctions (**or** propositions). In this system, the CF (certainty factor) of the rule, established upon the creation of the rule, is multiplied by the CF of the individual predicates used in the proposition to establish the CF of the conclusion. In any conjunction, the minimum CF of all the **and**ed facts is used as the CF of the whole. In disjunctions, the CF of the first predicate of the **or** proposition that is achieved is used. Thus, the overall certainty of a rule's conclusion uses the following formula:

CF(rule) * CF(premise) = CF(conclusion)

where

CF(premise) =
      premise case if,
          (or x y) = = > Cf of first x or y found to be TRUE
          (and x y) = = > Minimum CF of x and y

Examples

Facts:

```
(p 1)   [CF = 0.5]
(p 2)   [CF = 0.3]
(p 3)   [CF = 1.0]
```

Rules:

```
if: (p ?x)
then: (q ?x)
CF: 0.9
```

(and (p 1) (p 3)) = = > [CF = 0.5]

(or (and (p 1) (p 3)) (p 2)) = = > [CF = 0.5]

If you added (p 4) into the knowledge base and fired the rules, (q 4) would be obtained and added to the knowledge base, with a CF of 0.45 ($0.5 \times 0.9 = 0.45$).

For conjunctive premises, the certainty factor for the combined premise is the minimum of all certainty factors associated with each individual premise. Listing 9.5 shows a sample program for obtaining this minimum.

On the other hand, you can modify Listing 9.5 to derive a program for the combined certainty factor for disjunctive premises.

The uncertainty regarding a rule can be incorporated straightforwardly by multiplying the certainty factor of the rule by the certainty factor of the combined premises. As shown in Listing 8.2 (backward chaining, Chapter 8), this can be done as follows:

```
ret_pair->certainty = rp->certainty * temp1->certainty;
```

More sophisticated manipulation of certainty factors can be performed if you believe that autocorrelation exits between the rules and their premises.

Listing 9.5: Sample Program to Compute Minimum Certainty

```c
/*
** MIN.C
**
***/


#include <stdio.h>
#include "cons.h"
#include "goal.h"



/*-------------------------------------------------Min()-----------------*/

/*
**      Get the minimum certainty between two.
*/

double Min(cert1,cert2,cert3)
double cert1,cert2,*cert3;
{

        if(cert1 <= cert2)
        {
                (*cert3) = cert1;
        }
        else
        {
                (*cert3) = cert2;
        }
}
```

334

SUMMARY

- User interface is a weak but critical element of expert systems. Many current expert systems are equipped with menus and explanation modules to allow users to query expert systems and examine their output statements. Major research efforts have been undertaken in natural language interface, voice recognition, and voice synthesis to make expert systems more user friendly.

- It is also important to consider uncertainty in representing knowledge. Both Bayesian and belief-function approaches can be used under different circumstances. Modification of the approach is usually required to fully represent the flexibility of human probability judgment.

- The man-machine interface mechanism produces dialogue between the computer and the user. The current expert system may be equipped with menus or a natural language to facilitate its use and an explanation module to allow the user to challenge and examine the reasoning process underlying the system's answers.

- Menus are groups of simplified instructional statements that appear on the computer screen. Options can be selected by the user by pushing designated buttons on a mouse or designated keys on the keyboard. The user does not need to type instructions. A semi-natural or fully natural language interface is more sophisticated than a menu interface; it allows computer systems to accept inputs and produce outputs in a language closer to a conventional language such as English. Several expert systems incorporate primitive forms of natural language in their user interface to facilitate knowledge base development. Explanation modules generate output statements of expert systems in language that can be understood by noncomputer-professional users. Most expert systems are equipped with this type of module.

- Uncertainty arises from two sources, premises (facts or data) and rules themselves. A MYCIN approach is used for computing certainties of conjunctions (**and** propositions) and disjunctions (**or** propositions). In this system, the CF (certainty factor) of the rule, established upon the creation of the rule, is multiplied by the CF of the individual predicates used in the proposition to establish the CF of the conclusion. In any conjunction, the minimum CF of all the **and**ed facts is used as the CF of the whole. In disjunctions, the CF of the first predicate of the **or** proposition that is achieved is used.

REFERENCES

Lindsay, Robert K., B. G. Buchanan, E. A. Feigenbaum, et al. "Applications of artificial intelligence for organic chemistry." *The DENDRAL Project*. McGraw-Hill, 1980.

MACSYMA group. The MACSYMA reference manual. Computer Science Dept., Massachusetts Institute of Technology, 1974.

Swartout, W. "Explaining and justifying expert consulting programs." *IJCAI 7*, 1974, 815-822.

R. Davis. "Interactive transfer of expertise: Acquisition of new inference rules." *Artificial Intelligence*. vol. 12, 1979, 121-157.

Davis, Randall. "Expert systems: Where are we? And where do we go from here?" *The AI Magazine*, vol. 3, no. 2, Spring 1982.

Blaise Computing, Inc. *CView*, a commercial software package providing a mechanism for creating forms. Berkeley, CA (415) 540-541.

Business & Professional Software, Inc. *BPS Business Graphics*, a personal computer graphics package. Cambridge, MA, 1985.

Carbonell, J. G., W. M. Boggs, and M. L. Mauldin. "The EXCALIBUR project: A natural language interface to expert systems." *Proceedings, International Joint Conference on Artificial Intelligence*. vol. 26, 1983, 653-65.

P. J. Hayes and J. G. Carbonell. "Multi-start construction-specific parsing for flexible data B query and update." *Proceedings of the Seventh International Joint Conference on Artificial Intelligence*, August 1981, 432-439.

Hayes, P. J. and J. G. Carbonell. "Multi-strategy parsing and its role in robust man-machine communication." Tech. report CMU-CS-81-118. Computer Science Department, Carnegie-Mellon University, May 1981.

McDermott, J. "XSEL: a computer sales person's assistant." J. E. Hayes, D. Michie, and Y. H. Pao (eds.) *Machine Intelligence*, 10, Chichester, England: Horwood, 1982, 325-337.

McDermott, J. "R1: a rule-based configurer of computer systems." *Artificial Intelligence*, vol. 19, no. 1, September 1982.

Brodie Associates. *Language Workbench*, a programmer's toolkit for developing natural language interfaces to application softwares. Kurzweil AI (Waltham, MA), 1986.

Hendrix, G. G., E. D. Sacerdoti, and Slocum. "Developing a natural language interface to Com Data." Tech. report, Artificial Intelligence Center, International, 1976.

Hendrix, G. G. "The LIFER manual: A guide to build practical natural language interfaces." Tech. report, Tech. note 138, SRI, 1977.

Gasching, J. "PROSPECTOR: An expert system for mineral exploration." *Machine Intelligence*. Infotech State of the Art Report 9, no. 3, 1981.

Shortliffe, E. H. *Computer-based medical consultations: MYCIN*. New York: Elsevier, 1976.

Gordon, J. and E. H. Shortliffe, "The Dempster-Shafer theory of evidence." In B. G. Buchanan and E. H. Shortliffe, eds. *Rule-based expert systems: The MYCIN experiments of the Stanford Heuristic Programming project*, Reading, MA: Addison-Wesley, 1984, 272-292.

Shafer, G. (1985a). "Belief functions and possibility measures." In J. C. Bezdek, ed. *The Analysis of Fuzzy Information*, vol. 1, CRC Press, 1985.

Charniak E., and D. McDermott. *Introduction to Artificial Intelligence*, Reading, MA: Addison-Wesley, 1985.

Winston, P. *Artificial intelligence*, 2nd ed., Reading, MA: Addison-Wesley, 1984.

McCarthy, J. and P. J. Hayes. "Some philosophical problems from the standpoint of artificial intelligence." In B. Meltzer and D. Michie, eds. *Machine intelligence, 4*. Halsted Press, 1969, 463-502.

Vere, S. *Planning in time: Windows and durations for activities and goals*. Pasadena, CA: JPL, Nov. 1981.

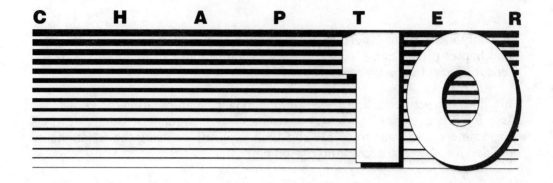

MAKING A C/C++ LIBRARY STRUCTURE FOR EXPERT SYSTEMS

The components of an expert system have been discussed in Chapters 7, 8, and 9. This chapter proposes a C/C++ library structure that can be modified by the user for efficient expert system development.

This library structure includes a set of functions for manipulating the knowledge base, inference engine, and user interface. It is intended for applications programmers who want to create run time applications using the functionality provided for database access and reasoning.

The scope of the library includes 1) the set of functions designed to access and modify data structures and 2) the set of functions tailored for the creation of end-user applications. Using the library functions, the programmer can create and modify knowledge base objects, natural language templates, and knowledge sources.

Limited error checking of the library files is accomplished when the files are loaded. When a name conflict occurs for objects of the same type, the last name used will replace any reference to the previous name; otherwise, an error will be displayed in the notification window. In addition, when a value does not satisfy a constraint, the slot does not assume that value and will remain unbound until a proper value is input.

Topics in this chapter include the library syntax, summary of library functions, object manipulation, reasoning, natural language, file interaction, and special applications.

THE LIBRARY SYNTAX

The following notation will be used to describe the library functions:

Uppercase	Function names; required verbatim text. Any combination of uppercase and lowercase letters is allowed.
Lowercase/*italics*	Specification for item. Replace lowercase letters with desired item of specific type.
[ ]	Item in brackets is optional (do not enter brackets themselves).
|	**or**. Select one item on either side of the vertical bar.

< >	Constraints for required inserted values.
*	Repetition. Indicates more than one (or none) of the preceding items may be specified.
"	String designator. Inserted text should be surrounded by double quotes.
()	Regular LISP-like parentheses.
{}	Braces separating **or** options from required text. **Note**: these braces are for notation only — not for use in commands.

In addition to the previous notations, the following special lowercase specifications will be used by a number of commands:

string =	*"any-message"*
slot-specs =	*(slot-spec*)*
slot-spec =	*(slotname [slot-attrib *])*
slot-attrib =	:CONSTRAINT *constraint-type* |
	:VALUE *value-satisfying-constraint* |
	:DESTINATION {MEMBER | OWN} |
	:DOC *string* |
	:PROMPT *string* |
	:CERTAINTY *certainty-number*
	:MANDATORY? {T | Nil}
filename =	*dos filename string where backslashes are duplicated.*
	{c:\autoexec.bat == > "c:\\autoexec.bat"}
var-subs =	*(var-instantiation *)*
var-instantiation =	*(var-name . value)*
var-name =	*?name*
multiple-var-subs =	*(var-subs *)*
cert-list =	*(certainty-number *)*
boolean =	T | NIL

The syntax appears to be LISP-like by design because LISP expressions are customarily easier to use for representing knowledge and concepts.

KEYS-and-VALS

Many of the command format descriptions of the library functions contain KEYS-and-VALS. KEYS-and-VALS are any number of optional keyword and value combinations that may be required arguments for the command. Each of the key-and-val combinations is in the following format:

> *:all-caps-keyword   value-satisfying-constraint*

Thus, if KEYS-and-VALS is in the command description, substitute any number of the KEYS definitions that follow the command syntax. As an example of the KEYS-and-VALS notation, the syntax definition for *slot-spec* could be abbreviated as follows:

slot-spec =   (*slotname* [*KEYS-and-VALS*])
with KEYS =   :CONSTRAINT *constraint-type*
                        :VALUE *value-satisfying-constraint*
                        :DESTINATION {MEMBER | OWN}
                        :DOC *string*
                        :WHEN-NEEDED {*LIBRARY-expression* | *value*}
                        :PROMPT *string*
                        :CERTAINTY *certainty-number*
                        :MANDATORY? {T | Nil}

Following are examples of slot-specs using KEYS-and-VALS:

```
(height :constraint number :doc "Height slot" :certainty
0.5)

(sex :constraint (member (m f)) :destination member)
```

SUMMARY OF COMMANDS

Summary of Library Functions

The proposed library functions include five groups: object manipulation, reasoning, natural language, file interaction, and special applications.

Object Manipulation

DELETE-LOCAL-CLASS-SLOT   Delete a local class slot.

CREATE-ENTITY   Create an entity object.

CREATE-LOCAL-ENTITY-SLOT   Add a slot to an entity.

DELETE-ENTITY   Delete an entity object.

DELETE-LOCAL-ENTITY-SLOT   Delete an entity slot.

CREATE-VARIABLE   Create a variable object.

DELETE-VARIABLE   Delete a variable object.

CLEAR-VARIABLES   Delete all variable objects.

CREATE-RULE   Create a rule structure.

DELETE-RULE   Delete a rule structure.

CLEAR-PKB   Remove all unstructured predicates.

Reasoning

ASSERT   Assert a proposition.

STASH   Stash a proposition.

UNSTASH   Remove a proposition.

ACHIEVE   Achieve a proposition.

ACHIEVE-ALL	Find all solutions to proposition.
LOOKUP	Achieve proposition, without rules.
LOOKUP-ALL	Achieve all solutions to proposotion, without rules.
QUERY-FIRST	Find first solution to proposition.
QUERY-NEXT	Find next solution to proposition.
QUERY-ALL	Find all solutions to proposition.
QUERY-RESET	Reset First/Next solutions to proposition.
REASSERT-CLASS	Assert class object.
REASSERT-ENTITY	Assert entity object.
REASSERT-VARIABLE	Assert variable object.
REASSERT-SLOT	Assert class or entity slot value.
REASSERT-CLASS-MEMBER-SLOT	Assert all inherit slots of class.
REASSERT-RULE	Assert RULE structure.
SET-PARAMETERS	Set system parameters.

Natural Language

DEFINE-NL-TEMPLATE	Specify natural language translation.
DELETE-NL-TEMPLATE	Remove natural language translation.
CLEAR-NL-TEMPLATES	Remove all natural language translations.

File Interaction

READ-LIBRARY-DATABASE	Read the library function file.
WRITE-LIBRARY-DATABASE	Write fact base to file.
READ-DBASE3-CLASS	Read dBASE III file into class object.
WRITE-DBASE3-CLASS	Write CLASS obect to dBASE III file.
READ-LOTUS123-CLASS	Read Lotus 1-2-3 spreadsheet to a class.

Special Applications

DEFINE-INTERFACE	Define an application interface.
DEFINE-MODE	Define a command mode for interface.
RUN-MODE	Execute a command mode.
DEFPROCEDURE	Define a sequence of the library commands.
START-HELP	Begin top-level help for application.
QUIT-INTERFACE	Exit an interface.
REDRAW-SCREEN	Redraw application screen.
CLEAR-OUTPUT-SCREEN	Clear main window of screen.
USER-PAUSE	Pause until user presses key.
NOTIFY	Print notification statement.

OBJECT MANIPULATION

Function: CREATE-LOCAL-ENTITY-SLOT *entity-name slot-spec*

Description: Creates an :OWN slot in an pre-defined entity. Any attempt to create a slot with a name of a slot that already exists will abort the command and signal an error.

Example: `(Create-local-entity-slot 'john '(occupation :constraint :name))`

Result: *slot-name*

if successful. If unsuccessful,

NIL

Function: DELETE-ENTITY *name*

Description: Deletes the named entity from the knowledge base.

Example: `(Delete-entity 'john)`

Result: *entity-name*

if successful.

NIL

if unsuccessful.

Function: DELETE-LOCAL-ENTITY-SLOT *entity-name slot-name*

Description: Deletes a local slot in the specified entity.

Example: `(Delete-local-entity-slot 'john 'occupation)`

Result: *slot-name*

if successful. If unsuccessful,

NIL

Function: CREATE-VARIABLE *name [keys-and-vals]*

KEYS: :VALUE *value*
        :CONSTRAINT *constraint-type*
        :CERTAINTY *certainty*
        :ASSERT? *boolean*

Description: Defines a variable object and places it in the knowledge base. Will assert variable value (depending on CF parameter) if ASSERT? is T.

Example: `(Create-variable 'count :value 0 :constraint :number)`

Result: *var-name* if successful

Function: DELETE-VARIABLE *name*

Description: Deletes a variable object.

Example: `(Delete-Variable 'count)`

Result: NIL

Function: CLEAR-VARIABLES

Description: Removes all variables from the working knowledge base. The function always succeeds.

Example: `(clear-variables)`

Result: NIL

Function:	CREATE-RULE *name* :PREMISE *proposition* :CONCLUSION *assertable-proposition* *[keys-and-vals]*
	
	KEYS: :ACTION *LIBRARY-expression*
	    :CERTAINTY *certainty-number*
	    :FIRED? *boolean*

Description:	Creates a rule object and places it in the knowledge base. The premise can be any proposition, but the conclusion must be an assertable proposition. Create-Rule will give an error if any of the variable terms in the conclusion are not present in the premise. The default for the direction of a rule is :BACKWARD.
Example:	```(Create-rule 'is-tall :rule-set 'person-rules :premise '(and (height ?x ?h) (>>> ?h 6.0)) :conclusion '(is-tall ?x) :certainty 0.9 :firing :single)```
Result:	*name*

Function:	DELETE-RULE *name*
Description:	Deletes a rule
Example:	```(Delete-rule 'is-tall)```
Result:	*rule* if successful. NIL if unsuccessful

Function:	CLEAR-PKB
Description:	Clear the predicate knowledge base (pkb). Always successful.
Example:	`(clear-pkb)`
Result:	NIL

REASONING

Function:	ASSERT *assertable-pc-or-nl-exp [keys-and-vals]*
	Keys: :CERTAINTY *certainty-factor* :STASH *boolean*
Description:	Asserts proposition. Two keys: -stash [Default: T]: If value = T, proposition is stashed and forward chained. If value = nil, value is not stashed, but will be forward chained. Note that asserting a conjunction is equivalent to asserting each element of the expression; asserting a negation is equivalent to unassertion; asserting a disjunction is not legal [Default: 1.0].
Example:	`(assert '(p 1) :certainty .4 :stash nil)` will stash the predicate (p 1) with a certainty of 0.4.
Result:	*assertable-pc-or-nl-expression*

Function:	STASH *pc-or-nl-exp [certainty-number]*
Description:	Stashes *pc-or-nl-exp* by first checking entities and classes, then variables, for unifications with predicate facts and, second, changing the appropriate slot values; if not found, stashes in pkb. Optional certainty factor.
Example:	`(stash '(p 1) .4)`
Result:	*pc-or-nl-expression*

Function:	UNSTASH *pc-or-nl-exp*
Description:	Unstashes *exp* by first checking entities and classes, then variables for unifications with predicate facts; if not found, removes in pkb.
Example:	(unstash '(p 1))
Result:	*predicate*

if found. Otherwise, the example function returns

NIL

Function:	ACHIEVE *pc-exp* *[prev-subs]*
	prev-subs = multiple-var-subs
Description:	Achieve any pc/nl expression (query). *Prev-subs* is optional previous substitutions list. If Back-Chain parameter enabled, function backchains.
Example:	(achieve '(p ?x))
	(achieve '(p ?x) '(((?x . 1)) ((?x . 2))))
Result:	NIL

if unsuccessful. If successful, the example function returns two values:

1) *var-subs*
2) *certainty*

Function: ACHIEVE-ALL *pc-exp*

Description: Achieves all solutions to any pc/nl expression (query).

Result: NIL

               if not successful. If successful, the example function returns two values:

               1) Solutions: *var-subs*
               2) Certainty list of each solution: *cert-list*

Example:
```
(achieve-all '(p ?x))
```

Result:
```
(stash '(and (p 1) (p 2) (p 3)))
(achieve-all '(p ?x))
==>>  (((?x . 3)) ((?x . 2)) ((?x . 1)))
         (1.0 1.0 1.0)
```

Function: LOOKUP *pc-exp [prev-subs]*

               prev-subs = *multiple-var-subs*

Description: Lookup allows the programmer to ascertain whether or not the goal is in the fact base only. It is equivalent to achieving the goal with the Back-Chain parameter off.

Example:
```
(lookup '(p ?x))
```

Result: NIL

               if unsuccessful. If successful, the example function returns two values:

               1) *var-subs*
               2) *certainty*

Function: LOOKUP-ALL *pc-exp*

Description: Looks up all solutions (no backchaining) to any pc/nl expression (query).

Example: `(lookup-all '(p ?x))`

Result: NIL

if unsuccessful. If successful, the example function returns two values:

1) Solutions: *var-subs*
2) Certainty-list of each solution: *cert-list*

Function: QUERY-FIRST *pc-exp*

Description: Finds the first satisfaction of the selected goal, establishing a series of previous satisfactions that have to be cleared. Stores *Pc-exp* goal and first substitutions for use of Query-Next to find others.

Example: `(query-first '(p ?x))`

Result: NIL

if unsuccessful. If successful, the example function returns two values:

1) *var-subs*
2) *certainty*

Function: QUERY-NEXT

Description: Finds the first satisfaction of the previous goal that is not a member of the internal previous substitutions list. Adds found substitutions to goal-substitutions list for additional use of Query-Next.

Example: `(query-next)`

Result: NIL

    if unsuccessful. If successful, the example function returns two values:

1) *var-subs*
2) *certainty*

Function: QUERY-ALL *pc-exp*

Description: Finds all satisfactions for the given goal and returns a list of all the instantiations of all variables. Equivalent to Achieve-All, except that recent goal used by Query-First and Query-Next is cleared.

Example: `(query-all '(p ?x))`

Result: NIL

    if unsuccessful. If successful, the example function returns two values:

1) Solutions: *var-subs*
2) Certainty-list of each solution: *cert-list*

Function:	QUERY-RESET
Description:	Resets the internal goal and previous substitutions list to NIL for the use of Query-First and Query-Next.
Example:	`(query-reset)`
Result:	NIL

Function:	REASSERT-CLASS *class-name*
Description:	Asserts all the slot values of a class

(<slot-name> <class> <value>)

and the class-subclass relation,

(subclass <class> <superclass>)

thereby forward chaining on the entire class. Used when class is modified and values should be asserted over entire knowledge base (especially the rule base).

Example:	`(reassert-class 'person)`
Result:	*class-name*

Function:	REASSERT-ENTITY *entity-name*
Description:	Asserts all the slot values of an entity

(<slot-name> <entity> <value>)

and the class-entity relation,

(<entity> is-a <class>)

thereby forward chaining on the entire entity. Used when entity is modified and values should be asserted over entire knowledge base (especially the rule base).

Example: `(reassert-entity 'joe)`

Result: *entity-name*

Function: REASSERT-VARIABLE *variable-name*

Description: Assert on the value of a variable. Asserts the structured variable predicate,

(value-of <variable-name> <value>)

thereby forward chaining on the variable value. Used when variable is modified and values should be asserted over entire knowledge base (especially the rule base).

Example: `(reassert-variable 'count)`

Result: *variable-name*

Function: REASSERT-SLOT *class-or-entity-name slot-name*

Description: Asserts the value of a slot of the specified entity or class. Asserts the structured entity/class-slot predicate,

(<slot-name> <class/entity-name> <value>)

thereby forward chaining on the value of the slot. Used when slot value is modified and value should be asserted over the entire knowledge base.

Result: *slot-name*

Function: REASSERT-CLASS-MEMBER-SLOT *class-name slot-name*

Description: For all entities of the class (and its subclasses) specified, asserts the value of the slot specified by *slot-name*. In other words, the function asserts the structured entity-slot predicate

(<slot-name> <class/entity-name> <value>)

in every member entity of the class, thereby forward chaining on the values of the slots. Generally used when a rule is created that will use the specified slot to apply a single class's slot values to that rule.

Result: *slot-name*

Function: REASSERT-RULE *rule-name*

Description: Reassert-Rule finds all unifications to the premise of the rule, and for those found, applies them to the conclusion of the rule, and fires the rule. Equivalent to Achieve-All on the premise, substituting all substitutes into the conclusion, and asserting the conclusion. Any rules that fire will also evaluate the action of the rule. Command is used when a new rule should be applied to the entire knowledge base to conclude all possible solutions to the rule.

Example: `(reassert-rule 'is-tall)`

Result: *rule-name*

Function: SET-PARAMETERS [*keys-and-vals*]

KEYS: :NAT-LANG *boolean*
    :TRACE {*boolean* | VERBOSE}
    :JUSTIFY *boolean*
    :FWD-CHAIN *boolean*
    :BACK-CHAIN *boolean*

Description: Sets the parameters for an application. The settings for each parameter must be either "t" or "nil" (except Trace, where "verbose" is also allowed). All parameters not specified are not affected. Can include any of the following, in any order:

nat-lang	predicate calculus or natural language
trace	debugging procedures, list search
justify	store search results for justification
fwd-chain	forward chain on assertions, creations, editing
back-chain	backward chain on queries, using rules.

Example:
```
(set-parameters :nat-lang nil :back-chain t :fwd-chain
t :justify nil :trace nil)
```

Result: NIL

NATURAL LANGUAGE

Function: DEFINE-NL-TEMPLATE *pc-exp* *"nl-exp"*

Description: Defines a template for the translation of predicate calculus expressions into natural language (or vice versa). If natural language parameter is set, all references to *pc-exp* will appear in *nl-exp* form.

Example:
```
(define-nl-template '(subsidiary ?x ?y)
"?x is a subsidiary company of ?y")
```

Result: T

Function: DELETE-NL-TEMPLATE *pc-exp*

Description: Removes one previously defined natural language template.

Example:
```
(delete-nl-template '(subsidiary ?x ?y))
```

Result: List of remaining templates.

Function:	CLEAR-NL-TEMPLATES
Description:	Removes all user-defined natural language templates.
Example:	`(clear-nl-templates)`
Result:	NIL

FILE INTERACTION

Function:	READ-LIBRARY-DATABASE *filename*
Description:	Loads an application environment (library file) into a knowledge base. If *filename* not specified, user will be prompted.
Example:	`(read-bpl-database "c:\\iq200\\examples\\icsint1.bpl")`

Function:	WRITE-LIBRARY-DATABASE *filename* [:SAVEABLE *objects*]
	:ALL-KB | :ALL-CLASSES | :CLASS | :ALL-RULE-SETS | :RULE-SET | :PKB | :VARIABLES | :ALL-TEMPLATES
Description:	Saves a knowledge base (classes, rules, entities, variables, etc.) into a library file. If *filename* not specified, user will be prompted. Saveable feature is used to save only a portion of the knowledge base (group of objects).
Example:	`(write-bpl-database "c:\\iq200\\examples\\ics.bpl")`

Function:	READ-DBASE3-CLASS *class-name* :FILENAME *filename* [KEYS-and-VALS]

	KEYS: :SUPERCLASS *superclass*
	     :SLOT-WITH-ENTITY-NAME *name*
	     :DOCUMENTATION *string*

Description: Creates the specified class by reading a dBASE III file. Fields become slots; records become entities. If :slot-with-entity-name is specified, entities will assume names from slots of dBASE III file; if it is not supplied, the entity names of the dbase3 class will be created, using the number of the proper record appended to the class name. If superclass is not specified, the class will be created as a subclass of Basic-Class.

Example:

```
(read-dbase3-class 'doctors :filename
"c:\\dbase\\doctors.dbf" :superclass 'person)
```

Function: WRITE-DBASE3-CLASS *class-name* :FILENAME *filename*

Description: Dbase3 class is written to the file specified. All entities become records, written in order of creation in IQ-200 (which is represented in all class-entity displays). Slots become fields.

Example:

```
(write-dbase3-class 'person :filename "c:\\dbase\\people.dbf")
```

Function: READ-LOTUS123-CLASS *class-name*
:FILENAME *filename*
:SLOT-NAMES-ROW *integer*
[:SUPERCLASS *class-name*]
[:DELETED-ROWS *list*] [:DELETED-COLUMNS *list*]

Description: Reads a Lotus 1-2-3 spreadsheet file into a class. Superclass is Basic-Class unless specified using the :Superclass option. Slot names of entities created are from the *:slot-names-row* specified.

Example:

```
(read-lotus123-class 'Sales-Records
:filename "c:\\123\\ware.wk1"
:slot-names-row 0
:deleted-rows '(1)
:deleted-columns '(1))
```

SPECIAL APPLICATIONS

Function: DEFINE-INTERFACE [*keys-and-vals*]

         Keys: :BANNER *string*
              :HOT-KEYS *hot-key-list*
              :HELP-FILE-PATHNAME *filename*

         hot-key-list = ((*keychord-integer LIBRARY-function*) *)

Description: Define-Interface is used to define an application interface. The banner will appear at the top of the screen of the new application. The help-file-pathname is used to access help for the application. Hot-keys are special functions that occur when the designated keychord is pressed (The F1 key is usually Help — keychord integer 224). To complete the application, modes and procedures must be defined.

Example:

```
(define-interface 'inventory-control
:banner " Inventory Control System "
:hot-keys '((224 (start-help 'inv-control))
(238 (quit-interface))
(225 (user-start-application-interface))
(#\c-d (dos)) (#\c-r (redraw-screen)))
:help-file-pathname "c:\\iq200\\examples\\icshelp.txt")
```

Function: DEFINE-MODE *interface-name mode-name docstring*
          command-list
        command-list = (*interface-function* *)
        interface-function = (*command-name-string LIBRARY-function*)

Description: Each application must have a mode named Toplevel-Mode that will replace the System Menu of the User-Interface; all other modes defined using the Define-Mode function are submodes of the application, and will place commands in the Mode Menu. Every mode contains a number of commands, which are defined by a *command-name-string* that will appear in the Command Menu and a library function that will be called when the command is selected by the user.

The command for running a submode (replacing the Mode Menu with the commands of a desired submode) is Run-Mode.

Note: Each command menu is 78 characters long. Attempts to define a mode whose sum of *command-name-string* lengths is greater than 78 characters will signify an error. In this case, either shorten the command strings or group similar commands into a submode.

Example:

```
(define-mode 'inventory-control
'TOPLEVEL-MODE "Inventory Toplevel"
'(("Dealership" (run-mode 'dealership-operations-mode))
("Warehouse" (run-mode 'warehouse-operations-mode))
("System" (run-mode 'system-operations-mode))
("Help" (start-help 'inv-control))
("Quit" (quit-interface))))
```

Function: RUN-MODE *mode-name*

Description: Run-Mode initiates a mode. When a mode is initiated, the *command-name-strings* given in the definition of the mode (another library command) will be placed in the Mode Menu. These items will become "sensitive" — each activates the corresponding library function in the Define-Mode command.

Example:

```
(run-mode 'dealership-operations-mode)
```

Function: DEFPROCEDURE *name library-function-list*

Description: Defprocedure is used to create new library functions; each new function is a list of system- or developer-defined library functions. To create a library function, just specify a name for the function and a list of the library functions that will be evaluated when the function is called. These functions are useful for creating mode commands, rule actions, eval functions, etc.

Example:
```
(defprocedure Order-Part
(reassert-rule 'order-new-part)
(user-pause)
```

Function: START-HELP *help-topic-name*

Description: Start-Help will display the specified help topic on the screen, with the subtopics of the topic in a menu list at the bottom of the screen.

Example:
```
(start-help 'inv-control)
```

Function: QUIT-INTERFACE

Description: Quit-Interface will exit from the application. The application will remain intact.

Example:
```
(quit-interface)
```

Function: REDRAW-SCREEN

Description: Redraw-Screen cleans up the screen by redisplaying the borders and menus and clearing output windows.

Example:
```
(redraw-screen)
```

Function: CLEAR-OUTPUT-SCREEN

Description: Clears the main output screen (main window) of the application.

Example:
```
(clear-output-screen)
```

Function:	USER-PAUSE
Description:	User-Pause temporarily suspends IQ-200 action until the user presses any key on the keyboard. The user is prompted with the following:

" Press any key or mouse button to continue "

Example:	(user-pause)

Function:	NOTIFY *string* [*format-arg* *]
Description:	Displays string in the monitor window. Strings may contain two format options:

~A   ASCII substitution
~%   New line

For every ~A in the string, there must be a corresponding item in the substitutions.

Example:	(notify "~%The price of ~A is ~A." ?stock ?cost)

If ?stock in IBM and ?cost is 35, this command print out, on a newline:

The price of IBM is 35.

SUMMARY

- This library structure includes a set of functions for manipulating the knowledge base, inference engine, and user interface. It is intended for applications programmers who want to create run-time applications using the functionality provided for database access and reasoning.

- The scope of the library includes the following:

  1) the set of functions designed to access and modify data structures
  2) the set of functions tailored toward the creation of end-user applications.

- Using the library functions, the programmer can create and modify knowledge base objects, natural language templates, and knowledge sources.

- The proposed library functions include five groups: object manipulation, reasoning, natural language, file interaction, and special applications.

REFERENCES

Baldur Systems Corporation. *User's Manual for IQ-200: Intelligent Data Base Communication*, Hayward, CA, 1988.

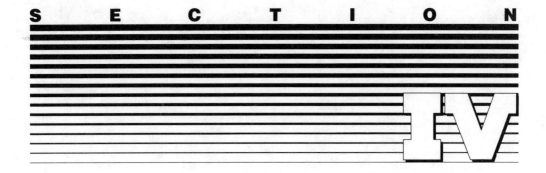

EXPERT SYSTEMS
APPLICATIONS

Section IV discusses methods to build expert systems by using the components developed in the previous chapters and other available packages and examines issues concerning delivery of expert systems.

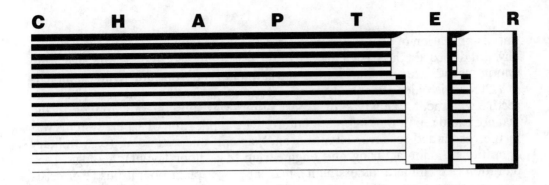

EXPERT SYSTEMS APPLICATIONS AND APPROACHES

Initial application of expert systems was in the diagnosis and treatment of human physical disorders; the basic purpose of these systems was to determine what the symptoms indicate and what remedial treatment is appropriate. One example is MYCIN, which identifies the type of infection a patient has and prescribes corrective treatment. This type of expert system was subsequently applied to the diagnosis and repair of equipment failure. The application of expert systems was further expanded to cover situation analysis and understanding (e.g., military operations), manufacturing and engineering (e.g., floor layout), geological exploration (e.g., mineral assessment), nuclear power plant operations (e.g., crisis management), software development (e.g., automatic programming), and financial services (e.g., bank loan applications). However, not every problem can be solved with expert systems; expert systems have their own limitations. For example, current expert systems are too slow, cost too much to develop, and are unable to recognize their own knowledge boundaries.

Topics in this chapter include tasks in which expert system technology may be helpful, two case studies, expert system limitations and difficulties, expert system development rules, and applying expert system technology to improve software programs.

TASKS IN WHICH EXPERT SYSTEM TECHNOLOGY MAY BE HELPFUL

The primary historical application areas can be classified into industrial applications (including chemistry, computer systems, electronics, engineering, geology, manufacturing, and other related areas such as space technology), medicine, military, information management, law, and agriculture. The most successful task types are control/monitoring, debugging, design, diagnosis, instruction, interpretation, planning, and prediction. Well-documented examples are used in this discussion. (The development status indicated in references to these examples is subject to change without notice). See Appendix C for representative expert systems.

Control/Monitoring

Control and monitoring systems usually perform sequential tasks and are closely integrated. Monitoring is required for effective control, and control is usually the ultimate objective of monitoring. The function of control/monitoring is the continuous interpretation of signals and activation of alarms when intervention is needed. Expert systems have been developed to perform control and monitoring for computer systems, nuclear power plants, and medicine. Examples include PTRANS, YES/MVS, and REACTOR. PTRANS, developed jointly by Digital Equipment Corporation and Carnegie-Mellon University, assists managers in controlling the manufacture and distribution of Digital Equipment computer systems. It monitors the progress of the technicians in the implementation of assembling plans in accordance with customer orders, diagnoses problems; predicts shortages or surpluses of materials; and prescribes solutions. YES/MVS, developed at the IBM T.J. Watson Research Center, assists computer operators on a real-time basis in monitoring and controlling the IBM MVS (multiple virtual storage) operating system. REACTOR, developed by EG&G Idaho, helps reactor operators diagnose and treat nuclear reactor accidents by monitoring instrument readings on a real-time basis.

The limitation with control/monitoring systems is that requirements and conditions for monitoring and control vary according to the process monitored and are time and situation dependent. Current expert technology cannot deal effectively with real-time problems.

Debugging

Debugging is performed to identify remedies for malfunctions in a physical system, e.g., machine. The search space for remedies is usually limited, and debugging can be performed admirably by expert systems. Debugging usually accompanies diagnosis, which is the best understood application area. The debugging task is most often used for chemistry, computer systems, electronics, engineering, geology, and medicine. Examples are TQMSTUNE (chemistry), TIMM/Tuner (computer systems), ACE (electronics), DRILLING ADVISOR (geology), and BLUE BOX (medicine). The purposes of these expert systems are summarized in Table 11.1.

Expert System	Application Area	Functions	Status
TQMSTUNE	Chemistry	Fine-tune a triple quadruple mass spectrometer.	Demonstration prototype
TIMM/Tuner	Computer systems	Tune VAX/VMS computers.	Production systems
ACE	Electronics	Troubleshoot faults in telephone networks.	Production systems
REACTOR	Nuclear power	Treat nuclear reactor accidents.	Research prototype
DRILLING ADVISOR	Geology	Correct oil right "drill stitching" problems.	Research prototype
BLUE BOX	Medicine	Treat various forms of depression.	Research prototype

Table 11.1   *Examples of expert systems specializing in debugging*

The limitation with the debugging task is that a single fault is usually assumed and an appropriate correction is prescribed for it. It may be difficult to develop expert systems capable of identifying remedies for multiple, sequential, or intermittent faults because the system anatomy may not be fully understood and represented in expert systems.

Design

The function of design is to establish specifications to configure objects that satisfy particular requirements and constraints. Design expert systems are developed mostly for chemistry (e.g., organic molecules), computer systems (e.g., configuration of computers), electronics (e.g., VLSI circuits), and the military (e.g., map labeling). Table 11.2 summarizes one example for each application area and its function. The systems listed in the table are research prototypes, with the exception of XCON. XCON was developed by Carnegie-Mellon University for Digital Equipment Corporation, and it configures VAX family computer systems at a very detailed level. XCON performs configuration at a level equal to that of an experienced technical editor, but at a speed 20 times faster than the editor.

Details of XCON are discussed in a later section.

Expert System	Application Area	Functions	Status
SECS	Chemistry	Synthesize organic molecules.	Research prototype
XCON	Computer systems	Configure VAX computers.	Production system
PALLADIO	Electronics	Design new VLSI circuits.	Research prototpye
ACES	Military	Design map labeling.	Research prototype

Table 11.2   Examples of expert systems specializing in design

The limitation of using expert systems specializing in design is that the scope of the problem may be so large that assessing the consequences of design decisions is impossible; consequently, subproblems may be partitioned. Subproblem interdependency can be difficult to resolve. Because of the complexity of the system, it may be difficult to evaluate the impact of design changes or to record design decisions because the design decisions were made sequentially by expert systems during the design process.

Diagnosis

Expert systems specializing in diagnosis perform troubleshooting of faults in a system based on interpretation of data. This task is the best understood and most highly developed task. These expert systems also perform debugging as discussed previously. They have been developed for computer systems (e.g., to locate defects in computers) and in electronics (e.g., to diagnose faults in telephone networks), nuclear power plants (e.g., to diagnose nuclear reactor accidents), geology (e.g., to locate problems related to drilling fluids used in drilling operations), and medicine (e.g., to diagnose lung diseases). Table 11.3 provides five examples; the three systems listed that have reached the production system stage are ACE, MUD, and PUFF.

Expert System	Application Area	Functions	Status
IDT	Computer systems	Locate defective units in PDP 11/03 computers.	Research prototype
ACE	Electronics	Diagnose faults in telephone networks.	Production system
REACTOR	Nuclear power	Locate nuclear reactor accidents.	Research prototype
MUD	Geology	Troubleshoot drilling fluid problems.	Field prototype
PUFF	Medicine	Diagnose lung diseases.	Production system

Table 11.3   Examples of expert systems specializing in diagnosis

With expert systems specializing in diagnosis, the limitation is similar to that of debugging. These systems tend to be based on single fault assumption and may not consider sequential, combinational, or intermittent faults. Many times, the faults originate with the diagnostic equipment rather than with the physical system being diagnosed. Full understanding of a physical system is often impossible because of the system's complexity. For some cases, e.g., nuclear power plants, diagnostic data are expensive and unavailable for testing.

Instruction

Instructional expert systems train students by diagnosing, debugging, and correcting student behaviors or knowledge in a particular field. These systems develop a basis of the student's acquired knowledge in a particular field, diagnose his or her deficiencies, and prescribe training drills to correct the deficiencies. These instructional systems are used in electronics (e.g., to teach the use of a CAD system), plant operation (e.g., to train operators of a steam-propulsion plant), and medicine (e.g., to instruct in methods of anesthesia management). Table 11.4 summarizes examples of instructional expert systems. Most of these systems have not yet reached the production system stage.

Expert System	Application Area	Functions	Status
CAD HELP	Electronics	Teach the use of a CAD subsystem for digital circuit design.	Research prototype
STEAMER	Plant operation	Instruct naval engineering students in operating a steam propulsion plant.	Field-test
ATTENDING	Medicine	Teach medical students in anesthesiology.	Research prototype

Table 11.4   Examples of expert systems specializing in instruction

One limitation of instructional expert systems lies in the complexity of interaction between teachers and students and the learning process of students. It is still too early to evaluate the effectiveness of instructional expert systems.

Interpretation

Expert systems for interpretation perform analyses of sensory data to determine their meaning. These systems deal with real data measured from sensing instruments in forms of data streams, wave forms, or pictures. Because of the real environment, these data may be flawed by noise and may be incomplete, unreliable, or erroneous. Interpretational expert systems are developed for chemistry (e.g., to infer a compound's moleculer structure from mass spectral data), nuclear power plants (e.g., to infer accidents from reactor data), geology (e.g., to interpret dipmeter logs), medicine (e.g., to interpret scanning densitometer data for inflammatory conditions), and the military (e.g., to interpret sonar sensor data for detecting and identifying ocean vessels). The main purpose of these systems is to explain what is taking place and to determine what the signals mean. Table 11.5 summarizes examples of expert systems specializing in interpretation. Data interpretation is also a well-understood and well-developed expert system task. DENDRAL and SPE are both commercial systems.

Expert System	Application Area	Functions	Status
DENDRAL	Chemistry	Infer the molecular structure of unknown compounds from mass spectral and nuclear magnetic response data.	Production system
REACTOR	Nuclear plants	Interpret instrument readings to evaluate system deviations.	Research prototype
DIPMETER ADVISOR	Geology	Infer subsurface geological structure by interpreting dipmeter logs.	Research prototype
SPE	Medicine	Interpret scanning densitometer data to diagnose inflammatory conditions.	Production system
HASP/SIAP	Military	Interpret sonar sensor data to detect and identify ocean vessels.	Research prototype

Table 11.5   Examples of expert systems specializing in interpretation

The drawback with interpretational expert systems is that the interpretation may be based on partial information or conflicting data from various sensors. These systems also require real-time processing of data that is still under development for the current technology.

Planning

Expert systems specializing in devising plans and programs to achieve given goals develop an entire course of action and occasionally reject a portion of a plan after implementation because it violates constraints. These systems are used in chemistry (e.g., to develop experiments in molecular genetics), computer systems (e.g., to develop plans for assembling and testing the computer system on order), electronics (e.g., to synthesize integrated circuit layouts of nMOS cells), and military operations (e.g., to develop plans for attacking enemy airfields). Table 11.6 summarizes examples of expert systems specializing in planning. Planning expert systems are new and relatively time-consuming to develop; all systems listed in the table are in the research prototype stage.

Expert System	Application Area	Functions	Status
GA1	Chemistry	Develop experiments in DNA structure.	Research prototype
PTRANS	Computer systems	Develop plans for assembling and testing the ordered computer system.	Research prototype
TALIB	Electronics	Synthesize integrated circuit layouts for nMOS cells.	Research prototype
TATR	Military	Develop a plan for air targeteer to attack enemy airfields.	Research prototype

Table 11.6   Examples of expert systems specializing in planning

The disadvantage of planning expert systems is the possible explosion of system complexity due to problem size and consequences of actions. These systems often contain great details of actions and relationships among actions and thus require substantial coordination among multiple players and subgoals.

Prediction

Expert systems specializing in prediction perform forecasts of the future from a model or program of the past and present that mirror real-world activity. To form the basis of predictions, predictive expert systems combine the traditional models and programs with the knowledge about the processes that originated them. These systems can be used in military applications (e.g., to forecast when and where a major armed conflict will next occur), agricultural applications (e.g., to foretell the damage due to the black cutworm), and economic applications (e.g., to predict effects of a change in economic policy). Few predictive systems have been developed. One system, I&W, was developed through a joint effort by ESL, Inc. (Sunnyvale, CA) and Stanford University. I&W assists an intelligence analyst in forecasting where and when an armed conflict will occur by analyzing incoming intelligence reports on troop locations, activity, and movements.

Another predictive system is PLANT/cd, which was developed by the University of Illinois to foretell black cutworm damage to corn, using a combination of rules and a set of black cutworm simulation programs. By using knowledge about a given field (e.g., moth trap count, weed density, larval age, soil condition, and corn variety), PLANT/cd produces predictions on the degree of damage the cutworm will cause in a particular field. The system has reached the research prototype stage.

The limitation of prediction expert systems lies in the integration of incomplete information, multiple possibilities of future courses, and diversity of data sources and reasoning methods.

TWO CASE STUDIES: XCON AND DELTA

XCON and DELTA are two interesting case studies because of the availability of detailed information for comparison, the frequent effective communication between the user and the developer, and the proven initial usefulness of these expert systems in industrial environments.

XCON

XCON is probably the most widely used and discussed expert system. As shown in Figure 11.1, XCON is used to interact with sales, manufacturing, and customer service departments. As of November 1985, it contained about 4500 rules and had been used to match the specifications on almost 100,000 customer orders against the parts and equipment shipped by the factory for VAX computer systems.

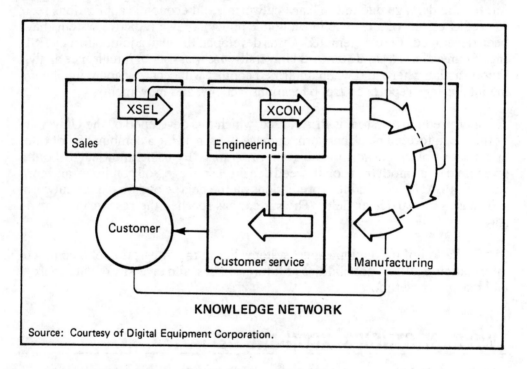

KNOWLEDGE NETWORK

Source: Courtesy of Digital Equipment Corporation.

Figure 11.1   How XCON configures VAX computer systems

XCON, also known as R1, was developed at Carnegie-Mellon University for Digital Equipment Corporation (DEC). It performs much faster and more accurately jobs that were previously undertaken by an experienced technical editor. For example, a VAX system order that may take the editor as long as 20 minutes to examine and determine what computer components need to be replaced or added, can typically be completed by XCON in less than a minute. Its performance is satisfactory in comparison with 20% of orders that had serious problems before XCON was installed; accuracy increased to 99% with only 1% repeated errors in 1985.

XCON configures VAX systems at a very detailed level based on its task-specific knowledge. It determines necessary modifications on each order, produces diagrams of spatial and logical relationships between hundreds of components in a complete system, and defines cable lengths between components. Rules and frames (e.g., templates) are used to represent knowledge on components. For example, the rule DISTRIBUTE-MB-DEVICES-3 for the distribution of massbus devices in VAX computer systems is expressed as follows:

Rule: Distribute-MB-Devices-3

IF: The most current active context is distributing massbus devices,

AND there is a single port disk drive that has not been assigned to a massbus,

AND there are no unassigned dual port disk drives,

AND the number of devices that each massbus should support is known,

AND there is a massbus that has been assigned at least one disk drive and that should support additional disk drives,

AND the type of cable needed to connect the disk drive to the previous device on the massbus is known,

THEN: Assign the disk drive to the massbus.

This rule shows that there are six conditions to be met before one of the single port disk drives on the order is assigned to one of the massbuses. The first condition indicates the task relevant to this rule is distributing massbus devices; the remaining five conditions specify constraints that must be satisfied before a disk drive can be assigned to a massbus.

The cabinet template that describes the space available in a particular CPU cabinet template (CPU-CABINET) resembles the following:

Template: **CPU-CABINET**

Class:	Cabinet
Height:	60 inches
Width:	52 inches
Depth:	30 inches
SBI module space:	CPU Nexus- (3 6 23 30)
	4-inch-option-slot 1 Nexus-3 (23 6 27 30)
	Memory Nexus-4 (27 6 38 30)
	4-inch-option-slot 2 Nexus-6 (38 5 42 30)
	4-inch-option-slot 3 Nexus-5 (42 5 46 30)
	3-inch-option-slot Nexus-6 (46 5 49 30)
Power supply space:	FPA Nexus-1 (2 32 1 0 40)
	CPU Nexus-2 (10 32 18 40)
	4-inch-option-slot 1 Nexus-3 (18 32 26 40)
	Memory Nexus-4 (26 32 34 40)
	4-inch-option-slot 2 Nexus-5 (34 32 42 40)
	Clock-battery (2 49 26 52)
	Memory-battery (2 46 26 49)
SBI device space:	10 (2 52 50 56).

This template displays information regarding the CPU cabinet's class, weight, width, depth, module space, power supply space, and device space requirements.

The early versions of XCON were implemented in OPS4; later versions were implemented in OPS5. Both OPS4 and OPS5 are expert system languages; OPS5 is the later version of OPS4. XCON initially covered only VAX-11/780; it was expanded to include VAX-11/780 in 1981, PDP-11/23 and VAX/730 in 1982, and Micro-VAX and Micro-PDP in 1983, as shown in Figure 11.2. The number of rules increased from an initial 777 in October 1983 to 3303 in January 1984; the number of parts included in the knowledge base increased from an initial 420 to 5481 during the same time period, as shown in Table 11.7.

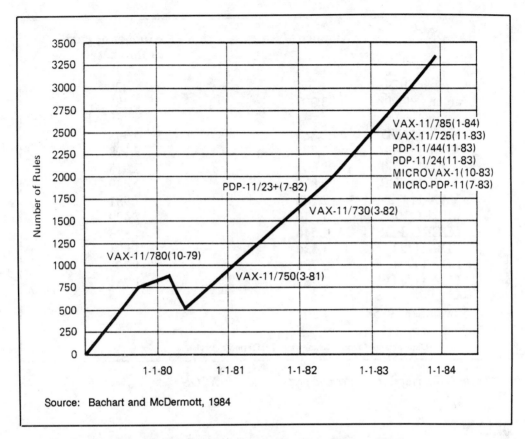

Figure 11.2   The growth of XCON — October 1979 to January 1984

XCON	Number of Rules	Number of Parts in Database
October 1979	777	420
January 1984	3,303	5,481
VAX-11/785	2,883	3,398
VAX-11/780	2,883	3,398
VAX-11/750	2,801	2,915
VAX-11/730	2,810	2,489
VAX-11/725	2,788	1,981
MICROVAX-1	1,516	1,490
MICRO-PDP11	1,516	1,828
PDP-11/23	1,516	1,894
PDP-11/24	2,786	1,763
PDP-11/44	2,786	1,764
November 1985	4,500	————

Source: Data obtained from Bachant and McDermott, 1984

Table 11.7   Number of rules and parts included in XCON

DELTA

DELTA (Diesel-Electric-Locomotive Troubleshooting Aid) was developed by General Electric to assist junior mechanics in analyzing and repairing complicated diesel-electric locomotives. DELTA is also known as CATS. The objective of DELTA is to ensure that proper and timely troubleshooting and repair action is taken by railroad maintenance personnel on GE products to reduce downtime, improve availability, and thus increase GE's market share of new locomotive sales.

DELTA's performance is built on more than 1,000 IF-THEN rules generated with an expert troubleshooter who had more than 40 years of experience in repairing diesel-electric locomotives. DELTA was field-tested on Burlington-Northern and Union-Pacific railroads in Nebraska in 1984-85.

DELTA was not developed with an expert system tool. It was originally implemented in LISP, but was later converted to FORTH (a high-level system-specific programming language). It then was rewritten to increase flexibility and to be operable in IBM PC-XT computers.

In assisting maintenance mechanics to diagnose and repair malfunctions, the system queries the user for symptoms and then uses the symptoms to select appropriate diagnostic strategies for locomotive repair. DELTA can also be used to train apprentice mechanics by leading the user through an entire repair procedure and giving specific repair instructions once the trouble is identified.

The organization of DELTA is shown in Figure 11.3. It requires a shop-hardened DEC-1170, a Sony video disk player, a color terminal for video, and a standard printer. Because it was going to be used in a railroad repair shop, GE had to design a hardened terminal that could withstand accidental collisions with wrenches and other equipment. During the consultation process, the system may retrieve diagrams of parts and subsystems from the repair manuals stored in the knowledge base and display videodisk still frames and movies of repair sequences in the color terminal.

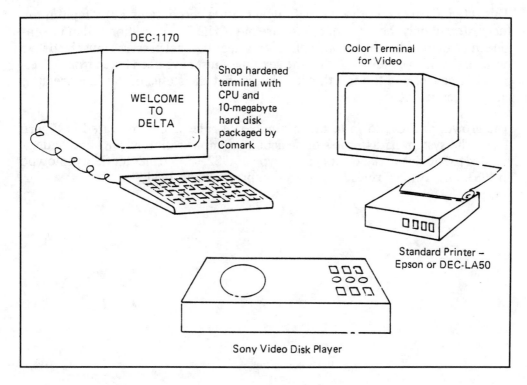

Figure 11.3   Major components required for Delta

DELTA is a rule-based system that consists of relatively simple rules. For example, the Fuel System Faulty rule is expressed as follows:

> IF: EQ (engine set idle) and
>
> EQ (fuel pressure below normal) and
>
> EQ (fuel-pressure-gauge used in test) and
>
> EQ (fuel-pressure-gauge status OK),
>
> THEN: WRITE (fuel system faulty) 1.0

This rule indicates that there is definitely (with a certainty of 1.0) a fault in the fuel system if only the four conditions are met. The first condition is that the engine must be set idle; the second condition is that the fuel pressure must be below normal; the third condition is that the readings must have been taken from a fuel-pressure-gauge; and the fourth condition is that the status of the fuel-pressure gauge must be OK.

The growth of DELTA in terms of number of rules is demonstrated in Figure 11.4. The system had 45 rules on feasibility demonstration in 1981 and had expanded to 350 rules in laboratory prototype in 1982, to 530 rules for field prototype in 1983, and to 1,200 rules for production prototype in 1984.

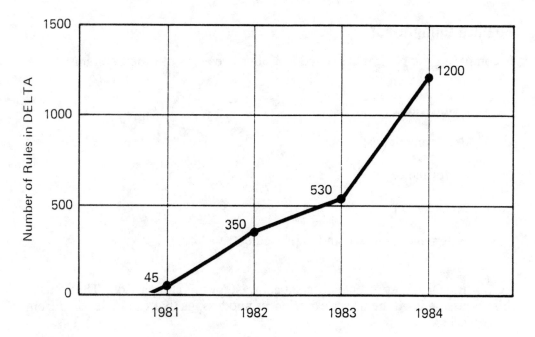

Figure 11.4   Growth of DELTA

DELTA can be used in the diagnosis of 50% of GE diesel locomotives, including Type E (CHECK/CMR) services. The slump in diesel locomotive sales slowed the development of the system after 1984. Because of the FORTH's system specificity and the difficulties with component interface hardware, the decision was made to convert DELTA to GEN-X (an expert system tool developed by GE that can be used on the IBM PC).

DELTA was also encoded in three microprocessors that would be implanted in new GE DASH 8 diesel locomotives to intelligently troubleshoot faults in these locomotives.

Feature Comparison

In comparing the two cases studied, consider five areas of expert systems:

- basic features

- development costs

- performance

- user reaction

- system maintenance and improvement

XCON and DELTA present sufficient contrast for this comparison. The focus of this discussion is on the user's experiences and lessons that can be learned from the two cases.

Basic Features

The basic features of the expert systems to be compared include application area, language used, knowledge source, knowledge representation, and inference engine. The results of these comparisons for XCON and DELTA are shown in Table 11.8. Examination of the table confirms that the selection of language, knowledge representation, and inference engine depend on the application. XCON is used for computer system configurations that consist of many data points regarding customer orders received by the sales department. Because the major element in configuration was the matching of customer order with the parts available, rules, frames, and data (or facts) were used to represent the bulk of information on parts and their constraints, and forward chaining was appropriate for XCON. Because OPS5 had excellent features for forward chaining, it was used to expedite XCON development.

Features	Expert System	
	<u>XCON</u>	<u>DELTA</u>
Application area	Computer system configuration	Diagnosis and training
Language used	OPS5	LISP/FORTH
Knowledge source	Manuals and experts	Single experienced expert
Knowledge representation	Rules, frames, and data (facts)	Rules and data (facts)
Inference engine	Forward chaining	Backward and forward chaining

Table 11.8   Basic features of expert systems

On the other hand, DELTA was used for diagnosing faults in diesel electric locomotives and for training apprentice mechanics. Backward chaining is effective for diagnosis because it performs efficiently in proving or disproving hypotheses regarding fault location. However, in training a new mechanic to troubleshoot locomotive faults, forward chaining is appropriate because during the training session, the expert system retrieves diagrams of parts and subsystems from the repair manuals stored in the knowledge base and displays videodisk slides and movies of repair sequences. Consequently, DELTA uses both backward and forward chaining. Because of the specific requirements of displaying videodisk information and having a combination of forward and backward chaining, LISP had initially been used to develop the system, which was later converted into FORTH for delivery. A single experienced expert was used to build the knowledge base for diagnosis in DELTA, as was the case in building other diagnostic expert systems, e.g., MYCIN.

Development Cost

Two aspects of development cost should be discussed: development stages (including time required) and manpower.

The six development stages for both XCON and DELTA as outlined in Table 11.9 are corporate R&D (research and development) proposal, feasibility demonstration, laboratory prototype, field test prototype, system implementation, and self-sufficiency; in many publications, system implementation and self-sufficiency stages may be included under "production system" or "commercial system." Table 11.9 shows the history of development and rule growth for XCON and DELTA. Both systems became useful products after two to three years: XCON was developed, tested, and revised from December 1978 to December 1980; DELTA was worked on from 1981 to 1984. This time period did not include the time required for approval of corporate R&D proposals for the expert system. In some cases it may take more than a year to obtain management approval to try new techniques such as expert systems. Table 11.9 also shows that about 1,000 rules are required for a commercially useful product.

	XCON		DELTA	
Stages	Time	Number of Rules	Time	Number of Rules
Corporate R & D proposal	N/A	N/A	1980	N/A
Feasibility demonstration	12/78-4/79	250	1981	45
Laboratory prototype	5/79-9/79	750	1982	350
Field test prototype	10/79-5/80	777	1983	530
System implementation	6/80-12/80	500*-850	1984	1,200
Self-sufficiency	1/81-present	850-4,500†	1985‡	N/A

* Prototype reimplemented in 500 rules, then increased to 850 rules.
† November 1985
‡ Conversion to IBM personal computers; six to nine person-months required

Source: Data obtained from Bachant and McDermott, 1984.

Table 11.9   Development stages of expert systems

The costs of developing XCON and DELTA are shown in Figure 11.5. XCON required about eight man-years; assuming a man-year cost of $150,000, the total development cost was about $1.2 million. DELTA cost about $800,000, which was shared equally by the GE corporate R&D and the diesel electric locomotive sales departments. You can conclude that about five man-years, or $800,000, is required to build a commercial expert system.

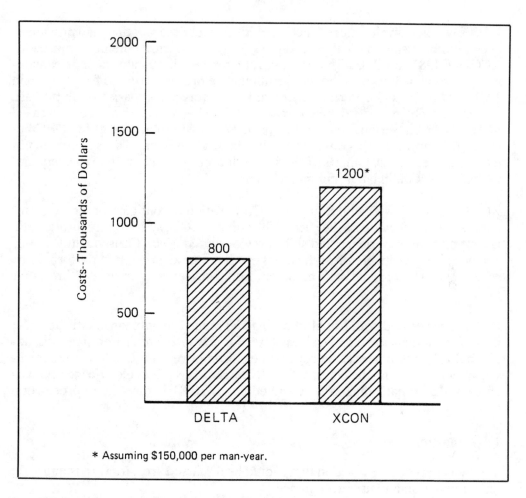

Figure 11.5   Costs of developing XCON and DELTA

System Performance

Both XCON and DELTA performed satisfactorily in solving the problems for which they were designed. They were then expanded to cover related problems not previously included as well.

XCON was performing more functions with greater accuracy than had previously been possible using manual procedures. Figure 11.6 shows the performance of XCON in 1982 and 1983. The serious problems were held stable at approximately 3% of total orders even though the number of orders increased from 26,986 in 1982 to 47,635 in 1983. Performance was satisfactory in comparison with the case of 20% of problematic orders before XCON had been used. Accuracy increased to 99% with 1% serious repeated error in 1985. The total savings for DEC between 1980 and 1985 was estimated to be about $12 million. This savings did not take into account customer satisfaction with accurate and on-time delivery and related reduction in labor and material cost.

XCON was used by Digital Equipment Corporation to configure orders for computer systems; because of the successful use of XCON, system configuration did not require the experience and skills previously required. Consequently, junior personnel were capable of performing the same tasks previously performed by specialists. The original staff members were subsequently transferred to other jobs.

DELTA performed both troubleshooting and regular maintenance satisfactorily; it also functioned as an ideal training tutor for new mechanics. For diagnosis, additional rules were needed to cover other locomotives and to allow users to restart any time during the consultation. New DASH 8 diesel electric locomotives implanted automatic diagnosis by embedding DELTA in three microprocessors.

User Reaction

The two areas of user reaction that should be discussed are hardware required in implementation and user acceptance.

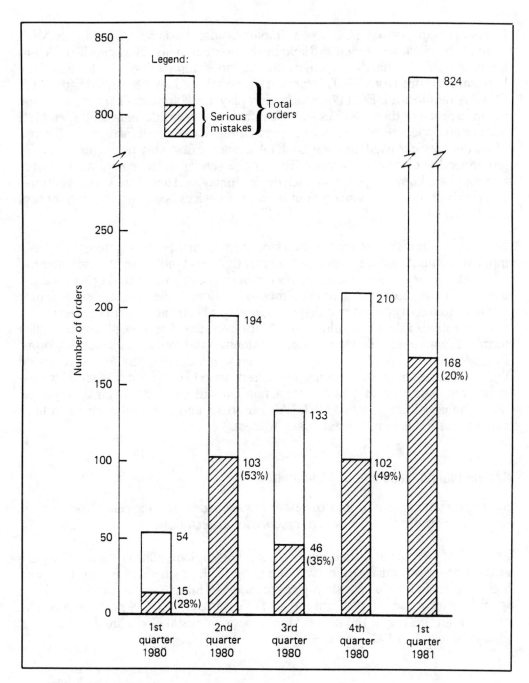

Figure 11.6   XCON's early performance by quarter in 1980-81

Hardware required for XCON was simple because it was developed in the VAX computers, which are owned and sold by the user company. Because the user was familiar with the hardware environment, no complication developed. The hardware required for DELTA was more sophisticated. As shown in Figure 11.3, DELTA required a DEC 1170, a videodisk player, a color terminal for video, and a printer; each of these devices was manufactured by a different vendor, and GE was not equipped to serve the user if any of these devices malfunctioned. Because of various devices used, moving DELTA around caused big problems in the interconnection of cables. Neither GE nor the vendor of the component devices had complete knowledge of how each device functioned under various conditions. Diagnosis of the interconnection of hardware devices became a substantial task in DELTA.

User acceptance is related to the interface mechanism of expert systems. XCON's input and output were arranged in a format that was familiar to the user, and the user was not required to use extra devices in employing it. DELTA provided the user with a numeric keypad for main menu selection, a videodisk player plus color terminal to display charts and diagrams, and hard copy at the end of the session of all questions asked and rules "fired." However, the videodisk player and color terminal sometimes failed to function as intended and could not display diagrams. Because DELTA could not be consulted in the middle of a problem, it repeated the entire series of questions when consulted; users became bored after a few sessions of use and after they had become familiar with the system. Usage dropped when the user knew most of DELTA's expertise, and more substance was then needed to stimulate and sustain user interest.

System Maintenance and Improvement

System maintenance and improvement require close working relationships with the user to ensure that the system meets user expectations.

XCON had significant difficulties in the earlier implementation stage. The percentage of serious mistakes in 1980 and early 1981, as shown in Figure 11.6, was high — more than 20% (the average percentage of human mistakes when human specialists were used to perform the job). Fortunately, XCON performance improved after 1981, and the percentage of serious mistakes declined from more than 20% to 3% in 1982 and 1983.

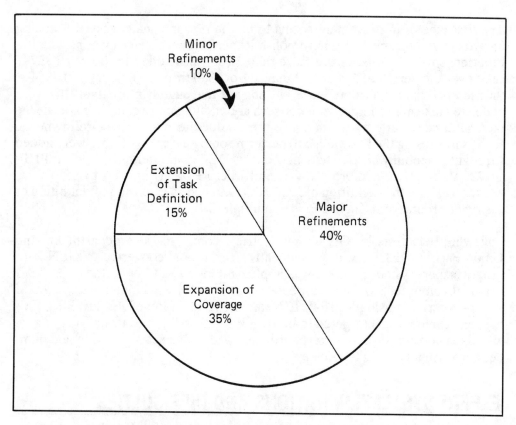

Figure 11.7   Four types of changes that improved XCON's accuracy

The many iterations between the user and the developer that have been made to improve XCON's performance, as shown in Figure 11.7, include the following:

- **Minor refinements**: adding knowledge to improve the expert system's performance on an existing subtask.

- **Major refinement**: adding knowledge to enable the expert system to perform a new subtask.

- **Expansion of coverage to new, related equipment**: expanding the coverage of the expert system significantly to include new equipment types.

- **Extension of the task definition**: extending new capacity of the expert system.

The first type of improvement seems to be the reason usually given for adding knowledge to an expert system to polish its performance. However, as with the experience with XCON, of the more than 2,500 rules added to the original 777 rules over the period of 4 years—January 1 of 1980 through January 1 of 1984— the recorded data shown in Figure 11.7 suggest that slightly more than 10% were added to make minor improvements, such as obtaining more complete knowledge on a subtask; slightly fewer than 40% were added to make major refinements, such as increasing the knowledge to perform some new subtask; 35% were added to provide capability needed to deal with new DEC computer types, such as PDP-11/23, VAX-11/730, Micro-VAX-1, and Micro-PDP11; and up to 15% were added to extend the definition of XCON's task, such as extension of definition of customer orders from single CPUs to multiple CPUs.

Following field tests by GE diesel electric locomotive sales departments and Union Pacific, DELTA was subsequently "frozen" and converted to GEN-X (a generic expert system tool that was implemented in C and operated on an IBM personal computer). A spreadsheet format of rules was implemented so that human experts could load in IF-THEN statements to improve DELTA. DELTA's host environment was targeted to be IBM PC-AT or XT, and its delivery system would include a push-button keyboard equipped with a set of function and number keys instead of a full-scale keyboard.

EXPERT SYSTEM LIMITATIONS AND DIFFICULTIES

The limitations of expert system development may originate from technology inheritance, environment, and cost.

Because current expert system technology is still evolving, limitations include the inherent shortcomings such as narrowness of expertise, inability to recognize knowledge boundaries, limited explanation facilities, and difficulty in validation.

Because building and maintaining a large knowledge base requires substantial effort, most expert systems cover a narrow range of expertise. Part of the reason is due to the current computing facility, which limits the speed and capability of searches in expert systems. Even when an expert system achieves a broad coverage of knowledge (e.g., INTERNIST, which covers some 500 diseases), it becomes shallow in representing associations between elements in the knowledge base. With the current limitations of technology, it seems that in building expert systems, you must be satisfied with a narrow scope of knowledge.

Inability of expert systems to recognize their knowledge boundaries is a serious problem: most expert systems do not deal competently with problems at the boundaries of their knowledge. They do not have the built-in knowledge to determine when a problem is beyond their capability or outside their field. Expert systems may need constant maintenance to reduce mistakes in complex or derived cases that are not fully represented in the knowledge base. The explanations are primitive, and a human expert may need to re-explain what the expert system has explained. Even with the success record of XCON, a complete overhaul was undertaken early in 1988.

Although validation of software programs is time-consuming, the effort required in validating expert systems is many times greater than the effort required for conventional software programs. Expert systems can be validated by human experts during actual use. Very few employees have both domain expertise and knowledge engineering. Communications between human experts and knowledge engineers in identifying and correcting mistakes in an expert system can be a formidable task.

The environment in which an expert system is developed or used is significant. The three potential limitations that exist within the current environment are hardware, software, and organization. The current computing facility is slow and is not equipped for symbolic processing; it was built for number-crunching only. Special AI workstations, e.g., LISP machines, may be required to develop expert systems. These stations are not only expensive, but they usually cannot execute existing software programs. Except for large expensive tools such as KEE, expert system tools have limited knowledge representation methods. Most of them use rule-based approaches that are not well suited to represent structural knowledge that has no immediate IF-THEN consequences. Because expert system technology is new, in the area of organization, management personnel expects either too much or too little from the technology, so initiating an expert system project can be a major undertaking.

Cost is another major source of problems in developing expert systems. At present, a knowledge engineer extracts knowledge from human experts and laboriously builds it into the knowledge base. The effort is time-consuming, and the knowledge engineer's services are costly due to supply shortage. Most expert system prototypes would require three man-months to develop, and a usable system would take about one man-year to build.

EXPERT SYSTEM DEVELOPMENT RULES

The four rules regarding system development learned from the two case studies are as follows:

- It is unwise to try to keep an expert system from regular use until its knowledge is complete.

- Like human specialists, expert systems always make mistakes and require time to advance from apprentice to expert status.

- A useful expert system advances incrementally over a long period of time.

- Selection of application fields is essential because it affects programming language, knowledge source, knowledge representation, and inference engines used.

The developers of XCON found that they did not have to wait until the system was near perfection for it to be useful because the system was providing significant assistance to technical editors during the field test prototype stage. It took 80,000 orders to uncover some of the deficiencies in XCON's configuration knowledge. Because the configuration task is continually redefined as new products are introduced, XCON will never have all the knowledge it needs and will require continual refinement. Refinement can be undertaken when the system is used and deficiencies are identified.

Unlike finished conventional software programs that have few bugs, however, expert systems always make mistakes. Expert systems must pass through a lengthy apprenticeship stage (more than one or two years) to become experts. Even after they become experts, they will, like all human experts, occasionally make mistakes. Fortunately, expert systems will not cover up their mistakes; these mistakes can be traced and corrected.

The developers of XCON and DELTA found that building a useful expert system is an unending process because it evolves with new task additions. Knowledge is continually added to correct or complement existing knowledge or to augment knowledge of new products. A significant portion of additions comes as the result of expert systems needing to obtain the knowledge to perform new tasks. Some of these tasks are the consequences of introduction of new products or inclusion of related products, and the rest are the result of the user's requirement to improve expert system performance to accomplish an additional task. Because of these additions, an expert system is likely to become too large to manage.

The selection of application types may consequently determine the programming language, knowledge source, knowledge representation method, and inference engine that can best fit the application. The developer of XCON found that the configuration problem was a good selection because the task of developing XCON entailed the appropriate degree of difficulty and allowed for use of a reasonable approach and computer language to show sufficient progress to anyone who was interested.

Hardware Requirements

The following two rules can be used as guidelines in selecting hardware requirements:

- Use available hardware equipment.

- Select easy-to-use equipment.

The experiences of XCON and DELTA indicate that the hardware equipment selected should be available and familiar to the user. XCON uses DEC computers that are available and familiar to DEC employees; thus, no computer training is needed. DELTA initially also used DEC computers, but its users (mainly mechanics) lacked computer knowledge; thus, training was required for both the computer and the expert system. The problems of adjusting to new tools were consequently compounded, the learning speed rate slowed, and the degree of user anxiety increased. DELTA was later converted to the IBM PC environment, and barriers to its use were partially removed.

In the case of DELTA, the Sony videodisk displayer, color terminal, and Epson printer were integrated with a hardened DEC computer. The idea was ingenious but caused problems in system integration and implementation. Selecting easy-to-use equipment may be mandatory for expert system acceptance by mechanics in the repair shop.

APPLICATION SELECTION RULES

The best candidate problems for expert systems are those that are small but important, in which data, test cases, and the knowledge and experience of human experts are available as a basis for expert system development and for validating the expert systems after they are developed.

Expert systems are more likely to be successful if certain conditions are met. Two essential prerequisites are as follows:

- The application (problem) area must be well bounded and understood.

- At least one human expert must be available to explain the knowledge required for the expert system being built.

Expert systems have been more successful in scientific and technical tasks in which a well-bounded field of knowledge and results of its application exist. The first necessary condition is that technical vocabularies can be enumerated and search space for a solution is relatively small so that computers can examine all feasible combinations and reach a conclusion. This can be illustrated by the diagnostic problem that has been most often dealt with by various expert systems in different fields. When diagnosing the fault in a machine, the number of possible faulty areas is limited, and these areas are understood and can be identified. Computers can be instructed to check feasible combinations and reach a conclusion on the faulty part.

Unbounded problem areas, such as linguistic concepts, can take on unlimited variations in meaning, depending on the context, e.g., language translation. Because of speed and memory limitations, this type of problem is difficult for today's computational technology to resolve. That is, the computer must examine almost endless combinational possibilities; it cannot accommodate the search space that is required.

Appropriate candidate problems are small but important, and it usually takes human experts a few hours to solve them.

The second necessary condition is that at least one human expert is available to explain the special knowledge and experience and the methods used to apply them to particular problems. If no human expertise has yet evolved—such as in the case of "Star Wars"—then an expert system for the task cannot be expected to fare any better than the human sources.

In addition to the two prerequisites just discussed, one or more of the following conditions must exist for any expert system to be worthy of development:

- shortage of human experts/specialists

- need to preserve experts' expertise

- high cost of expert advice or wrong decisions

- critical requirement of expert advice

- routine, detail-dependent decision making

The appearance of one or more of these elements plus the two prerequisites will make an expert system commercially attractive. Consider these elements individually, using examples of existing expert systems.

APPLYING EXPERT SYSTEM TECHNOLOGY TO IMPROVE SOFTWARE PROGRAMS

Expert system technology can be applied in five major ways to improve conventional software:

- **Intelligent "user"**: acts as a database and other software package users; interaction with the software package/database is not its primary objective, but merely a convenient means to access data.

- **Intelligent "representative"**: uses mathematical logic to represent general facts about data in the software package/database to increase the usefulness of the package/database to respond to queries.

- **Intelligent "prober"**: supports browsing through a database or program and also supports query modification either to narrow and broaden the scope of the request to make it more understandable.

- **Natural language "interface"**: provides natural language interface software packages and allows the user to search for and process information without having to learn the specialized command language of a software package.

- **Natural language text "analyst"**: processes a user's natural language input text to produce appropriate responses to user queries. The capability of the expert system to understand natural language text in a given field permits the user to enter data in a relatively flexible form.

Most of these approaches are implemented only in large AI workstations. Examples are given for each type.

Expert Systems As Intelligent Users

Expert systems can be developed to serve as intelligent users of complex conventional software programs such as database management systems or mixed-integer linear programs. Two distinctive types of expert systems can be developed to accomplish this objective: expert systems that act as "assistants" and expert systems that act as the "controllers."

Most commercial IBM PC packages in the joint application of expert systems and databases use knowledge-based systems that act as software package/database assistants in the areas of query optimization, data access through natural language front ends, and deductive databases. In most existing coupled systems, the expert makes direct calls to the standard DBMS through a hard-craft interface. This approach implements a tight coupling of the expert system to a designated database. Typical examples of intelligent front-end systems include Guru (by Micro Data Base Systems) Javelin (by Javelin Software), Paradox (by Ansa Software), REVEAL (by McDonnell Douglass), and Superfile ACLS (by Southdata). Most of these systems are tightly coupled to a specific DBMS. Each system contains varying levels of built-in, system-specific knowledge about its database/software packages. The coupling of standard software packages to a database is time-consuming and package-dependent. A hard-craft interface may be required for each new package added into the database.

The more flexible approach is an intelligent interface between the applications and the database when the expert system acts as a controller. The interface would integrate each standard software package on an as-needed basis without hard-craft linking and allow each component to function independently. The intelligent interface (an expert system) can reason about components and their requirements for interface and data communications of the packages being connected. It uses knowledge of the packages being linked to provide communication and data sharing and uses meta knowledge regarding the capabilities of the packages to optimally select and use software programs to meet the user's requirements. For example, a user may not be aware of the need to use a statistical package or may not know which statistical package to use; the intelligent interface will connect one when it determines from past experience that a particular statistical package would be cost-effective to show a particular aspect of the data the user has requested or acquired.

The flexibility of this interface mechanism relies on the expert system's reasoning capability, the content of the database and data spaces of standard software packages being interfaced in response to the need for data processing, and data descriptions of the software packages.

Transformation (semantic mapping) of data representations and translation (syntactic mapping) of data manipulation languages are required in communication between the database, standard software packages, and the user/preparer. Because each individual software package may use a different organization for equivalent data or may represent the data at different levels of detail, semantic mapping is required to transform data among software packages. Different software packages may use their own data manipulation languages. Mapping between these data manipulation languages is a syntactic translation. For example, the algebraic and calculus query languages used for relational databases may need to be translated syntactically for use in other software packages, e.g., graphics.

Two examples are cited to show how the two types of expert systems have served as intelligent users of software packages. SICAD (Standards Interfaces in CAD) acts as an expert-system assistant to standards processing in CAD. It uses a custom knowledge base and a hard-craft inference mechanism to gain access to design standards. The knowledge base contains three elements: classifier trees that relate engineering terminology to provisions of a standard; an information network that consists of decision tables written in FORTRAN, which represent the provisions of a standard; and mapping that relates data items in a standard to data items in a design database. SICAD was developed to assist a design program that performs compliance checking. SICAD acts as an assistant to the design program in identifying and checking applicable provisions. Compliance checking uses backward chaining to determine all data required to evaluate a provision.

KADBASE (Knowledge Aided Database Management System) acts as an expert-system controller to database management systems. The objective of KADBASE was to develop a flexible, intelligent interface that enables multiple expert systems and multiple databases to communicate as autonomous, self-descriptive units with a CAD system operating in a distributed computing environment.

KADBASE consists of three major parts: the knowledge-based system interface, which formulates the queries and updates sent to other components and processes replies from them; the knowledge-based database interface, which acts as an intelligent user of a DBMS that accepts queries from other components and returns appropriate replies regarding the database; and the database access manager, which actually performs interface by decomposing queries, issuing the appropriate subqueries to the local database, obtaining and processing the data, and formulating the replies.

Intelligent Representatives

Expert systems acting as intelligent "representatives" use logic to represent facts about data in the database or a complex software program to facilitate queries. They may be integrated to a complex database or software packages. If these intelligent "representatives" are integrated to databases, they also may be called intentional databases (IDB), which are a collection of axioms, such as rules, postulates, constraints, and general facts. These axioms may be viewed alternately as data integrity constraints, data definitions, or logical inference rules and are represented in mathematical logic.

Two examples are discussed to demonstrate the differences between the two categories, MRPPS and DADM. MRPPS (Maryland Refutation Proof Procedure System) is an integrated system based on mathematical logic. Knowledge and data are combined in a semantic network that consists of a semantic graph (a classificational structure), a database (including conventional database and the IDB), a dictionary (a listing of relations, constants, and functions), and a semantic form space (consisting of definitions of constraints to be imposed on predicates and their arguments). The elements of the semantic graph are referenced by the knowledge base index to facilitate quick access.

A query to MRPPS is a conjunction of clauses. The first step in query processing is to make sure the query is consistent with the acceptable syntax and structure. The system uses a refutation proof procedure search for a solution to the query. The refutation proof procedure first assumes the negation of the desired clauses and attempts to prove a contradiction from rules and facts in the knowledge base.

DADM (Deductively Augmented Data Management System) is an intelligent front-end system that represents a combination of a file in general knowledge with an inference engine and a file of specific knowledge with a searching mechanism. The general knowledge consists of a set of domain-specific assertions expressed in first-order predicate calculus, and the file of specific knowledge is supported by a single relational DBMS. The system was implemented in heterogeneous hardware environments: an inference engine running on a LISP machine, a relational database supported by a specialized database machine, and a query and reply translator running on a DEC VAX 11/780.

The inference engine uses the specific knowledge on the problem domain to develop search strategies for locating answers from the queries. The queries are then sent to the translator for conversion to database syntax and are then passed to the database machine for processing. Replies from the database machine follow a reverse path.

The applications of DADM include "Manager's Assistant" to aid in corporate project monitoring and planning and an intelligent assistant for information resources managers.

Intelligent Probers

Expert systems acting as intelligent probers provide support capability to browse through a database or program to probe for information the user seeks and make an attempt to determine specific information about alternative queries that may better suit the user's need, on the basis of rules that describe relationships between predicates. For example, if Employ (x, John) — i.e. find all persons who John employs — fails, the intelligent prober may try the queries Teach (x, John), Employ (x, Mary), or supervise (x, John) in accordance with the rules on relationships between predicates. One example is provided by A. Motro (1984), who discussed a system for browsing in a loosely structured database.

Natural Language Interfacers

Expert systems acting as natural language (NL) interfaces allow the user to search for information without having to learn a new, specialized command language. They can be divided into two categories: database front ends and bibliographic systems. A variety of systems have been implemented to provide restricted natural language front ends to databases and complex software packages. Examples include CO-OP (a portable NL interface for database systems) and XCALIBUR (a domain-independent NL interface for expert systems.) The CO-OP system provides several good examples of the types of queries that can be processed using current technology, for example, "Who advises projects in area 36?" Most of these systems can parse simple queries expressed in restricted conversational English into database access requests and request clarifications where ambiguities exist.

Natural language bibliographic retrieval systems allow users to enter English language queries. These systems work by selecting keyword matching and have little understanding of the actual meaning of the queries. Examples include ANNLODE and CITE. ANNLODE (A Navigator of Natural Language Organized Data) is a browsing system that accesses a full text knowledge base to search for paragraphs that match a natural language query issued by the user; 54 CITE (Current Information Transfer in English) is a natural language interface for an on-line bibliographic retrieval system.

Take ANNLODE as an example. It uses linguistic, probabilistic, and empirical techniques to determine the degree of similarity between the user's query and the candidate text. It uses three linguistic methods to process queries and candidate paragraphs:

- **Common word deletion**: elimination of nondescriptive words such as articles, prepositions, and conjunctions from consideration in the matching.

- **Word root isolation**: removal of suffixes from significant words in the queries and paragraphs.

- **Thesaurus expansion**: expansion of significant terms in the query by applicable synonyms, each having associated term weights that correspond to the degree to which the meaning of the original term and synonym overlap.

ANNLODE further takes advantage of heuristically derived functions to rank the paragraphs for similarity with the query:

- **Term weighting**: these factors are used to reduce the matching weight for synonyms.

- **Number of occurrences of each term in the paragraph**: absolute weight increases with number of occurrences, while incremental weight decreases.

- **Frequency of query terms in entire knowledge base**: for example, widely used terms contribute little to the search for relevant information.

- **Correction for paragraph length**: long paragraphs are likely to contain more of any given query term than short ones.

Natural Language Text Analysts

Expert systems acting as natural language text analysts examine a user's natural language input text to produce appropriate responses. Several prototype systems derive meaning from natural language texts in highly technical domains, e.g., chemical data (though you may wonder whether scientists in these domains write technical papers in natural languages). One example is the Retrieval of Numeric Chemical Data (RNCD).

Retrieval of Numeric Chemical Data is an expert system that locates specific numerical data for organic compounds in the text of chemical journal articles. It can recognize a variety of data regarding physical measurements such as **mp** (melting point) and **ir** (infrared spectra) in the chemical description. The system may be used to search for characterization data for a known compound or to identify an unknown compound for which some of the characterization data are known. It accumulates a descriptive and heuristic knowledge about how chemical characterization data are represented. Some of the knowledge is devoted to distinguishing paragraphs that contain characterization from those that describe compound synthesis, including keys based on style, sequence in the article, vocabulary, etc. Its knowledge base contains rules that distinguish the subject compound (e.g., a compound name mentioned in a heading) and the characterization data (e.g., synonyms for data types).

SUMMARY

- The most successful task types are control/monitoring, debugging, design, diagnosis, instruction, interpretation, planning, and prediction

- Two cases in industrial applications, XCON and DELTA, have also been examined in this chapter to demonstrate expert system development, cost, and benefit.

- The best use of expert system technology is to enhance conventional software programs in user friendliness and in intelligent interface of databases.

• Expert systems are more likely to be successful if certain conditions are met. Following are the two essential prerequisites:

1. The application (problem) area must be well bounded.

2. At least one human expert must be available to explain the knowledge required for the expert system being built.

In addition, one or more of five situations must exist for an expert system to be successful:

1. shortage of experts/specialists

2. need to preserve expert's knowledge

3. high cost of expert advice

4. critical requirements of expert advice

5. routine detail-dependent decision making

• Expert systems can act as intelligent users, intelligent representatives, intelligent probers, natural language interfacers, or natural language text analysts to conventional software packages or databases.

REFERENCES

Aikins, J. S., J. C. Kunz, and E. H. Shortliffe. "PUFF: an expert system for interpretation of pulmonary function data." *Computers and Biomedical Research*, vol. 16, 1983, 199-208.

Ansa Software. Paradox Product Description, Belmont, CA, 1985.

Bachant, J. and J. McDermott. "R1 Revisited: Four Years in the Trenches." *The AI Magazine*, vol. 5, no. 3, Fall 1984.

Bernstein, L. M. and R. E. Williamson. "Testing of a Natural Language Retrieval System for a Full Text Knowledge Base." *Journal of the American Society for Information Sciences*, vol. 35, no. 4, July 1984, 235-257.

Brown, H., C. Tong, and G. Foyster. "PALLADIO: an exploratory environment for circuit design." *IEEE Computer*, December 1983, 41-55.

Buchanan, B. G. and E. A. Feigenbaum. "DENDRAL and Meta-DENDRAL: their applications dimension." *Artificial Intelligence*, vol. 11, 1978.

Callero, M., D. A. Waterman, and J. R. Kipps. "TATR: a prototype expert system for tactical air targeting." Report R-3096-ARPA, Rand Corporation, June 1984.

Carbonell, J. G., W. M. Boggs, and M. L. Mauldin. "The XCALIBUR Project: A Natural Language Interface to Expert Systems." *Proceedings, International Joint Conference on Artificial Intelligence*, vol. 2, 1983, 653-656.

Cohen, P. and M. D. Liberman, "A report in FOLIO: An expert assistant for portfolio managers." *Proceedings IJCAI-83*, 1983, 212-214.

Cullingford, R. E., M. W. Krueger, M. Selfridge, et al. "Automated explanations as a component computer-aided design system." *IEEE Transactions on Systems, and Cybernetics*, vol. SMC-12, no. 2, April 1982, 168-181.

DELTA/CATS-1. *The Artificial Intelligence Report*, vol. 1, no. 1, January 1984.

Doszkocs, T. E. and B. A. Rapp. "Searching MEDLINE in English: A Prototype User Interface with Natural Language Query, Ranked Output, and Relevance Feedback." *Information Choices and Policies*. R.D. Meeting, Minneapolis, Minnesota, American Society for Information Science, Knowledge Industrial Publications, Inc., White Plains, N.Y., October 1979, 131-139.

Emrich, E. "Expert Systems Tools and Techniques." Oak Ridge National Laboratory, ORNL/TM-9555, August 1985.

EXSYS, Inc. EXSYS Product Description (EXSYS is written in C, using backward chaining and simple production rules, and uncertainly factors), Albequerque, NM, 1985.

Fox, M. "Knowledge-Based Systems: Applications in the Industrial Environment." Texas Instruments AI Satellite Symposium (A Project Management Expert System, developed for DEC), Nov. 1985, 109-114.

Fox, M. S. "Techniques for sensor-based diagnosis." *Proceedings IJCAI-83*, 1983, 158-163.

Griesmer, J. H., S. J. Hong, M. Karnaugh, et al. "YES/MVS: A continuous real time expert system." *Proceedings AAAI-84*, 1984.

Haley, P., J. Kowalski, J. McDermott, et al. "PTRANS: A rule-based management assistant." Technical Report, Computer Science Dept., Carnegie-Mellon University, Pittsburgh, PA, January 1983.

Hollander, C. R. and Y. Iwasaki. "The drilling advisor: an expert system application." In *Fundamentals of Knowledge Engineering*, Teknowledge Report, 1983.

Hollan, J. D., E. L. Hutchins, and L. Weitzman. "STEAMER: an interactive inspectable simulation-based training system." *The AI Magazine*, vol. 5, no. 2, 1984.

Howard, H. C. and D. R. Rehak. "Knowledge Based Database Management for Expert Systems." *ACM Sigart Newsletter*, Special Interest Group on Artificial Intelligence, Association for Computing Machinery, Spring 1985.

Javelin Software. Javelin Product Description, Cambridge, MA, 1985.

Kahn, G. and J. McDermott. "The MUD system." *Proceedings of the First Conference on Artificial Intelligence Appications*. IEEE Computer Society, December 1984.

Kaplan, S. J. "Designing a Portable Natural Language Database Query System." *ACM Transactions on Database Systems*, Association for Computing Machinery, vol. 9, no. 1, March 1984, 1-19.

Kellogg, C. "The Transition from Data Management to Knowledge Management." *Proceedings, International Conference on Data Engineering*. Los Angeles, CA, Institute of Electrical and Electronics Engineers, IEEE Computer Society Press, April 1984, 467-472.

Kim, J. and J. McDermott. "TALIB: an IC layout design assistant." *Proceedings AAAI-83*, 1983.

Kiremidjian, G., A. Clarkson, and D. Lenat. "Expert system for tactical indications and warning (I&W) analysis." *Proceedings of the Army Conference on the Application of AI to Battlefield Information Management*, Report AD-A139 685, Battelle Columbus Laboratories, Washington, D.C., 1983 (I&W).

Kogan, D. "The Manager's Assistant — An Application of Knowledge Management." *Proceedings, International Conference on Data Engineering*, Los Angeles, CA, Institute of Electrical and Electronics Engineers, IEEE Computer Society Press, April 1984, 592-595.

Kornell, Jim. "A VAX tuning expert built using automated knowledge acquisition." *Proceedings of the First Conference on Artificial Intelligence Applications*. IEEE Computer Society, December 1984.

Laffey, T. J., W. A. Perkins, and O. Firschein. "LES: a model-based expert system for electronic maintenance." *Proceedings of the Joint Services Workshop on AI in Maintenance*, October 4-6, 1984, 1-17.

Lopez, L. A., S. L. Elam, and T. Christopherson. "SICAD: A Prototype Implementation System for CAD." Proceedings, ASCE Third Conference on Computing in Civil Engineering, San Diego, CA, American Society of Civil Engineers (ASCE), April 1984, 84-94.

McDermott, J. "Building expert systems." In W. Reitman (ed.), *Artificial Intelligence Applications for Business*, Norwood, NJ: Ablex, 1984.

McDonnell Douglas. REVEAL Product Description, 1985.

Michalski, R. S., J. H. Davis, V. S. Bisht, and J. B. Sinclair, "PLANT/ds: an expert consulting system for the diagnosis of soybean diseases." *Proceedings of the Fifth European Conference on Artificial Intelligence*, Orsay, France, July 1982.

Micro Data Base Systems. Guru Product Description, Lafayette, IN 1985.

Miller, R. A., H. E. Pople, Jr., and J. D. Myers, "INTERNIST-1, an experimental computer-based diagnostic consultant for general internal medicine." *New England Journal of Medicine*, vol. 307, no. 8, August 1982, 468-476.

Minker, J. "Search Strategy and Selection Function for an Inferential Relational Database." *Transactions on Database Systems*, ACM, vol. 3, no. 1, March 1978, 1-31.

Motro, A. "Browsing in a Loosely Structured Database." ACM SIGMOD, vol. 14, no. 2, June 1984, 197-207.

Mulsant, B. and D. Servan-Schreiber. "Knowledge engineering: a daily activity on a hospital ward." *Computers and Biomedical Research*, vol. 17, 1984, 71-91.

Nelson, W. R. "REACTOR: an expert system for diagnosis and treatment of nuclear reactor accidents." *Proceedings AAAI-82*, 1982, 296-301.

Nii, H. P., E. A. Feigenbaum, J. J. Anton, et al. "Signal-to-symbol transformation: HASP/SIAP case study." *The AI Magazine*, Spring 1982, 23-35.

Polit, Stephen. "R1 and beyond: AI technology transfer at DEC," *The AI Magazine*. Winter 1985.

Pollock, J. J. "Quantification, Retrieval, and Automatic Identification of Numerical Data in Organic Chemistry Journals." *Journal of Chemical Information and Computer Sciences*, vol. 24, no. 3, August 1984, 139-147.

Rehak, D. and H. Howard. "Interfacing Expert Systems with Design Databases in Integrated CAD Systems." *Computer-Aided Design*, vol. 17, no. 9, November 1985.

Sager, N. and M. Kosaka. "A Database of Literature Organized by Relations." *Proceedings, The Seventh Annual Symposium on Computer Applications in Medical Care*, R. E. Dayhoff (ed.), Washington, D.C., Institute of Electrical and Electronics Engineers, October 1983, 692-695.

Shubin, H. and J. W. Ulrich. "IDT: an intelligent diagnostic tool." *Proceedings AAAI-82*, 1982, 209-295.

Smith, R. G. "On the development of commercial expert systems." *The AI Magazine*, vol. 5, no. 3, Fall 1984.

South Data. Superfile ACLS Product Description, U.K., 1985.

Stallman, R. M. and G. J. Sussman, "Problem solving about electrical circuits." In P. Winston and R. Brown (eds.), *Artificial Intelligence: An MIT Perspective*, vol. 1, MIT Press, 1979, 30-91.

Stefik, M. "Inferring DNA structures from segmentation data." *Artificial Intelligence*, vol. 11, 1978, 85-114.

Waterman, Donald A. *A Guide to Expert Systems*. Reading, MA: Addison-Wesley, 1986.

Weiss, S. M. and C. A. Kulikowski. "Developing microprocessor-based expert models for instrument interpretation." *Proceedings IJCAI-81*, 1981, 853-855.

Wipke, W. Tod, Glen I. Ouchi, and S. Krishnan. "Simulation and evaluation of chemical synthesis—SECS: an application of artificial intelligence techniques." *Artificial Intelligence*, vol. 11, 1978.

Wong, C. M. and S. Lanning. "Artificial intelligence in chemical analysis," *Energy and Technology Review*. Lawrence Livermore National Laboratory, February 1984.

Wright, J. M. and M. S. Fox. "SRL/1.5 user manual." Robotics Institute, Carnegie-Mellon University, Pittsburgh, PA, December 1983.

Wright, J. R., F. D. Miller, G. U. E. Otto, et al. "ACE: going from prototype to product with an expert system." *ACM Conference Proceedings*, October 1984.

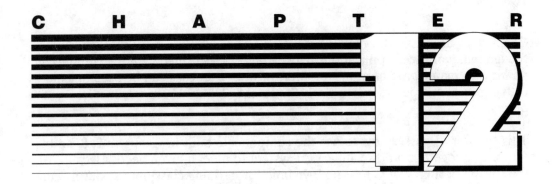

BUILDING AND DELIVERY OF EXPERT SYSTEMS

Chapter 11 discusses the main application of expert system technology. Even though many of these applications may be better performed with the computing power of a mainframe or minicomputer, most of the tasks can be accomplished with personal computers, particularly the Intel 80286- or 80386-based microcomputers.

This chapter discusses how to use the components built in Chapters 7, 8, and 9 for putting together a powerful expert system to meet a given need. Because of the special property of C++ (nondynamic for defining class objects during run time), you need to use an expert system tool to rapidly prototype a real-world problem in order to obtain a satisfactory structure of the problem before C++ is used to represent data and knowledge. Topics in this chapter include building expert systems in C++, structuring the problem, rapid-prototyping of the Inventory Control System, converting the prototype into C/C++, and delivering expert systems.

A GENERAL PROCEDURE FOR
BUILDING EXPERT SYSTEMS IN C/C++

The three major components of an expert system discussed in Chapters 7, 8, 9, and 10 are as follows:

- Knowledge Representation

    frame structure

    rule structure

    logic structure

- Inference engine

    forward chaining

    backward chaining

    reasoning/searching

- User interface

    input/output menus

    file operations (optional)

    graphics (optional)

    natural language interface (optional)

    window (optimal)

All or part of these components may be used to build expert systems. Because significant attention has been paid to the object-oriented programming rule, each program should be modular, and appropriate subcomponents can be selected to build an expert system shell that satisfies the current need. For example, if a small expert system is required for interfacing with large conventional programs to facilitate their input/output speed and convenience, only the following subcomponents may be required:

- rule structure

- forward chaining/reasoning/depth-first search

- input/output menus

- file operations

- natural language interface

To make this selection process convenient, you need to name the file of each subcomponent meaningfully and put the files in the library described in Chapter 10, for example,

      RULE.C   the file for the rule operation

      MOUSE.C   the file for the mouse operation

TOPLEVEL.C is needed to select various subcomponents:

- to tell the computer which subcomponents are included in this program

- to inform the user of the name of the program, the copyright logo, how to use the program, etc.

For the C++ class and function name overloading to be effectively used, the following procedure is recommended in building an expert system:

1. Structure the problem to do the following:

   - define the functions and modes to operate

   - select appropriate data types

   - establish communications links

2. Use an expert system tool (IQ-200) to rapidly prototype an expert system.

3. Debug and refine the prototype until it is satisfactory.

4. Use C++ and the library functions in Chapter 10 to convert the expert system.

The Inventory Control System that has been discussed throughout the book will be used to demonstrate this procedure.

STRUCTURING THE
INVENTORY CONTROL SYSTEM (ICS) PROBLEM

The ICS problem is as follows: three Mazda automobile dealers sustain small inventories on the parts most commonly requested by their customers. However, due to lack of communication between the dealers and the warehouse that supplies the parts, customers are often dissatisfied because the part is not available without a minimum two-week delay while the part is being ordered and shipped. In addition, a slight delay occurs on the turn-around between the time the dealer requests information on the current price or availability of the item and the time that information is received. Rules of thumb regarding how customers should be served can be extracted from experienced clerks and sales persons. Rules can also be obtained on the optimal inventory level that satisfies both the customer needs and capital requirement.

A communication system between the warehouse and the dealers is needed to maintain optimal supplies of the most requested Mazda parts at each of the dealer locations. Unfortunately, the database information available is in a variety of formats: the dealers maintain customer and inventory information in dBASE III files, while the warehouse uses dBASE III files for inventory and Lotus 1-2-3 files for sales information. In addition, there is no means of communication between the various computer networks.

The ICS is an intelligent information system that would allow a parts dealer or shop owner to control inventory, maintain an optimal level of stocks, record translations, reorder stocks, and check at any moment the condition of a given part (e.g., the cost, degree of customer satisfaction, and supplier's delivery schedule) in a cost-effective manner.

The minimum functionalities for such a system would include the following:

1. organization of parts inventory information in an easy-to-understand manner

2. accepting rules of how parts are sold, purchased, priced, and other heuristic knowledge

3. communicating with other information systems that contain necessary information, e.g., dBASE III

The first step in the creation of the application involves the decision as to what information is necessary, and in what forms, to create a product that is easy to use for both the dealers and the warehouse. Each dealer requires a number of functions at the time a new customer approaches the dealer for a particular part:

1. Check for the availability of the part at the approached dealer.

2. If part is not in stock, check nearby dealers for availability.

3. If part is not in stock at nearby dealers, notify warehouse of need to order.

4. For customer information, obtain listing of current orders and customers waiting for parts, and register customer complaints.

5. For dealer information, obtain listing of current prices of parts available at warehouse.

From the point of view of the warehouse, the following information would be helpful on a daily basis:

- statistics on the most requested parts — at individual dealerships and as a group

- access to the orders the dealers need to process orders and adjust inventories

- monitoring of inventory levels within the warehouse

IQ-200 (see detailed technical summary in Appendix A) will be used to prototype the ICS.

RAPID-PROTOTYPING THE ICS WITH IQ-200

Listing 12.1 shows the source code in IQ-200 for the ICS prototype. The listing includes the following files:

1. **ICSINT1.BPL**   interface commands
2. **ICSHOST2.BPL**   host, program, and operating system definitions
3. **ICSOBJ3.BPL**   knowledge base objects
4. **ICSKS4.BPL**   remote knowledge sources
5. **ICSHELP.TXT**   application help file

Listing 12.1:   A Sample Program for the Inventory Control System Prototype Using IQ-200

```
#| **********************************************************************


            1.    Inventory Control Demo INTERFACE


********************************************************************** |#


(define-interface 'inventory-control
  :banner " Inventory Control System Demonstration "
  :hot-keys '((224 (start-help)) (238 (quit-interface)) ; f1 and f2
            (#\c-d (dos)) (#\c-r (redraw-screen)) (#\c-m (mouse-initialize)))
  :hot-keys-doc " F1: Help  F10: Quit  C-D: Dos  C-R: Redraw  C-M: Init Mouse "
  :help-file-pathname "c:\\iq200\\examples\\icshelp.txt")


;;;_____MODES


(define-mode 'inventory-control 'toplevel-mode " Inventory Toplevel "
  '(("Dealership" (run-mode 'dealership-operations-mode))
    ("Warehouse" (run-mode 'warehouse-operations-mode))
    ("System"  (run-mode 'system-operations-mode))
    ("Help" (start-help 'toplevel-mode))
    ("Quit" (quit-interface))))
```

continued...

...from previous page

```
(define-mode 'inventory-control 'Dealership-Operations-Mode " Dealers "
  '(("Inventory" (view-dealer-inventory) :doc "Inventory of a dealer")
    ("Purchase" (request-sale) :doc "Purchase an item")
    ("Order" (order-part) :doc "Enter order from warehouse")
    ("Show Outstanding" (view-outstanding-orders)
                        :doc "Show outstanding orders")
    ("Show Processed" (view-processed-orders) :doc "Show processed orders")
    ("Check-Dealers" (check-dealers) :doc "Check dealers for part")))

(define-mode 'inventory-control 'warehouse-Operations-Mode " Warehouses "
  '(("View Inventory" (view-warehouse-inventory) :doc "View entire inventory")
    ("Price" (Get-Price) :doc "Get discounted price of part")
    ("Process Orders" (process-orders) :doc "Process Outstanding Orders")
    ("Low Inventories" (check-low-inventories) :doc "Check Low Inventories")
    ("Sales Percentage" (sales-percentage) :doc "Part % of total sales")))

(define-mode 'inventory-control 'system-operations-mode " System "
  '(("Redraw" (redraw-screen) :doc "Redraw the screen")
    ("Go to DOS" (dos))))


;;;_____DEALER PROCEDURES
;;;DEALER INVENTORY
(defprocedure view-dealer-inventory
  (deactivate-rule-set 'basic-rule-set)
  (activate-rule-set 'userint-rules)
  (activate-rule-set 'd-inv-rules)
  (query '(show-dealer-inventory))
  (user-pause))




;;;PURCHASE
(defprocedure request-sale
  (deactivate-rule-set 'basic-rule-set)
  (activate-rule-set 'userint-rules)
  (activate-rule-set 'request-rules)
  (query '(request-part))
  (user-pause))
```

continued...

...from previous page

```
;;;ORDER PART
(defprocedure Order-Part
  (deactivate-rule-set 'basic-rule-set)
  (activate-rule-set 'userint-rules)
  (activate-rule-set 'order-rules)
  (query '(order-part))
  (user-pause))


;;;VIEW CUSTOMER ORDERS
(defprocedure View-Outstanding-Orders
  (deactivate-rule-set 'basic-rule-set)
  (activate-rule-set 'userint-rules)
  (activate-rule-set 'view-outstanding-rules)
  (query '(view-orders))
  (user-pause))


;;;VIEW PROCESSED ORDERS
(defprocedure View-Processed-Orders
  (deactivate-rule-set 'basic-rule-set)
  (activate-rule-set 'userint-rules)
  (activate-rule-set 'view-processed-rules)
  (query '(view-processed-orders))
  (user-pause))


;;;CHECK DEALERS
(defprocedure Check-Dealers
  (deactivate-rule-set 'basic-rule-set)
  (activate-rule-set 'userint-rules)
  (activate-rule-set 'request-rules)
  (query '(dealer-check))
  (user-pause))
```

continued...

...from previous page

```
;;;_____WAREHOUSE PROCEDURES

;;;WAREHOUSE INVENTORY
(defprocedure View-Warehouse-Inventory
  (deactivate-rule-set 'basic-rule-set)
  (activate-rule-set 'userint-rules)
  (activate-rule-set 'w-inv-rules)
  (query '(show-warehouse-inventory))
  (user-pause))



;;;PRICE
(defprocedure Get-Price
  (deactivate-rule-set 'basic-rule-set)
  (activate-rule-set 'userint-rules)
  (activate-rule-set 'price-rules)
  (query '(display-price))
  (user-pause))



;;;PROCESS CUSTOMER ORDERS
(defprocedure Process-Orders
  (deactivate-rule-set 'basic-rule-set)
  (activate-rule-set 'userint-rules)
  (activate-rule-set 'process-order-rules)
  (stash '(value-of part-found nil))
  (query '(process-orders))
  (user-pause))

;;;LOW INVENTORIES
(defprocedure Check-Low-Inventories
  (deactivate-rule-set 'basic-rule-set)
  (activate-rule-set 'userint-rules)
  (activate-rule-set 'low-inv-rules)
  (stash '(value-of part-found nil))
  (query '(identify-critical-inventories))
  (user-pause))
```

continued...

...from previous page

```
;;;SALES PERCENTAGE
(defprocedure Sales-Percentage
  (deactivate-rule-set 'basic-rule-set)
  (activate-rule-set 'userint-rules)
  (activate-rule-set 'percentage-rules)
  (stash '(value-of total-sales 0))
  (stash '(value-of part-sales 0))
  (query '(get-sales-percentage))
  (user-pause))



#| **********************************************************************

            2.    Baldur Host Setup file.


 \'s for the c regexpr parser must be doubled (for lisp)
 ********************************************************************** |#

(define-host 'baldur :phone-number 7329715 :password 'changeme1
             :password2 'changeme2 :os 'dos
             :programs '((dbase3 "c:\\dbase\\") (sql "c:\\sqlbase\\"))
             :toplevel-program 'baldur-server
             :documentation "Hayward AT #1: God of light and Joy (Helios)")
(define-host 'odin :phone-number 7329716 :password 'changeme1
             :password2 'changeme2 :os 'dos
             :programs '((dbase3 "c:\\dbase\\") (sql "c:\\sqlbase\\"))
             :toplevel-program 'baldur-server
             :documentation "Hayward AT #2: Lord of the Gods (Zeus)")
(define-host 'thor :phone-number 3276521 :password 'changeme1
             :password2 'changeme2 :os 'dos
             :programs '((dbase3 "c:\\dbase\\") (sql "c:\\sqlbase\\"))
             :toplevel-program 'baldur-server
             :documentation "Menlo Park AT #1: The War-God (Ares)")
(define-host 'ymer :phone-number 3253860 :password 'changeme1
             :password2 'changeme2 :os 'dos
             :programs '((dbase3 "c:\\dbase\\") (sql "c:\\sqlbase\\"))
             :toplevel-program 'baldur-server
             :documentation "Menlo Park AT #2")
```

continued...

...from previous page

```
(define-host 'tyr :phone-number 3269106 :password 'changeme1
             :password2 'changeme2 :os 'dos
             :programs '((dbase3 "c:\\dbase\\") (sql "c:\\sqlbase\\"))
             :toplevel-program 'baldur-server
             :documentation "Stanford AT #2: The father of the Gods (Kronos)")
(define-host 'loki :phone-number 3234754 :password 'changeme1
             :password2 'changeme2 :os 'dos
             :programs '((dbase3 "c:\\dbase\\") (sql "c:\\sqlbase\\"))
             :toplevel-program 'baldur-server
             :documentation "Stanford AT #1: The mischievous God")
```

```
#| **********************************************************************

        3.    Inventory Control System Demo OBJECTS

   This file contains all the objects for use with the ICS Demo.
   ********************************************************************** |#


;;;_____RULE SETS

(create-rule-set 'dealer-rules)
    (create-rule-set 'request-rules :superset 'dealer-rules)
    (create-rule-set 'order-rules :superset 'dealer-rules)
    (create-rule-set 'd-inv-rules :superset 'dealer-rules)
    (create-rule-set 'view-outstanding-rules :superset 'dealer-rules)
    (create-rule-set 'view-processed-rules :superset 'dealer-rules)


(create-rule-set 'warehouse-rules)
    (create-rule-set 'w-inv-rules :superset 'warehouse-rules)
    (create-rule-set 'price-rules :superset 'warehouse-rules)
    (create-rule-set 'low-inv-rules :superset 'warehouse-rules)
    (create-rule-set 'process-order-rules :superset 'warehouse-rules)
    (create-rule-set 'percentage-rules :superset 'warehouse-rules)

(create-rule-set 'userint-rules)
```

continued...

...from previous page

```
;;; **************************************************************************
;;; Rules to determine what parts, dealers, and warehouses exist.

;;; Parts list rules
(create-variable 'parts-list :constraint :list)

(create-rule 'get-parts-list :rule-set 'userint-rules
          :premise '(and (format "~%Compiling list of parts...")
                         (set-of ?name
                                 (entity ?x is-a san-fran-inv
                                         with name = ?name)
                                 ?p)
                         (or (not (equal ?p nil))
                             (format "no parts found at San-Fran!!")))
          :action '(stash '(value-of parts-list ?p))
          :conclusion '(get-parts-list ?p))

(create-rule 'Part-List :rule-set 'userint-rules
          :premise '(and (cut)
                         (or (value-of parts-list ?list)
                             (get-parts-list ?list)))
          :conclusion '(get-list :part ?list))

;;; Warehouse & Dealer list rules

(create-rule 'Warehouse-List :rule-set 'userint-rules
          :premise '(set-of ?x (entity ?x is-a warehouse) ?list)
          :conclusion '(get-list :warehouse ?list))
(create-rule 'Dealer-List :rule-set 'userint-rules
          :premise '(set-of ?x (entity ?x is-a dealer) ?list)
          :conclusion '(get-list :dealer ?list))

;;;_____SPECIAL I/O RULES

;;; Supports types of :dealer :warehouse :part
```

continued...

...from previous page

```
;;; (achieve '(pick-value "Enter dealer to use" :dealer ?answer))

(create-rule 'pick-value :rule-set 'userint-rules
     :premise '(and (get-list ?type ?list)
              (cut)
              (menu-choose ?list ?string ?result))
     :conclusion '(pick-value ?string ?type ?result))


;;;**********************************************************************
;;;                     DEALERSHIP OPERATION RULES                     *
;;;**********************************************************************


;;;_____DEALER INVENTORY

(create-rule 'display-dealer-inv :rule-set 'd-inv-rules
     :premise '(and (pick-value "Enter dealer to use" :dealer ?dealer)
               (entity ?dealer is-a dealer with inventory = ?inv)
               (entity ?ent is-a ?inv with name = ?part-name
                      with cil = ?cil)
               (format "~%Part-Name: ~A, Number in Stock: ~A"
                      ?part-name ?cil)
               (fail))

     :conclusion '(show-dealer-inventory))

;;;_____REQUEST SALE

(create-rule 'new-request :rule-set 'request-rules
     :premise '(and (pick-value "Enter dealer to use" :dealer ?dealer)
            (or (and (remote-dealer ?dealer) (cut)
                (format "~%Sorry, ~A is a foreign dealer and cannot"
                       ?dealer)
                   (format "~%accept purchases at this location.")
                   (fail))
               (succeed))
            (pick-value "Enter part to use" :part ?part-name)
            (menu-input "Enter number desired" :integer ?num)
            (format "~%Looking in ~A's inventory for ~A"
                   ?dealer ?part-name)
            (request ?dealer ?part-name ?num))
       :conclusion '(request-part))
```

continued...

...from previous page

```
(create-rule 'process-request :rule-set 'request-rules
        :premise '(or (and (num-available? ?curr-deal ?part-name ?num)
                        (format
                        "~%Part ~A is in stock in ~A.  Reducing inventory..."
                                ?part-name ?curr-deal)
                        (reduce-inv ?curr-deal ?part-name ?num))
                    (format
                    "~%Part ~A not available at ~A.
                    ~%Try checking other dealers or ordering part."
                            ?part-name ?curr-deal))
        :conclusion '(request ?curr-deal ?part-name ?num))


(create-rule 'remote-dealer :rule-set 'request-rules
        :premise '(and (inventory ?dealer ?inv)
                    (entity ?ks is-a knowledge-source
                            with class-defined = ?inv))
        :conclusion '(remote-dealer ?dealer))

(create-rule 'reduce-inventory :rule-set 'request-rules
    :premise '(and (inventory ?curr-deal ?inv)
                (entity ?ent is-a ?inv with name = ?part-name
                        with cil = ?old)
                (- ?old ?num ?new)
                (format "~%Inventory at ~A reduced from ~A to ~A."
                        ?curr-deal ?old ?new))
    :conclusion '(reduce-inv ?curr-deal ?part-name ?num)
    :action '(stash '(cil ?ent ?new)))

(create-rule 'Available :rule-set 'request-rules
    :premise '(and (inventory ?source ?inv)
                (entity ?ent is-a ?inv with name = ?part-name
                        with cil = ?cil)
                (<= ?number ?cil))
    :conclusion  '(num-available? ?source ?part-name ?number))


;;;_____ORDER PART
```

continued...

...from previous page

```
;;; Top level backward chaining rule.
(create-rule 'order-new-part :rule-set 'order-rules
      :premise '(and (pick-value "From which dealer?" :dealer ?curr-deal)
                     (pick-value "Choose part to order" :part ?part-name)
                     (choose-values
                       ((num :prompt "Number to order: " :constraint :integer
                             :mandatory? t)
                        (cust :prompt "New customer name: " :constraint :name
                              :mandatory? t)
                        (date :prompt "Order date: " :constraint :date
                              :mandatory? t))
                       "Enter Customer information"
                       ?num ?cust ?date)
                     (print-arrival-info ?cust ?part-name))
      :conclusion '(order-part)
      :action '(create-entity '?cust :class 'Stanford-Custs
                              :name '?cust :dealer '?curr-deal
                              :part '?part-name :quantity '?num
                              :order-date '?date))

;;; Gets arrival information from the warehouse.
(create-rule 'calc-days-to-arrival :rule-set 'order-rules
          :premise '(and (entity ?ware is-a warehouse)
                         (format "~%Looking for a warehouse that stocks ~A"
                                 ?part-name)
                         (inventory ?ware ?inv)
                         (entity ?ent is-a ?inv with name = ?part-name
                                 with order-time = ?days)
                         (format
                         "~%Warehouse ~A has the part.  Computing arrival certainty"
                         ?ware)
                         (or (adjust-certainty ?part-name) (succeed)))
          :conclusion '(days-to-arrival ?part-name ?days)
          :certainty 0.9)

(create-rule 'print-arrival-info :rule-set 'order-rules
      :premise '(and (certainty-of (days-to-arrival ?part-name ?days) ?cf)
                     (format
                     "~%The certainty of the order for ~A arriving in ~A days is ~A."
                     ?cust ?days ?cf))
      :conclusion '(print-arrival-info ?cust ?part-name))
```
continued...

...from previous page

```
;;; Adjustment for unreliable part deliveries.
(create-variable 'unreliable-parts :value '(parking_brake cooling_fan)
                :constraint :list
                :documentation "Parts whose delivery is more uncertain")

(create-rule 'adjust-certainty :rule-set 'order-rules
     :premise '(and (value-of unreliable-parts ?up)
                    (eval (member '?part-name '?up) ?result)
                    (not (equal ?result nil))
                    (format
                    "~%Delivery of part ~A found unreliable; adjusting arrival certainty."
                    ?part-name))
     :conclusion '(adjust-certainty ?part-name)
     :certainty .7)


;;;_____VIEW CUSTOMER ORDERS


;;;need OR rule for no order condition
(create-rule 'view-order :rule-set 'view-outstanding-rules
     :premise '(and (pick-value "Which dealer's customers?" :dealer ?deal)
                    (entity ?deal is-a dealer with customers = ?deal-custs)
                    (entity ?cust-ent is-a ?deal-custs with name = ?n
                            with part = ?pd)
                    (entity ?cust-ent is-a ?deal-custs with quantity = ?nd
                            with order-date = ?od)
                    (format "~%Customer: ~A, Part: ~A, Quantity: ~A, Ordered: ~A"
                    ?n ?pd ?nd ?od)
                    (fail))
     :conclusion '(view-orders))


;;;_____VIEW PROCESSED ORDERS


(create-rule 'view-processed-order :rule-set 'view-processed-rules
     :premise '(and (pick-value "Which dealer to view orders from?" :dealer
                               ?dealer)
                    (or (processed-order ?dealer ?cust ?part-name ?num)
                        (and (format "~%No orders processed for ~A" ?dealer)
                             (cut) (fail)))
                    (format "~%Order Processed for ~A:  Cust: ~A,  Part: ~A, Number: ~A.
                    " ?dealer ?cust ?part-name ?num)
                    (fail))
     :conclusion '(view-processed-orders))
```

continued...

...from previous page

```
;;;_____CHECK DEALERS

(create-rule 'Dealer-Check :rule-set 'request-rules
            :premise '(and (pick-value "Enter part to check" :part ?part-name)
                           (menu-input "Enter number desired" :integer ?num)
                           (format "~%COMMENCING FOREIGN DEALER INQUIRY...")
                           (entity ?dealer is-a dealer)
                           (format "~%~A..." ?dealer)
                           (or (and (num-available? ?dealer ?part-name ?num)
                                    (format "has ~A ~As in stock" ?num ?part-name))
                               (format "does not have enough ~As" ?part-name))
                           (fail))
            :conclusion '(dealer-check))


;;;**********************************************************************
;;;                   WAREHOUSE OPERATION RULES                        *
;;;**********************************************************************




;;;_____WAREHOUSE INVENTORY

(create-rule 'display-warehouse-inventories :rule-set 'w-inv-rules
     :premise '(and (pick-value "Choose warehouse to display"
                                :warehouse ?ware)
                    (inventory ?ware ?inv)
                    (entity ?ent is-a ?inv with name = ?part-name
                            with cost = ?cost with discount = ?discount)
                    (format "~%Part-Name: ~A, Cost: ~A, Discount: ~A."
                            ?part-name ?cost ?discount)
                    (fail))
     :conclusion '(show-warehouse-inventory))


;;;_____GET PRICE
```

continued...

...from previous page

```
(create-rule 'display-price :rule-set 'price-rules
     :premise '(and (pick-value "Enter warehouse to use" :warehouse ?ware)
                    (pick-value "Pricing for which part?" :part ?part-name)
                    (format "~%Requesting pricing information from warehouse")
                    (or (and (inventory ?ware ?inv)
                             (entity ?ware-ent is-a ?inv with name = ?part-name
                                    with cost = ?cost with discount = ?discount)
                             (true-cost ?cost ?discount ?true-cost)
                             (format "~%Current price of ~A (including $~A discount): $~A"
                                  ?part-name ?discount ?true-cost))
                        (format "~%Pricing information on ~A not found."
                                  ?part-name)))
     :conclusion '(display-price))


(create-rule 'True-Cost :rule-set 'price-rules
     :premise '(and (format "~%Evaluating discount costs")
                    (- ?cost ?discount ?tcost))
     :conclusion '(true-cost ?cost ?discount ?tcost))


;;;_____PROCESS CUSTOMER ORDERS

;;; this will transfer a part for every customer
(create-rule 'Process-Order :rule-set 'process-order-rules
     :premise '(and (pick-value "Enter warehouse to process orders"
                                    :warehouse ?ware)
                    (subclass ?customer customer)
                    (entity ?cust is-a ?customer with name = ?name
                            with part = ?part-name)
                    (entity ?cust is-a ?customer with dealer = ?dealer
                            with quantity = ?num)
                    (format "~%Transfer needed for customer ~A:" ?name)
                    (format "~%  ~A ~A from ~A to ~A"
                            ?num ?part-name ?ware ?dealer)
                    (transfer ?part-name ?num ?cust ?ware ?dealer)
                    (eval (stash '(value-of part-found t)))
                    (fail))
     :conclusion '(process-orders))
```

continued...

...from previous page

```
(create-rule 'notify-no-orders-to-process :rule-set 'process-order-rules
    :premise '(and (value-of part-found nil)
                    (format "~%There are no more current orders."))
    :conclusion '(process-orders)
    :priority 5)

(create-rule 'transfer-from-ware/delete-cust :rule-set 'process-order-rules
    :premise '(and (inventory ?ware ?ware-inv)
                (or (and (entity ?dealer is-a dealer)
                        (not (remote-dealer ?dealer)))
                    (and (format "~%  Dealer ~A does not exist locally"
                            ?dealer)
                        (fail)))
                (or (entity ?part-inv is-a ?ware-inv with name = ?part-name
                        with cil = ?cil)
                    (and (format
                    "~%  Could not confirm that warehouse ~A stocks this part"
                    ?ware) (fail)))
                (or (and (<= ?num ?cil)
                        (- ?cil ?num ?new-cil)
                        (format "~%  ~A ~A transfered to ~A for ~A."
                                ?num ?part-name ?dealer ?cust))
                    (and (format "~%  Transfer unsuccessful, insufficient supply at ~A"
                    ?ware)
                            (fail))))
    :conclusion '(transfer ?part-name ?num ?cust ?ware ?dealer)
    :action
    '(do-all (delete-entity '?cust)
            (stash '(and (cil ?part-inv ?new-cil) ; only do this if local!!
                    (processed-order ?dealer ?cust ?part-name ?num)))))

;;;_____LOW INVENTORIES

(create-variable 'part-found :constraint :boolean)
(create-variable 'threshold-inventory :value .25 :constraint :fraction)
```

continued...

...from previous page

```
(create-rule 'quarter-inv :rule-set 'low-inv-rules
     :premise '(and (pick-value "Enter warehouse to use" :warehouse ?ware)
                    (value-of threshold-inventory ?thres)
                    (format "~%Parts for warehouse ~A." ?ware)
                    (inventory ?ware ?inv)
                    (entity ?ware-ent is-a ?inv with name = ?name
                            with cil = ?cil with oil = ?oil)
                    (/ ?cil ?oil ?ratio)
                    (< ?ratio ?thres)
                    (* ?ratio 200 ?%ratio)
                    (eval (stash '(value-of part-found t)))
                    (format "~%Critical inventory on ~A:" ?name)
                    (format "~%  Current inventory is ~A% of optimal" ?%ratio)
                    (fail))
     :conclusion '(identify-critical-inventories))

(create-rule 'notify-no-low-invs :rule-set 'low-inv-rules
     :premise '(and (value-of part-found nil)
                    (format "~%No parts with critically low inventories."))
     :conclusion '(identify-critical-inventories)
     :priority 5)

;;;_____SALES PERCENTAGE

(create-variable 'total-sales :constraint :number)
(create-variable 'part-sales :constraint :number)

(create-rule 'calc-sales-init :rule-set 'percentage-rules
     :premise '(and (pick-value "Enter warehouse to use" :warehouse ?ware)
                    (pick-value "Enter part to use" :part ?part-name)
                    (format "~%Initializing warehouse query for ~A at ~A."
                            ?part-name ?ware)
                    (get-part-totals ?part-name ?ware)
                    (calc-sales-perc ?part-name))
     :conclusion '(get-sales-percentage))
```

continued...

...from previous page

```
(create-rule 'calc-stats :rule-set 'percentage-rules
     :premise '(or (and (sales-records ?ware ?sr)
                        (entity ?ent is-a ?sr with total-sale = ?total-sale)
                        (add-value-to-variable total-sales ?total-sale)
                        ; if the part is the one we want, add its sales
                        (part ?ent ?part-name)
                        (add-value-to-variable part-sales ?total-sale)
                        (fail))
                   (succeed))
     :conclusion '(get-part-totals ?part-name ?ware))

(create-rule 'calc-sales-percentage :rule-set 'percentage-rules
     :premise '(and (value-of total-sales ?total-sales)
                    (value-of part-sales ?part-sales)
                    (not (= ?total-sales 0))
                    (eval (* 200 (/ ?part-sales ?total-sales)) ?per)
                    (format "~%Sales statistics on ~A: " ?part-name)
                    (format "~%Part Sales = $~A.  Total Sales = $~A"
                            ?part-sales ?total-sales)
                    (format "~%Percentage of Total Sales = ~A%" ?per))
     :conclusion '(calc-sales-perc ?part-name))

(create-rule 'notify-part-not-found :rule-set 'percentage-rules
     :premise '(format "~%No sales for part requested.")
     :conclusion '(get-sales-percentage)
     :priority 5)

(create-rule 'add-value-to-variable :rule-set 'percentage-rules
     :premise '(and (value-of ?variable ?old)
                    (+ ?old ?value ?new))
     :conclusion '(add-value-to-variable ?variable ?value)
     :action '(stash '(value-of ?variable ?new)))

;;;THE END
```

continued...

...from previous page

```
#| ***********************************************************************

    4.      Class and Knowledge Source definitions for ICS demo.

***********************************************************************|#

;;; Class definitions for dealer and warehouse inventories on car parts.
(create-class 'Location :documentation "Represents a location"
              :slots '((address :constraint :string)
                       (phone :constraint :number)
                       (inventory :constraint (:subclass inventory))))
(create-class 'Warehouse :documentation "Represents an actual warehouse"
              :superclass 'location
              :slots '((sales-records :constraint (:subclass sales-records))))
(create-class 'Dealer :documentation "Represents an actual dealer"
              :superclass 'location
              :slots '((customers :constraint (:subclass customer))))

(create-class 'Inventory :documentation "Inventory information on a part"
              :slots '((name :constraint :name)      ; part name
                       (cil :constraint :integer)     ;current invent level
                       (oil :constraint :integer)))   ;optimal invent level

(create-class 'Warehouse-Inv :superclass 'inventory
              :documentation "A Warehouse inventory on a part"
              :slots '((cost :constraint :number)
                       (discount :constraint :number)
                       (min-order :constraint :integer)
                       (order-time :constraint :integer)))

(create-class 'Dealer-Inv :superclass 'inventory
              :documentation "A dealer inventory on a part")

(create-class 'Customer :documentation "Dealership customer"
    :slots '((dealer :constraint :name)
             (name :constraint :name)
             (part :constraint :name)
             (quantity :constraint :number :when-needed 1)
             (order-date :constraint :date)
             (time :constraint :number)))
```

continued...

...from previous page

```
(create-class 'Sales-Records)

;;; ***********************************************************************
;;; Let's create a warehouse

(read-lotus123-class 'San-Fran-Sales-Records
                     :filename "c:\\iq200\\examples\\ware.wk1"
                     :superclass 'Sales-Records
                     :slot-names-row 0
                     :deleted-rows '(1)
                     :deleted-columns '(1))

(create-class 'San-Fran-Inv :superclass 'warehouse-inv
              :documentation "Inventory of parts for San Francisco Warehouse")
(define-knowledge-source 'San-FranKS :host :local
  :program 'dbase3
  :filename "c:\\iq200\\examples\\ware.dbf"
  :class-defined 'San-Fran-Inv
  :slot-with-entity-name nil
  :name-constrained-slots '(name)
  :slot-name-translations '((min-order min_ord) (order-time order_time)))

#|
(read-dbase3-class 'San-Fran-Inv
                   :superclass 'warehouse-inv
                   :filename "c:\\iq200\\examples\\ware.dbf"
                   :slot-with-entity-name nil
                   :name-constrained-slots '(name)
                   :slot-name-translations '((min-order min_ord) (order-time order_time)))
|#
(create-warehouse 'San-Fran :inventory 'san-fran-inv :phone 7329715
                  :address "230 Geary St."
                  :sales-records 'san-fran-sales-records)
```

continued...

...from previous page

```
;;; **********************************************************************
;;; Let's create some dealers

;;; Stanford dealer
(read-dbase3-class 'Stanford-Inv
                   :filename "c:\\iq200\\examples\\dealer1.dbf"
                   :superclass 'dealer-inv
                   :documentation "Stanford Inventory")

;;; local customers
(read-dbase3-class 'Stanford-Custs
                   :filename "c:\\iq200\\examples\\cust1.dbf"
                   :superclass 'customer
                   :slot-with-entity-name 'name
                   :name-constrained-slots '(name dealer part)
                   :slot-name-translations '((order-date order_date)))

(create-dealer 'stanford :inventory 'stanford-inv :phone 3269106
               :customers 'stanford-custs)


;;; Palo Alto dealer

(create-class 'Palo-Alto-Inv :superclass 'dealer-inv)
(define-knowledge-source 'Palo-AltoKS :host :local ; 'odin
  :program 'dbase3
  :filename "c:\\iq200\\examples\\dealer2.dbf"
  :name-constrained-slots '(name)
  :class-defined 'Palo-Alto-Inv)

(create-class 'Palo-Alto-Custs :superclass 'customer)
(define-knowledge-source 'Palo-Alto-CustKS :host :local  ; 'baldur
  :program 'dbase3
  :filename "c:\\iq200\\examples\\cust2.dbf"
  :slot-with-entity-name 'name
  :class-defined 'Palo-Alto-Custs
  :name-constrained-slots '(dealer name part)
  :slot-name-translations '((order-date order_date)))
```

continued...

...from previous page

```
(create-dealer 'palo-alto :inventory 'palo-alto-inv :phone 3276521
               :customers 'palo-alto-custs)

;;; Hayward Dealer
(create-class 'Hayward-Inv :superclass 'dealer-inv)
(define-knowledge-source 'HaywardKS :host :local
  :program 'dbase3
  :filename "c:\\iq200\\examples\\dealer3.dbf"
  :name-constrained-slots '(name)
  :class-defined 'Hayward-Inv)

(create-class 'Hayward-Custs :superclass 'customer)
(define-knowledge-source 'Hayward-custKS :host :local
  :program 'dbase3
  :filename "c:\\iq200\\examples\\cust3.dbf"
  :slot-with-entity-name 'name
  :name-constrained-slots '(dealer name part)
  :class-defined 'Hayward-Custs
  :slot-name-translations '((order-date order_date)))

(create-dealer 'hayward :inventory 'hayward-inv :phone 7329723
               :customers 'hayward-custs)

#| *********************************************************************

        5.   Help File

********************************************************************* |#



Title:
inventory-control
Text:

Welcome to the Mazda Inventory Control System (ICS).  This demo serves
as an introduction to IQ200 - the User Interface, Developers
Interface, and Communications.  The main function of the ICS is
to maintain inventories of automobile parts at a number of
dealerships and warehouses.
```

continued...

...from previous page

For assistance with the setup (loading demo files, setting up knowledge sources, hosts), see subsection SETUP.

Sub-Topics:
(Setup Dealership Warehouse System Help Quit)
Mode:
toplevel-mode

Title:
inventory-control.Setup
Text:

There are 4 files to be loaded before the demo can be used: ICSINT1.BPL, ICSHOST2.BPL, ICSOBJ3.BPL, and ICSKS4.BPL. The files can be in any directory. They should be loaded IN THE ORDER OF THEIR NUMBERS by using the IQ200 interface command Read (BPL). Otherwise, the file ICS.BPL can be loaded to do the loading automatically. The KS and HOST files may need to be edited to proper operation. The HOST file contains all the functions for setting defining external communications systems - computer modem lines, operating systems etc. You may want to change the NAME, PHONE NUMBER, and DBASE DIRECTORY of these hosts to represent the computers you will be working with. The KS file contains the descriptions of the sources (files external or local) you will be using for the dealerships and warehouse. Currently, all the knowledge sources are set up to use dBASE III files from the LOCAL computer. For these knowledge sources, you may wish to change the FILENAME slot to represent the location of the files. In order to make the knowledge sources remote for communications demonstration, change the HOST specifications of the individual knowledge sources (one of Hosts defined in ICSHOST2). In addition, you may wish to change the DB-FILE and CLASS-DEFINED to represent the names used for a particular situation. NOTE: the files ICSINT1 and ICSOBJ3 should never be changed; neither should any other slots than mentioned above; neither should any contents of the dbase and lotus files originally provided.

Title:
inventory-control.Dealership
Text:

continued...

...from previous page

The DEALERSHIP commands affect changes in the local dealership,
and gather knowledge from the external dealers and warehouses.
Each dealership maintains a limited selection (both in kind and
quantity) of the parts which are available at the warehouse.
This small inventory is used to satisfy the request of individual
customers at the dealership; if a part is not available (either
in kind or quantity) then the part can be ordered from the
warehouse, or other dealers can be checked for the part.

Sub-Topics:
(Inventory Purchase Order Show-Outstanding Show-Processed Check-Dealers)
Mode:
dealership-operations-mode

Title:
inventory-control.Dealership.Inventory
Text:

The inventory command has one input, the dealership to be used
for the command, and a listed output, the current inventory of
that dealer (part names and number in stock). If the dealer
chosen is an external source, the communications system will
automatically call up the proper host and obtain the information.
Note current inventories at a number of dealers before using
other commands (checking purposes).

Title:
inventory-control.Dealership.Purchase
Text:

Purchase is to discover if a part is available at a dealer in a
certain quantity. Its inputs are: dealer to use, part desired,
and number desired. The output depends on a) if the dealer
selected is local (cannot make purchases from remote dealers);
b) if the part is in stock in the proper quantity at the
dealership requested, the stock at the dealership is reduced and
the user is notified of the sale c) if the part is not in stock,

continued...

...from previous page

the user is asked to order the part (use ORDER command) or check
other dealers (CHECK-DEALERS). Note reduction in stock after a
successful sale using the INVENTORY command.

Title:
inventory-control.Dealership.Order
Text:

Order is used to tell the warehouse that a dealership REQUESTS a
new supply of a certain part. It is equivalent to writing a
letter to the warehouse - no reductions in inventory, sales, etc.
will occur upon completion of the procedure. The new order is
considered OUTSTANDING (as opposed to those processed by the
warehouse). Inputs are dealer, part, num desired, order name,
and date. Output is the creation of a customer internal to
Iq200.

Title:
inventory-control.Dealership.Show-Outstanding
Text:

Show-Outstanding merely displays the outstanding (non-processed)
orders at a certain dealer. Name of order, date, part, and
number are displayed. This list will be empty if all orders have
been processed.

Title:
inventory-control.Dealership.Show-Processed
Text:

This command shows all the orders which have been processed by
the warehouse. It will be the empty if their are no orders or
none of the available orders have been processed. Input is the
dealership whose orders you wish to display.

continued...

...from previous page

Title:
inventory-control.Dealership.Check-Dealers
Text:

The Check-Dealer command is useful for discovering which DEALERS have a certain part in stock. This is just a lookup procedure. The inputs are the part name and the quantity desired, while the output is a list of all dealers which have the quantity desired of the part in stock. When using communications, this command will sequentially call all of the hosts which are serving as dealers.

Title:
inventory-control.Warehouse
Text:

The WAREHOUSE commands operate on either local or non-local warehouse inventories. Warehouse inventories are much larger than dealer inventories, both in diversity of parts and in number available. The warehouse obviously serves as a backup for the dealers; if no dealership has a certain part, the part can be ordered by the warehouse. The warehouse also serves two other functions: the establishment of current pricing information for all dealerships, and the calculation of sales statistics on certain parts and groups of parts.

Sub-Topics:
(View-Inventory Price Process-Orders Low-Inventories)
Mode:
warehouse-operations-mode

Title:
inventory-control.Warehouse.View-Inventory
Text:

View-Inventory is a lookup command. It is used to display the current inventory of the warehouse at any period in time. The command will request the warehouse to use, and will exit by displaying a list of all parts and their current prices.

continued...

...from previous page

Title:
inventory-control.Warehouse.Price
Text:

PRICE obtains the current price of a part from the warehouse. It
will then attempt to evaluate any discounts on the part and
display the "true" cost of the part. Prices are shown for
quantity of one.

Title:
inventory-control.Warehouse.Process-Orders
Text:

Process-orders is used to satisfy the orders of the dealers by
transferring supplies of parts. For each order which is
outstanding at the dealers, the warehouse will attempt to reduce
its own inventory on the part and send the dealers the correct
quantity of the part. If the correct quantity is not available
at the warehouse, the order cannot be processed, and nothing
happens other than a notice to this effect. If the correct
quantity is available, the warehouse will reduce its own
inventory (note only possible if LOCAL; cant change external),
delete the customer entity, and store information about the
processed order. NOTE: the dealership inventory on the part is
NOT affected - the order is PROCESSED - meaning the order is
ready for pickup by the customer, and can be view using the
dealership SHOW-PROCESSED command.

Title:
inventory-control.Warehouse.Low-Inventories
Text:

Low inventories is a command which attempts to notify the user
about critically low inventories at the warehouse. The procedure
is to sequentially calculate the inventory ratio
(current-inv-level over optimal-inv-level) and display any parts

continued...

...from previous page

```
which are below 0.25.  Quarter inventory is therefore the
criteria for low inventory.  The command does not attempt to
alleviate any critical inventories.


Title:
inventory-control.System
Text:

System commands are commands for running the demonstration.
Commands are available for redrawing the screen, displaying the
rule structure, and exiting to Dos.

Sub-Topics:
(Redraw Go-To-Dos)
Mode:
system-operations-mode

Title:
inventory-control.System.Redraw
Text:

Redraws the screen.  Also available at any time by pressing C-R.


Title:
inventory-control.System.Go-To-Dos
Text:

Exits temporarily to DOS.  Type EXIT at the DOS prompt to return
to the demonstration.  Quick exit to DOS is also provided by
pressing C-X C-D.


Title:
inventory-control.Help
Text:
```

continued...

...from previous page

```
Help is available using the Help command, and by pressing the
<F1> function key.  Help from the command line is from top-level.
Help from <F1> is context sensitive (depending on the current
mode of operation).
```

```
Title:
inventory-control.Quit
Text:
```

```
The QUIT command is used to exit the demonstration and return to
IQ200.
```

Defining User-Interface Options

The ICS prototype is briefly explained below. To create a real application, first use the library command DEFINE-INTERFACE; to this you will add information concerning the functions you want to implement.

```
(define-interface :name 'inventory-control
    :banner " Inventory Control System "))
```

This command creates an interface that can be selected while in IQ-200 by pressing the F2 (go-to-interface) key or selecting Applications in the Utilities menu.

But first, you will define the list of top-level function calls that will control the various modes of operation (i.e., warehouse vs. dealer). Each one of these modes will have a "sensitive" item in the System Menu of the application.

```
(define-mode 'inv-control 'toplevel-mode "Inventory
Toplevel"
'(("Dealership" (run-mode 'dealership-operations-mode))
("Warehouse" (run-mode 'warehouse-operations-mode))
("Quit" (quit-interface))))
```

Selecting an item will present the commands of the mode in the Mode Menu. The previous command provides you with the following:

```
App Name:      inv-control
Mode Name:     toplevel-mode;top level mode of all applications
Doc:           "Inventory  Toplevel"
Choice-List:   Dealership, Warehouse, Quit ;three commands
```

You have now created the modes in which to run the functions and should declare function names for the functions themselves, placing them in the proper modes (dealership operations will be used as an example):

```
(define-mode 'inv-control 'Dealership-Operations-Mode "Dealers"
       '(("Request-Sale" (request-sale) :doc "Sell an item")
       ("View-Inventory" (view-inventory) :doc "View inventory")))
```

This command provides you with the following:

```
App Name:      inv-control
Mode-Name:     Dealership-Operations-Mode
Doc:           "dealers"
Choice-list:   Request-Sale, View-Inventory ;two commands
```

Now create the functions that will run when the commands created above are selected (use the View-Inventory function as an example):

```
(defprocedure view-inventory
(deactivate-rule-set 'basic-rule-set)
(activate-rule-set 'inventory-rules)
(assert-rule 'view-all-parts)
(user-pause)
(activate-all-rule-sets))
```

This procedure states that when View-Inventory is called, all the library functions in the procedure will be evaluated sequentially.

Creating Hosts/Knowledge Sources

Now you need to define the remote hosts and knowledge sources that will contain the external information. First, define the knowledge source for the warehouse.

The dBASE file contains fields for name, cil, oil, cost, and discount for the parts at the warehouse:

```
KNOWLEDGE-SOURCE    Warehouse-Parts
HOST                baldur
DBPROGRAM           dbase3
DB-FILE             "ware"
CLASS-DEFINED       san-fran
SUPERCLASS          warehouse-parts
FIELDS              (name cil oil cost discount)
```

Next, define the host computer Baldur:

```
HOST                  Baldur
phone-number          7329716
PASSWORD              changeme1
PASSWORD2             changeme2
OS                    baldur-dos
SETUP-STRINGS         ((dbase3 "c:\\rcd c:\\\\dbase\\r"))
TOPLEVEL-PROGRAM      baldur-server
```

Each knowledge (data) source, dealership, warehouse, and sales record has been defined in Listing 12.1. The ICS prototype has also been thoroughly tested and refined.

CONVERTING THE ICS TO C/C++

The ICS can be converted to C/C++ straightforwardly:

- Use C++ to convert frames, entities, slots, and member functions as shown in Listings 7.1 and 7.2 (Chapter 7). The organization of the ICS C/C++ programs is shown in Figure 12.1.

- Use the rule structure in Listing 7.4 (Chapter 7) to convert rules into C.

- Use the logic structure in Listing 7.5 (Chapter 7) to convert variable, unrelated facts to C.

- Prepare queries for the user by using Listing 9.3 (Chapter 9).

- Write additional user-interface subroutines to improve user convenience.

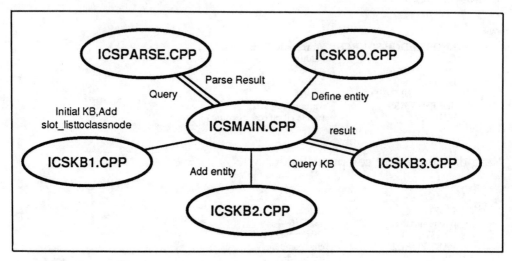

Figure 12.1   The organization of the ICS C/C + + programs

It is clear that the ICS conversion shown in Figure 12.1 is incomplete and requires further refinement for improved efficiency.

ISSUES OF EXPERT SYSTEM DELIVERY

After the expert system, such as ICS, has been successfully completed, you need to consider the delivery of the expert system. The issues of expert system delivery in the PC environment are slightly different from those for AI workstations and mainframe computers because PC expert systems tend to be smaller and less complicated. The main issues include user friendliness, convenience, usefulness, maintenance, and training.

User Friendliness

User friendliness is the most important criterion for winning user acceptance and overcoming any disincentives to using the system and to accepting the system as an office aid. Two important features identified with user friendliness are as follows:

- ease in getting into the system without training

- convenience in daily or occasional use without cumbersome memorization of operational procedures

With menus, help screens, graphics, and explanations, expert systems should be easier to get into and more convenient to use either routinely or occasionally than conventional software packages. In input queries during consultations and in output explanations stating consultation results, the following guidelines need to be observed carefully:

- Questions and explanations presented should be in the user's jargon.

- Explanations should be tailored to the user's level of expertise and adjusted accordingly.

- A reservoir of alternative questions or explanations should be available for use if the user fails to understand the initial set.

Convenience (Compatibility with the Working Environment)

Convenience to the user or compatibility with the working environment is generally overlooked by the developer until the expert system is field-tested. The example of DELTA illustrates the point vividly. DELTA was designed to be used by repair mechanics in railroad shops. DELTA calls for a hardened VAX computer, a videoplayer, a color terminal, and a printer; the cables connecting these individual units often become a formidable problem after a few relocations, i.e., transfers to other sites or even minor relocations in the same site.

When a system is designed, it is essential that the convenience to the user be carefully measured to prevent unexpected deficiencies. The following issues need to be assessed:

- Does the system call for overly complex facilities?

- Is an attempt made to use existing equipment in the working environment, e.g., personal computers?

- Does the system require an overly complicated assembly?

- Can the system tolerate the abuse of the intended/unintended user?

- Does the system require substantial additional effort on the part of the user to either carry or use it?

Usefulness of Products

Usefulness of products is the primary concern of many system designers because it is the objective of expert systems. Products include decisions recommended, advice given, or actions suggested, and training received by new users. Many PC expert system packages are compared with junior specialists or aides, such as loan officers, in their performance. Three useful strategies are as follows:

- First, target the performance of the system under development at the level of aides or junior specialists.

- Second, improve system performance to the level most suitable for the application after the system has been accepted.

- Third, be open to the user's suggestions; the usefulness of a product is determined by the user.

Usefulness of an expert system may also imply correctness of the advice it gives. Correctness of expert systems concerns accuracy of conclusions and reasoning they offer to the user. Conclusions should not be too vague to be useful; expert systems often provide the user with approximate, heuristic decisions or advice, making it difficult to assume the conclusions are accurate in the sense of numeric computation. Not all system designers are concerned about whether their expert systems reason correctly (i.e., whether they arrive at decisions in a human-expert-like manner) as long as the products they offer are appropriate.

However, in some applications (e.g., bank loan applications in which there are possible legal implications), the correctness of the reasoning mechanism of an expert system should receive as much emphasis as the conclusions themselves.

Maintenance

Maintenance may include improvement, expansion, and extension of an expert system: minor refinements, major refinements, expansion of coverage to a new related task, and extension of the task definition.

- **Minor refinements**: adding knowledge to improve the expert system's performance on an existing subtask.

- **Major refinements**: adding knowledge to enable the expert system to perform a new subtask.

- **Expansion of coverage to new, related equipment**: expanding the coverage of the expert significantly to include new equipment types.

- **Extension of the task definition**: extending new capacities of the expert system.

As discussed in Chapter 11, minor refinements is usually given as the reason for adding knowledge to an expert system to polish its performance. Using XCON as an example, of the more than 2,500 rules added to the original 777 rules over the period of four years, the recorded data indicate that slightly more than 10% of the rules were added to make minor improvements such as obtaining more complete knowledge on a subtask; 35% were added to provide capability needed to deal with new computer types, and up to 15% were added to extend the definition of XCON's task.

The four types of maintenance tasks may vary slightly for different expert systems. Appropriate maintenance procedures not only update the expert system but also assure the user's satisfaction.

Training

Training people to use large, complex expert systems and tools has been crucial because the many earlier versions of these systems and tools were not designed with the user in mind. For most PC expert systems and tools, training is less of a problem. A good training plan may be essential if a new expert system is to be widely used. The training requirement should not be more extensive than that required for WordStar or Lotus 1-2-3, for example, if the expert system is well designed to include sufficient user friendliness in system input and output.

SUMMARY

- This chapter has discussed how to use the components built in Chapters 7, 8, and 9 to put together a powerful expert system to meet a particular need. Because of C++'s special property (C++ is nondynamic for defining class objects during run time), you need to use an expert system tool to rapidly prototype a real-world problem so you can obtain a satisfactory model of the problem before using C++ to represent data and knowledge.

- Topics in this chapter include a general procedure for building expert systems in C++, structuring the problem, rapid-prototyping the Inventory Control System (ICS), converting the prototype into C/C++, and delivering expert systems.

- The ICS problem is as follows: three Mazda automobile dealers sustain small inventories on the parts most commonly requested by their customers. However, because of lack of communication between the dealers and the warehouse that supplies the parts, customers are often dissatisfied because the part is not available without a minimum two-week delay while the part is ordered and shipped. Rules of thumb regarding how to serve customers can be extracted from experienced clerks and sales persons. Rules can also be obtained on the optimal inventory level that satisfies both the customer needs and capital requirement.

- For the C++ class and function name overloading to be used effectively, the following procedure is recommended in building an expert system:

    1.　Structure the problem to do the following:

    　　a)　Define the functions and modes to operate.
    　　b)　Select appropriate data types.
    　　c)　Establish communications links.

    2.　Use an expert system tool (IQ-200) to rapidly prototype an expert system.

    3.　Debug and refine the prototype until it is satisfactory.

    4.　Use C++ and the library functions in Chapter 10 to convert the expert system.

- After an expert system, such as ICS, has been successfully completed, you need to be concerned with the delivery of the expert system. The main issues include user friendliness, convenience, usefulness, maintenance, and training.

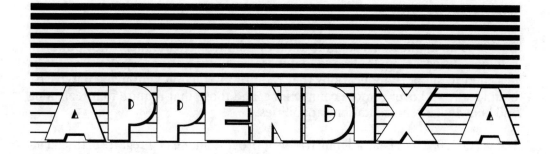

IQ-200 TECHNICAL SUMMARY

WHAT IS IQ-200?

IQ-200 is an applications support and development environment with powerful rule-based reasoning tools and database communication capabilities. It is designed to support applications that require interaction with many databases, both locally and over remote connections, and those that require rich reasoning and knowledge representation capabilities.

Using IQ-200, a database administrator or programmer can integrate artificial intelligence and object-oriented techniques with conventional databases and communications.

Data Integration

IQ-200 allows you to integrate and manage knowledge from many different sources: Data from the user or from static, relational, remote, or spreadsheet databases is handled all within one uniform, transparent data management mechanism. IQ-200 uses **knowledge sources** to define connections to remote databases. Once defined, all machine-specific protocols, such as logging on, opening files, making queries, etc., are handled by the knowledge source.

Rule-Based Reasoning

Additionally, IQ-200 allows you to accomplish **rule-based reasoning** over distributed knowledge sources. The integration of AI techniques with rule-based reasoning brings active power to previously static databases, allowing them to conclude new information based on inferences drawn from existing data.

FUNCTIONALITY OVERVIEW

Integration of Database Sources

IQ-200's **knowledge source** system enables it to connect to and reason over distributed databases. IQ-200 takes care of the headaches of multi-data-source management and provides the user with one uniform, powerful environment for manipulating all data sources. The following kinds of PC datafiles can be accessed directly from disk:

- Lotus 1-2-3 spreadsheet files

- dBASE III .dbf files

- IQ-200's own IQDB knowledge base files

Alternatively, if no direct access to datafiles is available, IQ-200 will allow you to link with programs that do have access, such as the following:

- a remote dBASE III database accessed via a modem

- a PC SQL database program accessed over a modem connection

- a mainframe-based SQL system such as DB2 over a network or modem connection

  Note: Please contact Baldur Systems regarding compatibility with specific SQL products.

Logic-Based Approach

Like most advanced database systems, IQ-200 is fully declarative in style: When making a query, you only need to specify *what* you want, but never how to get it; the rule-based logic will determine that for you. Additionally, the logic-based approach gives IQ-200 advantages over current DBMSs:

- **Deduction**: Through rules, IQ-200 can deduce information not explicitly represented in the database.

- **Recursion**: Queries that are difficult if not impossible to make in a typical database system can be solved easily using rules and recursive relations.

- **Explanation**: IQ-200 can be asked to explain the logic it used to solve a query. You can check that the answer is indeed what you asked for.

- **Uniformity**: Any fact or query can be represented in a uniform, first-order predicate logic language.

Knowledge and Data Representation

Object-Oriented Frames

- **Model-based reasoning**: You can create a model of your data universe by using objects to represent things in the real world.

- **Inheritance**: Unlike conventional database **tables**, IQ-200 **frames** simplify the creation of a structured database environment. By using frame inheritance, you can define parent-child relationships between frames, thus avoiding respecifying attributes that are common to both.

- **Active slot values**: An access to a slot of an object can automatically invoke any procedure or computation.

Knowledge Sources

Defining a connection to an external database system is easy. Linking a frame to a database table by using a knowledge source makes database communication details and information retrieval transparent to the user.

Predicate Fact Base

Any kind of information expressible through logic can be stored in the predicate fact base. Each piece of information has an associated certainty factor that can be used to express the validity of the information and results.

Rule Base

Logical dependencies, heuristic information, and computational procedures can be represented as **rules** in IQ-200.

Reasoning System

IQ-200's reasoning facilities were designed to provide maximum flexibilty for the programmer. Using the reasoning system, you can solve queries that depend on arbitrary combinations of objects, tables, variables, facts, spreadsheets, defaults, and even external functions. Reasoning system features include the following:

- Complete **pattern matching** of rules with variables.

- Complete combinations of **not, and**, and **or** in rules.

- **Backward** (goal-driven) reasoning, **forward** (event-driven) reasoning, or both kinds of reasoning can be used.

- **Rule sets** and **priorities** for meta-level control of inference.

- **Certainty factors**: Every fact in IQ-200 has an associated "degree of belief."

- **Justification system**: Every solved query can be explained by IQ-200.

- **Solutions with incomplete information**: defaults and when-needed active values.

- **Advanced reasoning constructs** like Prolog, such as cut, fail, succeed.

Communications System

IQ-200 includes a remote communications system, IQCOMM, which will allow IQ-200 to communicate with other computers.

- IQ-200 can enable a PC to automatically call up another computer, call up a database program, and retrieve information from a database file.

- The IQ-200 IQCOMM package provides a server program that will run on any PC, turning it into a database server. The PC can then be called up by the main IQ-200 system and queried for information.

- The user can directly use IQCOMM by setting up one PC to be the server and then dialing into it, using any standard modem software. The user can then log in and run command-line programs or transfer files.

- IQCOMM will also allow communications to other computers through networks. (Please contact Baldur Systems regarding compatibility with specific network systems.)

User Interface

An (optional) mouse-driven menu interface gives you access to most of IQ-200's functionality. Through this interface, you can create and modify data structures, query them, save them, interact with database files, and query remote database systems. A context-sensitive help facility allows you to obtain increasing levels of technical information on all aspects of the system.

IQ-200's natural language templates can shield the user or programmer from the details of a query language. The programmer can choose to use either predicate logic or simple English-like statements to create, modify, or query IQ-200 knowledge.

By means of IQ-200's interface-generation facility, the user can create screen-based, mouse-supporting, end-user interfaces to IQ-200 applications. You can even provide an IQ-200 context-sensitive help facility to the end user.

Interface to Other Programs

IQ-200 can bring expert system, object-oriented, database, and communications capabilities to other application programs. The IQDB extension library of functions is accessible both from the LISP and soon-to-be-released C languages. Also, support for the Microsoft Windows environment will soon be announced.

EXAMPLE

In this example, you will design a system that will allow a warehouse to get order information from dealers in several cities. Imagine that each of the dealers enters daily orders in a dBASE file in a PC and that the warehouse has a 1-2-3 spreadsheet with historical records of orders over the past year.

Using IQ-200, you would first define order classes representing each of the remote dealer order databases. Then, you would define knowledge sources to link each class to the respective remote data file. If you wanted to make adjustments based on seasonal variations, you could define rules to access the local 1-2-3 file to determine orders from historical ordering patterns. All of this could be done using IQ-200's mouse-driven menu system.

Now, the warehouse shipping agent wants to know how much of each part she should ship to each of the dealers this week. She would query the system (which is possible using natural language templates), asking IQ-200 to determine what the shipments should be. IQ-200 will take the query, see if the answer is already known (maybe somebody just asked five minutes ago), and if so, just display it. If the answer is not known, it will automatically call up the dealer PCs and retrieve the information from their dBASE III files.

If one of the dealers hasn't yet updated orders for the week, IQ-200 could examine the historical order records from last year and deduce a reasonable order quantity for that dealer. Say, for example, that even historical records aren't available; then, IQ-200 could ask the shipping agent directly for an order projection. If the agent has any doubt about how a projection was made, she can ASK IQ-200 to explain its reasoning.

SYSTEM REQUIREMENTS

The following equipment is required to run IQ-200:

- IBM AT or 100% compatible
- 1.5 megabytes extended memory

The following items are recommended:

- PC-compatible mouse
- Color monitor

The following items are required to use the IQCOMM communications system:

- a Hayes-compatible modem for each machine (workstation and servers)
- an installed dBASE III program for dBASE III database server

- an SQL database server (please contact Baldur Systems Corp. regarding connection to specific SQL products)

- 128 kilobytes for each server

To use the IQCOMM network communication system, please contact Baldur Systems Corp., 3423 Investment Blvd., Suite 12, Hayward, CA 94545 (415) 732-9715, regarding specific network requirements.

The following is required to use the IQ-DB library of functions:

- Gold Hill's Golden Common LISP version 2.2 or greater (please specify)

- up to 700K of LISP space (depending on subset used)

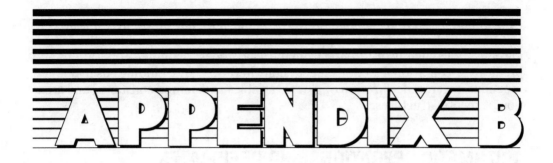

LISP FUNCTIONS THAT ARE SIMILAR BUT TOO COMPLEX TO EMULATE IN C/C++

LISP functions that are similar in purpose but may not be easily translated in C/C++ are discussed in this appendix. LISP allows you to perform the following operations slightly differently from the way C does: arithmetic operations and predicates, conditional actions, recursion, iteration and binding, user-defined functions, macros, declaration of global variables and named constants, and creation of record structures.

ARITHMETIC OPERATIONS AND PREDICATES

Mathematical calculations are not the principal use of the LISP language. The strength of the language is in symbolic manipulation.

Numbers in common LISP can be categorized as integers, ratios of two integers, floating point numbers, and complex numbers. The current version of GCLISP does not support complex numbers. Floating point numbers can be further divided into short, single, double, and long float; the precision for these floats can be short (13 bits), single (24 bits), double (50 bits), and long (50 bits). Actual precision varies among implementations. The basic arithmetic operations are listed below.

Arithmetic Operations

Function	Symbol	Arguments	Description	Example	Evaluation
Add	+	n	Add numbers	(+ 5 4)	9
difference	-		Subtract numbers from first	(- 5 3 1)	1
times	*	n	Multiply	(* 3 2 4)	24
quotient	/	2 or n	Divide first by second then third ...	(/ 4 5 2)	.4
add1	1+	1	Add one	(1+ 8)	9
sub1	1-	1	Subtract one	(1- 8)	7

continued...

Function	Symbol	Arguments	Description	Example	Evaluation
ex	exp	1	Exponent on e	(exp 3)	20.0855
expt	expt	2	Exponent on first	(expt 3 2)	9
log	log	1 or 2	A logarithm of first on second	(log 50 10)	1.699
sqrt	sqrt	1	Square root	(sqrt 9)	3
abs	abs	1	Absolute value	(abs -5)	5
sin	sin	1	Sine of radians	(sin 2.5)	
cos	cos	1	Cosine of radians	(cos 2.5)	
tan	tan	1	Tangent of radians	(tan 2.5)	
atan	atan	1 or 2	Arc tangent of radians	(atan 2.5)	
signum	signum	1	Sign of number if negative, -1 if zero, 0 if positive, 1	(signum -2)	-1
float	float	1 or 2	Convert first to float of same type as second	(float 6 3.0)	6.0
floor	floor	1	Greatest integer first	(floor 3.5)	3
ceiling	ceiling	1	Least integer not less than first	(ceiling 3.5)	4

continued...

Function	Symbol	Arguments	Description	Example	Evaluation
truncate	truncate	2	truncate first toward	(truncate 9 4)	2
round	round	1	round number	(round 9.8)	10
rem	mod	2	Smallest integer remainder	(mod 9 4)	1
incf	incf	2	Add value of second to first; the default for second is 1	setq m 0) (incf m) (incf m -3)	m = 0 m = 1 m = -2
decf	decf	2	Substract value of second from the first; default for second is 1	(setq m 0) (decf m) (decf m 5)	m = 0 m = -1 m = -6

Arithmetic Predicates

Nil and t are constants in Common LISP. **Nil** represents the logical false value and also the empty list ("F" in the following expressions). The value of **t** is always true ("T" in the following expressions). Arithmetic predicates are listed as follows:

Predicate	Symbol	Arguments	Description	Example	Evaluation
zerop	zerop	1	true if number is zero	(zerop 5)	F
plusp	plusp	1	true if number is positive	(plusp 5)	T
minusp	minusp	1	true if negative	(minusp -5)	T
oddp	oddp	1	true if odd integer	(oddp 7)	T
evenp	evenp	1	true if even integer	(even 8)	T
	=	n	true if arguments are all same	(= 2 2 2)	T
	/=	n	true if arguments are all different	(/= 2 3 4)	T
	<	n	true if arguments are increasing by 1s.	(2 3 4)	T
	>	n	true if arguments are decreasing by 1s	(7 6 5)	T
max	max	n	maximum argument	(max 2 3 4)	4
min	min	n	minimum argument	(min 2 3 4)	3

EVALUATION AND USER-DEFINED FUNCTIONS:
eval, apply, mapcar (apply-to-all), defun, lambda

So far, the expressions you have entered have been evaluated by an interpreter immediately, and the functions you used were written by someone else. In this section, five functions will be discussed — the first three for evaluation and the other two for writing your own functions to extend the convenience of the language. The function **eval** performs evaluation on lists, and **apply** and **mapcar** perform evaluation on functions. The eval function causes another evaluation beyond the one performed by the interpreter; each use of eval gives one more level of evaluation:

```
*(setq x 'y)

y

*(setq y 'z)

z

*x

y

*y

z

*(eval x)

z

*(eval (eval '''''Dave))

''Dave

*(eval (eval (eval '''''Dave)))

'Dave
```

The apply function takes a function name and its parameters, and evokes that function with the parameters; the parameters are not evaluated first:

```
*(apply #'cons '(because (I love you))

(because I love you)
```

Note that the symbol #' is required to tell LISP that it should expect a function name; the practice is similar to the symbol ' being required for the string of letters in an expression.

The mapcar function (sometimes called apply-to-all) applies a function to each element of the lists and returns a list of resultant elements. For example, if you want to add the elements of two equal-length lists, you can use the following statement:

```
*(mapcar #'+ '(1 5 10 20 25) '(1 2 3 4 5))

(2 7 13 24 30)
```

The defun and lambda functions allow you to write your own functions: **defun** defines named procedures, and **lambda** defines anonymous procedures.

The defun function has the following syntax format:

```
*(defun procedure name (parameter1, parameter2,...)

(things to be processed in this function)
    .
    .
    .

    )
```

All the parameters must appear in the main body of the function; it is all right to have a pair of parentheses instead of a parameter. For example, a very useful function in rapid-production of an expert system, **not-implemented-yet**, can be defined as follows:

```
*(defun not-implemented-yet ()

 (print 'This function is not implemented yet.)  ;print a message

 )
```

Defun can consist of any number of expressions, with the last expression determining the procedure's value.

The lambda function is used to define a function that will not be called upon too often (maybe once in a lifetime). The only difference between lambda and defun is that lambda does not have a procedure name. Lambda is particularly powerful for interfacing procedures to parameters in applying functions to more than one element in a list. For example, if you want to convert a list of miles to kilometers, you might attempt to write a statement such as

```
*(mapcar #'* '(1.6) (5 10 15 20 25))

(8)
```

Two problems cause the statement to be returned with a value (8). The two problems with this statement are as follows:

- The conversion factor list, (1.6), has only one element.

- Times (*), needs two arguments.

A lambda function will easily solve these problems:

```
*(mapcar #'(lambda (x)

(* x 1.6))

'(5 10 15 20 25)

)

(8 16 24 32 40)
```

CONDITIONAL ACTIONS: cond, if, ifn, when, unless, case

As in other programming languages, the **cond** structure is used with logical conditions to control the flow of a program. The general form of a cond expression is as follows:

```
*(cond (test1 result1)

      (test2 result2)

         .
         .
         .

  )
```

Each list is a cond clause. It is good practice to use a t in the last cond clause to show what will be done if none of the conditions of previous clauses are true. Cond expressions can be used to facilitate defun. For example, the following function member is enhanced by the use of cond:

```
*(defun member (element list)

  (cond ((null list) 'nil)

       ((eql element (car list)) list)

       (t (member element (car list)))))

     )
```

If takes three arguments as in the conventional if-then-else format: a condition (test), a true-part (then), and a false-part (else). In LISP, it is equivalent to cond as follows:

```
(if test then else)=(cond (test then) (t else))
```

If first evaluates the test. If the result is not nil, the expression **then** is selected; otherwise, the expression **else** is selected. The expression selected is then evaluated, and if returns the evaluation of the selected form. The else expression may be omitted; in this case, if the value of test is nil, then nothing is done and nil is returned. For example, the function made-even makes an odd number even by adding one to it, using if for conditional action:

```
*(Defun make-even (y)

    (if (oddp y)  (add1 y) y)

    )
```

Ifn is a derivative of if that is available from GCLISP only. Depending on the value of (not test), ifn evaluates the then clause or the else clause. The previous example and the example that follows illustrate the difference:

```
*(Defun make-odd (y)

    (ifn (oddp y) (add1 y) y

    )
```

Instead of making an odd number even, changing if to ifn will make an even number odd.

When performs a similiar function to cond or if; it has the following general format:

```
*(when (test) (action1) (action2)....)
```

If the result of evaluating test is non-nil, then action 1, action 2, etc. will be evaluated, and the result of the last action will be returned; otherwise, the actions are not evaluated and nil is returned. Consider the following examples:

```
*(when (not (zerop 3)) (list ' (This is a non-zero number)))

(This is a non-zero number)

*(when (zerop 3) (list '(This is a non-zero number)))

 nil
```

Unless is similiar to when except that the actions are evaluated, and the results of the last action are returned only when the result of the evaluating test is nil; otherwise, the actions are not evaluated and nil is returned. The general format of unless is as follows:

```
*(unless (test) (action1) (action2)....)
```

Following are two examples:

```
*(Unless (zerop 3) (List '(This is a non-zero nember.)))

(This is a non-zerop number.)

*(Unless (zerop 0) (List '(This is a non-zero number.)))

 nil
```

And can serve as a logical operator and a conditional control structure. If any form evaluates to nil, the value nil is immediately returned without evaluating the remaining forms. Its general format as a control structure is as follows:

```
(and  (test) (action1, action2,....))
```

For example,

```
*(and (not (zerop 3)) (List '(This is a non-zero number.)))

(This is a non-zerop number.)
```

Case is a conditional function that executes one of its clauses by a value (a key) to various constants; the key must be one of the following: symbol, integer, or characters (duplicate keys are not allowed). The general format of case is as follows:

```
*(case key

   (keylist1 consequent 1-1....)

   (keylist2 consequent 2-1....)
      .
      .
      .
      .
   )
```

Case evaluates the key first and then evaluates each clause in turn, except that a "t" or "otherwise" in the key list is evaluated last. If the key matches (eql to) one of the objects in a keylist, the consequents are evaluated and the value of the last consequent is returned. A clause containing no consequents other than the keylist is returned with a nil, for example,

```
*(defun odd-even (x)

(case  x  ((1 3 5 7 9) 'odd)

(( 2 4 6 8 10) 'even)

(otherwise '>10)

)
```

RECURSION

Recursion in LISP is similar to recursion in other programming languages such as C. A function is **recursive** if it calls itself. A recursive function is written to reduce a given problem to a part and remainder, solve the part, and pass the remainder to a copy of the function. The three basic rules in recursive programs are as follows:

1. Find out the initial (base) step.

2. Identify the next step, perform an action, and determine the remainder (the remainder should be smaller).

3. Know the last step (with an end test).

For example, a function for the factorial of n (n!) is defined as follows:

```
*(defun factorial (n)

(cond ((zerop n) 1); last step

(t (times n (factorial (sub1 n)))); first & next step

))
```

The program can be translated as follows:

1.   Define function factorial (n).

2.   Condition: if n is zero, then the factorial of n is 1; if n is not zero, then the factorial of n is equal to n * factorial (n-1).

The program, factorial, is recursive on itself by subtracting 1 from n each time that n is greater than 1. The three basic rules are applied as follows:

1.   The inital step is n = n.

2.   The next (iterative) step is n = n-1, and the action is n*(n-1).

3.   The stop point is n = 0.

ITERATION AND BINDING: prog, do, let, value

Prog (for "program") and do are the two LISP functions that allow you to repeat a sequence. **Prog, do,** and **let** allow you to bind local variables. Prog is most familiar to the conventional programmer; let and do are two powerful functions facilitating iterations in LISP that can reduce the abuse of prog. **Value** allows the programmer to control the return of multiple values.

prog, prog1, prog2, and progn

Prog enables you to write LISP programs that are similiar to the traditional program with statement and branches in familiar terms such as go, loop, and return. The general form of prog is as follows:

```
*(prog (local variable 1,variable 2,......);Bind local variables  to zero

(Setq....)      ;initialize variable

(Setq....)      ;initialize variable

Loop            ;start loop

(expression 1) ;actions

(expression 2)
    .
    .
    .
    .

 (Go Loop )      ;repeat

(Return variable-name) ;return the value of the variable
```

In a prog program, the first line lists the local parameters that are to be bound to nil when the program is called and become unbound when it returns. **Setq** is used to initialize these variables. The remaining expressions in the program are evaluated sequentially; the values of these expressions are not returned after evaluation. If an expression is a symbol, it is not evaluated. The symbol is referred to as a tag and is used with a **go** expression at some point in the program to perform iteration. After the last expression of the program has been evaluated, nil is returned. When a **return** expression is encountered, prog is terminated immediately and returns the value of the argument in the return expression. Return works only inside prog, but it need not always appear at the end of a program.

Prog allows the conventional programmer to write iterative loops to perform many tasks that might be performed more efficiently by other functions, such as a recursive function. It is thus advised that prog should not be abused. Prog expressions, if they absolutely must be used, should be kept simple to contain only a single tag and a single go, forming a single loop. Iterative solutions are preferably performed by do and are discussed in the next section.

The three functions prog1, prog2, and progn resemble prog semantically and are used to evaluate a series of expressions sequentially and return the value of one of the expressions. **Prog1** returns the value of the first expression, **prog2** returns the value of the second expression, and **progn** returns the value of the last expression. Examples are as follows:

```
*(prog1  (setq p 'a)

        (setq q 'b)

        (setq r 'c)

        )


*(progn (setq p 'a)

        (setq q'b)

        (setq r'c)

        )
```

do and do*

Do provides flexible variable binding and convenience for explicit iterations such as prog. Do supports a built-in loop that cycles through the expressions in its body until it is told to stop.

The general form of do is as follows:

```
*(do ((parameter-1 initial-value-1 update-expression-1)

      (parameter-2 initial-value-2 update-expression-2)

       .....)

     (condition action-1 action-2....)

     (expression 1)
             .
             .
             .
     (expression n)

)
```

Following is an example of a simple do:

```
*;count and print from 5 to 55 by 10

*(do i 5 (+ i 10)

(zerop (- 55 i))

(print i)          ;print i

(terpri)           ;print a new lin

 )
```

Do* is exactly like do except that do* performs serial (sequential) rather than parallel assignments of values. It is as if psetq were substituted by setq* in the previous section. The feature of sequential assignment of values is useful in knowledge representation, especially in a frame or unit.

Do* is particularly useful when certain variables in the initial assignment depend on other variables that have been assigned first, for example,

```
*(Defun do*-test (i j)

(do*

    ((bag1 i (sub1 bag1)

    (bag2 j (sub1 bag2))

    (payoff (sqrt (+(expt i 2) (expt j 2))) (+ payoff (sqrt

    (+(expt bag1 2)(expt bag2 2)))))

    (counter (sub1 bag2) (sub1 bag1))))

     ((zerop counter) payoff)

      ))
```

The above example shows that because do* performs sequential assignment of values, there is no unbound variable in the "payoff" expression. If do were used, then unbound variables bag1 and bag2 would be found in the "payoff" expression.

Binding Variables: let and let*

Let empowers the programmer to declare local variables and assign their initial values. Let does not accept tags, go, or return and is not an iteration function. The general form of a let expression is as follows:

```
*(let ((variable-1 value-1) (variable-2 value-2)......)

        (expression-1)

        (expression-2)
            .
            .
            .


        )
```

Let assigns each local variable to the initial value and then evaluates the expression in the programs; the value of the last expression is returned, for example,

```
*(let ((Class 'A)

        (Rule 'B)

        (Unit 'C)

(List Class Rule Unit)

    )

(A B C)
```

Let is useful in reducing repeated computations within a function. If an expression needs to be evaluated more than once in a program and setq is not desirable because it assigns a global variable, either prog or let can be used to assign a local variable. Because prog is often abused, let will be used here to illustrate. For example, the following function may be called to obtain the first and last element of a list:

```
*(defun first-and-last-element (x)

    (append ( car (last (reverse x)))

    (car (reverse x))

   )
```

The previous function can be enhanced by using let:

```
*(defund  first-and-last-element (x)

    (let  (y (reverse x)))

    (append (car (last (y))))

    (car (y))

    )
```

Let* is slightly different from let. While let assigns initial values in parallel, let* allows the user to assign initial values sequentially. The following two expressions demonstrate the difference:

Example 1:   `*(Let (a (b (con (1 a)) (c (cons (2 b)))`

`(values a b c )));  values will be discussed below.`

`Error`

`unbound variable a`

Example 2:   `*(let* (a (b (con (3 a)) (c (cons (5 b)))`

                    `(values a b c )`

       `nil`

       `(3)`

       `(5 3)`

In the first example, when let is used, the variables are assigned in parallel con(1 a), resulting in an unbound variable a.

However, when let* is used, because the variables are assigned sequentially, **a** has been assigned nil; therefore, there is no error in the expression.

Values

Values is used to produce multiple values; it takes and returns any number of arguments. If the last expression in the body of a function has **values** with five arguments specified, then a call to that function will return five values.

In the previous let example, values returned three values, nil, (3), and (5 3). If values is not used to explicitly return three values, then the first value is normally given to the caller, and all other values are discarded.

INPUT/OUTPUT:
print, princ, prin1, pprint, terpri, format, backquote, read

Input/Output (I/O) is one of the areas of great disagreement among LISP users, and no absolute standards exist.

Messages can be printed in LISP by placing a sequence of characters (a character string) in quotation marks, as shown in the following example:

`*"Good morning, this is an expert system."`

`" Good morning, this is an expert system."`

Like numbers, strings evaluate to themselves.

Print evaluates its arguments and prints the result preceded by a new line and followed by a space; its general format is as follows:

```
*(print object &optional output-stream)
```

The second argument, **output-stream**, is optional (indicated by **&optional**), and its default value is that of the variable ***standard-output***. Print returns the object, for example,

```
*;count and print 1 to 20 by 5

*(do i 1 (+ i 5)

(zerop (- 55 i))

(print i )

(terpri )

 )
```

Princ is similar to print except that it is not preceded with a new line and is not followed by a space. A symbol is printed as the characters of its name, and a string is printed without enclosing double quotes. Print returns the object.

Prin1 is the machine version of print; it is intended to be accepted by the function **read**. Prin1 does not start with a new line nor does it finish with a space. Escape characters are used as appropriate for read. Prin1 returns the object.

Pprint is just like print except that the subsequent space is omitted and the object is formatted for user readability. It returns no values. **Terpri** is a function that starts a new line as shown in the example for print.

484

Format is useful for producing a formatted document. The general format is as follows:

```
*(Format destination control-string other-arguments )
```

The characters of the control string and other arguments are outputted by format to the destination according to directions that are followed with a tilde (~), for example,

```
*(Setq p "you")

*(Format nil "We need  ~ A !" p)

"We need you!"
```

In this example, the destination is nil; format creates a string to contain its output and returns that string; the control string is "We need A !" in which A is a directive indicating that the argument (**p**) to be printed between "we need" and "!" is a LISP object and will be printed without a new line and space as in the case of princ. The resulting print is " We need you ! "

The destination must be either nil, t, or a stream. If the destination is t, the output is sent to the stream of the variable ***standard-output*** and format returns nil. If the destination is a string, the output characters are added to the end of the string and format returns nil.

A format directive includes a tilde character (~), optimal colon(**:**) and at-sign () modifiers, and a single character specifying the type of directives as follows:

Character	Meaning	Explanation
A	ASCII	Argument (arg) is printed as if by princ.
S	s-expression	Arg is printed as if by prin1.
D	decimal	Arg (which must be an integer) is printed in decimal radix with no trailing decimal point.
B	binary	Arg (which must be an integer) is printed in binary radix.
O	octal	Arg (which must be an integer) is printed in octal radix.
X	hexadecimal	Arg (which must be an integer) is printed in hexadecimal radix.
C	character	Arg (which must be a character) is printed.
%	new line	A #Newline character is printed.
&	freshline	Identical to newline.
~	tilde	A tilde character is printed.
<newline>	new line	The Newline character and any following white space is ignored. With a:, only the Newline is ignored. With a , only the white space following the new line is ignored.
:	[false~;true~}	If-Then expression. If arg is nil, false is processed as a format control string; otherwise, true is processed.
@	[true~] test	If arg is not nil, then arg is not consumed (i.e., it remains the next arg to be processed) and true is processed as a format control string; otherwise, arg is consumed and true is ignored.

Many of these directives are infrequently used, particularly by the beginner. Following are some more examples:

```
*(Setq *monitor-stream* "xyz data base")

*(Format *Monitor-stream* " Environment ~A Not saved."env ))

;example of format with control string

*(Format nil " ~& System loaded")
```

Backquote provides an easy way to create an expression that combines fixed and variable portions; the backquote character (') inserts the contents of the variable into the expression when a comma appears:

```
*(Setq x 5)

*'(x y ,x ,(+x z))

(x y 5 7)
```

The backquote before the parenthesis indicates that the expression is a template. When a comma occurs, the form following the comma is evaluated and its result replaces the original object after the comma.

If a comma is followed by an at sign (@), then the form subsequent to @ is evaluated to obtain a list and the elements of the list are substituted into the expression without the usual embracing parentheses, as shown in the following example:

```
*(Setq p'(x y z))

*'(p , p ,p,(cdr p),(cdr p))

(p (x y z) x y z (y z) y z)
```

Backquote can be used to help print arrange a hodgepodge of atoms and lists into a convenient and efficient format, for example,

```
*(print (p "=", p)

p = xyz
```

Read is a function that reads one LISP object from the terminal and returns that object as its value. Read causes the computer to wait for the user to type a response:

```
*(read) Hi

Hi
```

Because read prints nothing to warn the user that the computer is waiting for the user to enter an answer, it is usually preceded by a print expression to tell the user what kind of response is expected.

MACROS AND OTHER PROGRAMMING CONVENIENCES: defmacro

Macros allow the programmer to define arbitrary functions before evaluation or compilation. Unlike other computing languages, macros in LISP are performed at the expression level, not at the character-string level. Thus, using a macro does not introduce inefficiencies in a compiled program. Macros are not functions and cannot be used as functional arguments to such functions as **apply**. Macros are defined using the same general format as an ordinary procedure:

```
*(defmacro macro-name (parameter-1 parameter-2......)

   (expression-1 ....)

   (expression-2 ....)
           .
           .
           .
   )
```

A macro does not evaluate its arguments and returns an expression that is evaluated; the variables in a macro's argument are bound to the entire macro program. A macro when combined with backquote becomes a powerful programming technique. For example, you can define macro-when as follows:

```
*(defmacro macro-when (test &rest argument)

     '(cond (,test ,argument ))

   )
```

Lambda List Keywords: &rest and &optional

&rest in the previous example indicates that **argument** is optional, similar to **&optional**.

Both &optional and &rest provide the programmer with the option to supply arguments only when they are needed. The & of &optional or &rest tells the computer that &optional or &rest is not a parameter but a parameter separator, and the optional parameters are set to nil if there is no matching argument. For example, the output-stream in princ is optional:

```
*(Princ object &optional output-stream)
```

If output-stream is not specified, *standard-output*, a global variable, is assumed. The LISP printer writes to the output stream that is assigned to this variable.

If the number of optional parameters is known, then &optional suffices. The number can be one or more. However, if the number of optional parameters is not known to the programmer, &rest can be used to signal a single optional parameter that represents more arguments than the required and optional parameters. Macro-when mentioned previously can be used as an example because it contains an &rest in the argument; any number of arguments is permitted.

```
*(Macro-when (t (value 7 8 9)))

7 8 9

*(Setq x 3)

*(Macro-when ((zerop X) (Format nil "X is equal to ~ D." x)

(Format nil "X is zero."))
```

C++ also provides some of these features.

DECLARING GLOBAL VARIABLES AND NAME CONSTANTS: defvar, defparameter, defconstant, declare, proclaim

As discussed in the previous section, **set** evaluates its argument and works only with global (dynamic) variables. Because all variables in LISP are local (lexical) by default, a declaration of global variables for the argument may be required.

Defvar is the recommended way to declare the use of a special variable in a program. The general format of defvar is as follows:

```
*(defvar variable initial-value "documentation")
```

The variable name is customarily inserted with the beginning and ending asterisks (*) to signal that it is a global variable, for example,

```
*(defvar *menu-sensitive-items* nil "These are for menus that

enhance user-convenience in using the system")
```

Initial-value may not be required. If it is supplied, then variable is initialized to the result of evaluating initial-value, unless it already has a value.

Defvar suggests to the programmer that the value of the variable will be changed by the program during execution. The variable name will be returned.

Defparameter is similar to defvar except that defparameter requires an initial-value to initialize variable. Defparameter is intended to declare a variable that is normally constant but can be changed even during execution; however, such a change is considered a change to the program. Defparameter suggests to the programmer that the value of the variable will be changed by the user before program execution; it does not allow the compiler to assume the value for the program being executed, for example,

```
*(defparameter *system-file-list* '(until user;int slot toplevel)
```

In the above statement, the global variable is inserted with the beginning and ending asterisks (*).

Defconstant is similar to defparameter but does assert that the value of the variable will not be changed. Once a name has been declared by defconstant to be constant, any further assignment to that variable results in an error. The general format is the same as defvar or defparameter, for example,

```
*(defconstant *slot-attributes* '(value documentation type-
restriction inheritance) "Slot attributes that may be assigned by
the user")
```

Declare and **proclaim** should be used with caution because many implementations may not support them, and if they do support them, the effect varies over implementations. Declare has no effect on the variable in the current version of GCLISP, which does not support proclaim. The general formats for declare and proclaim are as follows:

```
*(declare (argument-1....))
```

```
*(proclaim '(argument-1....))
```

Declare has the effect only within executable code such as lambda and defun programs, while proclaim has the effect globally, for example,

```
*(defun declare-example (X))

*(declare (type float X))

*(proclaim '(type float *X*))
```

Type used in the above expressions is a common LISP function that specifies that the variables mentioned will take on values only of the given type. Its general format is as follows:

```
*(type variable-type variable-1 variable-2....)
```

CREATING RECORD STRUCTURES: defstruct

In representing structured knowledge, **defstruct** is a powerful mechanism for data abstraction and representation. It allows the programmer to organize fields and field values neatly. The general format for defstruct is as follows:

```
*(defstruct (name option 1 option 2....)

document-string

slot-description-1

slot-description-2
```

The name must be a symbol, and it is returned as the value of defstruct. Options are not required. If no options are given, the word defstruct can be omitted. Options include the following:

Use **:conc-name** to specify an alternate prefix to be used, for example,

```
*(defstruct (slot (:conc-name unit-))
```

Use **:include** to include a new structure definition as an extension of an old structure definition, for example, if an old structure called **student** resembles the following:

```
*(defstruct student person grade major sex)
```

If you want to make a new structure to represent a graduate student and would like to include all of the features of the **student** plus financial-aid, proceed as follows:

```
*(defstruct (graduate student (:include student) (:conc-name

graduate-)))

financial-aid)
```

The :include causes **graduate-student** to have the same slots as student plus the new slot financial-aid. The graduate-student can be further restricted by :include options, such as

```
*(defstruct (graduate-student (:include student (grade 3.8)))

financial-aid)
```

The **:print-function** prints a structure of this type; it requires three optional arguments, a structure to be printed, a stream to print to, and an integer indicating the current depth, for example,

```
*(defstruct (graduate-student (:print-function 'print-stext))
```

Print-stext is the stream to print to, and, as discussed before, quote (') signals to LISP that the subsequent form print-stext will not be evaluated.

The **:type** function specifies the representation to be used for the structure; it takes one argument, which can be either a vector or a list, for example,

```
*(defstruct (graduate-student (:type list) (:include student))

  financial-aid)
```

The :type and :print-function functions cannot appear in the same defstruct.

The **:initial-offset** function tells defstruct to skip over a certain number of slots before it starts allocating the slots in the structure, for example,

```
*(defstruct (graduate-student (:include student) (:initial-

offset 2))

  financial-aid)
```

The **document-string** in a defstruct is optional. If it is present, it is attached to the **name** as the document string of the structure. Each **slot-description** is in the following format:

```
*(slot-name default-initial

Slot-option-name-1 slot-option-value-1

Slot-option-name-2 slot-option-value-2
```

Consider the following example:

```
*(defstruct (slot (:print-function 'print-slot))

*(name nil)

*(value nil)
```

In the previous example, **name** and **value** are slot-names, and **nil** is the default-initial for these slots.

After the structure has been defined, the instances of the structure can be created by using the constructor function. Defstruct names the constructor function with a prefix of **make**. For example, if the structure name is slot, the constructor function is make-slot. The general format for a constructor function is as follows:

```
*(defun name-of-constructor-function

(slot-keyword-1 form1

slot-keyword-2 form2)
```

For example, the constructor function for slot appears as follows:

```
*(defun make-slot (&rest keys-and-values)
```

MESSAGE PASSING (OBJECT-ORIENTED PROGRAMMING): send, funcall

Send and **funcall** are identical; they enable the user to pass messages as in object-oriented programming. These two functions call a function with its arguments and return the results of this function call. The general format for message passing is as follows:

```
*(send message-receiver :message-name message-argument)

*(funcall message-receiver : message-name message-argument)
```

Consider the following example:

```
*(send *terminal-io* : set-attribute a)
```

In this example, **send** acts as the message-sending mechanism; ***terminal-io*** acts as the receiver of the message that is an output stream to the terminal; **set-attribute** is the message name (a function to perform a certain task); and **a** is an argument to indicate that the output stream is in the ASCII file format.

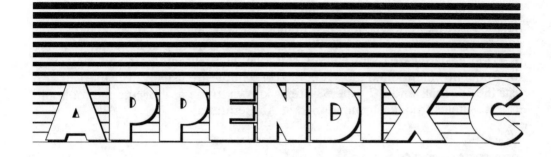

APPENDIX C

EXPERT SYSTEMS AND TOOLS

In addition to the AI/expert system programming language packages and tools detailed in Chapters 4, 5, and 6, a number of languages and development tools and systems are available for the PC environment. This appendix summarizes the description, hardware requirements, software requirements, cost, and contacts of the frequently mentioned tools (detailed brochures are usually available). It also lists the PC tools and PC expert systems known to the author and the tools and expert systems frequently mentioned in AI literature.

GENERAL DISCUSSION

The information contained in this section is based mostly on information provided by product developers and not on the author's own experience using the products, except for the products described in the text. This section does not contain a complete, up-to-date list of tools; it lists only selected representative products. This section is divided into three subsections. The first subsection contains summaries of expert system tools for IBM personal computers. The second subsection contains summaries of tools available for the Apple Macintosh; and the third subsection contains summaries of tools that run on both IBM and Macintosh personal computers.

Tools for IBM Personal Computers

APES 1.1

Description: APES 1.1 is an augmented version of Prolog specifically designed for developing expert systems. It retains the flexibility of Prolog while providing the modules common to many expert systems.

**Hardware
Requirements**:   IBM PC

**Software
Requirements**:   Micro-Prolog 3.1, which is included in the purchase price

Cost: $425. An academic discount is available.

Contact: Programming Logic Systems, Inc.
31 Crescent Drive
Milford, CT 06460
(203) 877-7988

ES/P ADVISOR

Description: ES/P ADVISOR is an expert system shell for rapid development of demonstration and prototype expert systems. Knowledge is represented by simple production rules. Uncertain knowledge cannot be directly handled. Language hooks to Prolog are supported. ES/P ADVISOR is written in Prolog.

**Hardware
Requirements:**   IBM PC/XT with a minimum of 128K RAM

**Software
Requirements:**   PC-DOS

Cost: $895
$626.50 for academic institutions

Contact: Expert Systems International
1150 First Avenue
King of Prussia, PA 19406
(215) 337-2300

Expertech

Description: Expertech is a "software laboratory" consisting of an integrated collection of expert system tutorials, case studies, on-line teaching programs, and expert systems building tools. Expertech includes eight rule-based expert system shells. A forward chaining and a backward chaining shell has been implemented in LISP, Prolog, dBASE, and Pascal. The emphasis of Expertech is on educating the user about expert system technology.

**Hardware
Requirements:**   IBM PC/XT with a minimum of 256K RAM

Cost:	$475. No academic discount is available.
Contact:	Intelliware, Inc. 4676 Admiralty Way, Suite 401 Marina del Rey, CA 90291 (213) 827-1334

Expert-Ease

Description:	Expert-Ease is an expert system tool that uses inductions made from examples to generate rules. Uncertain knowledge cannot be represented, and Expert-Ease doesn't support hooks to other languages. Expert-Ease is written in Pascal.
Hardware Requirements:	IBM PC with a minimum of 128K RAM
Software Requirements:	PC-DOS
Cost:	$695 per package, retail $278 per package for academic institutions
Contact:	Human Edge Software, Inc. 2445 Farber Place Palo Alto, CA 94303 (415) 493-1593

EXSYS 3.0

Description: EXSYS is an expert systems development tool implementation for the IBM PC. EXSYS uses a backward chaining inference mechanism and uses simple production rules for knowledge representation. Uncertain knowledge is handled through the use of simple probability measures or through uncertainty factors. EXSYS can execute external programs and can pass its results to external programs as well. EXSYS is written in C.

**Hardware
Requirements:**   IBM PC/AT with at least 256K RAM

**Software
Requirements:**   MS-DOS 2.0 or higher

Cost: $395 per package, retail
No academic discount is available.

Contact: Exsys, Inc.
P. O. Box 75158, Contract Station 14
Albequerque, NM 87194
(505) 836-6676

GCLISP and Goldworks

Description: GCLISP is a Common LISP package that implements most features available in Common LISP. GCLISP has two versions. One is for regular PC users and the other for expert system developers (286 developer) with IBM AT machines. Goldworks is an expert system environment.

**Hardware
Requirements:**   The PC version requires 512K RAM; the 286 developer version requires at least 2M RAM.

**Software
Requirements:**   PC-DOS

Cost:	The PC version is sold for $495; the developer version is sold for $1,195; and Goldworks is sold for $7,500.
Contact:	Gold Hill Computers 163 Harvard Street Cambridge, MA 02139 (800) 242-LISP

Guru

Description:	Guru is an expert system environment for business applications with easy access to database, spreadsheet, and word processing programs.
Hardware Requirements:	IBM PC
Software Requirements:	MS-DOS, OS/2
Cost:	$6,500
Contact:	Micro Data Base Systems, Inc. P. O. Box 248 Lafayette, IN 47902 (317) 463-2581

INSIGHT-1 and -2

Description:	INSIGHT-1 is a knowledge engineering software tool that provides an environment to design, create, and run prototype expert systems. INSIGHT-1 represents knowledge as simple production rules and allows both forward and backward chaining. INSIGHT-1 uses "confidence weighting" to represent uncertain knowledge and supports hooks to Pascal. INSIGHT-2 is an enhanced version of INSIGHT-1, for more serious applications. Expert systems developed with INSIGHT-2 can interface to external programs.

**Hardware
Requirements:** INSIGHT-1 requires an IBM PC/XT/AT with at least 128K
RAM; INSIGHT-2 requires at least 256K RAM.

**Software
Requirements:** MS-DOS 2.0 or higher

Cost: INSIGHT-1, $95; INSIGHT-2, $485

Contact: Level Five Research, Inc.
4980 South A-1-A
Melbourne Beach, FL 32951
(305) 729-9046

IQ-200

Description: IQ-200 is an applications support and development environment with powerful rule-based reasoning tools and database
communication capabilities. It is designed to support applications that require interaction with many databases, both
locally and over remote connections, and those that require
rich reasoning and knowledge representation capabilities.
Using IQ-200, a database administrator or programmer
can integrate artificial intelligence and object-oriented techniques with conventional databases and communications.

**Hardware
Requirements:** IBM AT or 100% compatible with 1.5 megabytes extended
memory

**Software
Requirements:** DOS 3.0

Price: $995.00

Contact: Baldur Systems Corp.
3423 Investment Blvd., Suite 12
Hayward, CA 94545
(415) 732-9715

KDS

Description: KDS is an expert system tool that uses inductions made from examples to generate rules. Uncertain knowledge cannot be represented. KDS supports both forward and backward chaining, can execute external programs, uses user-developed code, and can take input from external programs. KDS is written 100% in assembly language.

Hardware Requirements: IBM PC with at least 256K RAM

Software Requirements: PC-DOS

Cost: $795 for the development module, retail
$495 for the playback (inference engine) module, retail
A 20% discount is available to academic institutions.

Contact: KDS Corporation
934 Hunter Road
Wilmette, IL 60091
(312) 251-2621

KES

Description: KES is a family of software tools for developing, implementing, and supporting expert systems. KES uses production rules and frames to represent knowledge. Certainty factors are used to represent uncertain knowledge. Hooks to other languages are not supported.

Hardware Requirements: The IBM PC/XT version of KES requires the 8087 math coprocessor and at least 640K RAM.

Software Requirements: KES requires IQLISP, which must be purchased separately from Integral Quality in Seattle, Washington (206) 527-2918.

Cost: $4,000. A 75% discount is available to academic institutions. Training is available at a cost of $1,200 per student.

Contact: Software Architecture and Engineering, Inc.
1500 Wilson Boulevard, Suite 800
Arlington, VA 22209
(703) 276-7910

Micro-Expert

Description: Micro-Expert is a rule-based expert system development tool that provides the user interface and the inference engine. The user interface is equipped to allow the user to entertain questions, obtain results, and explain the sequence of reasoning used.

Hardware Requirements: 256K RAM

Software Requirements: PC-DOS

Cost: $99 with a book

Contact: McGraw-Hill Publishing
1221 Avenue of the Americas
New York, NY 10020
(212) 512-2000

M.1

Description: According to the manual, "M.1 is a knowledge engineering tool that provides training, exploration, and proof-of-concept capabilities for investigating applications of knowledge engineering. . . .M.1 is used to design, build, and run stand-alone knowledge systems." Its back-chaining inference engine is based on that of MYCIN. M.1 offers explanation and debugging facilities, as well as a hook to C. Uncertain knowledge is represented by certainty factors.

Hardware Requirements:	IBM PC/XT/AT with one disk drive and at least 192K RAM
Software Requirements:	Text editing program (such as the EDLIN program that accompanies MS-DOS)
Cost:	$10,000 $1,250 for academic institutions A four-day training course is available at a retail cost of $2,500 per student; the cost is $1,000 per student for academic institutions.
Contact:	Teknowledge, Inc. 525 University Avenue Palo Alto, CA 94301 (415) 327-6600

muLISP

Description:	muLISP is one of the earliest LISP packages for personal computers. It is not a Common LISP but contains a library of Common LISP primitives. Its functions can be linked to user-defined machine language subroutines. The commands available on muLISP are listed in Appendix B.
Hardware Requirements:	48K RAM
Software Requirements:	PC-DOS or CP/M
Cost:	$250
Contact:	Microsoft Corporation 10700 Northrup Way Bellevue, WA 98004 (206) 882-8088

Prolog-86

Description: Prolog-86 is an interpretative logic programming language to help the user learn and experiment with small problems. It is based on Clocksin's and Mellish's definitive Prolog work, *Programming in Prolog*, (New York: Springer-Verlag, 1984).

Hardware Requirements: 96K RAM

Software Requirements: PC-DOS or CP/M

Cost: $95

Contact: MICRO-AI (Solution Systems)
P. O. Box 91
Rheem Valley, CA 94570
(800) 821-2492

PROLOG-1 and -2

Description: PROLOG-1 is a logic-based (as opposed to algorithmic-based) programming language suitable for use in expert systems, robotic control, language processing, and other artificial intelligence applications. It incorporates advanced pattern machining, generalized record structuring, list manipulation, assertional database, and backtracking search strategy mechanisms.

PROLOG-2 is a logic programming language environment offering all the advantages of PROLOG-1, but also allowing for modules written in other languages as well. PROLOG-2 also runs about twice as fast as PROLOG-1.

Hardware Requirements: IBM PC/XT with a minimum of 128K RAM

Software Requirements: MS-DOS

Cost:	PROLOG-1 costs $276.50, and PROLOG-2 costs $1,326 per package for academic institutions.
Contact:	Expert Systems International 1150 First Avenue King of Prussia, PA 19406 (215) 337-2300

Personal Consultant

Description:	Personal Consultant is a set of programs and utilities that can be used to develop customized expert systems. Personal Consultant uses backward-chaining logic in a rule-based environment. Both structural and factual knowledge can be explicitly represented. Uncertain knowledge is represented by the use of certainty factors. Personal Consultant offers extensive explanation and debugging facilities, as well as the capability of translating knowledge base rules into plain English.
Hardware Requirements:	IBM PC/XT with one disk drive, a 10-megabyte hard disk, and 640K RAM
Software Requirements:	PC-DOS 2.0 or higher and IQLISP 1.7 or higher
Cost:	$950. A 35% discount is available for academic institutions.
Contact:	Texas Instruments, Inc. P. O. Box 2909 M/S 2151 Austin, TX 78769 (512) 250-7357

RuleMaster

Description:	The RuleMaster is based in C and can generate C and FORTRAN source codes; it also automatically induces rules from sets of examples supplied by the expert.

**Hardware
Requirements**:   IBM PC/XT, 640K of memory, and a 3-megabyte hard disk

**Software
Requirements**:   MS-DOS

Cost: depends on various arrangements

Contact: Radian Corporation
8501 MO-Pac Blvd.
Austin, TX 78720
(512) 454-4797

Smalltalk-AT

Description: Smalltalk-AT is a PC implementation of the original
Smalltalk-80 developed at Xerox Palo Alto Research Center.
It is an object-oriented programming language, featuring an
interactive debugger, inspectors, snapshotting, bit-mapped
graphics, windows, and a text editor.

**Hardware
Requirements**:   IBM PC/AT, 1 megabyte of RAM, a mouse, and an EGA
card

**Software
Requirements**:   DOS 3.0

Cost: $995

Contact: Softsmarts, Inc.
4 Skyline Drive
Woodside, CA 94062
(415) 327-8100

Smalltalk/v

Description: Smalltalk/v is an object-oriented language and has features
similar to those of Smalltalk-AT.

Hardware Requirements:	512K RAM, an EGA card, two diskette drives
Software Requirements:	PC-DOS 2.0
Cost:	$99
Contact:	Digitalk, Inc. 5200 West Century Boulevard Los Angeles, CA 90045 (213) 645-1082

Turbo Prolog

Description:	Turbo Prolog is a logic programming language. Turbo Prolog provides windows, simple menus, point- and line-based graphics, in addition to the normal Prolog features.
Hardware Requirements:	384K RAM
Software Requirements:	PC-DOS 2.0
Cost:	$95
Contact:	Borland International, Inc. 4585 Scotts Valley Drive Scotts Valley, CA 95066 CA: (800) 742-1133

VP-Expert

Description:	VP-Expert is an expert system developed tool that was built on C. It features simple backward and forward chaining, inductive front-end, windows, text editor, and confidence factors.

**Hardware
Requirements:** IBM PC with 256K RAM and graphics card

**Software
Requirements:** PC-DOS

Cost: $99.95

Contact: Paperback Software International
2830 Ninth Street
Berkeley, CA 94710
(415) 644-2116

XSYS

Description: XSYS is an expert system shell for the development of
prototype expert systems. Knowledge is represented by
simple production rules, and uncertainty is represented by
certainty factors. Hooks to other languages are not supported.

**Hardware
Requirements:** IBM PC/XT/AT with at least 640K. The 8087 math co-
processor is required if certainty factors are to be supported.

**Software
Requirements:** KES requires IQLISP, which must be purchased separately
from Integral Quality in Seattle, Washington: (206) 527-2918.

Cost: $995. No discount is available to academic institutions.

Contact: California Intelligence
912 Powell Street #8
San Francisco, CA 94108
(415) 391-4846

Tools for the Apple Macintosh

ExperOPS5

Description: OPS5 is a production system programming language. It uses a forward-chaining inference mechanism to make conclusions based on known facts and is thus best suited for data-driven applications. ExperOPS5 is an implementation of OPS5 in ExperLISP and offers no built-in explanation facilities or means of representing uncertainty.

Hardware Requirements: ExperOPS5 requires a 512K Macintosh equipped with an external disk drive or a hard drive.

Software Requirements: ExperOPS5 requires ExperLISP version 1.03 or higher.

Cost: $325. (ExperLISP required, $495 retail.) No academic discount is available. No training or formal support is available. Updates will be available for a nominal fee.

Contact: ExperTelligence, Inc.
559 San Ysidro Road
Santa Barbara, CA 93106
(805) 969-7871

MacKIT Level 1

Description: The stated purpose of MacKIT is to "provide a reasonably priced tool to support the technology transfer of basic Knowledge Engineering skills to you. . . .You will build your own knowledge systems to provide the productivity tools you require." MacKIT uses back-chaining inference on simple production rules and does not support variables or calculations of any type. Uncertain knowledge is represented as a variant of certainty factors.

Hardware Requirements: MacKIT Level 1 requires a 512K Macintosh.

**Software
Requirements:** A word processing program (e.g., MacWrite).

Cost: $149. Updates will be available for a nominal fee.

Contact: Knowledge System Environments, Inc.
201 S. York Road
Dillsburg, PA 17019
(717) 766-4496

Tools for IBM and Macintosh Computers

OPS5+

Description: OPS5+ is a programming language principally designed to implement forward chaining production systems. Knowledge is represented by simple production rules, and control structures can be built into these rules as well. A development and debugging environment is included. OPS5+ is written in C and supports hooks to Lattice/Microsoft C (not included).

**Hardware
Requirements:** OPS5+ runs on an IBM PC/XT/AT with at least 640K RAM, the standard IBM graphics card, and a Mouse Systems mouse; or on an Apple Macintosh 512K.

**Software
Requirements:** None

Cost: $3,000
$960, academic institutions

Contact: Artelligence, Inc.
14902 Preston Road, Suite 212-252
Dallas, TX 75240
(214) 437-0361

NEXPERT

Description: As an expert system development environment. NEXPERT represents knowledge by using a combination of simple production rules, as well as contexts, and categories. Knowledge base structure can be represented either as a tree or a network. NEXPERT supports backward chaining, forward chaining, or a combination of both. It automatically generates a graphical representation of the knowledge structure and supports both text and image associations with rules.

Hardware Requirements: NEXPERT requires a 512K Macintosh.

Software Requirements: None

Cost: $5,000. No academic discount is available. Training is available for an additional fee.

Contact: Neuron Data, Inc.
444 High Street
Palo Alto, CA 94301
(415) 321-4488

List of PC Tools and Systems

PC tools and systems are listed in separate subsections.

PC Tools

Name of Tool	Applicable PC	Developer	Telephone	Note
LISP				
BYSCO LISP	IBM AT	Levien Instrument	(703) 396-3345	
CLISP	IBM	Westcomp	(714) 982-1738	
Cromenco LISP	Z-80	Cromenco	(415) 964-7400	
ExperLISP	Macintosh	ExperTelligence	(805) 969-7874	
Golden Common LI	IBMSP	Gold Hill Computers	(617) 492-2071	
IQLISP	IBM	Integral Quality	(206) 527-2918	
LISP/80	IBM	Software Toolworks	(818) 986-4885	
LISP/88	IBM	Norell Data Systems	(213) 748-5978	
MuLISP	all	Soft Warehouse	(206) 455-8080	
TLC-LISP 86	all	LISP Company	(408) 353-2227	
UO-LISP	IBM	Northwest Computer Algorithms	(213) 426-1893	
Waltz LISP	all	Pro Code	(800) LIP-4000	
XLISP	all	N.Y. Amateur Computer Club	(603) 924-9820	
Prolog				
IF/Prolog	IBM	Interface Computer	089/984444	W. Germany
LPA Micro-Prolog	IBM	Logic Programming Associates	018740350	UK

Name of Tool	Applicable PC	Developer	Telephone	Note
Prolog (cont.)				
MPROLOG	all	Logicware	(714) 476-3634	
Micro-Prolog	IBM	Programming Logic Systems	(203) 877-7988	
PC-Prolog	IBM	SuInfologics AB		Stockholm, Sweden
PROLOG-1 and -2	IBM	Expert Systmes Int'l	(215) 337-2300	
PROLOG V	IBM	Chalcedody Software	(619) 483-8513	
Prolog-86	IBM	Solution Systems	(800) 821-2492	
Shells				
ADS	IBM	Aion	(415) 328-9595	
ADVISOR	all	Ultimate Media	(415) 924-3644	
APES	IBM	Logic Programming Associates	01-874-0350	UK
ES/P ADVISOR	IBM PC	Expert Systems International	(215) 337-2300	
EX-TRAN 7	IBM	Intelligent Terminals	0415521353	Scotland, Induction
Expert Choice	PC-DOS	Decision Support Software, and MS-DOS Inc.	(703) 442-7900	
EXPERT 4	IBM	Elsevier-Biosoft	02-23-31-5961	UK
Expert-Ease	IBM	Human Edge Software Corp.	(415) 431-9562	Induction
EXSYS	IBM PC	EXSYS, Inc.	(505) 836-6676	
1st Class	IBM PC	Mountain View Press		

Name of Tool	Applicable PC	Developer	Telephone	Note
Shells (cont.)				
Inference Manager	IBM	Intelligent Terminals	041-552-1353	Inference
INSIGHT-1 and -2	IBM	Level Five Research, Inc.	(305) 729-9046	Linked to dBASE
KDS	IBM PC	KDS Corp	(312) 251-2621	
KES	IBM	Software A&E	(703) 276-7910	
M.1 M.1a	IBM PC	Teknowledge, Inc	(415) 327-6600	
MO-LRO	IBM PC &	Conception et Realisation Industri- elles de Logiciel	1-776-34-37	France
MP-LRO	IBM	Conception et Realisation Industri- elles de Logiciel	1-776 34-37	France
Micro Expert	IBM	McGraw-Hill Books	(212) 512-2000	
NEXPERT	Macintosh	Neuron Data	(415) 321-4488	
OPS5	IBM, Apple	Artelligence, Inc.	(214) 437-0361	
Personal Consultant	TI PC and IBM PC (soon)	Texas Instruments	(800) 527-3500	
Reveal	IBM	Tymshare U.K. Heiron House	04862 26761	UK
RuleMaster	IBM	Radian Corp.	(512) 454-4797	
Savoir	IBM, HP	ISI	0737-71327	UK
TESS	IBM	Helix Expert Systems	01-248-1734	UK
Think!	Commodore 64, Apple II, and Atari 800	UME	(805) 488-2972	

Name of Tool	Applicable PC	Developer	Telephone	Note
TIMM-PC	IBM PC	General Research Corp.	(703) 893-5915	Induction
Texpert	all	Texpert Systems	(713) 469-4068	Linked to dBASE
Topsi	IBM	Dynamic Master Systems	(404) 565 0771	Based on OPS5
XSYS	IBM	California Intelligence	(415) 391-4846	
Xi	IBM	Expertech House	0753-821321 UK	

PC Expert Systems

System Name	Developer	Application Areas	Telephone	Note
Capital Investment Expert Systems	Palladian Software	Capital Investment	(617) 661-7171	
Clout	Microrim (Bellevue, WA)	Database front end	(206)883-0888	Linked to R:Base
Expert Choice	Decision Support Software	Decision support	(800) 368-2022	Linked to Lotus 1-2-3
Guru	Micro Data Base Systems	Database management	(317) 463-2581	
HAL	GNP Development (Pasadena, CA)	Spreadsheet front end	_____	Linked to Lotus 1-2-3
HULK II	Brainstorm Computer Solutions	Rule founder	01 263 6926	UK, also Unix
Hypnotist	Intelligence Products	Expert analysis on Lotus 1-2-3, Symphony	016777583	UK

System Name	Developer	Application Areas	Telephone	Note
Javelin	Javelin Software (Cambridge, MA)	Database management	(617) 494-1400	
Lightyear	Lightyear	Decision analysis	(408) 985-8811	
Manufacturing & Logistics Expert System	Palladian Software	Manufac-turing and logistics	(617) 661-7171	
Micro-Synthese	Ecole Nationale Superieure Chimie de Paris	Organic molecule	133625235	France; Apple II
Paradox	Borland, Intern'l	Database Management	(403) 438-8400	
Parys	Business Information Techniques	Personnel management	0274736766	UK
Plan Power	Applied Expert Systems (Cambridge, MA)	Financial planning	(617) 492-7322	
Q&A	Symantec (Cupertino, CA)	Database	(408) 235-9600	
REVEAL	McDonnell Douglas	Data management	(408) 446-7406	
Superfile ACLS	Southdata	Database management	017277564	UK
Wizdom XS	Software Intelligence Lab	Commercial and financial	(212) 747-9066	

List of Frequently Mentioned Tools and Systems

Frequently mentioned tools and systems are listed here in separate subsections.

Tools

Tool	Representation Method	Developer
ACLS	Aid	
ADVISE	Aid	University of Illinois
AIMDS	Frame based and procedure oriented	_____
AL/X	Rule based	Intelligent Terminals, Ltd.
ALICE	Logic based	Institute de Programmation (France)
AMORD	Rule based	Massachusetts Institute of Technology
APES	Logic based	Imperial College of London (United Kingdom)
APLICOT	Logic based	University of Tokyo
ARBY	Rule based	Yale University
ARS	Rule based	Massachusetts Institute of Technology
ART	Rule and frame based; procedure oriented	Inference Corporation
C	Procedure oriented	Bell Laboratories
COMMON LISP	Procedure oriented	Carnegie-Mellon University
CONCHE	Aid	University of Leeds

Tool	Representation Method	Developer
CSRL	Frame based	Ohio State University
DETEKR	Aid	Tektronix, Inc.
DPL	Frame based	Massachusetts Institute of Technology
DUCK	Logic and frame based	Smart Systems Technology
EMYCIN (a shell of MYCIN)	Rule based	Stanford University
ERS	Rule based	PAR Technology Corp.
ES/P ADVISOR		———————
ETS	Aid	Boeing Computer Services
EXPERT	Rule based	Rutgers University
EXPERT-2	Rule based	Helion Inc.
EXPERT-EASE	Aid	Intelligent Terminals Ltd. (Great Britain)
EXPRS	Rule based	Lockheed Palo Alto Research Laboratory
FIT	Logic based	University of Hamburg
FLAVORS	Object based	Symbolics
FRL	Frame based	Massachusetts Institute of Technology
GEN-X	Rule based	General Electric's Research and Development Center
GLIB	Rule based	Tektronix, Inc.

Tool	Representation Method	Developer
GOLDWORKS	Frame, rule based	Gold Hill
GUESS/1	Rule based	Virginia Institute and State University
HCPRVR	Logic based	University of Texas at Austin
HEARSAY-III	Rule based	Information Sciences Institute
HPRL	Frame based	Hewlett-Packard
HSRL	Logic and frame based	Robotics Institute of Carnegie-Mellon University
INSIGHT 1, 2	Rule based	Level Five Research
INTERLISP	Procedure oriented	Xerox Corporation
INTERLISP-D	Procedure oriented	Xerox Corporation
IQ-200	Frame, rule, and logic based	Baldur Systems
KANDOR	Frame based	Fairchild Laboratory for Artificial Intelligence Research
KAS (a shell of PROSPECTOR)	Rule based	SRI International
KC	Rule and frame based; object and procedure oriented	Carnegie Group
KEE	Rule and frame based; procedure and object-oriented	Intellicorp
KES	Rule and frame based	Software Architecture and Engineering
KL-ONE	Frame based	Bolt, Beranek and Newman

Tool	Representation Method	Developer
KMS	Frame based	University of Maryland
KRYPTON	Frame based	Fairchild Laboratory for Artificial Intelligence Research
LES	Rule based	Lockheed Palo Alto Research Laboratory
LISP	Procedure oriented	Massachusetts Institute of Technology
LOOPS	Rule based; object and procedure oriented	_____
M.1	Rule based	Teknowledge, Inc.
M.1	Frame based	Teknowledge, Inc.
MARS	Rule based	Stanford University
MEL	Rule based	Westinghouse Research and Development Center
MORE	Aid	Carnegie-Mellon University
MRS	Rule and logic based	Stanford University
MUMPS	Procedure oriented	_____
NETL	Frame based	Massachusetts Institute of Technology
OPS5	Rule based	Carnegie-Mellon University; available from Verac Corporation and from DEC
OPS83	Rule based	Carnegie-Mellon University; available at Production Systems Technologics

Tool	Representation Method	Developer
OWL	Frame based	Massachusetts Institute of Technology
PERSONAL CONSULTANT	Rule based	Texas Instruments Inc.
PICON	Rule and frame based; object oriented	LISP Machines Inc.
PICON	Aid	LISP Machines Inc.
PLUME	Aid	Carnegie Group Inc.
PRISM	Rule based	IBM Palo Alto Scientific Center
PROLOG	Logic based	Available from various vendors
PSL	Procedure oriented	University of Utah
PSYCHO	Rule based	Imperial Cancer Research Fund and Queen's Medical Center
RADIAL	Rule based and procedure oriented	Radian Corporation
RITA	Rule-based	Rand Corporation
RLL	Frame based	Stanford University
ROGET	Aid	Stanford University
ROSIE	Rule based and procedure oriented	Rand Corporation
RULEMASTER	Aid	Radian Corporation
S.1	Rule and frame based; procedure oriented	Teknowledge, Inc.

Tool	Representation Method	Developer
SAIL	Procedure oriented	Stanford University
SAVOIR	Rule based	ISI, a joint venture between ISIS Systems Ltd., and ICI Ltd. (United Kingdom)
SEEK	Aid	Rutgers University
SMALLTALK	Object based	Xerox Palo Alto Research Center
SOAR	Rule based	Carnegie-Mellon University
SRL	Frame based	Robotics Institute of Carnegie-Mellon University
SRL+	Rule, frame, and logic based; object oriented	Carnegie Group Inc.
STROBE	Object based	Schlumberger-Doll Research
T.1	Aid	Teknowledge, Inc.
TEIRESIAS	Aid	Stanford University
TIMM	Aid	General Research Corporation
UNIT PACKAGE	Frame based	Stanford University
ZETALISP	Procedure oriented	Massachusetts Institute of Technology

Expert Systems

Expert System	Application	Developer/User
ACE	Diagnoses and debugs telephone networks	Bell Laboratories of Whippany, New Jersey

Expert System	Application	Developer/User
CES	Designs map labeling	Developed by ESL
ATTENDING	Instructs medical students in anesthesiology	Yale University School of Medicine
BLUE BOX	Treats various forms of depression	Stanford University
CADHELP	Instructs in use of CAD subsystem for digital circuit design	University of Connecticut
CELLISTO DELTA	Provides field service for diesel-electric locomotion troubleshooting	General Electric
DENDRAL	Infers molecular structure of unknown compounds	Stanford University
DIPMETER ADVISOR	Infers subsurface geological structure by interpreting dipmeter loop	Schlumberger-Doll Research
DRILLING ADVISOR	Corrects oil right "drillsticking" problem	Teknowledge in cooperation with Societe National Elf Aquitaine
EL	Performs a steady-state analysis of resistor-diode-transistor circuits	Massachusetts Institute of Technology
FOLIO	Assists portfolio managers in determining client investment goals and selecting portfolios	Stanford University
GA1	Development experiments in DNA structure	Stanford University

Expert System	Application	Developer/User
HASP/SIAP	Interprets sonar sensor data to detect and identify ocean vessels	Joint effort of Stanford University and Systems Control Technology
I&W	Analyzes intelligence reports and predict when and where armed conflict will occur	Joint effort by ESL and Stanford University
IDT	Locates defective units in PDP11/30 computers	Digital Equipment Corporation University of Pittsburgh
INTERNIST	Diagnoses disease	Carnegie-Mellon University in cooperation with NL Baroid
MUD	Troubleshoot drilling fluid problems	_____
MYCIN	Assists in selection of appropriate antimicrobial therapy for patients	Stanford University
PALLADIO	Designs new VLSI circuits	Stanford University
PLANT/cd	Predicts degree of damage caused by cutworms	University of Illinois
PROSPECTOR	Aids geologists in their search for ore deposits	SRI International
PTRANS	Develops plans for assembling and testing the ordered computer system	Digital Equipment Corporation and Carnegie-Mellon University
PUFF	Diagnoses presence and severity of lung diseases	Stanford University
REACTOR	Diagnoses and treats nuclear reactor accidents/abnormal events	EG&G Idaho

Expert System	Application	Developer/User
SECS	Synthesizes organic molecules	University of California at Santa Cruz
SEL	Production	_____
SPE	Interprets scanning densitometer data to diagnose inflammatory conditions	Rutgers University (Incorporated in CliniScan and marketed by Helena Labs)
STEAMER	Instructs navy engineering students in steam plant propulsion operation	Naval Personal Research and Development Center in cooperation with Bolt, Beranek and Newman
TALIB	Electronics — automatically synthesizes integrated circuit layouts for nMOS cells	Carnegie-Mellon University
TATR	Develops plan for air targeteer to attack enemy airfields	Rand Corporation
TIMM/TUNER	Tunes VAX/VMS computers	General Research Corporation
TQMSTUNE	Fine tunes a triple quadruple mass spectrometer	Lawrence Livermore Labs
XCON	Configures VAX computers	Carnegie-Mellon University and Digital Equipment Corporation
XPS-E	Production planning	Carnegie-Mellon University and Digital Equipment Corporation
XSEL	Assists design/distribution selection	Carnegie-Mellon University and Digital Equipment Corporation

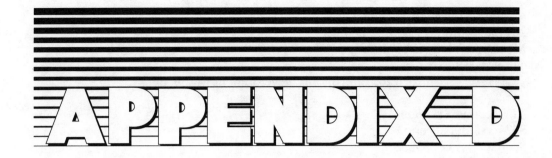

SELECTED EXPERT
SYSTEM COMPANIES

Advanced Decision Systems
201 San Antonio Circle, #286
Mountain View, CA 94049
415-941-3912
CONTACT: Clifford Reid, Program Development Manager

AI Decision Systems
8624 Via del Sereno
Scottsdale, AZ 85258
602-991-0599
CONTACT: Ralph Lunt, President

Aion Corporation
101 University Avenue, 4th Floor
Palo Alto, CA 94301
415-328-9595
CONTACT: Joel Voelz, Director, Marketing

Apollo Computer Inc.
330 Billerica Rd.
Chelmsford, MA 01824, MS 37
617-256-6600

Applicon (Schlumberger)
32 Second Avenue
Concord, MA 01803
617-272-7070
CONTACT: Sales Department

Applied Expert Systems (APEX)
5 Cambridge Center
Cambridge, MA 02142
617-492-7322
CONTACT: Fred Luconi, President

Arity Corporation
358 Baker Avenue
Concord, MA 01742
617-371-2422

Arthur D. Little
25 Acorn Park
Cambridge, MA 02140
617-864-5770
CONTACT: Karl Wiig, Director, AI Programs

Artificial Intelligence Research Group
921 N, La Jolla Avenue
Los Angeles, CA 90046
213-656-7368
CONTACT: Steve Grumette, Proprietor

Artificial Intelligence Software S.r.1
Casella Postale 198-45100 Rovigo
Italy
0425/27151

AT&T/Bell Laboratories
Crawford's Corner Road
Holmdel, NJ 07733
201-949-3000
CONTACT: Gregory Vesonder, Director, Tech Group

Automated Reasoning Corporation
290 W. 12th Street, Suite 1-D
New York, NY 10014
212-206-6331
CONTACT: Richard Cantone, Project Director

Baldur Systems Corporation
3423 Investment Boulevard, Suite 12
Hayward, CA 94545
415-732-9715
CONTACT: Rob Romers

Battelle Columbus Laboratories
505 King Avenue
Columbus, OH 43201
614-424-7728
CONTACT: Harry Templeton, Corporate Communication

Boeing Computer Services
P. O. Box 24346/MS 7A-03
Seattle, WA 98124
206-763-5392
CONTACT: George Roberts, GM, Advanced Tech

Bolt Beranek and Newman Inc.
10 Moulton Street
Cambridge, MA 02238
617-491-1850
CONTACT: Robert Harvey, VP, Development

Brattle Research Corporation
215 First Street
Cambridge, MA 02142
617-492-1982
CONTACT: John Clippinger, President

California Intelligence
912 Powell Street, Suite 8
San Francisco, CA 94108
415-391-4846
CONTACT: Ray Winestock, President

Carnegie Group, Inc.
Commerce Court and Station Square
Pittsburgh, PA 15219
412-642-6900
CONTACT: Jack Geer, Marketing Director

Center for Machine Intelligence
2001 Commonwealth Blvd.
Ann Arbor, MI 48105
313-995-0900

Cognitive Systems
234 Church Street
New Haven, CT 06510
203-773-0726

Computer Thought Corporation
1721 W. Plano Parkway, Suite 125
Plano, TX 75075
214-424-3511

Control Data Corporation
Post Office Box O
Minneapolis, MN 55440
612-853-6137
CONTACT: Joanne Henry, Marketing Comm Mgr.

Decision Support Software
1300 Vincent Plain
McLean, VA 22101
703-442-7900
CONTACT: Mary Ann Selly, President

Digital Equipment Corporation
77 Technology Way
Westboro, MA 01580
617-366-8911
CONTACT: Neil Pundit, Director, AI Program

Digitalk Inc.
5200 West Century Blvd.
Los Angeles, Ca 90045
213-645-1082
CONTACT: Mike Tang

ESL, Inc.
495 Java Drive
Sunnyvale, CA 94088-3510
408-738-2888
CONTACT: George Hodder, Marketing Director

ExperTelligence, Inc.
559 San Ysidro Road
Santa Barbara, CA 93108
805-969-7871

Expert Technologies, Inc.
2600 Liberty Avenue
Pittsburgh, PA 15230
412-355-0900
CONTACT: James Gay, President

Expert-Knowledge Systems, Inc.
6313 Old Chesterbrook Road
McLean, VA 22101
703-734-6966
CONTACT: James Naughton, CEO

Exsys, Inc.
P. O. Box 75158, Con. Station 14
Albuquerque, NM 87914
505-836-6676
CONTACT: Dustin Huntington, President

Ford Aerospace and Communications Corporation
Aeronutronic Division
Dept. A703-001
Ford Road
Newport Beach, CA 92660
714-720-1700

Fountain Hills Software, Inc.
6900 E. Camelback Road, Suite 1000
Scottsdale, AZ 85251
602-945-0261
CONTACT: Loretta Mahoney, Vice President

General Motors Research Laboratories
Computer Science Department
Warren, Michigan 48090-9057
313-575-3101
CONTACT: Dr. George G. Dodd, Head

General Research Corporation
7655 Old Springhouse Road
McLean, VA 22102
703-893-5915
CONTACT: Wanda Rappaport, Marketing Director

Gold Hill Computers
163 Harvard Street
Cambridge, MA 02139
617-492-2071

Gould Electronics
6901 West Sunrise Blvd.
Fort Lauderdale, FL 33313-4499
303-587-2900
CONTACT: Dr. Stephen Coles, Ph.D

Grumman-CTEC, Inc.
1355 Beverly Road, Suite 200
Dept. 13
McLean, VA 22101
703-448-0226

GTE Laboratories
Box A3, 40 Sylvan Road
Waltham, MA 02254
617-890-8460

Hewlett-Packard Labs
1501 Page Mill Road
Palo Alto, CA 94304
415-857-5356
CONTACT: Ira Goldstein, AI Director

Honeywell, Inc.
1000 Boone Avenue North
Golden Valley, MN 55427
612-541-6579
CONTACT: Paul D. Christopherson, Section Chief
Intelligent Systems, Technology Strategy Center

Hughes Research Laboratories
3011 Malibu Canyon Road
Malibu, CA 90265
213-317-5000

IBM
1501 California Avenue
Palo Alto, CA 94303 0821
415-855-3938
CONTACT: Peter J. Smith

Iconics
8502 E. Via de Ventura
Scottsdale, AZ 85258
602-948-2600
CONTACT: Roger Phillips, President

Inference Corporation
5300 W. Century Boulevard
Los Angeles, CA 90045
213-417-7997
CONTACT: Dr. Alex Jacobson, President

Intellicorp
708 Laurel Street
Menlo Park, CA 94025
415-323-8300
CONTACT: Thomas Kehler, Executive VP

Intelliware, Inc.
4676 Admiralty Way, Suite 401
Marina del Rey, CA 90291
213-305-9391

Jeffrey Perrone and Associates
3685 17th Street
San Francisco, CA 94114
415-431-9562
CONTACT: Jeffrey Perrone, President

KDS Corporation
934 Hunter Road
Wilmette, IL 60091
312-251-2621
CONTACT: Barbara Wallace, President

Knowledge Quest (search firm)
1210 Park Newport, #106
Newport Beach, CA 92660
714-760-2527
CONTACT: Gary C. Anderson

Level Five Research
4980 South A1A
Melbourne Beach, FL 32951
305-729-09046
CONTACT: Henry Seiler, President

Lockheed Software Technology Center
Department 700-20
P. O. Box 17100
Austin, TX 78760
512-386-0000

Lucid, Inc.
1090 East Meadow Circle
Palo Alto, CA 94303
415-424-8855

MacKintosh Consulting
14395 Saratoga Avenue, Suite 150
Saratoga, CA 95027
408-867-9800
CONTACT: Jim Kent

Martin Marietta Data Systems
98 Inverness Drive East, Suite 135 (P193)
Englewood, CO 80112
303-790-3404

McDonnell Douglas — Knowledge Engineering
20705 Valley Green Drive, VG2-BO1
Cupertino, CA 95014
408-446-6553
CONTACT: Ron Engdahl, Marketing Contact

MDBS (Micro Database Systems)
P.O. Box 248
Lafayette, IN 47902
317-463-2581
CONTACT: Ron Grimsley, Marketing Representative

Mitre Corporation
Burlington Road
Bedford, MA 01730
617-271-2000
CONTACT: Richard Brown, Group Leader, AI

Naval Underwater Systems Center
Personnel Staffing Division, A1
Newport, Rhode Island 02841-5047
401-841-3585

Palladian
41 Munroe Street
Cambridge, MA 02142
617-661-7171
CONTACT: Philip A. Cooper, Chairman

Perceptronics
21111 Erwin Street
Woodland Hills, CA 91367
818-884-7572
CONTACT: Azad Mahdni, VP, AI & Man-Mach Systems

Programming Logic Systems, Inc.
31 Crescent Drive
Milford, CT 06460
203-877-7988

Quintus Computer Systems, Inc.
2345 Yale Street
Palo Alto, CA 94306
415-494-3612

Radian Corporation
P.O. Box 9948
Austin, TX 78766
512-454-4797
CONTACT: Ben Finkel, Marketing Manager

Reasoning Systems
1801 Page Mill Road
Palo Alto, CA 94303
415-494-6201
CONTACT: Joseph Rockmore, Vice President

Schlumberger-Doll Research
P.O. Box 307/Old Quarry Road
Ridgefield, CT 06877
203-431-5000
CONTACT: Peter Will, Director

Scientific DataLink
850 Third Avenue
New York, NY 10022
212-838-7200

Semantic Microsystems
1001 Bridgeway, Suite 543
Sausalito, CA 94965
415-332-8094

Shell Development Company
Research Recruitment
P. O. Box 1380
Houston, TX 77001
713-241-6161

Smart Systems Technology
6870 Elm Street, Suite 300
McLean, VA 22101
703-448-8562
CONTACT: Eamon Barrett, President

Software Architecture & Engineering, Inc.
1500 Wilson Boulevard, Suite 800
Arlington, VA 22209
703-276-7910
CONTACT: Joseph Fox, Chairman

Soft Warehouse
P. O. Box 11174
Honolulu, HI 96828-0174
808-734-5801

Sperry Corporation (Unisys)
Systems Management Group
Employment Department RB-522
12010 Sunrise Valley Drive
Reston, VA 22091
703-620-7000

SRI International
333 Ravenswood Avenue
Menlo Park, CA 94025
415-326-6200
CONTACT: Stan Rosenchein, Director AI Lab

Syntelligence
1000 Hamlin Court
Sunnyvale, CA 94088
408-745-6666
CONTACT: Dennis G. White, Marketing Director

Systems Designers Software, Inc.
444 Washington Street, Suite 407
Woburn, MA 01801
617-935-8009

Systems Research Laboratories, Inc.
Computer Systems Division
2800 Indian Ripple Road
Dayton, OH 45440-3639
513-426-6000

Teknowledge, Inc.
525 University Avenue
Palo Alto, CA 94301
415-327-6600
CONTACT: Mike Dolbec, Corporate Marketing

United Technologies Research Center
Silver Lane
East Hartford, CT 06108
203-727-7000

Verac, Inc. (Applied Computer Science Group)
9605 Scranton Road, Suite 500
San Diego, CA 92121
619-457-5550
CONTACT: Dr. Charles Moorefield, President

PUBLISHERS

Addison-Wesley Publishing Co.
Reading, MA 01867
ATTN: Carolyn Berry
617-944-3700

Cambridge University Press
32 East 57th Stret
New York, NY 10022
212-688-8885

Computational Intelligence
Distribution, R-88
National Research Council of Canada
Ottawa, Canada K1A 0R6
613-933-9101

Electronic Trend Publications
10080 N. Wolfe Road
Suite 372
Cupertino, CA 95014
408-996-7416

Harper & Row
10 East 53rd Street, Suite 3D
New York, NY
212-207-7000

Howard W. Sams & Co.
4300 West 62nd Street
Indianapolis, IN 46268

John Wiley & Sons, Inc.
605 Third Avenue
New York, NY 10158
1-800-526-5368

Kluwer Academic Publishers
190 Old Derby Street
Hingham, MA 02043
617-749-5262

MIS: Press
P.O. Box 5277
Portland, OR 97208-5277
1-800-MANUALS

The MIT Press
28 Carleton Street
Cambridge, MA 02142
617-253-5251

Morgan Kaufman Publishers, Inc.
Dept. A1, 95 First Street
Los Altos, CA 94022
415-965-4081

Pitman Publishing, Inc.
1020 Plan Street
Marshfield, MA 02050
617-837-1331

W. W. Norton & Company, Inc.
500 Fifth Avenue
New York, NY 10010
212-354-5500

Westcomp
Software Engineering Group
517 N. Mountain Avenue
Upland, CA 91786-5016
no number

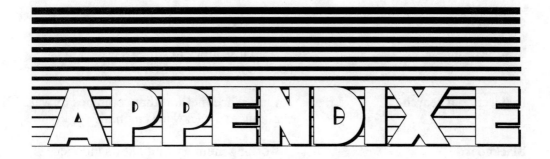

GLOSSARY FOR EXPERT SYSTEMS

Attribute

A property of an object.

Best Search

A search strategy in which a criterion is used to minimize search time.

Bidirectional search

An inference method that combines forward chaining and backward chaining.

Blackboard

A working memory that allows independent knowledge sources to communicate with one another.

Blackboard architecture (also HEARSAY architecture)

An expert system design in which several independent knowledge sources each examine a common working memory, or a "blackboard."

Breadth-first search

A search strategy in which the rules or objects on the same level of the hierarchy are examined before any rules or objects on the next lower level are checked.

C/C++

A programming language initially associated with the UNIX operating system.

Certainty factor

A number that measures the certainty or confidence in a fact or rule.

Declarative knowledge

Facts about objects, events, or situations.

Deep knowledge

Knowledge of basic theories, first principles, axioms, or models, in contrast to surface knowledge.

Demon

A procedure activated by the chaining of values in a database.

Depth-first search

A search strategy in which one rule or object on the highest level is examined, and then rules or objects immediately below that one are examined, in contrast to a breadth-first search.

Domain

The application area of an expert system.

Domain expert

A person with expertise in a particular domain.

Expert system

A computer program containing knowledge and reasoning capability that imitates human experts in problem-solving in a particular domain.

Expert system building tool

The computer programming language and support package designed for building the expert system.

Explanation facility

The component of an expert system that explains how solutions were reached and justifies the steps used to reach them.

Forward chaining

An inference technique in which the IF portion of rules are matched against facts to establish new facts.

Frame

A knowledge representation method that associates an object with a collection of features (e.g., facts, rules, defaults, and active values). Each feature is stored in a slot.

Heuristic

A rule-of-thumb approach that suggests a procedure to solve a problem; a heuristic approach does not guarantee a solution to a specific problem.

Induction system

An example-driven system that has a knowledge base consisting of examples.

Inference	The process by which new facts are derived from known facts.
Inference engine	The component of an expert system that controls its operation by selecting the rules to use, executing those rules, and determining when an acceptable solution has been reached.
Inheritance	A process by which characteristics of one object are assumed to be characteristics of another in the same class.
Knowledge acquisition	The process of identifying, interviewing, collecting, and refining knowledge.
Knowledge base	The component of an expert system that contains the system's knowledge.
Knowledge-based system	Another name for an expert system.
Knowledge engineer	An AI programmer responsible for capturing and encoding human expert knowledge.
Knowledge representation	The technique used to encode and store facts and relationships in a knowledge base.
LISP	An AI programming language based on list processing.
LISP Machine	A single-user computer designed to facilitate the development of AI programs.
Logic-based method	Programming technique that uses predicate calculus to structure the program.
Logical Inferences Per Second (LIPS)	A method of measuring the speed of computers used for AI applications.
Man-machine interface	See user interface.

Model-based expert system

A type of expert system that is based on a model of the structure and behavior of the physical system it is designed to understand.

Modus ponens

A basic rule of logic that asserts that if you know that A implies B and also know for a fact that A is true, then you can assume B.

Monotonic reasoning

A reasoning technique based on the assumption that once a fact is determined, it cannot be altered during the course of the consultation process.

Natural Language Interface (NLI)

A program that allows a user to communicate with a computer in the user's natural language, such as English.

Nonmonotonic reasoning

A reasoning method that allows multiple approaches to reach the same conclusion and the retraction of facts or conclusions given new information.

Object

Physical or conceptual entities that have attributes. A collection of attributes or rules are organized around an object.

Object-oriented programming

Programming technique based on the use of objects that communicate with one another by means of messages.

Predicate calculus

A classical logic that uses functions and predicates to describe relations between individual entities. Each elementary unit in predicate calculus is called a term (an object). Statements about objects are called predicates.

Procedural knowledge

Information about courses of action.

Procedure-oriented programming
Conventional programming techniques using nested subroutines to organize and control program execution.

Production rule
A rule in the form of an IF-THEN or CONDITION-ACTION statement.

Prolog (Programming in Logic)
An AI programming language that is popular in Europe and Japan.

Rapid Prototype
In expert system development, a prototype is an initial version of an expert system, usually a system with from 10 to 300 rules, used to demonstrate effectiveness of knowledge representation and inference strategies.

Reasoning
The process of drawing inferences or conclusions, either by human experts or by expert systems.

Representation
The method by which an expert system stores knowledge about a domain.

Rule
A conditional statement of two parts. The first part, comprised of one or more IF clauses, establishes conditions that must be satisfied; the second part, comprised of one or more THEN clauses, is to be acted upon.

Rule-based method
Programming technique using IF-THEN rules to perform forward or backward chaining.

Search
The process of examining the set of possible solutions to a problem to find an acceptable solution.

Searchspace
The set of all possible solutions to a problem that might be evaluated during a search.

Semantic network

A method for representing associations between objects and events.

Skeletal system

A computer program designed for building expert systems; it was derived by removing all domain-specific knowledge from an existing expert system.

Slot

A component in a frame that contains a specific attribute of an object.

Smalltalk

An object-oriented programming language.

Speech recognition

An area of AI research that attempts to enable computers to recognize words or phrases at human speed.

Symbolic reasoning

Problem-solving based on the application of strategies and heuristics to manipulate symbols, in contrast to traditional numeric processing.

Tool

A short name for an expert-system-building tool, which is a computer software package that simplifies the effort of building expert systems.

Tree structure

A way of representing knowledge as a connected graph in which each node can branch into other nodes that are deeper in the structure.

User Interface (or man-machine interface)

The component of an expert system that allows communication between the expert system and its user.

Unit

A frame-like knowledge representation method using slots with values and procedures attached to them.

Value

A quantity or quality that can be used to describe an attribute in a frame of knowledge representation.

Width-first search

A search strategy in which rules or objects on the same level are searched first before moving down to the next level.

Working memory

The component of an expert system that is composed of all attribute-value relationships temporarily established while the consultation is in progress.

C++

Guidelines Software, Inc. *Guidelines C++: Installation Guide and Release Notes,* Orinda, CA, 1988.

Lifeboat Associates, Inc. *Advantage C++: User's Guide*, Tarrytown, NY, 1986.

OASYS. "Designer C++," Product description, Waltham, MA, 1987.

Oregon Software, Inc. "Oregon C++: Software Product Description," Portland, OR, 1988.

Stroustrup, B. *The C++ Programming Language.* Reading, MA: Addison-Wesley, 1986.

Usenix Association. "C++ Workshop, Santa Fe, NM, Proceedings, November 9-10, 1987," Berkeley, CA, 1987.

Wiener, R. and L. Pinson. *An Introduction to Object-Oriented Programming and C++.* 1988.

Zortech, Inc. "Zortech C++," Product description, Arlington, MA, 1988.

EXPERT SYSTEMS: MAGAZINES AND JOURNALS

AI Expert. San Francisco.

AI Journal. Published by North-Holland.

AI Magazine. An informal quarterly magazine included in membership in the American Association for Artificial Intelligence (Menlo Park, CA).

Computer Language. San Francisco.

IEEE Expert. Published by IEEE Computer Society.

Proceedings of the IJCAI. From the International Joint Conference on Artificial Intelligence, a biannual conference held in odd-numbered years.

Proceedings of the AAAI. From the Amercian Association for Artificial Intelligence Conference, held every year.

AI/EXPERT SYSTEMS: SELECTED BOOKS AND ARTICLES

Aleksander, I. *Designing Intelligent Systems: An Introduction.* New York: UNIPUB, 1984.

Baldur Systems Corporation. User's Manual for IQ-200: *Intelligent Data Base Communication.* Hayward, CA 1988.

Bachant, J. and J. McDermott. "R1 Revisited: Four Years In the Trenches," *The AI Magazine,* 5, No. 3, Fall, 1984.

Barr, A., and E. A. Feigenbaum (eds.). *The Handbook of Artificial Intelligence,* vol's. I and II. Los Altos, CA: William Kaufman, Inc., 1981.

Brachman R. and Levesque, H. (ed.) *Readings in Knowledge Representation,* Morgan Kaufman Publishers, Los Altos, CA, 1985.

Brownston, L., R. Farrel, E. Kant, and N. Martin. *Programming Expert Systems in OPS5. An Introduction to Rule-Based Programming.* Reading, Mass: Addison-Wesley Publishing Co, Inc., 1985.

Buchanan, B. G. and E. H. Shortliffe (eds.). *Rule-Based Expert Systems: The MYCIN Experiments of the Stanford Heuristic Programming Project.* Addison-Wesley: Reading, Mass. 1984.

Campbell, J.A. (ed.), *Implementations of Prolog.* New York: Halsted Press, 1984.

Charniak, E. and D. M. McDermott. *Introduction to Artificial Intelligence.* Reading, MA: Addison-Welsey, 1985.

Clancey, W. J. and E. H. Shortliffe. *Readings in medical artificial intelligence: The first decade.* Reading, Mass: Addison-Wesley, 1984.

Clocksin, W. F. and C. S. Mellish. *Programming in Prolog.* New York: Springer-Verlag, 1984.

Coombs, M.J. *Development in Expert Systems.* London: Academic Press, 1984.

Danicic, I. *LISP Programming.* Boston: Blackwell Scientific Publications, 1983.

Davis, Randall. "Expert Systems: Where Are We? And Where Do We Go From Here?" *The AI Magazine,* vol. 3, no. 2, Spring 1982.

Davis, R. and D. B. Lenat. *Knowledge-Based Systems in Artificial Intelligence.* New York: McGraw-Hill International Book Co., 1982.

Digitalk, Inc. *Smalltalk/V: Tutorial and Programming Handbook.* Los Angeles, 1986.

Emrich, M. L. "Energy Division, Expert Systems Tools and Techniques." Prepared by Oak Ridge National Laboratory for the U.S. Department of Energy under contract No. DE-AC05-840R21400, August 1985.

Ennals, J.R. *Beginning Micro-Prolog* (2nd rev. ed.), New York: Harper & Row 1984.

Forsyth, R (ed.). *Expert Systems: Principles and Case Studies.* New York: Methuen, 1984.

Gevarter, W. B. *Artificial Intelligence, Expert Systems, Computer Vision, and Natural Language Processing.* Park Ridge, New Jersey: Noyes Publications, 1984.

Glorioso, R. M. and F. C. C. Osorio. *Engineering Intelligence Systems: Concepts, Theory, and Applications.* Bedford, Mass: Digital Press, 1980.

Harmon, P. and D. King. *Expert Systems: Artificial Intelligence in Business.* New York: John Wiley, 1985.

Hayes, J. E. and D. Michie (eds.). *Intelligent Systems: The Unprecedented Opportunity.* New York: Halsted Press, 1983.

Hayes-Roth, F., A. Waterman, and D. B. Lenat (eds.). *Building Expert Systems.* Reading, Mass: Addison-Wesley, 1983.

Hu, D. *Programmer's Reference Guide to Expert Systems, #22566.* Indianapolis, IN: Howard Sams, 1987.

Hu, D. *Expert Systems for Software Engineers and Managers.* New York: Chapman & Hall, 1987.

Johnson, T. *The Commercial Application of Expert System Technology.* London: Ovum Ltd., 1985.

Kelly, D. P. *Expert Consulting Systems in Construction Management Engineering.* Thesis, Dept. of Civil Engr., Stanford University, Calif. 1984.

McDermott, John. "R1: The Formative Years," *The AI Magazine*, vol. 2, no. 2, Summer 1981.

McDermott, John. "R1: A Rule-Based Configurer of Computer Systems," *Artificial Intelligence,* 1982.

Miller, R. D. (ed.). *The 1984 Inventory of Expert Systems,* SEAI Institute, Madison, GA; Technical Insights, Inc., Fort Lee, NJ 1984.

Naylor, Chris. *Build Your Own Expert System.* Halstead Press, A Division of John Wiley & Sons, 1983.

Negoita, C. V. *Expert Systems and Fuzzy Systems.* Menlo Park, CA: Benjamin/Cummings Pub. Co., 1985.

Polit, Stephen. "R1 and Beyond: AI Technology Transfer at DEC," *The AI Magazine*, vol. 5, no. 4, Winter 1985.

Reboh, R. *Knowledge Engineering Techniques and Tools for Expert Systems,* Software Systems Research Center, Linkoping University, Sweden 1981.

Rich, E. *Artificial Intelligence.* New York: McGraw-Hill, 1983.

Sell, Peter S. *Expert Systems—A Practical Introduction.* MacMillan Publishers Ltd. (in Great Britain) and Halstead Press, A Division of John Wiley & Sons, Inc. (in the U.S.), 1985.

Shafer, G. "Probability judgment in artificial intelligence and expert systems," Working paper 165. School of Business, the University of Kansas, 1984.

Sleeman, D., J. S. Brown (eds.) *Intelligent Tutoring Systems.* New York: Academic Press, 1982.

Steele, Guy L., Jr. "Common LISP Reference Manual." Spice Project Internal Report. Pittsburgh: Carnegie-Mellon University, Digital Press, 1982.

Tello, E. *Mastering AI Tools and Techniques, #22612.* Indianapolis, IN: Howard Sams, 1988.

Tversky, A. and D. Kahneman. "Judgment under uncertainty: heuristics and biases," in D. Kahneman, P. Slovix, and A. Tversky, *Judgment Under Uncertainty: Heuristics and Biases*, Cambridge University Press, 1982.

Waterman, Donald A. A Guide to Expert Systems. Reading, Mass: Addison-Wesley, 1986.

Weiss, S. M. and C. A. Kuliwoski. *A Practical Guide to Designing Expert Systems*, Totwa, N.J: Rowman and Allanheld, 1984.

Winston, P.H. and B. K. P. Horn. *LISP* (2nd edition). Reading, Mass: Addison-Wesley Publishing Company, 1984.

Winston, P.H. and K. A. Prendergast (eds.). *The AI Business: The Commercial Uses of Artificial Intelligence* (2nd edition). Cambridge, Mass: MIT Press, 1984.

INDEX

RELATED TITLES FROM MIS:PRESS

Please send additional information on the following products:

☐ **C/C++ For Expert Systems Source Code Disks**
($25.00 plus $2.00 for shipping and handling)

☐ **C/C++ Expert System Library**
($49.50 plus $5.00 for shipping and handling)

☐ **IQ-200 Intelligent Database Communication System**
($995.00 plus $15.00 for shipping and handling)

☐ **IQ-DB Developer's Toolkit for IQ-200**
($450.00 plus $10.00 for shipping and handling)

Name: _____

Address: _____

City: _____ State: _____ Zip: _____

Telephone: _____

Or call 415/732-9715 (FAX:415/732-9716) for more information.

Baldur Systems Corp.
3423 Investment Blvd., #12
Hayward, CA 94545
U.S.A

Cut on dotted line, fold, and affix postage on back

Baldur Systems Corp.
3423 Investment Blvd., #12
Hayward, CA 94545
U.S.A